GOVERNING PRIVACY IN KNOWLEDGE COMMONS

Governing Privacy in Knowledge Commons explores how privacy impacts knowledge production, community formation, and collaborative governance in diverse contexts, ranging from academia and IoT, to social media and mental health. Using nine new case studies and a meta-analysis of previous knowledge commons literature, the book integrates the Governing Knowledge Commons framework with Helen Nissenbaum's Contextual Integrity framework. The multidisciplinary case studies show that personal information is often a key component of the resources created by knowledge commons. Moreover, even when it is not the focus of the commons, personal information governance may require community participation and boundaries. Taken together, the chapters illustrate the importance of exit and voice in constructing and sustaining knowledge commons through appropriate personal information flows. They also shed light on the shortcomings of current notice-and-consent style regulation of social media platforms. This title is also available as Open Access on Cambridge Core.

Madelyn Rose Sanfilippo is Assistant Professor at the School of Information Sciences, University of Illinois at Urbana-Champaign. She studies sociotechnical governance, broadly exploring privacy, inequality, and political consequences of information technology. She is the co-author of three previous books: *Online Trolling and Its Perpetrators: Under the Cyberbridge* (2016); *Social Informatics Evolving* (2015); and *Multiculturalism and Information and Communication Technology* (2013).

Brett M. Frischmann is the Charles Widger Endowed University Professor in Law, Business and Economics, at Villanova University. He is also an affiliated scholar of the Center for Internet and Society at Stanford Law School and a trustee for the Nexa Center for Internet and Society, Politecnico di Torino. Specializing in intellectual property and Internet law, he is the co-author of *Re-Engineering Humanity* with Evan Selinger (2018). He has also published foundational books on the relationships among infrastructural resources, governance, commons, and spillovers, including *Governing Medical Knowledge Commons*, with Michael Madison and Katherine Strandburg (2017); *Governing Knowledge Commons*, with Michael Madison and Katherine Strandburg (2014); and *Infrastructure: The Social Value of Shared Resources* (2012).

Katherine J. Strandburg is the Albert Engelberg Professor of Law at New York University School of Law. She directs NYU's Information Law Institute and interdisciplinary Privacy Research Group and is a faculty director of the Engelberg Center on Innovation Law and Policy. Professor Strandburg co-developed the Governing Knowledge Commons framework and researches information privacy, automated decision-making, patents, and innovation policy. Before obtaining her JD, she was a computational physicist at Argonne National Laboratory.

CAMBRIDGE STUDIES ON GOVERNING KNOWLEDGE COMMONS

The mission of the series is to provide an authoritative space for high quality scholarship on the governance of knowledge commons. Following the path pioneered by Elinor Ostrom, recipient of the Nobel Prize in Economics for her work on institutional analysis of commons regimes in the natural environment, and the editors' work in *Governing Knowledge Commons*, this series uses a similar framework to systematically study knowledge commons in various sectors. Readers seeking more information on knowledge commons and this series can visit http://knowledge-commons.net, a repository for scholarship produced by an international, interdisciplinary group of knowledge commons researchers.

Series Editors
Katherine J. Strandburg
Brett M. Frischmann
Michael J. Madison

Other Books in the Series

Katherine J. Strandburg, Brett M. Frischmann and Michael J. Madison, *Governing Medical Knowledge Commons*

Governing Privacy in Knowledge Commons

Edited by

MADELYN ROSE SANFILIPPO
University of Illinois at Urbana-Champaign

BRETT M. FRISCHMANN
Villanova University School of Law

KATHERINE J. STRANDBURG
New York University School of Law

CAMBRIDGE
UNIVERSITY PRESS

CAMBRIDGE
UNIVERSITY PRESS

University Printing House, Cambridge CB2 8BS, United Kingdom

One Liberty Plaza, 20th Floor, New York, NY 10006, USA

477 Williamstown Road, Port Melbourne, VIC 3207, Australia

314–321, 3rd Floor, Plot 3, Splendor Forum, Jasola District Centre, New Delhi – 110025, India

79 Anson Road, #06–04/06, Singapore 079906

Cambridge University Press is part of the University of Cambridge.

It furthers the University's mission by disseminating knowledge in the pursuit of education, learning, and research at the highest international levels of excellence.

www.cambridge.org
Information on this title: www.cambridge.org/9781108485142
DOI: 10.1017/9781108749978

When citing this work, please include a reference to the DOI 10.1017/9781108749978

First published 2021

A catalogue record for this publication is available from the British Library.

Library of Congress Cataloging-in-Publication Data
NAMES: Sanfilippo, Madelyn R., author. | Frischmann, Brett M., author. | Strandburg, Katherine Jo, 1957– author.
TITLE: Governing privacy in knowledge commons / Madelyn R. Sanfilippo, University of Illinois, Urbana-Champaign; Brett M. Frischmann, Villanova University School of Law & Katherine J. Strandburg, New York University School of Law.
DESCRIPTION: Cambridge, United Kingdom ; New York, NY : Cambridge University Press, 2021. | Series: Cambridge studies on governing knowledge commons | Includes bibliographical references.
IDENTIFIERS: LCCN 2020046714 (print) | LCCN 2020046715 (ebook) | ISBN 9781108485142 (hardback) | ISBN 9781108749978 (ebook)
SUBJECTS: LCSH: Privacy, Right of. | Secrecy – Law and legislation. | Data protection – Law and legislation. | Information networks – Law and legislation. | Information commons. | Knowledge management.
CLASSIFICATION: LCC K3263 .S25 2021 (print) | LCC K3263 (ebook) | DDC 342.08/58–dc23
LC record available at https://lccn.loc.gov/2020046714
LC ebook record available at https://lccn.loc.gov/2020046715

ISBN 978-1-108-48514-2 Hardback

Contents

Figures

Tables

Contributors

Noah Apthorpe is an Assistant Professor of computer science at Colgate University.

Brett M. Frischmann is the Charles Widger Endowed University Professor in Law, Business, and Economics at Villanova University Charles Widger School of Law, Villanova, Pennsylvania.

Felix Gille is a researcher in the Health Ethics and Policy Lab in the Department of Health Sciences and Technology, Swiss Federal Institute of Technology (ETH) Zürich.

Katherine Haenschen is an Assistant Professor in the Department of Communication Studies and Political Science, Northeastern University.

Kyle M. L. Jones is an Assistant Professor in the Department of Library and Information Science in the School of Informatics and Computing at Indiana University-Indianapolis (IUPUI).

Michael J. Madison is a Professor of Law and Faculty Director of the Future Law Project at the University of Pittsburgh School of Law, Pittsburgh, Pennsylvania.

Michael Mattioli is an Associate Professor of Law at the Indiana University Bloomington Maurer School of Law, Bloomington, Indiana.

Chase McCoy is a Lecturer in informatics at Indiana University-Bloomington Luddy School of Informatics, Computing, and Engineering.

Darakhshan J. Mir is an Assistant Professor of computer science and Jane W. Griffith faculty fellow at Bucknell University.

Madelyn Rose Sanfilippo is an Assistant Professor in the School of Information Sciences at the University of Illinois at Urbana-Champaign.

Scott J. Shackelford is an Associate Professor of Business Law and Ethics at the Kelley School of Business, as well as the Cybersecurity Program Chair and

Executive Director of the Ostrom Workshop Program on Cybersecurity and Internet Governance at Indiana University-Bloomington.

Katherine J. Strandburg is the Alfred B. Engelberg Professor of Law and Director of the Information Law Institute at New York University School of Law, New York.

Yan Shvartzshnaider is an Assistant Professor and faculty fellow in the Courant Institute of Mathematical Sciences at New York University.

Effy Vayena is a Professor of Bioethics and Director of the Health Ethics and Policy Lab in the Department of Health Sciences and Technology at Swiss Federal Institute of Technology (ETH) Zürich.

Ari Ezra Waldman is a Professor in the School of Law and Khoury College of Computer Sciences at Northeastern University.

Acknowledgments

We are grateful to the Governing Knowledge Commons (GKC) community, as well as the broader community of commons scholars, for their continued engagement and interdisciplinary feedback. We also thank the publishing team at Cambridge University Press – including Matt Gallaway, Shalini Bisa, and Cameron Daddis – for making this book possible, as well as Jason Livingood and the Comcast Innovation Fund for their support.

Introduction

Madelyn Rose Sanfilippo, Brett M. Frischmann, and Katherine J. Strandburg

Privacy, in contrast with secrecy, is a relational concept, achieved when personal information is shared appropriately between actors. Viewed in this way, privacy is necessarily contextual and complex because norms about appropriate flows and use of personal information are socially negotiated and often contested (Nissenbaum, 2009). Privacy is thus a problem of collective action. Moreover, personal information is often among the knowledge resources pooled and managed by knowledge commons. Even when that is not the case, personal information can be important in shaping knowledge commons participation and governance. The Governing Knowledge Commons (GKC) framework is thus well suited for studying and analyzing how communities or populations evaluate and shape governance of privacy in particular contexts. (Sanfilippo, Frischmann & Strandburg, 2018)

Chapter 1 of this volume introduces the theoretical basis for applying the GKC framework to study privacy, explores how that framework complements and supplements Nissenbaum's contextual integrity theory, and describes a privacy-focused meta-analysis of previous GKC case studies. Previous case studies within the GKC tradition did not explicitly address questions of privacy. Nonetheless, the meta-analysis presented in Chapter 1 demonstrates that personal information shaped governance – and was itself pooled and governed – in previously published GKC cases. By studying how the strength and enforcement of particular types of "rules-in-use" for personal information varied among those cases, the privacy-focused meta-analysis uncovers three patterns of commons governance: member-driven, public-driven, and imposed.

Drawing on insights from the theory and meta-analysis reviewed in Chapter 1, the chapters gathered in this volume were solicited from an interdisciplinary group of scholars studying personal information governance in a variety of contexts. Chapters 2 through 5 in this volume present case studies of knowledge commons in which personal information is pooled and governed as a critical knowledge resource. Chapters 6 and 7 present case studies in which privacy's role is primarily instrumental to the creation and management of other sorts of knowledge resources; commons governance of personal information enables trust and cooperation. Chapters 8 through 10 explore some of the failures and complexities of privacy commons governance, particularly with respect to the representation of information subjects, and suggest potential paths toward greater inclusion and legitimacy.

In Chapter 2, "How Private Individuals Maintain Privacy and Govern Their Own Health Data Cooperative: MIDATA in Switzerland," Felix Gille and Effy Vayena explore the Swiss MIDATA cooperative. MIDATA's members exert cooperative control over the uses of their personal health data through a combination of individual decisions and collective review of project proposals for biomedical research. Within this privacy commons, the board, which reviews research proposals, provides governance and builds trust, while participants across the Swiss population supply the critical resources, namely personal health data.

Chapter 3, "Pooling Mental Health Data with Chatbots," by Michael Mattioli, presents a critical analysis of applications of conversational agents to treat clinical anxiety. In addition to treating anxiety and depression in real time, these chatbot apps are designed to improve quality of care with time, not only by learning about individual users, but also by creating and using a larger pool of user conversations. Patients who use these chatbots are thus both the source of personal information used as a resource for generating new knowledge and part of the community most directly impacted by its use. Unlike MIDATA, the chatbot governance model does not involve information subject participation, but relies instead on the ethical commitments of its physician creators and patient-informed consent.

In Chapter 4, "Privacy in Practice: A Socio-Technical Integration Research (STIR) Study of Rules-in-Use within Institutional Research," Chase McCoy and Kyle M. L. Jones study the governance and practice of university data mining and learning analytics using a sociotechnical integration research (STIR) design. Their study probes the value of student data to institutional research, the institutional participants involved with its collection and use, and the ways in which the creation and use of student data knowledge resources are governed. In this case, student information subjects do not participate directly in governance, nor is governance premised on their consent. Instead, privacy governance is based on legal regulation, university policies, and, importantly, collective norms reflecting the ethical commitments of the researchers.

Chapter 5, "Public Facebook Groups for Political Activism," by Madelyn Sanfilippo and Katherine Strandburg, studies governance of personal information in online social movements that use Facebook as a primary locus for activity. Their empirical study of the Day Without Immigrants movement, the March for Science, and the Women's March explores the variety of personal information – ranging from personal narratives to contact information – contributed by participants and the complex and polycentric ways in which personal information resources are governed by movement leaders and organizers, informal responses from other participants, and the design of Facebook's platform. This chapter also serves as a bridge to the group of studies focused on the ways that privacy governs participation and co-creation of knowledge resources because these movements also must deal with collateral flows of personal information associated with the creation and governance of other types of knowledge resources.

In Chapter 6, "The Republic of Letters and the Origins of Scientific Knowledge Commons," Michael Madison explores how privacy shaped the historical knowledge sharing practices of "The Republic of Letters," an early open science regime. The knowledge resources created by this sharing regime were public, both in the sense that they were not secret and in the sense that they were intended to include general, rather than personal, knowledge. Nonetheless, as Madison describes, privacy practices were key to self-organization processes of the Republic of Letters. For example, rules-in-use about personal information sharing both underlay reputational compensation and significantly limited the types of personal information deemed appropriate to share.

In Chapter 7, Brett M. Frischmann, Katherine Haenschen, and Ari Ezra Waldman address "Privacy and Knowledge Production across Contexts." They compare the rules-in-use governing personal information flows in three distinct contexts: meetings governed by the Chatham House Rule, Gordon Research Conferences, and Broadband Internet Tech Advisory Group (BITAG). Their study shows how these communities use different forms of privacy governance to create trusted environments for information sharing, thereby encouraging participation by diverse contributors to the creation of knowledge resources.

Chapter 8, Scott J. Shackelford's "Governing the Internet of Everything," considers the problem of cybersecurity governance in a global Internet system that increasingly involves connected smart devices. He emphasizes the complexity and polycentricity of the cybersecurity governance regime, which involves international, state, commercial, and private actors. Cybersecurity has many aspects, including governance of the ways that various commercial, governmental, and criminal players can exploit users' personal information. Shackelford warns that the regime complexes addressing cybersecurity may not adequately represent the interests of personal information subjects, particularly those who live in less developed and less powerful states. He argues that the GKC framework and Ostrom's IAD framework can be used to critically analyze cybersecurity governance in order to develop novel interventions to address these concerns.

In Chapter 9, "Contextual Integrity as a Gauge for Governing Knowledge Commons," Yan Shvartzshnaider, Madelyn Sanfilippo, and Noah Apthorpe use contextual integrity (CI) as a gauge for evaluating the governance of personal information revealed by users participating in the Internet of Things. Through a survey of public perceptions regarding privacy and IoT devices, they find large gaps between the norms and expectations articulated by some sub-groups of users and the ways that commercial suppliers of smart connected devices govern the aggregation and use of such information. These gaps are evidence that current governance fails to account for the interests of information subjects. Their study also explores how some smart device users cooperate through user forms to create a distinct knowledge resource of information about how personal information flows in the IoT environment and strategies that users can use to limit the collection of their information, at least to some extent.

Chapter 10, Darakhshan J. Mir's "Designing for the Privacy Commons," examines how the tools and methodologies of design might be used to assess the appropriateness of entrenched norms or rules-in-use associated with privacy. Mir argues that Participatory Design methodology, with its political and ideological commitments to democratic decision-making, may be a particularly promising way to address the deficits in representation of information subjects' interests identified in some cases of personal information governance.

While each of these chapters and case studies is fascinating in its own right, the concluding chapter provides a critical meta-perspective. Taken together, this book's exploration of personal information and its unique connection to information subjects add nuance to our earlier analysis of member-driven, public-driven, and imposed commons governance and bring new themes into focus. Newly salient themes include the role of personal information governance in boundary negotiation and socialization, the potential for conflicts between knowledge contributors and information subjects; the potential adversarial role of commercial infrastructure in imposing commons governance; the role of privacy work-around strategies in responding to those conflicts; the importance of trust; the contestability of commons governance legitimacy; and the co-emergence of contributor communities and knowledge resources. These new studies also confirm and deepen insights into recurring themes identified in previous GKC studies (Frischmann, Madison & Strandburg, 2014; Strandburg, Frischmann & Madison, 2017).

REFERENCES

Frischmann, Brett M., Michael J. Madison, and Katherine Jo Strandburg, eds. *Governing Knowledge Commons*. Oxford University Press, 2014.

Nissenbaum, Helen. *Privacy in Context: Technology, Policy, and the Integrity of Social Life*. Stanford University Press, 2009.

Sanfilippo, Madelyn, Brett Frischmann, and Katherine Strandburg, Privacy as commons: case evaluation through the Governing Knowledge Commons framework, *Journal of Information Policy* (8), pp. 116–166 (2018).

Strandburg, Katherine J., Brett M. Frischmann, and Michael J. Madison, eds. *Governing Medical Knowledge Commons*. Cambridge University Press, 2017.

1

Privacy and Knowledge Commons

Madelyn Rose Sanfilippo[1], *Brett M. Frischmann*[2], *and Katherine J. Strandburg*[3]

1.1 INTRODUCTION

Although "privacy" and "commons" might on first impression seem conceptually orthogonal or even opposed, a deeper analysis suggests there are insights to be gained from studying information privacy as a question of knowledge commons governance. Privacy often is taken to connote constraint and control over information, while commons often connotes openness and sharing. Neither of these stereotypes, however, are accurate reflections. A more nuanced perspective reveals that sharing and constraint are two sides of the same coin, acting as complements, both in social situations ordinarily conceived in privacy terms and in institutions aimed at creative production through knowledge sharing. Privacy is not simply a matter of constraint, but is more usefully understood, as Helen Nissenbaum has argued, as a matter of "*appropriate flow* of personal information" for specific social contexts (2009, p. 127). When defined as such, it becomes apparent both that privacy is not secrecy and that privacy often involves knowledge sharing. Indeed, true secrecy, in which information is completely unshared (Friedrich, 1971; Neitzke, 2007), is a rarity. Privacy

The original version of this chapter was published in *The Journal of Information Policy* as: Sanfilippo, Frischmann, and Strandburg . "Privacy as Commons: Case Evaluation through the Governing Knowledge Commons Framework." *Journal of Information Policy*, 8 (2018): 116–166.

1 Assistant Professor, School of Information Sciences, University of Illinois at Urbana-Champaign; Affiliate Scholar, The Vincent and Elinor Ostrom Workshop in Political Theory and Policy Analysis, Indiana University, Bloomington; Former: Postdoctoral Research Associate, Center for Information Technology Policy, Princeton University and Information Law Institute, New York University; Ph.D., Indiana University, Bloomington; M.I.S., Indiana University, Bloomington; B.S., University of Wisconsin-Madison.

2 Charles Widger Endowed University Professor in Law, Business and Economics, Villanova University, Charles Widger School of Law; Affiliated Faculty, The Vincent and Elinor Ostrom Workshop in Political Theory and Policy Analysis, Indiana University Bloomington; Affiliate Scholar, Center for Internet and Society, Stanford Law School; Affiliate of the Princeton Dialogues on AI and Ethics, Princeton University; Trustee, Nexa Center for Internet & Society, Politecnico di Torino. J.D. Georgetown University Law Center; M.S., Columbia University; B.A., Columbia University.

3 Katherine J. Strandburg is the Alfred Engelberg Professor of Law and Director of the Information Law Institute at New York University.

ordinarily entails both constraint and flow. Similarly, commons-based knowledge production, at least as understood within the Governing Knowledge Commons (GKC) framework, is rarely free-for-all open sharing, but ordinarily combines sharing practices with constraints to overcome social dilemmas (Frischmann, Madison, and Strandburg, 2014). Thus, privacy may aptly be described not only as contextually appropriate information flow but also as governance of personal information resources.

Given the close affinity between privacy and knowledge commons governance, progress may be made in theoretical and empirical studies of privacy by employing tools developed for the study of knowledge commons governance. In earlier work, Frischmann, Madison, and Strandburg (2014) adapted Elinor Ostrom's Institutional Analysis and Development (IAD) framework for natural resource commons (1990, 2005) to devise a GKC framework for studying commons-based knowledge production. This framework has now been successfully employed in a number of case studies (Frischmann, Madison, and Strandburg, 2014; Strandburg, Frischmann, and Madison, 2017). There is also surprisingly close correspondence between the GKC framework and Nissenbaum's contextual integrity framework for privacy, given their construction for quite different social concerns. Comparing the two, we identify two specific ways in which the knowledge commons approach can help to move the privacy research ball forward.

First, we propose to supplement Nissenbaum's conceptions of "transmission principles" and "context-relevant information norms" with the more politically and procedurally grounded conceptions of rules-in-use and governance employed in commons studies. In Nissenbaum's framework, appropriate flows of information are distinguished, in the first instance, by compliance with "transmission principles," defined as "terms and conditions under which such transfers ought (or ought not) to occur" (Nissenbaum, 2009, p. 145) between specific parties in a specific context. The "transmission principles" observed in a specific situation are examples of what Ostrom called "rules-in-use." Ostrom's concept of "rules-in-use" differentiates between nominal rules "on the book" and the actual (and perhaps unanticipated) practices that emerge from interactions within often complex structures of formal and informal institutional arrangements. Ostrom further taxonomized "rules-in-use" into an "institutional grammar" that encompasses rules, social norms, and strategies (Crawford and Ostrom, 1995), as well as individual tactics of compliance and avoidance, power dynamics, and enforcement mechanisms. This approach can be used to add depth to our understanding of the privacy transmission principles observed in various real-world situations. The "rules-in-use" concept allows sweeps beyond information transmission to include the possibility of other sorts of constraints, such as rules-in-use governing how personal information may appropriately be exploited.

Under Nissenbaum's framework, when transmission principles are contested, eroded, or changed as a result of social and technological changes, their normative validity is tested against "context-relevant informational norms" and overarching ethical principles. The origins of contextual norms governing appropriate information flow are exogenous to Nissenbaum's analysis. The commons governance perspective encourages us to look behind the curtain to investigate the *origins* and dynamic characters of both nominal rules and rules-in-use, and to interrogate the potentially contested legitimacy of the formal and informal processes that produce them. We believe that issues of procedural legitimacy and distinctions between nominal rules and rules-in-use are central both to descriptive understanding of privacy and to normative evaluation and policymaking. Governance and legitimacy may be particularly important for the most perplexing privacy issues, which often involve overlapping ethical contexts or contested values.

Second, we propose the knowledge commons framework as a rigorous, yet flexible, means to systematize descriptive empirical case studies of real-world contexts; it is primarily an explanatory approach, rather than a descriptive theory, and structures analysis of nested and networked policy instruments and management strategies (Bennett and Raab, 2006). Accurate empirical understanding is an essential basis for constructing and evaluating theory and for effective policy design. Privacy, understood as "appropriate" personal information flow, takes complex and variable forms that can only be understood by delving deeply into specific real-world situations. If general principles are to be gleaned from case studies of such various and heterogeneous situations, a systematic framework is needed. The IAD framework was applied successfully by Ostrom and collaborators to derive general "design principles" from case studies of natural resource commons (Ostrom, 1990). The accumulation of case studies employing the IAD-derived GKC framework is at an earlier stage, but general insights and testable hypotheses have already started to emerge (Frischmann, Madison, and Strandburg, 2014; Strandburg, Frischmann, and Madison, 2017). We anticipate that using the enhanced GKC framework proposed here to structure systematic case studies of how personal information flows are governed in various real-world contexts will lead to similar progress in our understanding of privacy.

This chapter aims to convince readers that the commons approach to information privacy has a good chance of producing new and useful insights. We thus supplement our conceptual discussion of the approach with a demonstration study in which we identify and analyze privacy issues that were implicit in previously studied knowledge commons cases. Those studies have produced insights into a variety of aspects of knowledge production within communities, ranging from the various social dilemmas communities may face when seeking to achieve their objectives to the institutional governance choices they rely on to overcome those dilemmas. A previous analysis of knowledge-sharing regimes elucidated differences along four distinct community designs: centralized, intermediate distributed, fully distributed, and noncommons (Contreras and Reichman, 2015). Similarly, our meta-analysis, focusing on personal information sharing, uncovered three distinctive patterns of rules-in-use based on whether the governance was public driven, member driven, or imposed by leadership or a platform. This reanalysis of previous case studies is intended to be exemplary, rather than representative of the range of situations in which privacy debates arise, so it is likely that additional patterns will emerge from case studies undertaken with privacy in mind. Nevertheless, the meta-analysis presented here uncovers interesting empirical patterns and raises issues that are worthy of further exploration; in particular, the knowledge commons perspective highlights the interdependence between knowledge flows aimed at creative production and personal information flows. It also demonstrates that a contextualized understanding of privacy requires a broad conception of "personal information" that extends well beyond information that is ordinarily deemed "sensitive." For example, inappropriate flows of information such as an individual's views, opinions, or ideas can stifle socially valuable information sharing or have other undesirable effects.

This meta-analysis demonstrates that those who systematically study knowledge commons governance with an eye toward knowledge production routinely encounter privacy concerns and values, along with rules-in-use that govern appropriate personal information flow. In the same way, we anticipate that many, if not most, communities within which privacy is a hotly contested issue are also dealing with corresponding questions about knowledge production, sharing, curation, and use – or more generally, knowledge governance. In sum, while this chapter does not attempt a new conceptualization of privacy per se, it contends that institutional analysis can be an important conceptual and empirical aid to privacy research and that understanding privacy as governance of personal information flows can illuminate otherwise underappreciated facets of knowledge commons arrangements.

1.2 THEORETICAL BACKGROUND

In order to explore the utility of integrating the GKC framework (1.2.1) with Nissenbaum's Contextual Integrity framework (1.2.2), it is first necessary to understand and compare them, and to identify points of synergy and possibilities for augmentation (1.2.3), including research questions to be explored in further developing the GKC framework.

1.2.1 *The GKC Framework*

Commons governance of natural resources is often explored through Ostrom's IAD framework. Commons, as used in the literature upon which we build here, refers to community management or governance of resources. "The basic characteristic that distinguishes commons from non-commons is *institutionalized sharing of resources* among members of a community" (Madison, Frischmann, and Strandburg, 2009, p. 841). Commons governance can take many forms and need not involve the kind of complete openness often associated with discussions of "the commons" or "the public domain" in the legal literature, nor should it be conflated with the type of resources that are managed.

Ostrom's work initially emphasized the appropriateness of commons governance for "common pool resources," meaning "a natural or man-made resource system that is sufficiently large as to make it costly (but not impossible) to exclude potential beneficiaries from obtaining benefits from its use" (Ostrom, 2015, p. 4). In economic terms, common pool resources are rivalrous and nonexcludable and commons governance of such resources generally aims to address so-called tragedies of the commons, social dilemmas associated with overuse – congestion, depletion, and destruction. Commons governance is used by a wide variety of communities to manage many different types of resources, however, and responds to various obstacles to sustainable sharing and cooperation. Some of those obstacles derive from the nature of the resources and others derive from other factors, such as the nature of the community or external influences.

When we refer to knowledge commons, we mean commons governance applied to knowledge resources, broadly defined, where:

> Knowledge refers to a broad set of intellectual and cultural resources. ... We emphasize that we cast a wide net and that we group information, science, knowledge, creative works, data, and so on together. (Frischmann, Madison, and Strandburg, 2014, p. 2)

In this sense, knowledge resources may lie at any point along the data, information, knowledge, and wisdom hierarchy (Henry, 1974). Personal information, broadly defined, is one type of knowledge resource, which can produce value when it is shared and managed appropriately.

As recognized by Hess and Ostrom (2007) and confirmed by later GKC studies, "sharing of knowledge often is sustained by commons governance." Indeed, case studies of knowledge commons have illustrated the use of commons governance to manage not only knowledge, which is a classic public good,[4] but also classic private goods, such as money, that must be shared to accomplish a community's goals and objectives.

We anticipate that commons governance will often be applied to flows of personal information for related, but somewhat distinct reasons. If personal information can flow without constraint, the subjects of the information may either be disinclined to share it at all, opting for secrecy, or, if secrecy is not possible, may be unfairly harmed by the flow. Commons governance can provide for the beneficial and managed flow of personal information within a legitimate and trusted institutional structure, thus encouraging subjects to share it in a particular social setting and reducing the potential that harm will result from doing so.

The GKC framework (which is adapted for knowledge resources from Ostrom's IAD framework) is represented in Figure 1.1.

[4] More extensive discussions of the public goods nature of knowledge are presented by Frischmann, Madison, and Strandburg (2014, introduction, p. ix) and Ostrom and Hess (2007).

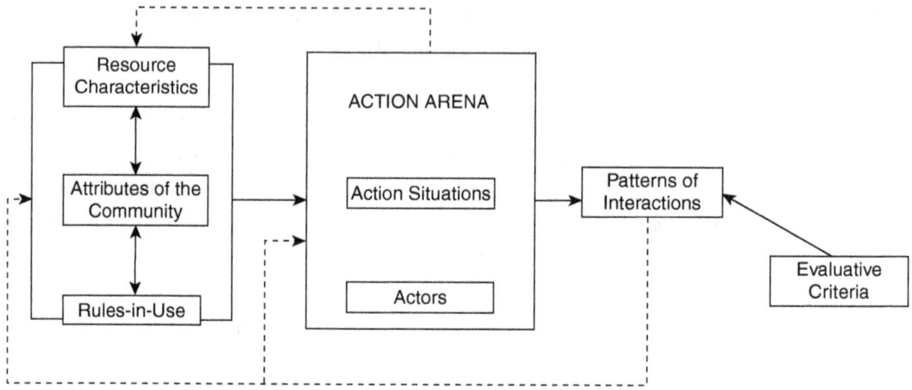

FIGURE 1.1 The GKC framework

Using the IAD framework, Ostrom and colleagues explored patterns of community interactions (McGinnis, 2011). *Action arenas* serve as the core units of IAD and GKC analysis, functioning as policy analysis equivalent of social action and interaction settings (Burns and Flam, 1987 or Goffman's frames, 1974). An action arena is simply a recurring type of situation in which community actors interact with one another. Interactions in an action arena produce outcomes, denoted here as patterns of interaction, which can then be evaluated according to some community or socially generated criteria. The figure depicts how effects flow between conceptual building blocks. Thus, resource characteristics, community attributes (including members and roles), and a set of governing "rules-in-use" are inputs to an action arena. Patterns of interactions accumulate, feeding back to create new action situations and influencing resource characteristics, community attributes, and rules-in-use. Knowledge resources are often produced and defined by the community. The knowledge outputs of some knowledge commons action arenas must themselves be managed by the community and may be inputs to further knowledge production. This feedback, between a community's activity and its available knowledge resources, justifies community-level analysis, emphasizing questions related to group interactions and outcomes, rather than user-level analysis, emphasizing questions about individual experiences.

Focusing on action arenas facilitates examination of resource sharing in dynamic local contexts, as opposed to simply examining interactions in broad contexts (Ostrom, 2005). The "action arena" concept is flexible and can be applied at a variety of levels of generality, depending upon the question of interest to the analyst. Analyzing an action arena is meaningful only if one can specify resource characteristics, community attributes, and rules-in-use that are "exogenous" or fixed over a number of action situations and if one can describe meaningful "patterns" in the outcomes of the interactions. If an action arena is too general, such a description will not be possible, while if an action arena is defined too specifically, meaningful patterns cannot emerge. Finally, note that the concept of an action arena can also apply to governance activities that determine rules to govern knowledge creation and flow or membership qualifications.

The IAD and GKC frameworks include a step in which "evaluative criteria" are applied but do not explicitly provide a yardstick for normative assessment. In the classic studies of natural resource commons, the normative goal is often implicitly assumed to be sustainable use of the resource by the community. Applications of the GKC framework to innovation and knowledge production have generally focused on whether the community is successful in terms of its internally defined goals and objectives, while recognizing that the goals of a knowledge commons community could, in principle, be out of step with, or adverse to, the values and objectives of society at large.

For purposes of analysis and empirical study, the high-level GKC framework shown in Figure 1.1 can be unpacked into a more detailed set of research questions, as shown in Table 1.1.

TABLE 1.1 *A revised GKC framework*

Knowledge Commons Framework and Representative Research Questions
Background Environment
What is the background context (legal, cultural, etc.) of this particular commons?
What normative values are relevant for this community?
What is the "default" status of the resources involved in the commons (patented, copyrighted, open, or other)?
How does this community fit into a larger context? What relevant domains overlap in this context?
Attributes
What resources are pooled and how are they created or obtained?
What are the characteristics of the resources? Are they rival or nonrival, tangible or intangible? Is there shared infrastructure?
What is personal information relative to resources in this action arena?
What technologies and skills are needed to create, obtain, maintain, and use the resources?
What are considered to be appropriate resource flows? How is appropriateness of resource use structured or protected?
Who are the community members and what are their roles?
What are the degree and nature of openness with respect to each type of community member and the general public?
Which noncommunity members are impacted?
What are the goals and objectives of the commons and its members, including obstacles or dilemmas to overcome?

TABLE 1.1 *(continued)*

Who determines goals and objectives?
What values are reflected in goals and objectives?
What are the history and narrative of the commons?
What is the value of knowledge production in this context?
Governance
What are the relevant action arenas and how do they relate to the goals and objective of the commons and the relationships among various types of participants and with the general public?
Are action arenas perceived to be legitimate?
What legal structures (e.g., intellectual property, subsidies, contract, licensing, tax, and antitrust) apply?
What are the governance mechanisms (e.g., membership rules, resource contribution or extraction standards and requirements, conflict resolution mechanisms, and sanctions for rule violation)?
What are the institutions and technological infrastructures that structure and govern decision-making?
What informal norms govern the commons?
What institutions are perceived to be legitimate or illegitimate? How are institutional illegitimacies addressed?
Who are the decision-makers and how are they selected? Are decision-makers perceived to be legitimate?
How do nonmembers interact with the commons? What institutions govern those interactions?
Are there impacted groups that have no say in governance?
Patterns and Outcomes
What benefits are delivered to members and to others (e.g., innovations and creative output, production, sharing, and dissemination to a broader audience, and social interactions that emerge from the commons)?
What costs and risks are associated with the commons, including any negative externalities?
Are outcomes perceived to be legitimate by members? By decision-makers? By impacted outsiders?

1.2.2 *Nissenbaum's Contextual Integrity Framework*

Commonalities between Nissenbaum's contextual integrity framework (2009) and the GKC framework are immediately apparent. Nissenbaum's framework centers around "contexts," which she defines as "structured social settings characterized by canonical activities, roles, relationships, power structures, norms or rules and internal values (goals, ends, purposes)." (Nissenbaum, 2009, p. 129) A context, in Nissenbaum's framework, is a social setting in which people undertake "activities," depending on their "roles," subject to "norms (or rules)" (broadly defined), guided by "internal values (goals, ends, purposes)." This is in parallel to rule-in-use determination by community goals and objectives in an action arena.

For purposes of discussing privacy as contextual integrity, Nissenbaum focuses on "context-relative informational norms" characterized by four key parameters: contexts, actors, attributes (or information types), and transmission principles. In knowledge commons terms, one can imagine an action arena involving communication of personal information. Nissenbaum's "attributes" are the resource characteristics of the knowledge commons framework; her "actors" are the community members who are the subjects, senders, or recipients of the information, and her "transmission principles" are the "rules-in-use" of the knowledge commons framework that specify what information resources can be shared with whom and on what terms. Note that Nissenbaum's framework, like the GKC framework, does not depend on defining any particular type of information as innately "private" or "sensitive." Indeed, the impossibility of such global characterization of information is one of the insights of her theory. "Personal" information is simply information about or connected to an individual and the issue of contextual integrity is simply whether the information flows according to a transmission principle that is appropriate for the context.

Having set out the parameters of the descriptive framework, Nissenbaum constructs a three-step process for normatively evaluating new information practices. First, determine whether the information practice appears to violate the entrenched informational norms of its context and identify the norm that is violated. If there is such a violation, the practice should be deemed in prima facie violation of contextual integrity. Second, consider whether the new practice has problematic ramifications for high-level moral and political values, such as autonomy and freedom. Third, consider whether the new practice aligns with the values and goals of the particular context in which it occurs. If it does, the practice might signify that the entrenched contextual norms themselves are no longer appropriate and should evolve. Such a conclusion would rebut the prima facie determination that the new practice violates contextual integrity (Nissenbaum, 2009).

Nissenbaum describes three ways in which the contextual integrity framework could be employed in confronting privacy controversies. First, the framework has explanatory power, in that it identifies why a new information practice produces resistance or discomfort. She argues that simply understanding what is going on in a particular instance may affect the debate. Second, she argues that contextual integrity provides a framework for evaluating a changing information practice. Finally, an information practice that violates an entrenched informational norm in a way that has problematic ramifications for high-level moral and political values should be redesigned or abandoned. The framework focuses debate on real disagreements about the values at stake.

1.2.3 *Some Comparative Notes*

While there are many commonalities between the GKC framework and the contextual integrity framework, there also are some interesting differences that we believe point the way to fruitful application of the knowledge commons perspective to privacy.

The most important difference between the two constructs for present purposes is that Nissenbaum's framework envisions actors as individual participants in a broadly defined social context, such as education, healthcare, or the commercial market. In contrast, the GKC framework envisions actors as members of a "community" involved in producing or managing a set of resources, with the broader context ordinarily accounted for as part of the "background environment," as with the nested contexts navigated by privacy advocates (Bennett, 2010) or subject to polycentric governance (Deitz, Ostrom, and Stern, 2003; Ostrom, 1990, 2005). This distinction is by no means categorical; depending on the resources in question, one can imagine applying a commons-based analysis to a large "community" consisting, for example, of healthcare professionals or teachers. One might also imagine applying the contextual integrity framework to a local community.

The difference in perspective between the frameworks does lead the analysis in somewhat different directions, however. Most significantly, the knowledge commons perception of actors as members of a community, rather than as individuals situated in a broad, exogenously defined context, shifts the focus from questions of consistency with externally defined norms and rules to questions of community governance, involving not only what background norms and rules are in force in a given action arena but also how – and by whom – those rules are determined. The GKC framework inquires into how the rules-in-use of a particular community are co-determined by the background environment, including rules and norms determined at higher contextual and societal levels. Emphasis on governance adds a layer to empirical analysis that will be quite useful in analyzing privacy issues.

Comparing and combining insights from the Contextual Integrity and GKC frameworks may also shed light on the normative analysis of personal information flows. The GKC framework has focused primarily on community goals and objectives, while the normative phase of Nissenbaum's contextual integrity analysis has emphasized values from higher-level social contexts or foundational ethical and moral principles. Focusing on governance thus raises key questions: Who should be in charge of deciding appropriateness of information flows? How is appropriateness evaluated? How is the legitimacy of privacy as knowledge commons governance contested and reinforced? As with substantive appropriateness, procedural legitimacy is contextual (Pinkerton and John, 2008; Suzor and Woodford, 2013). Legitimacy, as consensus about social good or appropriateness as reached through participatory decision-making of all potentially impacted (Habermas, 1996), raises governance issues that may be addressed through commons institutions.

The GKC emphasis on community governance as a co-determinant of rules-in-use thus brings the tool of procedural legitimacy into play in assessing whether the transmission principles for personal information are normatively "appropriate." The question becomes not only whether the rules affecting the flow of personal information are substantively appropriate for a given specific context but also whether the rules have been adopted through a governance process that imparts legitimacy to the, sometimes unequal, ways they affect particular individuals or groups. Procedural legitimacy is at issue in three distinct ways. First, one may consider whether the commons governance structure constructs rules-in-use via procedures (whether formal or informal) that are perceived as legitimate by various types of community members. Previous GKC cases have focused primarily at this level of inquiry. Second, one may ask whether governance practices of a given community are legitimate in that they adequately account for the interests of impacted outsiders. The interests of outsiders may sometimes, but not always, be legitimately accounted for by exogenous rules or norms that constrain the development of rules-in-use. Third, and finally, one might ask whether the exogenous rules and norms to which a community is subject are adequately responsive to member interests. In principle, all three of these questions are important to the normative evaluation of any knowledge commons. However, questions of legitimacy promise to be of particular importance in analyzing privacy issues, because rules-in-use governing flows of personal information may often pay inadequate attention to the interests of the subjects of the information, who may or may not be participants.

By drawing attention to procedural legitimacy, the knowledge commons framework may be particularly helpful in confronting challenges faced by the contextual integrity framework by assessing the appropriateness of transmission principles for personal information flows in real-world nested or overlapping social contexts, as identified throughout the literature (Bennett, 2010), or unresolved substantive ethical disagreements. Indeed, focusing on governance may provide the only practical way forward for normative evaluation and policymaking when information flows involve overlapping contexts with differing values or communities in which values are contested.

In addition, we believe that integration of these two perspectives also facilitates examination of the meaning of privacy in a more nuanced and multidimensional way. For example, while Solove has drawn attention to the ambiguity surrounding privacy as a concept (Solove, 2002) and its diversity of meanings (Solove, 2006), and Bennett has addressed the diversity of potential harms with respect to possible missuses and inappropriate flows of privacy (Bennett, 2010; Bennett and Raab, 2006), our exploration of privacy as governance of knowledge production and flow in the cases discussed later highlights issues of appropriate information flow pertaining to information about individuals that might not traditionally have been deemed "personal" or "sensitive."[5]

Moreover, viewing privacy as governance of information flow highlights the sense in which privacy may pertain not only to individuals but also to communities. First, constructing boundaries, within which information can be controlled by community members, is often important in encouraging participation in knowledge sharing or for other community goals and objectives. Second, knowledge commons structures often constrain not only the flow of information about the identities of participants but also the sharing of ideas and opinions, which, while not traditionally considered to be "personal information," may in fact be intensely personal. In such cases, privacy constraints on personal information flow enable knowledge production by encouraging trust. Third, what is personal differs from one situation to another, just as privacy harms and appropriateness of flows do. While some types of information, such as health or sexuality information, are often denoted "sensitive," these types of information may be shared freely and appropriately in some situations, while transmission of less traditionally sensitive types of information may be appropriately constrained or barred in other situations. In this sense, an understanding of "personal information" need not be laid out in advance or once and for all. Instead, the "personal information" issue is reflected in a set of questions to raise in each case: In what context is particular information "personal"? What is personal in this particular context?

Analysis in the section "Conceptual Background" suggests that the GKC framework, modified as indicated in Figure 1.1, may be usefully applied to study privacy, understood as governance of personal information flow. The framework does not adopt a specific normative stance about the ends of personal information flow governance or how they should be prioritized. It begins by uncovering and understanding the contextualized goals and objectives reflected in the governance of personal information flows in each case, the ways in which they reflect the interests of various community members, and how they are instantiated in rules-in-use for information flow in light of the larger social environment. We believe that such empirical understanding of how personal information flow is governed in practice is valuable in and of itself. We also anticipate, as discussed earlier, that studies employing the GKC framework will provide a fruitful basis for identifying normative issues or conflicts and analyzing potential resolutions.

[5] The broader perspective on "personal information" illuminated by existing knowledge commons case studies is consistent with, though distinct from, arguments about the need for a broad understanding of "personal information" in an era of data aggregation and mining (e.g. Omer Tene and Jules Polonetsky. "Privacy in the age of big data: a time for big decisions." *Stan. L. Rev. Online* 64 (2011): 63–69).

1.3 METHOD

To validate our argument that privacy can be conceptualized as knowledge commons governance and evaluate the utility of the GKC framework in the study of privacy issues, we conduct meta-analysis of several existing information production case studies, drawing on the diverse set generated through previous analysis under the GKC or IAD framework. Here, these examples are systematically structured according to Yin's (2013) guidelines for exploratory case-study design, in contrast to their initial analysis according to an explanatory design.

Selection of cases was guided by the following criteria for inclusion: (1) previously analyzed as knowledge commons using the GKC or IAD framework and (2) involving personal information flows, broadly understood, in addition to impersonal shared knowledge. The final set of fourteen cases included:

A. Galaxy Zoo
B. Online Creation Communities
C. Biobanks
D. Local and indigenous knowledge systems (LINK) indigenous knowledge (IK) commons
E. The Rare Disease Clinical Research Network
F. The Oncofertility Consortium
G. Patient Innovation Project
H. The Sentinel Initiative
I. The Open Neuroscience Movement
J. Aviation Clubs
K. Nineteenth-century newspaper editors
L. Congress
M. Biomedical Data Commons
N. Genome Commons

Many of these cases were selected from edited volumes on governance of knowledge commons and medical commons (Frischmann, Madison, and Strandburg, 2014; Strandburg, Frischmann, and Madison, 2017), though others were selected from the Ostrom Workshop's Digital Library of the Commons. The units of analysis for this reanalysis include both individuals and collectives within the commons, as well as their information flows, so as to support a holistic design. Given the parallel frames through which these cases were evaluated, it is possible to understand how concepts of privacy, personal information flow, and appropriateness of information flows shaped knowledge practices in commons arrangements. However, it is important to note that reliance on previously published studies limits evidence to the observations made by the authors of those previous studies.

Sources of evidence considered include the original explanatory analysis of each case, which emphasized the framework and research questions summarized in

TABLE 1.2 *Institutional grammar applied from Crawford and Ostrom*

Institution			Component	Definition
Rules	Norms	Strategies	Attributes	To whom does this apply? Individual, organizational variables Stage or role in research
			Aims	Specific action
			Conditions	When, where, how aims apply
			Deontics	Modal operators Examples: permitted, obliged, forbidden
			Or else (Consequences)	Sanction for noncompliance

Table 1.1. The principle of multiple sources of evidence was further satisfied by comparing multiple analyses of the same cases or other contextual sources, for all cases. This design, overall, supports evaluation of the flexibility of the framework through multiple examples, as well as analytic generalization for further development of the GKC framework and conceptualization of privacy as commons governance through pattern matching.

To analyze and compare the rules-in-use uncovered in existing case studies, we employed the institutional grammar, as developed by Crawford and Ostrom (1995). As previously mentioned, the concept of "rules-in-use" in the IAD and GKC frameworks refers broadly to multiple levels of institutionalization. Rules-in-use can be divided into strategies, norms, and rules based on components, defined in Table 1.2.

To further explore commonalities and differences in the governance of personal information among these cases, we employ Daniel Solove's (2006) taxonomy of privacy values to code institutions and underlying values or priorities within cases. Solove identified four major dimensions of privacy concerns: information collection, information processing, information dissemination, and invasion. Table 1.3 lays out more specific concerns within these major categories.

1.4 COMPARATIVE ANALYSIS OF CASE STUDIES

In order to reexamine knowledge commons cases as grounds for privacy as knowledge commons governance, it is necessary to seek ways in which evidence of commons governance of personal information flows and institutionalization of appropriateness in these flows will be elicited by the GKC framework. Section 1.4.1, "Governance of Privacy within Knowledge Commons," provides brief synopses

TABLE 1.3 *Privacy taxonomy as applied from Solove*

Privacy Dimension	Specific Concerns
Information collection	Interrogation Surveillance
Information processing	Aggregation Identification Insecurity Secondary use Exclusion
Information dissemination	Breach of confidentiality Disclosure Exposure Increased accessibility Blackmail Appropriation Distortion
Invasion	Intrusion Decisional interference

of the cases listed in Table 1.4 and discusses some of the governance patterns and features that were observed across cases. Section 1.4.2, "Patterns of Privacy Governance as Delineated by Institutional Origins," employs more detailed representations of each case to explore three patterns of knowledge commons development observed in these cases. These patterns are associated with distinctive governance arrangements, community goals and objectives, and origins. Finally, Section 1.4.3, "Implications," discusses meta-analysis implications and the proposed synthesis of frameworks.

1.4.1 *Governance of Privacy within Knowledge Commons*

The knowledge commons described in Table 1.4 prioritize privacy of personal information to some degree, despite the fact that privacy sometimes conflicts with other knowledge commons values, such as transparency in government, individual health benefits, and accountability. The guided meta-analysis focuses on those GKC framework questions associated with the identification and description of resources and those associated with patterns and outcomes. It also emphasizes questions about legitimacy, since appropriateness and sustainability in context are dependent on the legitimacy of commons institutions. This section provides examples of the ways in which these communities govern and manage personal information.

TABLE 1.4 *Examples of privacy commons within empirical case studies of knowledge commons*

Knowledge Commons	Case Synopsis	Privacy Concerns	Personal Information
Biomedical Data Commons National Center for Biotechnology Information (NCBI)	*Biomedical data commons govern large-scale collaborative repositories of sensitive clinical and scientific medical data*	State stakeholder roles – including creators, funders, convenors, collaborators, endorsers, and consumers – are central to tensions surrounding appropriateness of knowledge flows within biomedical data commons. Given the sensitive nature of health information, including its personally identifiable nature, the potential for misuse, and breaches of patient expectations and privacy is high and contentious.	Clinical medical records; Research subject and Researcher personally identifiable information; Researcher activities and uses of resources
Indigenous Knowledge Commons Local and indigenous knowledge systems (LINKS)	*Indigenous knowledge commons pool, structure, preserve, and control access to threatened, local knowledge, in order to ensure persistence for future generations and conserve language and knowledge diversity*	Access, dissemination, and use controls for indigenous knowledge (IK) are both important and contentious issues, given the sensitive nature of indigenous knowledge within traditional and context specific cultures. While IK may not be personal with respect to an individual, it is highly personal with respect to the	Participant personal information; traditional knowledge associated with private community and spiritual practices

		community, making trust and legitimacy within IK commons imperative to appropriate preservation and control of knowledge resources, particularly given the involvement of community outsiders in providing and maintaining infrastructure for the commons.	
Biobanks	*A collaborative commons established to aggregate biological data, including tissue samples, supporting large-scale biomedical research*	Externalities of research collaborations relative to biomedical specimens center largely on harms to individuals who have provided data and samples, due to inappropriateness of information flows, including: privacy invasions, social stigma or discrimination, and anxiety.	Clinical medical records; Biological samples and test results; Research subject and Researcher personally identifiable information; Researcher activities and uses of resources
Genome Commons Genetic Association Information Network (GAIN) 1000 Genomes Encode	*Genomic data as a common pool resource, rather than a public good, within large-scale, collaborative investigations and shared repositories*	Given the intensely personal nature of genomic information being aggregated, exchanged, shared, and commercialized through a variety of projects and communities, there is disagreement about appropriate information flows and different commons have created different rules about permissible data flows. These range from full genome commons,	Genetic information associated with individuals and populations; Research subject and Researcher personally identifiable information; Researcher activities and uses of resources

TABLE 1.4 *(continued)*

Knowledge Commons	Case Synopsis	Privacy Concerns	Personal Information
		with open access to all for any use, to much more restricted regimes. Privatization is a disruptive force in this community, at the expense of insights.	
Rare Disease Clinical Research Network	A *network connecting patients of rare diseases to clinical researchers for treatment development*	Given the sensitive nature of health information, a variety of concerns about privacy and appropriate information flow have arisen, including appropriate consent for release of patient contact information to researchers, control over release of data to third parties.	Clinical medical records; Research subject and Researcher personally identifiable information; Patient contact information; Researcher activities and uses of resources
Oncofertility Consortium	A *collaborative interdisciplinary research network connecting scientists, practitioners, and patients around fertility issues for cancer patients and survivors*	Governance issues in this case center on institutionally enforcing appropriate flows between practitioners and researchers, with strong boundaries guarding the collaborations, given the intensely personal nature of patient information.	Clinical medical records; Research subject and Researcher personally identifiable information; Researcher activities and uses of resources
Patient Innovation Project	A *knowledge sharing community established among patients and their nonprofessional caregivers*	This community emphasizes active knowledge production within patient support systems, pooling patient	Research subject and Caregiver personally identifiable information; Participant activities and uses of

		networks in an open online environment and, in some subcommunities, sharing data with pharmaceutical companies. Boundaries and enforcement of appropriateness of flows, for the benefit of patients, is critical to encouraging participation.	resources; Relationship and interaction information between patients and pharmaceutical companies
Sentinel Initiative	*This system supports active monitoring of food and drug safety and health information*	This US Food and Drug Administration (FDA) initiative fosters collaborative aggregation by supporting the autonomy of contributors in determining appropriateness of their own data flows.	Clinical trial data; Participant and research subject personally identifiable information; Participant activities and uses of resources; Proprietary health and safety information
Galaxy Zoo	A *data-intensive, peer-produced, global citizen-science project*	A key contentious issue within this commons regarding privacy relates to appropriate use of the information, rather than to access to the information. The consensus is that the data is public, but noncommercial in nature.	Participant activities and uses of resources; Participant personally identifiable information
The Open Neuroscience Movement	*Collaborative aggregation of clinical brain imaging data for neuroscience and neurological technology innovation*	Privacy concerns, beyond patient privacy issues, are central to encouraging participation; without clear boundaries and enforcement of use constraints toward nonproprietary	Clinical medical records; Research subject and Researcher personally identifiable information; Patient contact information; Researcher activities and uses of resources

TABLE 1.4 *(continued)*

Knowledge Commons	Case Synopsis	Privacy Concerns	Personal Information
		adaptations, contributions would be minimal and collaborators would not feel secure in the network.	
Online Creation Communities (OCCs) Wikipedia Flickr wikiHow, Openesf	*Peer production communities that exist to generate and share knowledge*	A majority of OCCs support publicly visible exchanges between members of the commons, yet this institutionalized openness often affords privacy to members, given that participation is possible in anonymous and pseudonymous ways. Some OCCs provide control of information flows to subcommunities or individuals, as in Openesf and Flickr, respectively.	Participant activities and uses of resources; Participant and nonparticipant personally identifiable information; Relationships and interactions between participants; Images of participants and nonparticipants
Aviation Clubs	A *community of practice emerged around early aviation enthusiasts and their efforts to make scientific progress, supported by extensive correspondence*	Secrecy and inaccessibility, as barriers to information flow within the commons, presented a threat, in that "if the secret-holders were more successful than the commons participants, then the point of the commons would largely have evaporated."[a] In this sense,	Participant activities and uses of resources; Participant and nonparticipant personally identifiable information; Relationships and interactions between participants

			appropriate information flow was uninhibited within the commons.	
Nineteenth-Century US Newspaper Editors	*Newsgathering as a collective, collaborative enterprise among journalists, editors, and news organizations*		Contention and negotiation within these commons were visible, not only to members, but also to outsiders. Privacy in disagreements was minimal, given the cost-minimizing exchange practices of editors to dispute through their papers, rather than through private correspondence.	Participant and nonparticipant personally identifiable information; Relationships and interactions between participants; Participant decisions and opinions
Congress			Openness – in terms of membership, access to members, and access to knowledge – presents some of the most significant information flow issues associated with Congress as a lawmaking commons. Issues of secrecy, transparency, and control over information flows informing lawmaking, as well as about lawmakers, including relative to conflicts of interest, are important to understanding how Congress operates.	Participant and nonparticipant personally identifiable information; Relationships and interactions between participants; Participant decisions and opinions

[a] Meyer.

1.4.1.1 Limiting Participation

One way for a community to manage personal information flows is to limit participation. Specific governance mechanisms for limiting participation, including membership rules, resource contribution standards and requirements, and sanctions for rule violation, vary across these cases. Diverse membership rules apply. Some communities, such as Online Creation Communities (OCCs), are open to any anonymous user who wants to contribute, while others have caveats about participant identifiability or exclude antisocial or disruptive users, such as trolls. In contrast, distinct participation thresholds, such as disease or public funding recipient status, manage flows of personal information in some communities. Interests and expertise delineate boundaries in many research and innovation commons, ranging from biomedical to early aviation, whereas status delineates membership, formally and informally, in other cases. Diverse governance mechanisms pertaining to who participates are usually implemented through clear rules that are transparent to both insiders and outsiders. Congress is an exception to this observation. There, ambiguity, perpetuated by norms and strategies, is used to allow members to develop knowledge with the help of experts and advocates who are known within Congress and invisible or anonymous to those outside; this relates to privacy associated with decisional interference, a form of invasion in Solove's taxonomy.

Constraints on personal information flow to or use by outsiders also protect the value of knowledge resources for intended beneficiaries, whether community members or the general public. Many of these knowledge commons prohibit the commercial use of personal information shared within the commons because such secondary uses outside the knowledge or consent of original data subjects are of concern to participants. For example, strict sanctions are imposed against commercialization of genomic information, given the significant public investment and its representative nature of humanity at large, and of traditional knowledge, given both the associations with intellectual property and the religious connotations of cultural heritage in that context. In both cases, personal information is contributed for aggregation and public uses but not for appropriation. These concerns are distinct from those motivating prohibitions of secondary commercial uses of Wikipedia or Galaxy Zoo knowledge products, which reflect participants' intentions to produce public resources.

1.4.1.2 Rules-in-Use

The rules-in-use and technological infrastructures that structure and govern interactions can be categorized according to the institutional grammar described in Table 1.1 and compared across cases. In many cases, informal sharing and subversion *strategies* allow individuals and subgroups to ensure their practices are consistent with their values, even when overarching norms and rules conflict with their preferences. Formal strategies are also observed, in which communities innovate in their knowledge production and privacy practices, prior to normalization. The Patient Innovation Project provides examples of each, in that courses of action for collaboration with medical researchers are specified, but there are no modal operators or pressure for actions. There are also subgroups within the Patient Innovation community that adopt informal strategies, such as sharing information with pharmaceutical companies and sacrificing privacy protections provided by overarching institutions, in pursuit of more rapid innovation.

Norms, more often than strategies, are shared within and across cases. Formal norms concerning anonymity are observed across many cases in which there is open crowdsourcing, made explicit by written, but unenforced, policies and platform designs that reinforce the protection of contributor identities. Informal norms regarding personal information also are observed, such as the norms of publishing debates that impact the public in the case of nineteenth-century newspaper editors or keeping debates private so as to garner more useful input from critical contributors observed in the studies of Congress and the Sentinel Initiative.

More structured *rules* for personal information management also may be either formal or informal. For example, endogenous rules against commercialization of personal information varied in their features. Some case studies observed formal rules with top-down imposed penalties, often excluding violators from future participation and enforcing cease and desist orders (e.g., Wikipedia and some genome commons), while others featured informal rules, in which anticommercialization rules were enforced by social exclusion (e.g., Galaxy Zoo and some genome commons). Within the Galaxy Zoo, the Astrophysical Research Consortium (ARC) formally maintains the right to allow some commercial uses, but contributors are extremely opposed to such uses, leading to divergence between the formal rule on the books and rules-in-use enforced among participants.

Exogenous rules also shape many of the cases. For example, the Health Insurance Portability and Accountability Act (HIPAA) forces a degree of de-identification in aggregated health data sets and strictly constrains sensitive health information flows, applicable to biobanks, the Open Neuroscience Movement, genome commons, and the Oncofertility Consortium. The Patient Innovation Project, by contrast, is by design not subject to these rules, because its information flows are managed by patients and their nonprofessional caregivers, who may disclose at will. Other legal structures (e.g., intellectual property, subsidies, contract, licensing, tax, antitrust) also impose exogenous rules in some cases.

Commons governance of personal information flows is highly situation specific based on a range of institutional components: from endogenous values and strategies, norms, and rules to exogenous rules and other multivalent, sometimes competing, exogenous sociocultural constraints.

1.4.2 *Patterns of Privacy Governance as Delineated by Institutional Origins*

Despite the diversity of institutional arrangements, we observe three primary patterns[6] in the relationship between the origins of institutions and the rules-in-use that emerge (1) public-driven patterns (section "Pattern 1: Public-Driven Commons," cases A and B), (2) member-driven patterns (section "Pattern 2: Member-Driven Commons," cases C–L), and (3) imposed patterns, from leadership or platforms (section "Pattern 3: Imposed Commons," cases M–N). OCCs and the Galaxy Zoo primarily exemplify Pattern 1, while aviation innovation groups, the Patient Innovation Project, and the US Food and Drug Administration's (FDA) Sentinel Initiative, which all emphasize member autonomy, predominantly exemplify Pattern 2; both patterns reflect a local, endogenous structure. Genome Commons are structured by various institutions that exemplify Pattern 3, which is primarily about exogenous constraint.

These patterns fundamentally reflect and influence community goals as well as the types of participants and relationships with the public. Community goals in these cases broadly pertain to the development of information resources. Governance mechanisms and rules-in-use are constructed to achieve those objectives, promoting both compliance and participatory buy-in. Institutional designs that effectively support these objectives are not necessarily domain specific but rather reflect the specific combinations of actors, resources, and goals of each knowledge commons, as situated in its broader environment. The patterns of rules-in-use we observe are associated with how open each community is to the public, with the nature of community contributions, as well as with governance design. It is important to note that while we identify three specific patterns in these cases, other patterns may better describe the origins of rules-in-use in other cases. Moreover, multiple patterns are sometimes observed in a single case. The Galaxy Zoo, for example, while generally public in nature, is not always so; some action arenas, including decision-making arenas, are members-only for instrumental reasons. As a result, Galaxy Zoo has developed and arranged rules-in-use that are more typical of other patterns. This overlap of patterns should not be surprising. When we abstract patterns from empirical observations, we necessarily reduce the complexities of reality, removing meaning. One benefit of IAD-based approaches, including the GKC framework, is in allowing overlap and recognizing the polycentric nature of reality (McGinnis, 2011).

6 Here we draw on the concept of a "pattern" used by the IAD framework literature (McGinnis, 2011).

1.4.2.1 Pattern 1: Public-Driven Commons

Some communities employ commons governance of information flows to ensure appropriateness, and by extension privacy, within open environments, which welcome public participation and public consumption of knowledge products. Among the cases we study, various OCCs, as well as citizen science projects, such as the Galaxy Zoo, facilitate the solicitation and management of participation from a large and diverse group of members of the public using online platforms.

A. GALAXY ZOO. The Galaxy Zoo project, organized by the ARC, fundamentally opens scholarly processes to the public, establishing commons with open borders for participation and open dissemination of data within a crowdsourced classification project pertaining to astronomy (Madison, 2014). Issues of privacy, as well as profit, are central to rules-in-use for sharing and use of data within this case (Madison, 2014; Raddick et al., 2017). Participant actions, knowledge contributions, and interactions are captured by the platform. Moreover, participants are personally identified and credited with their contributions to the project. Thus, they are encouraged to share "the name you'd like to be known by (not necessarily your username)" so as to be credited for their work by scholars using the knowledge resources. In addition, individuals may disclose personal information to other participants when posting to the project's online forum. While there is no requirement that all scholarly publications based on knowledge produced by this community be made publicly available on the ARC archive, those publications that are contributed to the archive are not to be used for commercial publication or commercial purposes. ARC formally maintains the right to grant exceptions to this constraint (Madison, 2014), but the possibility of such exceptions runs contrary to motivations for participation by the public (Raddick et al., 2017). Exceptions, such as those made for commercial educational materials, thereby threaten the stability of the commons. Violations of community expectations reduce knowledge production, and thus future information flows; appropriateness is key to the viability of the commons.

B. ONLINE CREATION COMMUNITIES. Various, diverse OCCs that produce public resources such as Wikipedia, Flickr, wikiHow, and Openesf employ similar forms of commons governance, in which distributed, autonomous participants generate knowledge resources, but strong expectations around appropriateness of information flows exist (Fuster Morell, 2010). For example, Wikipedia is not to be used for commercial purposes (Fuster Morell, 2011) but is open to any and all to consume; transparency with regard to contributions leads many participants to conceal their offline identities, but many nonetheless reveal personal information as a means of establishing expertise or credibility in order to influence knowledge construction (Hara and Sanfilippo, 2016). In contrast, Openesf has more variability in public access to specific projects, but personally identifiable information about contributors is more publicly available (Fuster Morell, 2014). Participation roles are adaptive to the community and fit specific niches in knowledge creation (Hara and Doney, 2015; Fuster Morell, 2010).

While these platforms impose exogenous rules and technological infrastructure to structure interactions between participants, participant influence on rules-in-use is apparent. Table 1.5 presents institutional patterns emerging from Pattern 1, including grassroots strategies, norms, and rules about information flows and exogenously imposed enforceable rules. Pattern 1 is identifiable as the emergence of institutions over time based on unbounded participations.

Certain varieties of rules-in-use are often observed across this diverse set of public-driven knowledge commons, whether they are engaged in developing knowledge across broad (e.g., Wikipedia) or specific (e.g., the Galaxy Zoo) topics, and whatever those topics might be. Governance of appropriate uses of knowledge products and documentation surrounding the production process, which includes personal metadata, is primarily structured through strategies and norms, given the social challenges of enforcing rules. Public-driven cases also tend to be strongly influenced by exogenous rules about intellectual property rights relative to knowledge resources.

Commons governance of personal information flows within these publicly oriented communities emphasizes privacy values related to dissemination of personal information, in the sense of Solove's privacy taxonomy (2006). While these knowledge commons focus on public knowledge, as opposed to traditionally personal information, governance structures aim to ensure appropriate flows (or to prevent flows) related to five of the seven subdimensions of dissemination identified by Solove: disclosure, exposure, accessibility, appropriation, and distortion. These dissemination-related values are manifest in information disclosure strategies among participants, as well as in a variety of norms shared across cases, including norms about anonymous contributions.

Other categories of privacy concerns reflected in the governance of these communities include information collection and information processing. Concerns about secondary use, a form of information processing, were reflected in widespread noncommercialization norms. The Galaxy Zoo participants were also concerned about (re)identification of individuals from data included in their comments and discussions, and with association of participation information with true identities from contribution lists, perhaps in part due to the community's expertise in identifying meaning from large data sets.

Within these public-driven commons, work-arounds are sometimes used by individual participants or subgroups to avoid overarching imposed rules-in-use. Work-arounds reflect the diversity of actors' and contributors' values and preferences in these public-driven commons. They emerge when the overarching rules are hard to enforce and when the benefits of violation to a specific individual or subgroup outweigh

TABLE 1.5 *Illustrative governance features of pattern 1, public-driven commons*

Institution Type Concern	Strategies	Norms	Rules
Participation		Participation should be anonymous in crowd-sourced commons (e.g., Online Creation Communities (OCCs) and the Galaxy Zoo)	
Information Resources	Users that see value become knowledge contributors (e.g., aviators, OCCs, and the Galaxy Zoo)	Contributions are valuable when justified with references, expertise, or experience (e.g., OCCs)	Resources may only be contributed when participants' have rights to share the information or else participants' will be removed (e.g., OCCs and the Galaxy Zoo)
Appropriate Flows		Knowledge products may only be shared beyond the community for non-commercial purposes (e.g., the Galaxy Zoo and Genome Commons)	
Decision-Making	Personal disclosures to establish credibility or expertise (e.g., OCCs and the Patient Innovation Project)	Subcommunity decisions are democratic (e.g., the Patient Innovation Project and OCCs)	Decisions are made by those who provide the commons platform (e.g., the Galaxy Zoo, nineteenth-century newspaper editors, and Biobanks)

potential penalties. For example, in many crowd-sourced commons, including OCCs and the Galaxy Zoo, some actors leverage personal information for personal (though noncommercial) gain, despite overarching community constraints on flow and norms about identifiability. Wikipedia contributors, whose personal information is ordinarily masked for their own protection in the fully transparent logs of Wikipedia contributions and debates, sometimes nonetheless leverage their personal information to validate their expertise and credibility in seeking acceptance of their contributions.

1.4.2.2 Pattern 2: Member-Driven Commons

Pattern 2 institutional arrangements are shaped largely by the normative values of their members; this pattern is defined as emergence from democratic processes among bounded participants. Cases in which we observed Pattern 2 included aviation clubs, LINK IK commons, nineteenth-century newspaper editors, Congress, biobanks, the Rare Disease Clinical Research Network, the Oncofertility Consortium, and the Open Neuroscience Movement.

C. BIOBANKS. Biobanks are established through collaboration among researchers in order to mutually benefit from access to data produced through analysis of tissue samples and medical tests and specimens (Boggio, 2017). Collaboration is extremely valuable, given that samples are rivalrous, while the associated knowledge may be easily shared. Thus, biobanks seek to maximize available data and minimize costs to researchers (Boggio, 2017; Roden et al., 2008). However, there is a trade-off between privacy of data subjects and sharing of data and samples among researchers, since the possibility of inappropriate flows of tissue-related information can raise concerns about discrimination and stigma, and produce anxiety about breach of trust and consent. Biobanks have sought to deal with this trade-off by enhancing the security of repositories, controlling access, and de-identifying data prior to sharing (Boggio, 2017). In this sense, there are strict boundaries surrounding participation in the commons and access to or use of the resources within. Additionally, frameworks have been developed for informed consent at the point of collection, so that subjects and patients fully understand and can control future uses of data related to their biological and medical characteristics (Hansson et al., 2006; UK Biobank, 2017).

D. LINK INDIGENOUS KNOWLEDGE COMMONS. Indigenous Knowledge (IK) commons, such as United Nations Educational, Scientific and Cultural Organization's (UNESCO) Local and indigenous knowledge systems (LINKS), are established within and between indigenous communities, often in collaboration with librarians and information professionals with access to knowledge infrastructure, in order to protect and document IK (Joranson, 2008). Collaborations are critical to best utilize infrastructural technologies, given the danger of extinction of IK, coupled with threats of piracy. Control over knowledge is central to the identity and persistence of many native cultures (Brown, 2009). Given the incongruence between Western knowledge structures and many forms of IK (Joranson, 2008), concerns about misappropriation and misinterpretation pose serious risks to trust and legitimacy within IK commons. While IK knowledge resources may not pertain to a single individual, they often are highly personal to the community and thus commons arrangements, such as LINKS, must adhere to the preferences of indigenous communities about appropriateness of information flows if there is to be continued cooperation in the knowledge archiving processes.

E. RARE DISEASE CLINICAL RESEARCH NETWORK. Various Pattern 2 knowledge commons exist within the domain of medical research and practice, including for patients with specific conditions (Strandburg, Frischmann, and Cui, 2014; West and Camidge, 2012). To generate participation in clinical studies for rare diseases, commons are constructed in which privacy safeguards for participants' personal information are strong but sharing with researchers is open. Despite the openness and unrestricted nature of information flows within the community, boundaries excluding and controlling information flows to outsiders are maintained, particularly with respect to for-profit (Strandburg, Frischmann, and Cui, 2014). Sustaining commons involving medical information is possible only with strong institutions. Buy-in from patients who provide data for research and development of treatments is crucial and is afforded by governance regimes perceived to be legitimate (Webber and Kremer, 2001). Perceptions of legitimacy are increased by informed consent provisions, participation of patient advocacy groups in research governance, and strong safeguards for patient privacy in such commons regimes (Strandburg, Frischmann, and Cui, 2014). It is also notable that participation in clinical research is more consistent in instances in which patients benefit from the support of others like them, in addition to treatment (Frost and Mssagli, 2008).

F. ONCOFERTILITY CONSORTIUM. Efforts by the National Institutes of Health (NIH) to establish interdisciplinary research consortia led to the development of the Oncofertility Consortium, which includes diverse stakeholders, such as "reproductive endocrinologists, oncologists, molecular biologists, biological engineers and cryobiologists" (Pedraza-Fariña, 2017). Within this consortium, a serious health and research priority – fertility in cancer patients and survivors – is addressed through collaboration between scientists, practitioners, and patients (Gorman et al., 2014; Woodruff, 2010). Commons governance of appropriate information flows within this community of practice is critical not only to support buy-in for social knowledge construction and innovation but also to protect patient data as a resource for the consortium. In other words, strong institutions governing participation, access, and use are important to encourage participation and develop knowledge for the benefit of patients. In this case, questions of appropriate data stewardship center on managing knowledge sharing across institutional and disciplinary boundaries. Though the patient data used in this research would need to be managed carefully within any research project (Pedraza-Fariña, 2017), governance of this interdisciplinary community focuses on facilitating sharing at points of intersection between diverse commons participants and enforcing use restrictions and managing commons boundaries to mitigate potential privacy harms.

G. PATIENT INNOVATION PROJECT. Collaborative sharing and knowledge production among patients and nonprofessional caregivers through the Patient Innovation online platform represents an inverse medical commons arrangement in which researchers and medical professionals essentially become passive consumers, while patients and their personal support systems become active knowledge producers (Oliveira, Zejnilović, and Canhão, 2017). Participation is generally open, as with communities in Pattern 1, yet members sometimes choose to share information in ways that are contrary to general public norms regarding personal health information flows, thereby driving governance, as with communities in Pattern 2. This case is somewhat unique, among biomedical cases, in that the participants are not constrained by professional codes of ethics in handling personal information, though the platform imposes some features of medical ethics in its rules regarding the types of materials that can be posted and by employing physician moderators. Innovation within the Patient Innovation commons is dependent on sharing and disclosure; without openness in the community, there is no value; yet boundaries are necessary to encourage participation (Zejnilović, Oliveira, and Canhão, 2016). Some subcommunities of patients even establish linkages with pharmaceutical companies, outside the scope of the Patient Innovation Project, to capitalize upon their data sharing (Oliveira, Zejnilović, and Canhão, 2017). These subcommunities thus recharacterize appropriate personal information flow to include some commercial uses (von Hippel, 2010). In this sense, rules-in-use for personal information flow are not governed solely at the platform level within the Patient Innovation Project but rather are significantly driven by member subcommunities.

H. THE SENTINEL INITIATIVE. Aggregated food and drug safety and health information, as amassed by the FDA, is stored within the Sentinel system in order to support active monitoring (Abbott, 2017). The initiative requires data collector cooperation and represents a complex commons design in which exogenous rules and the disproportionate power of the FDA dominate decision-making, yet governance institutions have been designed to mitigate that dominance (Robb et al., 2012). For example:

> the sentinel team engaged in an extensive and successful campaign to engage data holders by giving them the opportunity to participate in sentinel's creation. the end result was that sentinel was structured as a primarily distributed model, meaning

that data holders almost entirely maintain control over their own data and only share aggregated results with fda.

In this sense, each stakeholder contributing knowledge resources to this commons governance system is autonomous and is able to collaborate with the FDA to determine what an appropriate information flow is for its data (Abbott, 2017). Differential treatment of data is important, given the diversity of data and constraints, ranging from HIPAA restrictions on patient data to stakeholder concerns about sharing preliminary proprietary data in competitive medical innovation environments (Abbott, 2017; Robb et al., 2012).

I. THE OPEN NEUROSCIENCE MOVEMENT. Within the emerging neuroscience data commons, the Open Neuroscience Movement represents a commons arrangement that aggregates clinical data and brain scans for meta-analysis across studies and uses big data analytics to analyze the aggregated data so as to improve imaging technologies (Larson and Chon, 2017). The diverse origins of the aggregated knowledge resources reflect different information practices, for example: "Data should be made as widely and freely available as possible while safeguarding the privacy of participants, and protecting confidential and proprietary data" (NIH, 2003). Privacy issues within this context range from subject privacy, including concerns about reidentifiability, to competitive advantages associated with proprietary data, to researcher willingness to participate at all, given that early publicity and dissemination of research results can lead to misinterpretation (Choudhury et al., 2014; Larson and Chon, 2017).

J. AVIATION. Early aviation and invention in airplane design depended on "the use of the common expertise and designs" of community members (Meyer, 2014, p.350), with the community consistently seeking to expand and constantly threatened by secrecy and inaccessibility of knowledge needed for progress. Aerial navigation enthusiasts were eager to benefit from shared expertise and the innovations of others. There were persistent incentives to defect and keep one's innovations secret. Individuals could gain comparative advantage by keeping their successes to themselves (Meyer, 2014), yet were unlikely to make enough progress on their own to want to isolate themselves from the commons entirely (Allen and Potts, 2016). The community developed strong institutions, in the form of rules, to address these dilemmas. Those rules-in-use structured interactions and communication patterns within the community and maintained open boundaries, while supporting rigorous initiation into community-sharing practices for new members. Such commons-based sharing arrangements have been recognized as important to success in innovation prior to commercialization (Vermeulen and Guffarth, 2017).

K. NINETEENTH-CENTURY NEWSPAPER EDITORS. Knowledge commons surrounding news and journalistic practice emerged among nineteenth-century newspaper editors in a way that hinged on a set of norms of sharing certain disagreements and controversies through the practice of public dispute in the pages of newspapers, rather than confining conflict to private communication. Clear commons boundaries existed in terms of contribution, yet knowledge sharing and debates regarding sourcing, appropriation, and misappropriation were pervasively public, as editors revealed personal stances and private conflict through published open letters, rather than private correspondence or secrecy. Norms of interaction were shaped largely by exogenous rules, including the omission of news reporting from the coverage of then-current copyright law, the existence of significant postal subsidies to the distribution of newspapers and the implications of then-existent communications technology (Murray, 2014). Over time, information flows change dramatically, particularly due to the introduction of the telegraph, which decreased the cost and increased the speed of private communications, relative to distribution through publication in newspapers. These historical developments resulted in dramatic changes to historical practices of social interaction among journalists (Schudson, 1981).

L. CONGRESS. The US Congress has also been characterized as representing knowledge commons governance, in order to systematically evaluate knowledge production surrounding the legislative process (Daniels, 2014). The extent to which there is openness with respect to the influence and contributions of congressional staff, lobbyists, and advocates is an important determinant of the public's access to information about the drivers of legislative cycles (Schickler, 2001). The rules-in-use governing knowledge flows within the Congressional "commons" and between Congress and the public reflect an interesting and contentious design for balancing trade-offs between privacy and transparency in public politics and policy (Fox, 2010). Different stakeholders have different views about what constitutes appropriate information flows. Despite frequent demands for greater transparency, those with the power to impact governance of this specific knowledge commons have great vested interest in constraining the flows of information about communications among lawmakers and between lawmakers and others seeking to influence and inform them. The result is commons governance with strict filtering of information flows, despite strong public claims to transparency (Daniels, 2014).

Despite diverse domains and differing degrees of exogenous influence, we observe similar processes relating to participation in knowledge construction and decision-making in these Pattern 2 communities, spanning all four categories of Solove's taxonomy (2006): information collection, information processing, information dissemination, and invasion. Commonalities are discernable through the GKC framework's parallel structure for analysis even though there are significant differences in the range of empirical contexts and mediums of interaction, including the online and offline divides between cases such as the Patient Innovation

Project and nineteenth-century newspaper editors. While values and theoretical explanations for actual practices and objectives may differ, the GKC framework is strong in revealing a common member-driven approach and similar governance features. Shared features associated with Pattern 2, presented in Table 1.6, arise

TABLE 1.6 *Illustrative governance features of pattern 2, member-driven commons*

Institution Type Concern	Strategies	Norms	Rules
Participation	Community members will participate when they view knowledge production as threatened without commons (e.g., LINK and Rare Disease Clinical Research Network)	Participants' patient status is a prerequisite for membership (e.g., Rare Disease Clinical Research Network and Oncofertility Consortium)	
Information Resources	Users that see value become knowledge contributors (e.g., aviators, OCCs, and the Galaxy Zoo)	Patient participants must contribute personal health information (e.g., Oncofertility Consortium and Patient Innovation Project)	Information must be disclosed or else funding is revoked (e.g., the Sentinel Initiative and the Open Neuroscience Movement)
Appropriate Flows	Direct flows toward pharmaceutical research, when patients benefit (e.g., Patient Innovation Project)	Flows should not leave the commons to encourage valuable participation (e.g., Congress and the Sentinel Initiative)	Knowledge produced subject to publicly financed grants must be available to the public (e.g., Genome Commons and the Open Neuroscience Movement)
Decision-Making	Personal disclosures to establish credibility or expertise (e.g., Wikipedia and patients)	Subcommunity decisions are democratic (e.g., the Patient Innovation Project and OCCs)	Some decisions are made by those who provide the commons platform (e.g., the Galaxy Zoo, nineteenth-century newspaper editors, and Biobanks)

from an emphasis on member interests, sometimes in contrast to the interests of other impacted stakeholders or even to members' interests in other communities.

In these communities, whether members are required to participate by exogenous rules (e.g., the Open Neuroscience Movement or the Sentinel Initiative) or participation is entirely voluntary (e.g., the Patient Innovation Project or aviation interest groups), rules-in-use governing personal information flows within Pattern 2 attempt to foster productive and good-faith participation, reflecting the value placed on knowledge production. Various strategies and norms reflect privacy concerns surrounding the secondary use aspect of information processing; for example, the LINK project, designed by UNESCO to protect traditional knowledge and languages, depends on design principles that control uses. These principles also notably reflect concerns about appropriation as a particularly threatening form of information dissemination. Norms about flows beyond community boundaries, as in the Sentinel Initiative, also reflect concerns regarding information dissemination. Constraining dissemination encourages participants to embrace the community, despite its mandatory nature. Additional values also guide this community, in that allowing participants to determine appropriate information processing and internal flows provides a degree of autonomy, despite exogenous constraints and enforcement by funding agencies. Though Solove's taxonomy does not explicate autonomy in this precise sense, autonomy is frequently cited as underlying the need for privacy protection.

In general, rules-in-use observed in cases within the member-driven commons pattern reflect these two branches of privacy conceptualizations: concerns about secondary uses as information processing and concerns about information dissemination as appropriation and inappropriate disclosures. It is notable that these cases reflected less concern with information collection than cases in either the first or third patterns. Pattern 2 communities appear more comfortable with the types and amounts of personal information in flow within the commons, perhaps in part because personal information is directly relevant to the knowledge production objectives of these member-driven cases, in contrast to the public-driven patterns, in which personal information flow is often an unintended by-product. Alternatively, member-driven communities may tend to be created or emerge precisely when buy-in is needed to encourage the personal information flows necessary to produce certain knowledge products.

Members of Pattern 2 commons that were heavily influenced by exogenous institutions often used work-around strategies and norms to subvert exogenous constraints. Rules and norms of privacy for information flow in Congress, for example, reflect tension between exogenous political demands for transparency and members' own desires for privacy to get legislative sausage made – sometimes for better and sometimes for worse from a social perspective. Because Congress makes the laws, this trade-off may be involved even when the rules-in-use are compliant with legal requirements for transparency as a mechanism of democratic accountability. Other work-arounds are similar to those observed for Pattern 1. Subgroups of Patient Innovation participants share personal information with pharmaceutical companies to support development of targeted treatments, despite exogenous legal protections and platform protections designed to constrain such flows. Patient Innovation participants also sometimes leverage personal, sensitive health information to negotiate status in communities. In Pattern 2 commons, work-arounds by subgroups may reflect inequalities and contested legitimacies within commons governance.

When membership in commons arrangements does not include everyone affected by the community's decisions and information practices, additional issues concerning the legitimacy and social benefit of commons decision-making arise. Some exogenous rules are intended to force the rules-in-use of member-driven commons to accommodate the interests of such outside parties. For example, HIPAA regulations and professional ethics applicable to commons whose members are medical researchers or professionals are designed to reflect the interests of the patients about whom the personal health data is collected. In other cases, the exclusion of affected parties from membership in a community leads to contestation of membership boundary rules. The membership rules of both the Rare Disease Clinical Research Network and Oncofertility Consortium, for example, reflect efforts to move toward better representation and empowerment for data subjects. These examples provide evidence that the concept of legitimacy is central to understanding rules-in-use and thus ought to be incorporated into the GKC framework.

Contestation over community rules-in-use and decision-making processes may sometimes lead to commons failure. In other cases, commons persist despite contestation because of beneficial outcomes, because work-arounds are sufficiently effective, or simply because of disparities in power.

1.4.2.3 Pattern 3: Imposed Commons

Biomedical data commons and genome commons, as Pattern 3 arrangements driven almost entirely by exogenous decision-makers, are influenced by the relationship between public funding for biomedical research and the establishment of accessible pooled resources. Pattern 3 can be identified by emergence from a subset of powerful participants.

M. BIOMEDICAL DATA COMMONS. Given increasing transparency requirements associated with public funding for scientific research (Contreras, 2014) and opportunities afforded by technological advancement relative to large data sets (Roski, Bo-

Linn and Andrews, 2014), scientific and clinical research data is increasingly aggregated in large, collaborative repositories (Contreras, 2016, 2017). Uses of data aggregated in this way raise a number of concerns, not only relative to the informed consent of data subjects relative to secondary uses, but also relative to privacy, given the sensitive nature of health information (Malin, Emam and O'Keefe, 2013). These repositories represent commons, established between a diverse group of stakeholders – private and publicly funded researchers, data subjects and curators, and state actors – yet are also importantly impacted by complex exogenous rules, such as "laws governing intellectual property and data privacy" (Contreras, 2016, 2017). The state plays multiple distinct roles within these commons, and is particularly important in ensuring that data flows are appropriate in both private and publicly funded biomedical knowledge construction; it is for this reason that the National Center for Biotechnology Information (NCBI) molecular biology information resource, for example, was established to curate an unparalleled biomedical research common, drawing diverse researchers in, subject to constraints on data flows (Contreras, 2016).

N. GENOME COMMONS. Collections of genomic data, beginning with the human genome project, have been designed as large-scale and collaborative projects that require data governance as common pool resources and shared repositories (Contreras, 2014; Van Overwalle, 2014). Within this context, governance of appropriate information flows addresses: information and types, de-identification, data production, who can access data, how data can be used, and rights regimes with respect to the information (Contreras, 2014; Lee, 2017; Van Overwalle, 2014). There is also further differentiation between the "community per se" and the community at large, surrounding the commons, based on generation of the data versus subjects, users, and beneficiaries, respectively (Van Overwalle, 2014). Concerns and treatment vary from group to group, ranging from full commons and open access to privatized repositories (Contreras, 2014; Van Overwalle, 2014), with privatization as a threat to genome commons, given that supra-governance, institutionalized through the Bermuda Principles (Contreras, 2017), guarantee access to genetic data, but not use (Van Overwalle, 2014). Numerous examples have been documented in which participants reject a specific commons in favor of alternatives when they perceive rules-in-use, particularly surrounding knowledge resources uses, to be illegitimate or contrary to their objectives. The diversity of communities and arrangements surrounding repositories, coupled with guarantees that apply only to access, result in diverse use provisions (Contreras, 2014). However, the increasing prevalence of genome-wide association studies (GWAS), which link genotypes and phenotypes, have led to regulation by the NIH across genome commons regimes, prohibiting identification of individuals from data and subjecting commons to strict standards regarding subject confidentiality (Lee,

TABLE 1.7 *Illustrative governance features of pattern 3, imposed commons*

Institution Type Concern	Strategies	Norms	Rules
Participation			Membership must be revoked when participants misuse information resources (e.g., Genome Commons)
Information Resources			All knowledge produced via publicly funded research must be contributed (e.g., Genome Commons and the Open Neuroscience Movement)
Appropriate Flows		Knowledge products may only be shared beyond the community for noncommercial purposes (e.g., the Galaxy Zoo and Genome Commons)	Knowledge produced subject to publicly financed grants must be available to the public (e.g., Genome Commons and the Open Neuroscience Movement)
Decision-Making			Publicly funded research is subject to exogenous institutional constraints, as decided by lawmakers (e.g., Genome Commons and the Sentinel Initiative)

2017). Regulation instantiating the inappropriateness of documenting and sharing subject identities extends to consumer genome data and commons, as well (Evans, 2017).

Examples of shared governance features for Pattern 3 are presented in Table 1.7, including overlap with a subset of institutional arrangements, or rules-in-use, found in other patterns. Pattern 3 examples that are not centrally dependent upon the state can also be identified, though none have been studied using the GKC framework so far. Such examples might include Facebook communities, where many or most of the important rules-in-use concerning information flow are embedded in platform-level infrastructure.

Relevant privacy concerns embodied in Pattern 3 rules-in-use regulating information flow primarily reflect information processing and dissemination concerns. Consistent with the imposed commons pattern, information collection concerns of members, and invasion concerns of impacted stakeholders may be overlooked and are emphasized in criticisms of these communities. Secondary uses, as information processing, are particularly important – and frequently criticized – aspects of personal information rules-in-use across both cases. Knowledge production is mandatory in these Pattern 3 cases, with few documented strategies or workarounds. Instead, many rules with enforced consequences structure these communities.

The absence of strategies within these communities is notable because, by design, grassroots and informal practices are difficult to enact, given the constraints on the community. While many of the rules-in-use present here are also observed in communities from Patterns 1 and 2, Pattern 3 is institutionally defined by rigidity of structure and limits on participatory decision-making, despite a commons governance arrangement to support sharing.

1.4.3 *Implications*

This meta-analysis provides proof of concept for the proposed GKC framework in structuring the study of privacy. It also begins to provide interesting insights into patterns of institutional organization and rules-in-use and into the specific privacy concerns that appear to ground those structures. Observed patterns vary primarily according to whether the commons approach is public-driven, member-driven, or imposed. Endogenous and exogenous sources of rules-in-use also affect compliance and perceptions of legitimacy. Those who experience negative consequences of information flow rules-in-use that are adopted without their participation contest legitimacy, either directly or by engaging in workaround strategies.

This reanalysis also situates the examination of privacy governance within a nuanced exploration of privacy values, drawing on Solove's taxonomy. The distinctive origins of institutions and the nature of knowledge work within specific communities lead different sorts of communities to emphasize different categories of privacy concerns (e.g., with respect to information collection or dissemination). These different concerns (e.g., secondary uses or decisional interference) yield different rules-in-use and structure. The study also highlights a set of concerns associated with information collection that does not appear in Solove's taxonomy. These concerns stem not from surveillance or interrogation, per se, but from the participatory nature of knowledge commons and the discontinuity between typical top-down collection arrangements and the grassroots arrangements of knowledge commons. In these cases, collection concerns emphasize the group and intermediaries, rather than governments or firms.

Our analysis also highlights the importance of stakeholder perceptions of legitimacy regarding commons decision-making, both by members and by impacted individuals who are not members of the commons community. Legitimacy concerns differ by role, consistent with work by Bennett (2010). Legitimacy failures and issues are likely underrepresented in the set of cases studied here, given the skew toward successful commons governance regimes and the absence of questions explicitly targeting legitimacy from the original set of questions posed within the GKC framework, and should be addressed in future work.

The observed procedural legitimacy issues are related to impacts of the commons on the outside community, to work-arounds and attempts to subvert constraints, to contestation of appropriateness of information flows, and to negative externalities. While many of these issues appear most starkly when focusing on privacy concerns, this analysis of privacy from a governance perspective draws attention to legitimacy questions that may be of more general importance in the study of knowledge commons but may have been overlooked. Thus, this study has helped to identify important questions to augment the GKC framework more generally. Furthermore, this analysis illustrates that diverse examples of knowledge resources shared or produced between two or more participants in a specific context or set of contexts can be explored from this perspective. Table 1.1 displays a revised version of the GKC framework based on what has been learned from the reanalysis reported here. Overall, the meta-analysis reported here illustrates that commons governance of privacy and the nature of privacy as sharing are useful conceptualizations.

The revisions to the GKC framework shown in Table 1.1 highlight the patterns and recurring concepts gleaned from the meta-analysis. It is also important to note that the language within these questions is conceptually intentional. For example, questions about how communities fit into contexts and how contexts are nested in polycentric arrangements shaped by domains reflect theorization based on previous IAD-driven studies, as well as an effort to reconcile differences between Contextual Integrity and the GKC framework. Whereas "communities" can be understood as groups of participants with structured interactions, "contexts" are either the nested arrangements of institutions, infrastructure, organizations, technologies, and/or platforms or specific constructed environments within which communities function. In contrast, the term "domain" is intentionally employed to differentiate the IAD conceptualization of context from the CI approach to context as higher-level social contexts, such as education or healthcare or politics. For example, a community of parents may share personal expertise and information about local health resources through many channels, including discussions or groups on global platforms, such as Baby Center, with structure imposed by the community of participants, the context of the online platform, and the overarching domains of health and protections for children (Hara and Sanfilippo, 2016).

1.5 CONCLUSIONS

There are many advantages of systematically studying privacy using the GKC framework for structured case-study analysis. The framework allows researchers to explore variance among communities with respect to knowledge resources and participation, obstacles and dilemmas surrounding knowledge formation and flows, objectives of participants, and rules-in-use structuring knowledge and privacy commons. Case studies will illuminate both commonalities and differences among the rules-in-use governing privacy in various specific situations. The GKC framework helps to structures these observations by sorting findings into coherent conceptual categories. The emphasis on the role of privacy in knowledge formation and the establishment of sharing as a dimension of privacy facilitates the exploration of intersections of privacy with commons arrangements focused on knowledge production and sharing. That intersection is at the heart of current debates about big data. Given the framework's focus on investigating how practices and normative values play out on the ground, there is potential to learn what people really care about and why, as well as to improve institutional design or develop design principles, based on patterns of success across commons cases, coupled with detailed understanding of values, legitimacy, and trust within nested contexts.

Personal information itself is contextually and situationally dependent, as the case studies discussed here demonstrate. Thus, not only the appropriateness of information flows, but also the personal or sensitive nature of information depends on context. Knowledge production may depend on understanding this point, since ideas and data processes themselves are sensitive in some cases. Appropriateness of information flow is thus critical not only to traditional privacy concerns, but to knowledge governance generally.

Validating the proposed framework against cases in our meta-analysis helped us to enhance the GKC framework with additional questions to structure future inquiry. While higher level categories in the framework are general, applicable to diverse research questions, and have remained unchanged when applied to many cases, the more specific questions are intended to evolve, and have evolved throughout this project so as to apply to questions about privacy as governance. This grounded development approach also illustrates the diversity of privacy commons and common privacy governance mechanisms. An agenda for future cases ought to address diverse, emerging, and changing settings for information privacy governance that address: the interplay between the public and corporate actors on social media platforms, private and secret knowledge sharing practices relative to public policy development, and mechanisms of accommodating information governance to overlapping contexts and contested or conflicting social values.

Finally, it is important also to acknowledge the limitations of this approach, as well as areas for future conceptual development. One of the framework's virtues is its focus on descriptive empirical understanding of contextualized situations. The flip side of that focus on observation is that more is needed to resolve contested normative issues about privacy. Integration of this approach with normative analysis is extremely important for future conceptual work. Combining the GKC approach with contextual integrity, while adding in questions of governance and procedural legitimacy, is a step in that direction. Finally, this approach requires its own knowledge commons to succeed. The GKC framework's systematic structure facilitates comparison across cases, yet generalizability comes when patterns can be divined across sets of many cases based on detailed understanding of their similarities and differences. Thus, application of the GKC framework is time-consuming and requires an effective research community, so as to support the cross-context comparisons and extrapolation needed for the development of design principles that can guide policy-makers and communities in structuring knowledge commons governance to promote appropriate information flows. Diversity in cases, including in community objectives, resources, participants, domains, and institutional arrangements, will better reveal how privacy structures knowledge management and production. It is important to study cases ranging from those pertaining to small communities designed for exchange to those that involve explicit privacy policies in commercially oriented environments, both online and offline.

REFERENCES

Abbott, R. "The Sentinel Initiative as a Knowledge Commons." In *Governing Medical Knowledge Commons*, Katherine J. Strandburg, Brett M. Frischmann, and Michael J. Madison, eds. Cambridge University Press, 2017, 121–143.

Allen, Darcy and Jason Potts. "How Innovation Commons Contribute to Discovering and Developing New Technologies." *International Journal of the Commons* 10, no.2 (2016): 1035–1054.

Bennett, Colin J. *The Privacy Advocates*. Cambridge, MA: MIT Press, 2010.

Bennett, Colin J. and Charles D. Raab. *The Governance of Privacy: Policy Instruments in Global Perspective*. Cambridge, MA: MIT Press, 2006.

Bennett, Colin J. and Charles D. Raab. *Revisiting the Governance of Privacy*. Cambridge, MA: MIT Press, 2017.

Boggio, Andrea. "Population Biobanks' Governance: A Case Study of Knowledge Commons." In *Governing Medical Knowledge Commons*, Katherine J. Strandburg, Brett M. Frischmann, and Michael J. Madison, eds. Cambridge University Press, 2017, 102–120.

Brown, Michael F. *Who Owns Native Culture?* Cambridge, MA: Harvard University Press, 2009.

Burns, Tom R. and Helena Flam. *The Shaping of Social Organization: Social Rule System Theory with Applications*. Sage Publications, 1987.

Choudhury, Suparna, J. R. Fishman, M. L. McGowan, and E. T. Juengst. "Big Data, Open Science and the Brain: Lessons Learned from Genomics." *Frontiers in Human Neuroscience* 8 (2014): 239.

Contreras, Jorge L. "Constructing the Genome Commons." In *Governing Knowledge Commons*, Brett M. Frischmann, Michael J. Madison, and Katherine J. Strandburg, eds. New York: Oxford University Press, 2014.

Contreras, Jorge L. "Leviathan in the Commons: Biomedical Data and the State." In *Governing Medical Knowledge Commons*, Katherine J. Strandburg, Brett M. Frischmann, and Michael J. Madison, eds. Cambridge University Press, 2017, 19–45.

Contreras, Jorge L. "Optimizing Access Policies for Big Data Repositories: Latency Variables and the Genome Commons." In *Big Data Optimization: Recent Developments and Challenges*, Ali Emrouznejad, ed. Cham: Springer, 2016, 201–215.

Contreras, Jorge L. "Prepublication Data Release, Latency, and Genome Commons." *Science* 329, no. 5990 (2010): 393–394.

Contreras, Jorge L. and Jerome H. Reichman. "Sharing by Design: Data and Decentralized Commons." *Science* 350, no. 6266 (2015): 1312–1314.

Crawford, Sue E. and Elinor Ostrom. "A Grammar of Institutions." *American Political Science Review* 89, no. 3 (1995): 582–600.

Daniels, Brigham. "Legispedia." In *Governing Knowledge Commons*, Brett M. Frischmann, Michael J. Madison, and Katherine J. Strandburg, eds. New York: Oxford University Press, 2014, 445–468.

Dietz, Thomas, Elinor Ostrom, and Paul C. Stern. "The Struggle to Govern the Commons." *Science* 302, no. 5652 (2003): 1907–1912.

Digital Library of the Commons. 2009. https://dlc.dlib.indiana.edu/

Evans, B. J. "Genomic Data Commons." In *Governing Medical Knowledge Commons*, Katherine J. Strandburg, Brett M. Frischmann, and Michael J. Madison, eds. Cambridge University Press, 2017, 74–101.

Fagundes, David. "Labor and/as Love: Roller Derby as Constructed Cultural Commons." In *Governing Knowledge Commons*, Brett M. Frischmann, Michael J. Madison, and Katherine J. Strandburg, eds. New York: Oxford University Press, 2014, 417–444.

Fox, Jacqueline. "The Hidden Role of Cost: Medicare Decisions, Transparency and Public Trust." *University of Cincinnati Law Review* 79 (2010): 1–52.

Friedrich, Carl J. "Secrecy versus Privacy: The Democratic Dilemma." *Nomos XIII: Privacy* (1971): 105–120.

Frischmann, Brett M., Michael J. Madison, and Katherine J. Strandburg, eds. *Governing Knowledge Commons*. Oxford University Press, 2014.

Frost, Jeana H. and Michael P. Massagli. "Social Uses of Personal Health Information within PatientsLikeMe, an Online Patient Community: What Can Happen When Patients Have Access to One Another's Data." *Journal of Medical Internet Research* 10, no. 3 (2008): e15.

Fuster Morell, Mayo. "Governance of Online Creation Communities for the Building of Digital Commons: Viewed through the Framework of the Institutional Analysis and Development." In *Governing Knowledge Commons*, Brett M. Frischmann, Michael J. Madison, and Katherine J. Strandburg, eds. New York: Oxford University Press, 2014, 281–312.

Fuster Morell, Mayo. "Governance of Online Creation Communities: Provision of Infrastructure for the Building of Digital Commons." PhD diss., European University Institute, 2010. https://cadmus.eui.eu//handle/1814/14709

Fuster Morell, Mayo. "The Unethics of Sharing: Wikiwashing." *International Review of Information Ethics* 15 (2011): 9–16.

Goffman, Erving. *Frame Analysis: An Essay on the Organization of Experience*. Cambridge, MA: Harvard University Press, 1974.

Gorman, Jessica R., Samantha C. Roberts, Sally A. Dominick, Vanessa L. Malcarne, Andrew C. Dietz, and H. Irene Su. "A Diversified Recruitment Approach Incorporating Social Media Leads to Research Participation Among Young Adult-Aged Female Cancer Survivors." *Journal of Adolescent and Young Adult Oncology* 3, no. 2 (2014): 59–65.

Habermas, Jurgen. *Between Facts and Norms: Contributions to a Discourse Theory of Law and Democracy*. Cambridge, MA: MIT Press, 1996.

Hansson, Mats G., Joakim Dillner, Claus R. Bartram, Joyce A. Carlson, and Gert Helgesson. "Should Donors Be Allowed to Give Broad Consent to Future Biobank Research?" *The Lancet Oncology* 7, no. 3 (2006): 266–269.

Hara, Noriko and Jylisa Doney. "Social Construction of Knowledge in Wikipedia." *First Monday* 20, no. 6 (2015). Accessed March 31, 2017. http://dx.doi.org/10.5210/fm.v20i6.5869.

Hara, Noriko and Madelyn Rose Sanfilippo. "Co-constructing Controversy: Content Analysis of Collaborative Knowledge Negotiation in Online Communities." *Information, Communication & Society* 19, no. 11 (2016): 1587–1604.

Henry, Nicholas L. "Knowledge Management: A New Concern for Public Administration." *Public Administration Review* 34 (1974): 189–196.

Joranson, Kate. "Indigenous Knowledge and the Knowledge Commons." *The International Information & Library Review* 40, no. 1 (2008): 64–72.

Larson, Maja and Margaret Chon. "The Greatest Generational Impact: The Open Neuroscience Movement as an Emerging Knowledge Commons." In *Governing Medical Knowledge Commons*, Katherine J. Strandburg, Brett M. Frischmann, and Michael J. Madison, eds. Cambridge University Press, 2017, 166–191.

Lee, Peter. "Centralization, Fragmentation, and Replication in the Genomic Data Commons." In *Governing Medical Knowledge Commons*, Katherine J. Strandburg, Brett M. Frischmann, and Michael J. Madison, eds. Cambridge University Press, 2017, 46–73.

Madison, Michael J. "Commons at the Intersection of Peer Production, Citizen Science, and Big Data: Galaxy Zoo." In *Governing Knowledge Commons*, Brett M. Frischmann, Michael J. Madison, and Katherine J. Strandburg, eds. New York: Oxford University Press, 2014, 209–254.

Madison, Michael J., Brett M. Frischmann, and Katherine J. Strandburg. "Constructing Commons in the Cultural Environment." *Cornell Law Review* 95 (2009): 657.

Malin, Bradley A., Khaled El Emam, and Christine M. O'Keefe. "Biomedical Data Privacy: Problems, Perspectives, and Recent Advances." *Journal of the American Medical Informatics Association* 20, no. 1 (2013): 2–6.

McGinnis, Michael D. "An Introduction to IAD and the Language of the Ostrom Workshop: A Simple Guide to a Complex Framework." *Policy Studies Journal* 39, no. 1 (2011): 169–183.

Meyer, P. B. "An Inventive Commons: Shared Sources of the Airplane and its Industry." In *Governing Knowledge Commons*, Brett M. Frischmann, Michael J. Madison, and Katherine J. Strandburg, eds. New York: Oxford University Press, 2014, 341–364.

Murray, Laura J. "Exchange Practices among Nineteenth-Century US Newspaper Editors: Cooperation in Competition." In *Governing Knowledge Commons*, Brett M. Frischmann, Michael J. Madison, and Katherine J. Strandburg, eds. New York: Oxford University Press, 2014, 365–390.

Neitzke, Gerald. "Confidentiality, Secrecy, and Privacy in Ethics Consultation." In *HEC Forum*, vol. 19, no. 4, pp. 293–302. Springer Netherlands, 2007.

NIH. "NIH Data Sharing Policy and Implementation Guidance." National Institute of Health. March 5, 2003. https://grants.nih.gov/grants/policy/data_sharing/data_sharing_guidance.htm.

Nissenbaum, Helen. *Privacy in Context: Technology, Policy, and the Integrity of Social Life*. Stanford, CA: Stanford University Press, 2009.

Oliveira, Pedro, Leid Zejnilović, and Helena Canhão. "Challenges and Opportunities in Developing and Sharing Solutions by Patients and Caregivers: The Story of a Knowledge Commons for the Patient Innovation Project." In *Governing Medical Knowledge Commons*, Katherine J. Strandburg, Brett M. Frischmann, Michael J. Madison, eds. Cambridge University Press, 2017, 301–325.

Ostrom, Elinor. *Governing the Commons*. Cambridge: Cambridge University Press, 1990.

Ostrom, Elinor. *Governing the Commons: The Evolution of Institutions for Collective Action*. Cambridge: Cambridge University Press, 2015.

Ostrom, Elinor. *Understanding Institutional Diversity*. Vol. 241. Princeton, NJ: Princeton University Press, 2005.

Ostrom, Elinor and Charlotte Hess, eds. *Understanding Knowledge as a Commons: From Theory to Practice*. Cambridge, MA: MIT Press, 2007.

Pedraza-Fariña, Laura G. "Constructing Interdisciplinary Collaboration: The Oncofertility Consortium as an Emerging Knowledge Commons." In *Governing Medical Knowledge Commons*, Katherine J. Strandburg, Brett M. Frischmann, Michael J. Madison, eds. Cambridge University Press, 2017, 259–284.

Pinkerton, Evelyn and Leonard John. "Creating Local Management Legitimacy." *Marine Policy* 32, no. 4 (2008): 680–691.

Raddick, M. Jordan, Georgia Bracey, Pamela L. Gay, Chris J. Lintott, Carie Cardamone, Phil Murray, Kevin Schawinski, Alexander S. Szalay, and Jan Vandenberg. "Galaxy Zoo: Motivations of Citizen Scientists." *arXiv preprint arXiv:1303.6886* (2013). Accessed March 31, 2017. https://arxiv.org/abs/1303.6886

Robb, Melissa A., Judith A. Racoosin, Rachel E. Sherman, Thomas P. Gross, Robert Ball, Marsha E. Reichman, Karen Midthun, and Janet Woodcock. "The US Food and Drug Administration's Sentinel Initiative: Expanding the Horizons of Medical Product Safety." *Pharmacoepidemiology and Drug Safety* 21, no. S1 (2012): 9–11.

Roden, Dan M., Jill M. Pulley, Melissa A. Basford, Gordon R. Bernard, Ellen W. Clayton, Jeffrey R. Balser, and Dan R. Masys. "Development of a Large-scale de-identified DNA Biobank to Enable Personalized Medicine." *Clinical Pharmacology & Therapeutics* 84, no. 3 (2008): 362–369.

Roski, Joachim, George W. Bo-Linn, and Timothy A. Andrews. "Creating Value in Health Care Through Big Data: Opportunities and Policy Implications." *Health Affairs* 33, no. 7 (2014): 1115–1122.

Sanfilippo, Madelyn, Brett Frischmann, and Katherine Strandburg (2018). "Privacy as Commons: Case Evaluation Through the Governing Knowledge Commons Framework." *Journal of Information Policy* 8 (2018): 116–166.

Schickler, Eric. *Disjointed Pluralism: Institutional Innovation and the Development of the US Congress*. Princeton, NJ: Princeton University Press, 2001.

Schudson, Michael. *Discovering the News: A Social History of American Newspapers*. Printed in the United States of America, Basic Books, 1981.

Schweik, Charles M. and Robert C. English, *Internet Success: A Study of Open-Source Software Commons*. Cambridge, MA: MIT Press, 2012.

Solove, Daniel J. "A Taxonomy of Privacy." *University of Pennsylvania Law Review* 154 (2006): 477–564.

Solove, Daniel J. "Conceptualizing Privacy." *California Law Review* 90 (2002): 1087–1155.

Strandburg, Katherine J., Brett M. Frischmann, and Michael J. Madison, eds. *Governing Medical Knowledge Commons*. Cambridge Studies on Governing Knowledge Commons. Cambridge: Cambridge University Press, 2017.

Strandburg, Katherine J., Brett M. Frischmann, and Can Cui, "The Rare Diseases Clinical Research Network and the Urea Cycle Disorders Consortium as Nested Knowledge Commons." In *Governing Knowledge Commons*, Brett M. Frischmann, Michael J. Madison, and Katherine J. Strandburg, eds. Oxford University Press, 2014, 155–208.

Suzor, Nicolas P. and Darryl Woodford. "Evaluating Consent and Legitimacy Amongst Shifting Community Norms: An EVE Online Case Study." *Journal of Virtual Worlds Research* 6, no. 3 (2013): 1–14. Available at SSRN: https://ssrn.com/abstract=2330108

Tene, Omer and Jules Polonetsky. "Privacy in the Age of Big Data: A Time for Big Decisions." *Stan. L. Rev. Online* 64 (2011): 63.

UK Biobank. "UK Biobank Ethics and Governance Framework." *UK BIOBANK* 3.0 (2007). Accessed March 31, 2017. www.ukbiobank.ac.uk/wp-content/uploads/2011/05/EGF20082.pdf.

Van Overwalle, G. "Governing Genomic Data: Plea for an 'Open Commons'." In *Governing Knowledge Commons*, Brett M. Frischmann, Michael J. Madison, and Katherine J. Strandburg, eds. New York: Oxford University Press, 2014, 137–154.

Vermeulen, B. and D. Guffarth "A Process Model of Invention and the Role of Government, Institutions, and Geography. Anecdotal Evidence from the Aerospace Industry in the Years 1800–1950." In *Innovation Networks for Regional Development*, Vermeulen, Ben and Paier, Manfred, eds. Cham: Springer, 2017, 97–129.

Von Hippel, Eric. "Open User Innovation." In *Handbook of the Economics of Innovation*, Bronwyn H. Hall and Nathan Rosenberg, eds. Vol. 1, North-Holland: Elsevier, 2010, 411–427.

Webber, David and Michael Kremer. "Perspectives on Stimulating Industrial Research and Development for Neglected Infectious Diseases." *Bulletin of the World Health Organization* 79, no. 8 (2001): 735–741.

West, Howard Jack and D. Ross Camidge. "Have Mutation, Will Travel: Utilizing Online Patient Communities and New Trial Strategies to Optimize Clinical Research in the Era of Molecularly Diverse Oncology." *Journal of Thoracic Oncology* 7, no. 3 (2012): 482–484.

Woodruff, Teresa K. "The Oncofertility Consortium – Addressing Fertility in Young People with Cancer." *Nature Reviews Clinical Oncology* 7, no. 8 (2010): 466.

Yin, Robert K. *Case Study Research: Design and Methods*. Thousand Oaks, CA: Sage Publications, 2013.

Zejnilović, Leid, Pedro Oliveira, and Helena Canhão. "Innovations by and for Patients, and Their Place in the Future Health Care System." In *Boundaryless Hospital*, Horst Albach, Heribert Meffert, Andreas Pinkwart, Ralf Reichwald, and Wilfried von Eiff, eds. Berlin, Heidelberg: Springer, 2016, 341–357.

PART I

Personal Information as a Knowledge Commons Resource

2

How Private Individuals Maintain Privacy and Govern Their Own Health Data Cooperative

MIDATA in Switzerland

Felix Gille and Effy Vayena

2.1 BACKGROUND

We as private individuals provide a wide range of data about our personal lives via our smartphones, loyalty cards, fitness trackers, and other digital health devices. These devices collect increasingly diverse and comprehensive data about us. Depending on the mobile applications we use, devices collect data about our daily routines, location, preferences, desires and interests, shopping behaviors, mood, illness, and more. When this personal data is linked to health records – including genome data and phenotype data – or linked to other data collected in our environment, such as that collected by state administrations or financial systems, the data has huge potential for public health research and society in general (Wellcome Trust, 2015; Vayena and Blasimme, 2017). Precision medicine, including pharmacogenomics, particularly depends on the potential of data linkage (Huang, Mulyasasmita, and Rajagopal, 2016). New advanced data processing techniques help researchers to make sense of data in a way that was not possible before. With this new capacity to analyze linked data, researchers today can retrieve and assess valuable and clinically relevant information (Blasimme, Vayena, and Hafen, 2018). One way to develop such linked data sets and to make them available for research is through health data cooperatives. An example of such a health data cooperation is MIDATA – a health data cooperative recently established in Switzerland and the main focus of this chapter.

In practice, our society cannot yet fully exploit the potential of linked data sets, even though data cooperatives similar to MIDATA are slowly multiplying. This is because private people act as data sources, but they have minimal control over the data collected and do not know where the data is stored. Health apps are a case in point: these private services operate under a particular business model, that is to harvest a private individuals' data and exploit it for the company's own financial

We thank Ernst Hafen, co-founder of MIDATA and Professor at ETH Zürich; Madelyn Sanfilippo, an editor of this volume; and Shannon Hubbs and Stephanie Bishop, from our research group, for their valuable feedback. We thank Personalized Health and Related Technologies (grant 1-000018-025) for their support.

profit. In this business model, data is market capital (Sadowski, 2019). This is a lucrative business, and with an estimated annual growth rate of 20 percent, by 2020 utilizing personal data could deliver an annual economic benefit of €330 billion to enterprises in Europe. Furthermore, the combined total digital identity value of individuals could comprise around 8 percent of the EU-27 gross domestic product (Boston Consulting Group, 2012). Despite these impressive figures, the pressing question is: to what extent do we as data providers and as a society benefit from these business models? One could argue, as ETH Zürich Professor Ernst Hafen does, that '*the data economy is broken, because we do not have control over our data*' (SWISS RE, 2018). Ordinary individuals are dispossessed of control over their data and cannot access the revenue their data generates.

Exacerbating this sense of powerlessness for private individuals, several large companies recently used personal data in ways misaligned with public norms and values. These scandals led to public outcry against privacy breaches as well as abuse of power. Facebook has been a chief offender, with noteworthy failings such as providing the political consultancy firm Cambridge Analytica access to over 50 million user profiles, which they used to influence the 2016 USA election and the UK Brexit campaign (Cadwalladr and Graham-Harrison, 2018). In the healthcare sector, the contract between the Royal Free NHS Foundation Trust, London, and Google Deep Mind breached the United Kingdom's Data Protection Act with controversial implications for patient privacy. The Trust provided Deep Mind with about 1.6 million patients' personal data as part of a study to test a detection and diagnosis system for acute kidney injury (Information Commissioner's Office, 2018; Powles and Hodson, 2017).

In addition to lack of control and privacy breaches, security breaches present a further challenge to the management of personal data. Whereas a privacy breach refers to a company inappropriately sharing data, a security breach occurs when hackers access data repositories, or data is leaked due to poor data security mechanisms. For example, think of the computer software updates that could have contained the WannaCry ransomware attack in 2017, had they been performed. Instead, staff neglected the updates, nefarious ransomware exploited the vulnerability, and the English NHS performance was compromised for days (National Audit Office, 2018).

These improprieties led to increased public skepticism over whether data-driven private (and to some degree, public) enterprises can be trusted, including within the healthcare system (Symantec, 2015; Hafen, 2018). We can easily observe the uptake of the term "trust" as a prominent concept in the public sphere, which hints at a public need to discuss issues of trust. This is alarming evidence that healthcare systems need to be reformed, including the data economy within them (Gille, Smith, and Mays, 2014). Prevailing public trust in the healthcare system is paramount for a healthcare system to function well (Gille, Smith, and Mays, 2017). If the public does not trust organizations in the healthcare system to protect and appropriately manage the data entrusted to them, value generation is at risk. In particular, the healthcare industry depends on access to personal data, with an estimated 40 percent of the healthcare system's benefit generated on the basis of personal identity data (Boston Consulting Group, 2012).

To complicate the picture, Mhairi Aitken and colleagues concluded that in fact conditional support for sharing and linking health data exists. This seems to contradict the concerns raised earlier. Public concerns pertain to issues such as confidentiality, individuals' control over their data, uses and abuses of data, and potential harms that may ensue. However, the public also supports private companies' research when actual or potential public benefits from research are foreseeable, as well as when the public trusts the individuals or organizations leading and overseeing the research, data linkage, and data sharing (Aitken et al., 2016). Other studies in the field similarly highlight the importance of trust and clear public benefit of research (Wellcome Trust, 2015; Audrey et al., 2016).

To restore the data economy – that is, to build public trust toward data-rich enterprises, as well as trust for how data flow between different enterprises is managed; to establish individual control over personal data; and to ensure privacy as well as data security – we need to answer several practical, ethical, legal, and social questions. Ultimately, these issues can be addressed through an appropriate governance model, but this is no easy feat. What governance model do we need for aggregated personal data sets? Who should have legitimate control over personal data, and how can we foster digital self-determination? How can personal data be securely stored? How can we increase transparency about who uses people's data, and how they use it? Who is accountable for aggregated data sets stored in research facilities?

In response to these questions, health data cooperatives can perhaps provide a suitable model to govern aggregated data sets. Private individuals in cooperatives democratically control the governance processes of the cooperative itself and the data stored within the cooperative. Health data cooperatives therefore may be able to provide a fair governance model for health data ecosystems that may benefit society through innovation, knowledge generation, improved quality of healthcare, or advances in diagnostics and therapy (Hafen, 2019). Furthermore, health data cooperatives empower private people, as control of personal data shifts from corporate enterprises back to individuals who provide their data for research. This is of particular importance, as private individuals are the legitimate controllers of their own data, especially when it comes to health data (Wilbanks and Topol, 2016). Moreover, health data cooperatives uniquely combine a list of attributes that are crucial for legitimate data aggregation. Examples include open and collective governance principles; not-for-profit status, as revenues are re-invested into the cooperative itself; and the use of open-source software to simplify the creation of new data cooperatives (Van Roessel, Reumann, and Brand, 2018).

Prior to this chapter, examples of health-related cooperatives are presented in the previous volume in this series: *Governing Medical Knowledge Commons* (Frischmann, Strandburg, and Madison, 2017). Among these, the authors of the book discuss health data commons, such as Genomic Data Commons (Evans, 2017). Evans describes the legal and practical obstacles of aggregating genomic data in commons for the US context. In particular, these obstacles relate to decentralized data storage, consent alignment and data access, as well as aggregation (Evans, 2016). Evans encourages the professional community to overcome these obstacles and to find appropriate ethical governance mechanisms for such commons.

Also, in the 2014 volume *Governing Knowledge Commons*, both Contreras and Van Overwalle analyze the construction of genome commons (Van Overwalle, 2014; Contreras, 2014). However, in this example commons are constructed in a different format in which data is not aggregated, but a public network was built allowing data sets to be shared. They observe that the rapidly growing data volume, described by some as a data tsunami, will flood data cooperatives. Importantly, they observe that commons structures should be designed to fit the complex and highly specialized nature of genetic research structures:

> Failing to appreciate the structural rules implemented to address these issues, or seeking to dispense with them in favor of a more broadly "open" public goods models . . . could have adverse consequences. In particular the elimination of rules regulating human subject protection could limit the willingness of individuals to participate in genomic research, and the elimination of data-generator priorities could weaken the incentives of data-generating scientists. Each of these effects could negatively impact the growth of the commons itself. (Contreras, 2014, 130)

Taken together, the two examples present several structural, practical, ethical, and legal challenges that are inherent in the development of medical commons and likely also apply to the development of health data cooperatives, such as the example presented in this chapter. Tying in with the previous examples and in response to the societal challenges described earlier, the *Data and Health Association*, founded in 2012, aimed to establish a health data cooperative for Switzerland. As a result of these efforts, the health data cooperative MIDATA was co-founded by a group of researchers of ETH Zürich and the University of Applied Sciences Bern, in 2015 (MIDATA Genossenschaft, 2017; Mòdol, 2019). The basic idea behind MIDATA is conceptually similar to a bank account. A person can open an account to deposit copies of her data (which was collected and stored elsewhere), and then she can choose to make the data accessible to researchers to advance science. This is shown in Figure 2.1.

In addition, people can become formal cooperative members, in contrast to those who only open an account. Eventually, each individual's account will contain a wide range of different data sets that belong to that one person. The data stored by MIDATA on servers located in Switzerland is encrypted and can only be accessed

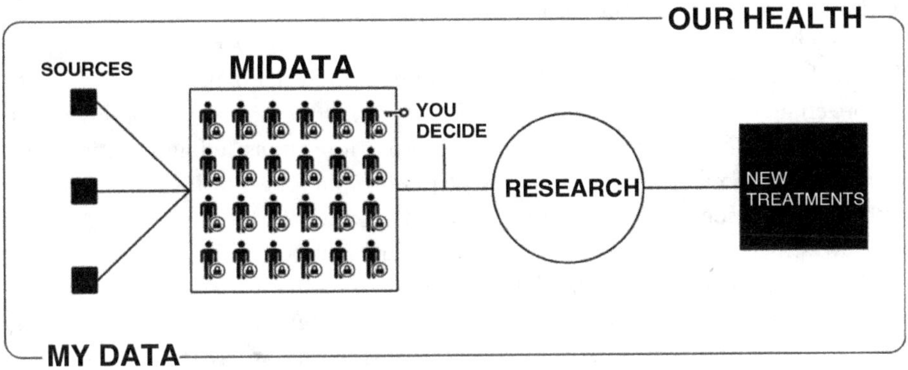

FIGURE 2.1 Simplified overview of the MIDATA cooperative (MIDATA Genossenschaft, 2019c)

by the account owner, unless they release it for a specific purpose. To access this rich data source, external parties can submit a proposal for data use. If the proposal is positively reviewed by the ethics committee, each account holder can consent to release her data to the specific project. Account holders need to release their data for each project individually, as this action is a central privacy control mechanism of the data cooperative.

Culturally, MIDATA is embedded in a society with a cooperative tradition in many fields apart from healthcare. This is arguably an advantage for the implementation of MIDATA, as the Swiss society is well familiar with the basic principles of cooperatives. Nowadays, some of the most prominent enterprises in the Swiss public sphere are cooperatives. Two notable examples are the grocery chain Migros and the car sharing platform Mobility, run by the Swiss Federal Railways (SBB). Migros is one of the most recognized grocery stores in Switzerland. The Migros cooperative comprises 2.1 million members (growth rate 0.7 percent in 2016), about 50 enterprises that are linked to the Migros group, and the Mirgos group had total sales of 27738 million CHF in 2016. Migros' roots stretch back to 1925, when five Ford Model T cars started selling groceries in Zürich. Gottlieb Duttweiler (1888–1962), the founder of Migros and a well-known Swiss personality, aimed to build a direct link between producers and consumers, similar to the health data cooperative described in this chapter. Also, Duttweiler with his wife formulated fifteen theses that make up the moral spirit of Migros. To highlight a few key theses, Duttweiler pointed out the importance of transparency, accountability, and the involvement of women in the decision-making and governance of the cooperative. The cooperative is present in the public sphere, and Migros recently broadcasted a TV advertising campaign called the "Migros Besitzer" – the Migros owner – showing the benefits of membership in the Migros cooperative (Migros, 2017). Similarly, Mobility started as a cooperative in 1987, and is now the largest car sharing platform in Switzerland.

Mobility is present in every village with more than 10,000 inhabitants. Today, Mobility has more than 50,000 cooperative members and over 120,000 customers. The declared goal is to minimize the traffic burden in Switzerland and contribute to a more efficient and individualized mobility solution for customers (Mobility, 2019). Mobility's signature red cars help distinguish Mobility as a highly visible and recognizable cooperative within the Swiss public sphere. Mobility and Migros are just two prominent examples among many that indicate the cooperative idea is already well established in the Swiss media landscape and public sphere.

Given that people in Switzerland are familiar with the concept of cooperatives, and in light of the pressing need to find an alternative governance model for the use of personal data in research, the founders of MIDATA currently have high hopes that MIDATA is a platform that could resolve the challenges raised earlier.

2.1.1 *Tool of Analysis: Governing Knowledge Commons Framework*

To describe the MIDATA cooperative in a structured and detailed way, the remainder of this chapter will apply the Governing Knowledge Commons (GKC) framework to MIDATA. Brett Frischmann, Michael Madison, and Katherine Strandburg developed the GKC framework, drawing inspiration from Elinor Ostrom and her colleagues' work on the institutional analysis and development framework (Ostrom, 1990; Frischmann, Madison, and Strandburg, 2014; Strandburg, Frischmann, and Madison, 2017). This framework allows researchers to analyze "institutionalized community governance of the sharing and, in some cases, creation, of information, science, knowledge, data, and other types of intellectual and cultural resources" (Frischmann, Madison, and Strandburg, 2014, 3). In combination with Helen Nissenbaum's theory that understands privacy as contextual integrity (Nissenbaum, 2010), the GKC framework is useful when examining how individuals maintain privacy and govern their own health data cooperative. Broadly, the framework considers the background environment, attributes, governance, patterns, and outcomes of knowledge commons. The remainder of this chapter will follow the structure of the GKC framework to ease comparison across the different case studies of this and earlier volumes of the knowledge commons book series (Strandburg, Frischmann, and Madison, 2017, 16–17).

At present, MIDATA is in the buildup phase. Several small research projects, as presented later, contribute to the testing and refinement of MIDATA. This chapter is part of an ongoing (2018–2021) health ethics and policy research project at ETH Zürich, Switzerland, where we aim to develop further the existing governance model of MIDATA. Our main purpose in this research is to create a systemic oversight model for MIDATA (described later) that is considered trustworthy by the general public and MIDATA members. In this research we engage with governance theory, law, and policy, and will conduct interviews with different stakeholders, such as researchers who work within the cooperative, members of the cooperative, and members of the general public. For this chapter we gathered background information by interviewing MIDATA co-founder Ernst Hafen. For the interview we developed questions that follow the content of the GKC framework and Nissenbaum's privacy theory. In addition, we examined the statutes of MIDATA as well as further policy and administrative documents of the cooperative. The advantage of applying the GKC framework and insights from privacy theory as contextual integrity at this stage is the possibility to leverage the perspective the framework provides to inform MIDATA's ongoing development. Applying the GKC framework to MIDATA can help us better understand how MIDATA processes and structural components contribute to the community governance of MIDATA. The systematic design of the GKC framework allows us to dissect MIDATA to unfold the involved attributes, the present governance structure, and anticipated outcomes. In addition, the theory of privacy as contextual integrity can help us to improve the governance processes and structures that apply to privacy within MIDATA.

2.2 ATTRIBUTES OF MIDATA

MIDATA is a member-owned cooperative that aims to store and aggregate personal data from people who open an account at MIDATA. Cooperative members are the main actors in the cooperative as well as the main resource providers for the cooperative itself. Ultimately, the goal of MIDATA is to provide a secure storage for personal data, in which account holders themselves retain full control over their data. As MIDATA members, people contribute to research by granting others access to their data. The following sections will describe MIDATA's resources, goals, and objectives in more detail, and the role private individuals take in this cooperative.

2.2.1 *MIDATA Resources*

The resources pooled in the MIDATA cooperative are copies of account holders' personal data. Such data can be transferred to the account by the account holder him/herself; or in some cases apps use MIDATA to store data, and account holders using such an app can allow the data to be deposited in to their MIDATA accounts directly. Accessing copies of personal data has been simplified within the European Union with the newly established European Union's General Data Protection Regulation. This regulation emphasizes in Article 20 that individuals have the right to copies of their data. This right applies to EU residents, and non-EU residents can ask for copies of data stored by companies based within the EU (European Parliament Council of the European Union, 2016). It is anticipated that this European regulation will supportively affect the data transfer processes for MIDATA, even though the regulation does not apply in Switzerland as

Switzerland is not an EU member state (Ngwa and Hafen, 2017). Swiss residents can make use of the GDPR when they request data that is stored within the EU.

The allergy app Ally Science is an example of an app that stores data on MIDATA. Launched by Bern University of Applied Sciences and University Hospital Zurich, Ally Science is part of a research project to collect pollen allergy symptoms data in combination with location data. Thereby, the study investigates pollen allergies in Switzerland (MIDATA Genossenschaft, 2019a). If the app user has no MIDATA account, the app user is asked to open a MIDATA account before s/he uses the app. By July 2018, 8,100 app users had registered (Hafen, 2018). Another use case example is a research study involving multiple sclerosis patients. Study participants use an app called MitrendS to capture their neurological development over time. Generally speaking, each citizen generates a huge amount of data that can be stored in MIDATA accounts so that each citizen can contribute to the development of the cooperative's resource pool (Mòdol, 2019).

2.2.2 *MIDATA Account Holders, Cooperative Members, and the Swiss Community*

Because the cooperative model of MIDATA is designed to be regional, MIDATA is open to any person residing in Switzerland. To open an account on MIDATA, one does not need to be a member of the cooperative. Yet, if a person would like to actively participate in the governance of MIDATA, a community member needs to become a cooperative member for a fee of 40 CHF. The cooperative has an altruistic motivation that goes beyond the MIDATA community itself and seeks to benefit the general society, and this is evident in the objectives outlined later.

2.2.3 *Goals and Objectives of MIDATA*

The overarching goal of MIDATA is to establish regional, member-owned data cooperatives that contribute to research and ultimately to the benefit of society via their stored data. In more detail and as stated by Article II of the MIDATA statutes, the objectives are:

(1) "The Cooperative pursues as a non-profit organization the following objectives:
   (a) it operates a secure IT platform ('MIDATA platform') for storage, management, and sharing of personal data of any kind, in particular health and education data, and to provide related services;
   (b) it makes the MIDATA platform available to natural persons (members and non-members) who may use the platform as personal data account holders ('account holders');

(c) it promotes broad Cooperative membership among account holders, thus allowing them to partake in the governance of the Cooperative, and it helps members pursue common interests;
(d) it promotes the digital self-determination of the population by enabling account holders to use their personal data as self-determining agents and according to their wishes, in particular to support research purposes;
(e) it promotes the collective interests of the account holders and it enables the utilization of their personal data as a common resource. This is achieved by enabling individual account holders to accept requests for the analysis of their data and to give explicit informed consent for the secondary use of their personal data by third parties in return for an economic remuneration to the cooperative;
(f) by providing the MIDATA platform, it fosters the development of an innovative ecosystem in which third parties can offer data-based services to the account holders;
(g) it promotes medical research projects and projects that aim to realize a fair digital society and that promote the digital self-determination of the population; and
(h) it employs the scientific results and income derived from the secondary usage of personal data in the framework of the aforementioned objectives.

(2) With its operative and commercial activities, the Cooperative strives to achieve a positive effect upon society and the environment.
(3) The Cooperative may engage in all activities that are directly or indirectly related to its purpose.
(4) The Cooperative may support the founding of cooperatives of equal purpose in Switzerland and abroad, and it may form a federation of cooperatives together with them.
(5) The Cooperative may establish branches and subsidiaries in Switzerland and abroad, hold interests in other companies in Switzerland and abroad, and acquire, hold and sell real estate." (MIDATA Genossenschaft, 2017, 2,3)

Key values represented by the objectives are data security, being open to all people, promotion of cooperative membership, promotion of digital self-determination, promotion of collective interest, fostering innovation and medical research, and re-investment in the goals of the cooperative. Together these values eventually lead into the overarching aim to achieve a positive effect on society and environment. Furthermore, to build a network of cooperatives, MIDATA may help to facilitate similar cooperatives. To finance itself, the cooperative may engage in financial investment activities.

All key values are relevant to this cooperative's character, but we consider *promotion of digital self-determination* the one value that makes this cooperative distinctive. As we presented in the introduction of this chapter, outside of the cooperative model, private individuals' ability to determine how their personal data is used is limited, if not impossible. Therefore, MIDATA aims to foster *digital self-determination* as one of the key incentives for members of the general public to participate in MIDATA and eventually become MIDATA cooperative members. Objective 1 (d) underlines this clearly by promoting the personal use and free choice over what one wishes to do with his/her data, focusing in particular on research.

When we compare the MIDATA objectives to the cooperative principles as stated by the International Co-operative Alliance (Voluntary and Open Membership; Democratic Member Control; Member Economic Participation; Autonomy and Independence; Education, Training, and Information; Cooperation among Cooperatives; and Concern for Community), it becomes clear that MIDATA is in line with the cooperative tradition (International Co-operative Alliance, 2019). Based on the similarity between the MIDATA cooperative values and general cooperative principles, and given the prevalence of cooperative membership already present in Switzerland, it seems likely people will easily familiarize themselves with the governance principles of MIDATA as they participate in MIDATA activities. This should facilitate easy access and participation in MIDATA. Nevertheless, MIDATA's focus on scientific data is clearly different from grocery trading and car sharing. It is essential to educate participants so they are equipped to contribute to the MIDATA governance in a meaningful way. Yet, MIDATA participants can build on their previous familiarity with cooperatives in other areas of their lives.

As MIDATA focuses at present on healthcare and public health research, data stored within MIDATA may contribute to the improvement of health for all. Furthermore, it is anticipated that the cooperative as a whole could advance public literacy and public control in the field of digital self-determination. These two aspirations together comprise the key value of knowledge production within the cooperative.

2.3 GOVERNANCE OF MIDATA

The legitimate action arena for MIDATA is research, development, and education. At the moment, MIDATA focuses on healthcare research, in particular research that exploits aggregated data sets. We anticipate that in the future MIDATA will extend to other research fields such as education. In doing so, MIDATA's success depends on cooperative members investing significant trust in MIDATA, and in the public and research institutions that apply to access their data. Therefore, MIDATA needs to maintain not only an appropriate governance model but also trustful relationships with all stakeholders to be able to compile meaningful data sets, and also to appear as a valuable partner for researchers, so that they invest their resources into MIDATA. When it comes to the involvement of private companies, it will be fundamental to adhere to robust governance structures within MIDATA. In particular, it will be necessary to show how corporate research will benefit the wider society. Furthermore, private companies will need to show how privacy is maintained and disclose their accountability structures (Aitken et al., 2016). That is to show, in an understandable way, who is accountable for the research conducted with the data provided by MIDATA members. Such structures need to not only meet ethical values but also align with good governance. A governance model that is likely to be particularly suitable for MIDATA is the *systemic oversight approach* (Vayena and Blasimme, 2018). As data volume increases, the situation requires adaptive governance models that are able to respond to the challenges that come with big data and the accumulation of data ecosystems. Among other challenges, experts anticipate that current informed consent processes are limited in their capacity to provide a meaningful choice to data donors about how they control large volumes of their data. In addition, broad consent to a frankly unlimited future use of data, as often seen in current consent designs for medical research, is not only ethically questionable but also provides the donor with no control over future use of their data. Finally, the increasing use of machine learning algorithms in data-intense research challenges research accountability in a way that an informed consent process is not able to cover appropriately (Vayena and Blasimme, 2018). In response to these challenges, which are also relevant to MIDATA, systemic oversight is a governance model that builds on the principles of adaptivity, flexibility, monitoring, responsiveness, reflexivity, and inclusiveness. These principles should not be understood as fixed mechanisms but rather as a Leitmotiv for MIDATA governance. As data handling is at the core of MIDATA, it will be pivotal to implement governance mechanisms that are adaptive to new types of data as well as increasing data volumes. Also, as different research projects apply for data use, MIDATA governance mechanisms need to be flexible to meet the requirements of how the data will be used, as opposed to governance mechanisms that are tailored towards the origin of data. Furthermore, as nowadays data sets are linked, and therefore source data will be used to develop new data sets, it is essential to monitor data use beyond the initial research proposal approval, especially since novel data mining and machine learning methods potentially pose risks to privacy and may lead to discrimination. To accommodate for potential malicious privacy breaches or other failures, governance mechanisms need to be responsive and prepared to address such problems. Also, data sets provide information not only about the data donor but also potentially about his/her environment. Therefore, governance needs to be reflexive about these issues. This requires reflexive analysis of assumptions and biases that are embedded in machine learning algorithms. Lastly, governance should include all relevant stakeholders in governance processes to not exclude underrepresented groups. This engagement should foster public dialogue and learning (Blasimme and Vayena, 2018; forthcoming). As mentioned earlier, our present research activities in the field of governance at MIDATA precisely test the suitability of systemic oversight for health data cooperatives.

Currently, MIDATA comprises four bodies: the general assembly, administration, audit office, as well as an ethics committee. The general assembly is the highest body, qualified among other competences to elect members for the administration, audit office, and ethics committee, as well as to amend the statutes and close down MIDATA. The management contains the management board and coordinates the operational work of the cooperative. The auditor is an independent body in line with the Swiss Code of Obligations. Last, the ethics committee reviews the quality of projects that apply for the use of data stored in the cooperative. This review also assesses how applicants aim to ensure privacy and what privacy preserving mechanisms are proposed by the applicant. Furthermore, the ethics committee advises the general assembly regarding reviewed proposals (MIDATA Genossenschaft, 2017).

Actors involved in the governance process can be divided roughly into four groups: first, cooperative members – membership confers formal governance powers; second, private individuals who have an account on the MIDATA platform but who lack formal governance power as they are not cooperative members. Governance power can easily be acquired by becoming a member of the MIDATA cooperative; third, professionals who are members of different committees and provide expertise and make decisions, for example about the ethical validity of research applicants; and fourth, administrative staff that run the cooperative on a daily basis and maintain the IT infrastructure. From a decision-making point of view, three decision points are of crucial importance. First and foremost, account holders have the exclusive decision power on what data should be stored within the cooperative as well as which data they would like to release into a research project. Then, elected members of the ethics committee (elected by the general assembly) review and decide which research projects are deemed to be in line with ethical as well as cooperative norms and therefore are approved to request data from account holders. Last, the general assembly is the highest decision-making body within the cooperative and therefore has the last word when it comes to committee elections, statutes amendments, or any other structural and far-reaching decision. At the current stage of governance development, people who have an account but are not cooperative members have no powers over cooperative governance. Nonmembers of MIDATA who do not hold an account with MIDATA can open an account at any time. The public visibility of MIDATA mainly relies on media coverage and academic events related to either research projects that work with MIDATA, as described earlier, or related to professionals who are involved in MIDATA. So far, MIDATA was covered in several local and national news articles in Switzerland, as well as in scientific journals (MIDATA Genossenschaft, 2019b).

With respect to privacy governance, at present MIDATA operates two mechanisms to maintain privacy. On the institutional level, there are ethics committee reviews. At the account holder level, there is the dynamic consent process, whereby account holders must actively consent to research as well as release their data into a research project in order for an applicant to access it. Here, MIDATA's Privacy Policy in articles 5 and 6 clearly puts the account holder in the center of activities that are related to the account holder's data. Only law enforcement can override the exclusive data access rights of account holders (MIDATA Genossenschaft, 2018). Both measures are crucial to maintain account holders' privacy. The ethics committee works with professional expertise to review how the applying research projects will preserve privacy within their research projects. Both mechanisms together also control appropriate data flow. In the last instance, it is the account holder's decision to consent to data sharing depending on whether s/he finds the data flow appropriate.

2.4 PATTERNS AND OUTCOMES OF THE MIDATA

It is anticipated that MIDATA will lead to a range of benefits for not only cooperative members but also society in general. Considering the objectives of MIDATA, cooperative members and account holders will benefit foremost from the ability to control and manage their own personal data repository due to their exclusive control rights over their data. Nested within a governance framework designed to promote ethical, secure, and transparent data sharing, account holders should find a dependable platform to store and collect copies of their personal data. In addition, cooperative members have governance powers over the cooperative itself, and can therefore directly and in a democratic manner influence the governance processes within the cooperative. By personal control over data as well as the possibility to take part and shape governance processes, cooperative members maintain high levels of control over their own privacy.

Furthermore, as the cooperative is open to the general public, everybody has the opportunity to open an account on the MIDATA platform and to become a cooperative member. MIDATA membership growth will not only strengthen the cooperative by increasing the data volume and thereby the value for research, but a growing cooperative will also democratize the data economy within Switzerland. This is because ultimately MIDATA provides a governance tool that allows individuals to determine what happens with their data. Now, if a high proportion of Swiss residents store copies of their data in data cooperatives, they will eventually take back the legitimate control of their own data, which was one of the driving motivations for the foundation of MIDATA. This entire process is supported by the coordination role MIDATA plays by connecting its members and building an exchange network for members and account holders.

The expected social benefit of MIDATA will depend on the research conducted with data stored in MIDATA and MIDATA's actions in the area of public relations, advocacy, and education. MIDATA understands itself as a platform that drives innovation, facilitates medical research projects, and promotes the digital self-determination of private individuals. With this focus, MIDATA may also be able to raise digital literacy among the general public and to act as an advocate for a fair data economy within Switzerland. In addition to the focus on Switzerland, the founders of MIDATA also work actively to develop relationships with other research institutions across Europe, to spread the MIDATA model and to drive the health data cooperative movement. At the moment, MIDATA is building a cooperative ecosystem with the Berlin Institute of Health, Charité, Germany; Medical Delta, City of Rotterdam, the Netherlands; Vito Research Institute, Belgium; Oxford University Hospital Foundation Trust, UK; and the INDEPTH-Network.org. Together, they focus on informing health policy through improved health information in low- and middle-income countries (Hafen, 2018).

Considering the benefits for cooperative members, wider society, and international partners, MIDATA has the potential to contribute to legitimate research outputs and innovation in society. As MIDATA is structured following cooperative principles, in combination with the Swiss tradition of corporativism, the actions and outputs of MIDATA are likely to be perceived as legitimate by the general public as well as cooperative members. Nevertheless, it will be crucial to maintain and build a governance structure that addresses the concerns raised in the introduction of this chapter to make MIDATA a true alternative for member-controlled data sharing, and eventually a competitive data platform that attracts stakeholders from across society and research.

2.5 CONCLUSION

This chapter discussed the Switzerland-based health data cooperative MIDATA. In response to concerns about the present health data economy, MIDATA was founded to provide a governance structure for data storage that supports individuals' digital self-determination, by allowing MIDATA members to control their own personal data flow and to store such data in a secure environment. The aim of MIDATA is to give data control back to the legitimate data controllers, the people, and thereby allows individuals to regulate their own personal privacy. In addition, in line with basic cooperative principles and considering MIDATA's aim to advance science, MIDATA may contribute to the advancement of society and innovation.

MIDATA will refine its governance structure to account for the challenges that burgeoning data volumes and diversity present. In particular, current research activities focus on making the governance structure even more robust by adopting the systemic oversight approach. Then, it is anticipated that MIDATA will grow and that the cooperative data storage model will establish itself as a serious alternative to existing data repository models.

REFERENCES

Aitken, Mhairi, Jenna de St. Jorre, Claudia Pagliari, Ruth Jepson, and Sarah Cunningham-Burley. "Public Responses to the Sharing and Linkage of Health Data for Research

Purposes: A Systematic Review and Thematic Synthesis of Qualitative Studies." *BMC Medical Ethics* 17, no. 1 (2016): 73. https://doi.org/10.1186/s12910-016–0153-x.

Audrey, Suzanne, Lindsey Brown, Rona Campbell, Andy Boyd, and John Macleod. "Young People's Views about Consenting to Data Linkage: Findings from the PEARL Qualitative Study." *BMC Medical Research Methodology* 16, no. 1 (2016): 34. https://doi.org/10.1186/s12874-016–0132-4.

Blasimme, Alessandro and Effy Vayena. 2018. "Systemic Oversight: A New Approach for Precision Medicine and Digital Health." Bill of Health, Petrie-Flom Center at Harvard Law School. 2018. http://blog.petrieflom.law.harvard.edu/2018/04/04/systemic-oversight-a-new-approach-for-precision-medicine-and-digital-health/.

Forthcoming. "Towards systemic oversight in big data health research: implementation principles" In *CUP Handbook of Health Research Regulation*. Editor Graeme Laurie. Cambridge University Press.

Blasimme, Alessandro, Effy Vayena, and Ernst Hafen. 2018. "Democratizing Health Research Through Data Cooperatives." *Philosophy and Technology*. Springer Netherlands. https://doi.org/10.1007/s13347-018–0320-8.

Boston Consulting Group. 2012. "The Value of Our Digital Identity."

Cadwalladr, C. and E. Graham-Harrison. 2018. "The Cambridge Analytica Files Cambridge Analytica Revealed: 50 Million Facebook Profiles Harvested for Cambridge Analytica in Major Data Breach." *The Guardian UK Edition*, 2018. www.theguardian.com/news/2018/mar/17/cambridge-analytica-facebook-influence-us-election.

Contreras, Jorge L. "Constructing the Genome Commons." In *Governing Knowledge Commons*, Brett M. Frischmann, Michael J. Madison, and Katherine J. Strandburg, eds. Oxford University Press, 2014, 99–136. https://doi.org/10.1093/acprof:oso/9780199972036.003.0004.

European Parliament Council of the European Union. 2016. "Regulation (EU) 2016/679 of the European Parliament and of the Council of 27 April 2016 on the Protection of Natural Persons with Regard to the Processing of Personal Data and on the Free Movement of Such Data, and Repealing Directive 95/46/EC General Da." https://eur-lex.europa.eu/legal-content/EN/ALL/?uri=CELEX:32016R0679.

Evans, Barbara J. "Barbarians at the Gate." *American Journal of Law & Medicine* 42, no. 4 (2016): 651–685. https://doi.org/10.1177/0098858817700245.

"Genomic Data Commons." In *Governing Medical Knowledge Commons*, Brett M. Frischmann, Katherine J. Strandburg, and Michael J. Madison, eds. Cambridge Studies on Governing Knowledge Commons. Cambridge: Cambridge University Press, 2017, 74–101. https://doi.org/DOI:10.1017/9781316544587.005.

Frischmann, Brett M., Michael J. Madison, and Katherine J. Strandburg. "Governing Knowledge Commons." In *Governing Knowledge Commons*, Brett M. Frischmann, Michael J. Madison, and Katherine J. Strandburg, eds. New York: Oxford University Press, 2014, 1–44. https://doi.org/10.1093/acprof:oso/9780199972036.003.0001.

Frischmann, Brett M., Katherine J. Strandburg, and Michael J. Madison. "Governing Medical Knowledge Commons." In *Cambridge Studies on Governing Knowledge Commons*, Brett M. Frischmann, Katherine J. Strandburg, and Michael J. Madison, eds. Cambridge: Cambridge University Press, 2017. https://doi.org/DOI:10.1017/9781316544587.

Gille, Felix, Sarah Smith, and Nicholas Mays. "Why Public Trust in Health Care Systems Matters and Deserves Greater Research Attention." *Journal of Health Services Research & Policy* 20, no. 1 (2014): 62–64. https://doi.org/10.1177/1355819614543161.

"Towards a Broader Conceptualisation of 'Public Trust' in the Health Care System." *Social Theory & Health* 15, no. 1 (2017): 25–43. https://doi.org/10.1057/s41285-016–0017-y.

Hafen, Ernst. 2018. "Data to the People – MIDATA Personal Data Cooperatives." In *FEAM Conference*. www.feam.eu/wp-content/uploads/FINAL-2019-04-25-precision-medicine-report_final-1.pdf.

2019. "Personal Data Cooperatives – A New Data Governance Framework for Data Donations and Precision Health BT – The Ethics of Medical Data Donation." In, edited by Jenny Krutzinna and Luciano Floridi, 141–149. Cham: Springer International Publishing. https://doi.org/10.1007/978–3-030–04363-6_9.

Huang, Bevan E., Widya Mulyasasmita, and Gunaretnam Rajagopal. "The Path from Big Data to Precision Medicine." *Expert Review of Precision Medicine and Drug Development* 1, no. 2 (2016): 129–143. https://doi.org/10.1080/23808993.2016.1157686.

Information Commissioner's Office. 2018. "Royal Free – Google DeepMind Trial Failed to Comply with Data Protection Law." ICO. 2018. https://ico.org.uk/about-the-ico/news-and-events/news-and-blogs/2017/07/royal-free-google-deepmind-trial-failed-to-comply-with-data-protection-law/.

International Co-operative Alliance. 2019. "Cooperative Identity, Values & Principles." 2019. www.ica.coop/en/cooperatives/cooperative-identity.

MIDATA Genossenschaft. 2017. *Statuten Der MIDATA Genossenschaft Mit Sitz in Zürich*. https://midata.coop/docs/MIDATA_Statuten_20170905.pdf.

2018. "Privacy Policy." 2018. https://test.midata.coop/#/portal/terms/midata-privacy-policy.

2019a. "Ally Science." 2019. https://allyscience.ch/en/home/.

2019b. "MIDATA MEDIA." 2019. www.midata.coop/en/media/.

2019c. "My Data – Our Health."

Migros. 2017. "Die Migros Gehört Den Leuten." 2017. www.migros.ch/de/migros-gehoert-den-leuten.html.

Mobility. 2019. "Mobilitys Unternehmenszweck: Nachhaltig Handeln." 2019. www.mobility.ch/de/nachhaltigkeit/.

Mòdol, Joan Rodon. 2019. "Citizens' Cooperation in the Reuse of Their Personal Data: The Case of Data Cooperatives in Healthcare." In *Collaboration in the Digital Age*, Kai Riemer, Stefan Schellhammer and Michaela Meinert, eds., 159–185. Cham: Springer. https://doi.org/10.1007/978–3-319–94487-6_8.

National Audit Office. 2018. "WannaCry Cyber Attack and the NHS." www.nao.org.uk/report/investigation-wannacry-cyber-attack-and-the-nhs/.

Ngwa, Elsy M. and Ernst Hafen. 2017. "MIDATA Cooperatives – Democratizing the Personal Data Economy." www.the-stars.ch/media/381219/elsy-ngwa_midata-cooperatives-democratizing-the-personal-data-economy.pdf.

Nissenbaum, Helen. 2010. *Privacy in Context : Technology, Policy, and the Integrity of Social Life*. Stanford, California: Stanford Law Books, an Imprint of Stanford University Press.

Ostrom, Elinor. 1990. *Governing the Commons: The Evolution of Institutions for Collective Action*. The Political Economy of Institutions and Decisions. Cambridge: Cambridge University Press.

Overwalle, Geertrui Van. "Governing Genomic Data: Plea for an 'Open Commons.'" In *Governing Knowledge Commons*, Brett M. Frischmann, Michael J. Madison, and Katherine J. Strandburg, eds. New York: Oxford University Press, 2014, 137–154. https://doi.org/10.1093/acprof:oso/9780199972036.003.0005.

Powles, Julia and Hal Hodson. "Google DeepMind and Healthcare in an Age of Algorithms." *Health and Technology* 7, no. 4 (2017): 351–367. https://doi.org/10.1007/s12553-017–0179-1.

Roessel, Ilse Van, Matthias Reumann, and Angela Brand. "Potentials and Challenges of the Health Data Cooperative Model." *Public Health Genomics* 20, no. 6 (2018): 321–331. https://doi.org/10.1159/000489994.

Sadowski, Jathan. "When Data Is Capital: Datafication, Accumulation, and Extraction." *Big Data & Society* 6, no. 1 (2019): 205395171882054. https://doi.org/10.1177/2053951718820549.

Strandburg, Katherine J., Brett M. Frischmann, and Michael J. Madison. 2017. "The Knowledge Commons Framework." In *Governing Medical Knowledge Commons*, Brett M. Frischmann, Katherine J. Strandburg, and Michael J. Madison, eds. 9–18. Cambridge Studies on Governing Knowledge Commons. Cambridge: Cambridge University Press, 2017, 9–18. https://doi.org/DOI:10.1017/9781316544587.002.

SWISS RE. 2018. *The Future of Personal Data with Ernst Hafen*. https://youtu.be/wyx5sS5I_QQ.

Symantec. 2015. "State of Privacy Report 2015."

Vayena, Effy and Alessandro Blasimme. "Biomedical Big Data: New Models of Control Over Access, Use and Governance." In *Journal of Bioethical Inquiry* 14 (2017): 501–513. Springer Netherlands. https://doi.org/10.1007/s11673-017–9809-6.

2018. "Health Research with Big Data: Time for Systemic Oversight." *The Journal of Law, Medicine & Ethics*. https://doi.org/10.1177/1073110518766026.

Wellcome Trust. 2015. "Enabling Data Linkage to Maximise the Value of Public Health Research Data: Full Report." London. https://wellcome.ac.uk/sites/default/files/enabling-data-linkage-to-maximise-value-of-public-health-research-data-phrdf-mar15.pdf.

Wilbanks, John T. and Eric J. Topol. "Stop the Privatization of Health Data." *Nature* 535, no. 7612 (2016): 345–348. https://doi.org/10.1038/535345a.

3

Pooling Mental Health Data with Chatbots

Michael Mattioli [1]

3.1 INTRODUCTION

For an invisible condition, clinical anxiety casts a long shadow. In the United States, about 40 million adults – a full 18.1 percent of the population – suffer from an anxiety disorder, making it the most common type of mental health problem in the country [1]. Anxiety is insidious; it can crop up like a weed at any point in life, coloring one's days and nights with unaccountable feelings of dread. Anxiety is expensive. A recent study estimated that in the United States, the total costs of treatment, lost productivity, and lost wages are about $42 billion every year (Du Pont et al., 1996) [2]. This amount exceeds the most recent annual revenues of Facebook, Coca-Cola, Nike, and Morgan Stanley. Anxiety is thriving. There is a shortage of mental health workers (clinicians) in the United States, and experts believe that this problem of supply and demand will worsen substantially by 2025. Even when help is available, high prices and perceptions of social stigma prevent many people from seeking help [1].

This chapter explores a new type of technology that relies in part upon large sets of patient data to relieve anxiety symptoms (Dobbs, 2017). The technology is software that can simulate certain kinds of conversations with human therapists. Referred to as "conversational agents" or "therapy chatbots," the idea might sound like science fiction, but it is a commercial reality. Recent studies indicate that conversational agents are useful in helping to reduce the symptoms of anxiety and depression. A recent peer-reviewed study showed that the program highlighted in this chapter, "Woebot," can significantly reduce depressive symptoms in two weeks of regular use [3]. Some therapy chatbots have also been able to predict the onset of panic attacks or depressive episodes based on patterns in user behavior (Mathotaarachchi, et al., 2017). A key feature of therapy chatbots is their ability to improve over time by drawing insights from the ever-

[1] Professor of Law, Indiana University Maurer School of Law (Bloomington). Affiliated Faculty and Member of Advisory Board and Governance Committee, The Vincent and Elinor Ostrom Workshop in Political Theory and Policy Analysis, Indiana University Bloomington; Affiliated Faculty, Center for IP Research, Indiana University Maurer School of Law; J.D., Penn Law; B.S., Tufts University; Previously held fellowships at Berkeley Law and Michigan Law.

growing pools of information they receive from their conversations with users.[2] The potential for good seems significant.

An even more tantalizing possibility is that therapy chatbots offer can solve the problem of collecting, pooling, and drawing helpful insights from large sets of mental health data. In the past, only individual therapists or scientists have been able to collect such information in the course of their work. Patient confidentiality, funding constraints, a lack of technological infrastructure and expertise, and limited numbers of patients have made it infeasible to build useful pools of mental health data in treatment or research settings. One such problem is the fact that many people regard their mental health conditions as private. As mentioned, the desire for privacy often stems from a sense of social stigma that many attach to mental health care. Individuals struggling with, say, anxiety, might prefer to benefit from the insights of a data pool without contributing to it themselves. If everyone felt this way, there would be no data to collect in the first place. The effort would fail – a classic free-rider dilemma.[3]

Woebot and conversational agents like it address this problem in a unique way. The system obscures its most valuable asset – broad knowledge or wisdom about how to help people – behind an automated chat interface that the company tightly controls. Unlike a database, this information cannot easily be copied or otherwise expropriated. The asset, so to speak, can be accessed only indirectly through conversing with the software. Chatting in this way requires users to share information with the system. (Importantly, the company keeps all user data private and has pledged not to monetize any user data.) Woebot shows how a chat interface might be able to regulate the flow of mental health data, and in doing so, ameliorate the collective action problems that make aggregating mental health data difficult.

Students of commons governance could regard chatbots like Woebot as technologies that provide an "imposed pattern" for governing the flow of private information. Like other "imposed commons" that scholars have examined in this series of volumes, therapy chatbots are affected by a vast number of exogenous factors, such as laws. The Governing Knowledge Commons ("GKC") helps situate these new technologies in their broader cultural, medical, legal, and technological contexts.

Drawing upon the GKC framework, this chapter presents an ethnographic study of Woebot – a therapy chatbot designed to administer a form of Cognitive-Behavioral Therapy ("CBT"). Section 3.1 explains the methodology of this case study. Section 3.2 describes the background contexts that relate to anxiety as a public health problem. These include the nature of anxiety and historical approaches to diagnosing and treating it, the ascendency of e-Mental Health therapy provided through apps, and relevant laws and regulations. Section 3.3 describes how Woebot was developed and

2 See, e.g., "Digital Me," created by Patients Like Me.

3 As Elinor Ostrom wrote in her pathbreaking book, Governing the Commons, "Whenever one person cannot be excluded from the benefits that others provide, each person is motivated not to contribute to the joint effort, but to free-ride on the efforts of others. If all participants choose to free-ride, the collective benefit will not be produced."

what goals its designers pursued. Section 3.4 describes the kinds of information that users share with Woebot. Section 3.5 describes how the designers of the system seek to manage this information in a way that benefits users without disrupting their privacy.

3.2 METHODOLOGY

This chapter's approach follows the GKC framework developed by Katherine Strandburg, Brett Frischmann, and Michael Madison (2014). The framework is an adaptation of Elinor Ostrom's Institutional Analysis and Development (IAD) (Ostrom, 1990; Strandburg, Frischmann, and Madison, 2014). I followed the following process.

- A literature review. To gather general information about the state of e-mental health apps and services, I surveyed recently published books, newspaper articles, and academic works related to this topic. This research also covered general interest publications on anxiety and treatments such as Cognitive-Behavior Therapy. From these sources, I identified software and services (apps) designed to help people manage their anxiety. I then contacted individuals who led the companies that produce these apps.
- Semi-structured interviews. I interviewed ten experts with knowledge of either Woebot or the e-mental health landscape more generally. I selected some of these individuals because they were cited or quoted commonly in news articles, books, and academic works. I learned of others in the interview group by asking for contacts and referrals in the first interviews I conducted for this project. Interview subjects included professors, technologists, and CEOs. In keeping with the GKC framework, these interviews were semi-structured and focused on the following topics: (1) the scientific, technological, and social contexts in which this form of information-sharing takes place; (2) the various types of data and related informational assets this group seeks to aggregate and organize access to; (3) the "default" status of these assets; (4) the players involved, including corporations and health-care institutions; (5) the community's goals; (6) rules and related internal governance mechanisms; (7) the technological infrastructure supporting the community.

I conducted all interviews by telephone and recorded them through handwritten notes. The average duration of the interviews was 45 minutes. Some interviews were supplemented with brief follow-up email exchanges. In keeping with Internal Review Board procedures, I furnished each interview subject with an information sheet describing the goals of this study.

3.3 BACKGROUND ENVIRONMENT: CONTEXTS

This section focuses on the most prominent landmarks in the anxiety landscape: how the disorder has been understood and treated historically, how anxiety sufferers typically encounter and experience the problem, the evolving nexus between mental health and technology, and relevant laws and regulations in the United States.

3.3.1 *A Brief History of Anxiety*

Culture has shaped how people have understood and treated anxiety throughout history (Horwitz, 2013). The very language we use to describe the problem is rooted in cultural lore: The word "panic" derives from the Greek god Pan, whose battle cry was said to fill his enemies with uncontrollable fear. In ancient Greece, soldiers who experienced panic in battle were often regarded as cowards and imprisoned or executed. Some historians credit Aristotle (384–320 BCE) for taking the first step toward understanding anxiety as a pathological condition. In exploring the idea of fear, he wrote, "For the man who is by nature apt to fear everything, even the squeak of a mouse, is cowardly with a brutish cowardice, while the man who feared a weasel did so in consequence of disease." In other words, fear can sometimes be healthy and warranted and other times a sign of illness. (We can surmise that in Aristotle's time, mice were generally considered a rational source of fear, whereas weasels were not.)

Other Greek philosophers made some of the earliest and most enduring contributions toward Western understandings of anxiety. Hippocrates (460–367 BCE), for example, sought to understand medical disorders by observing his patients in a systematic, scientific manner. This process led him to develop a system for classifying mental disorders, including anxiety. Today, a similar classification system called the *Diagnostic and Statistical Manual* (*DSM*) is widely used in the medical profession to identify mental health disorders (Ghinassi, 2010). Hippocrates conjectured that the key to treating anxiety was in achieving a kind of harmony between the body and mind (Kleisiaris, Sfakianakis, and Papathanasiou, 2014).

Socrates (470–399 BCE) expanded the set of tools that experts had to investigate anxiety. The Socratic Method, a process of deeply questioning one's underlying assumptions, is perhaps his most lasting methodological contribution. Like Hippocrates, Socrates also believed that the key to mental health had to do with the relationship between the body and the mind. Understanding this relationship, he believed, required not only physical examination but also introspection on the part of the patient. The idea is captured well in his famous injunction to his followers, "know thyself" (Ghinassi, 2010). Plato (427–347 BCE) believed that anxiety was rooted in incorrect or distorted beliefs about the world. His solution was straightforward: educating sufferers about their erroneous beliefs, and through persistent reminding and reasoning, attempts to alter those beliefs.

Arguably, even more nuanced insights about mental health appear in Buddhist teachings from the fifth century BCE. In his teachings, Siddhartha Gautama (The Buddha) explains that people fundamentally misperceive the true nature of the world. The path away from anxiety and other afflictions, he explains, lies in gaining an accurate view of reality as it is, rather than how we imagine it to be. Buddhist traditions usually focus on better aligning the body and mind to gain this clearer view. As Thich Nhat Hanh, a widely known Vietnamese Buddhist master, explains, "Wrong-thinking causes us to see the world in an upside-down way. Our mind is often thinking about one thing while our body is doing another. Mind and body are not unified."

The Middle Ages, which lasted roughly from the year 476 to 1000 BCE, saw a retreat from the scientific methods developed in ancient Greece in favor of the supernatural. In some cultures, the belief emerged that mental disorders are evidence of demonic possession. This idea is likely the historical root of the stigma that many sufferers of anxiety and depression experience today. In some cultures, the notion of demonic possession persists.

The European renaissance sparked a return to ancient insights. In the fifteenth century, for instance, Descartes developed the idea of "mind-body dualism" – the notion, as Descartes described it, that the mind and the body "compose a certain unity." This insight led to the modern recognition of the fact that the mind and the body influence each other – "bidirectionality" – a core principle of contemporary treatment. These ideas were not new, of course. The Latin phrase "mens sana in corpore sano" ("a healthy mind in a healthy body") dates to the second century.

Psychology, the modern scientific study and treatment of behavior and the mind, took root and flourished in the late nineteenth and early twentieth centuries. Some leaders in the field, such as Sigmund Freud and Carl Jung, focused heavily on the subjective experiences of patients. Freud believed, for instance, that the roots of anxiety, depression, and related mental health disorders lay in repressed sexual energy. Although this view is not widely credited today, Freud made a lasting contribution to the modern understanding of anxiety by classifying it into different forms: generalized anxiety, panic disorders, phobias, and obsessions (Horwitz, 2013).

Others in the then-emerging field searched for objective sources of information on the disorder. Ivan Pavlov (1849–1936) illustrated that anxiety responses could be conditioned in animals – a discovery that suggested people might develop anxiety disorders as a learned response to life experiences. Pavlov's work inspired the field of behavioral psychology, which explores the theory that people acquire mental conditions entirely through learning. John Watson (1878–1959), Rosalie Rayner (1899–1935), and B.F. Skinner (1904–1990) are widely known names in this field.

In the 1950s, researchers challenged the notion that anxiety is *solely* a learned behavior. These experts argued that cognition, or how one sees and appraises the world, must play a role too. George Kelly (1905–67) advanced the idea that people perceive the world as a series of mental constructs. Mental disorders may arise when these constructs are inaccurate. This view seems to align remarkably well with the core teachings of Buddhist philosophy, as well as Plato's teachings, both mentioned earlier. Recent research indicates that life experiences, including stressful environments and incidents, particularly in childhood, can "activate" the disorder.

Cognitive-behavioral therapy (CBT), one of the most effective techniques to treat anxiety today, is grounded in the idea that anxiety is a self-reinforcing behavior that stems from our misunderstanding of the world. Patients who undergo CBT treatment learn about common types of cognitive distortions, and then learn to spot these distortions in their thinking. For instance, some people who suffer from anxiety tend to think about future events in binary or black-and-white terms. In the mind of a person experiencing anxiety, the results of a routine blood test for cholesterol, for instance, will reveal either perfect health or imminent death. The simple act of recognizing this form of thinking and placing a label on it has been shown to drain it of its power.

In the 1950s, the American Psychiatric Association published the first edition of the *DSM*. Now in its fifth edition, the *DSM* is the primary tool that medical professionals use to diagnose mental health disorders, including anxiety. Some critics of the modern psychological establishment argue that the *DSM*'s focus on classification implies a level of clarity and precision to the diagnosis of mental health disorders that does not exist. This line of criticism is mostly academic, however, and removed from the day-to-day business of treating people with mental health disorders.

Alongside CBT, another important set of tools for treating anxiety are drugs. People have used chemicals derived from plants to manage stress and anxiety for millennia. Alcohol, one of the earliest such substances, remains one of the most popular. Opium, a drug derived from a type of poppy plant, has been used as a sedative at least since 4000 BCE. In the late nineteenth century, a chemist working at the Bayer Company successfully diluted the active molecule in opium – diacetylmorphine. Bayer branded the chemical as "heroin" and commercialized it in 1898. The drug's dangerousness and addictive qualities were evident within just a few years of public use. Opiates were eventually replaced by barbiturates, another depressant, which were developed chiefly by a German chemist and Nobel Prize winner named Adolf von Baeyer.

In the 1950s, the pharmaceutical company Smith-Kline began selling a drug it called Thorazine. The drug's popularity for treating mental health disorders fueled research into the development of new drugs designed to address specific disorders. The first drug that was developed specifically to target anxiety was called Miltown. Although highly effective, it was, unfortunately, also highly addictive. Continued research led to the creation of benzodiazepines, including diazepam (Valium) and alprazolam (Xanax). These drugs are often prescribed to treat acute episodes of panic, but like earlier drugs, they can be highly addictive. In the 1970s, Eli Lilly and Company introduced Fluoxetine (Prozac), a new kind of medicine called a selective serotonin reuptake inhibitor (SSRI). Approved by the FDA in 1987, the drug remains widely used and highly regarded, along with other SSRIs, such as Zoloft, Paxil, Luvox, Celexa, and Lexapro. SSRIs are the most commonly prescribed drugs in the United States and by far the frontline defense against anxiety. Despite the significant advances in drug development that took place in the twentieth century, very few new drugs have been developed to target anxiety since the 1990s.

Recent studies have shown that today, drugs (serotonin inhibitors) and CBT are the two most effective and standard tools to manage clinical anxiety [4]. Several complementary and integrated health treatments have also been shown to reinforce the benefits offered by conventional medical treatment. These include stress and relaxation techniques, yoga, meditation, and acupuncture [5]. Getting adequate sleep, regular exercise, maintaining a healthy diet, having a robust social support system, and living with low levels of stress are also important [6]. For people who have access to adequate mental health care, educational resources, and the ability to follow a beneficial lifestyle, anxiety can be highly manageable. Unfortunately, as discussed in the following section, there is a shortfall in access to mental health care.

3.3.2 *The Patient Context*

Nearly all anxiety disorders involve intense feelings of fear and the anticipation of imminent harm (Hilty and Mucic, 2016; Rachman, 2020). A short review of several types of anxiety shows subtler aspects of the problem. Under the heading of Anxiety, the *DSM* identifies the following: (i) generalized anxiety disorder, (ii) panic disorder, (iii) social anxiety disorder, (iv) obsessive-compulsive disorder, (v) post-traumatic stress disorder, and (vi) specific phobias:

(i) In generalized anxiety disorder, feelings of worrying and fear permeate everyday life. Sometimes, these feelings are tied to real causes for worry, but they are disproportionately intense. (Recall Aristotle's mouse.) Other times, the feelings may be disconnected from any cause that the sufferer can identify – a kind of free-floating dread. These feelings are often accompanied by physical discomfort, such as muscle tension, restlessness, queasiness, and nausea. Those with generalized anxiety disorder are focused heavily on the future, both near- and long-term, and unable to tolerate feelings of uncertainty (Rachman, 2020).

(ii) Panic disorders, another class of anxiety disorder, are typified by intense physical and mental episodes of uncontrollable fear brought on by a perceived threat that typically does not exist. These episodes are different from the chronic worrying and fear that generalized anxiety disorder brings on: they are more physically intense and often mistaken by sufferers for heart attacks.

(iii) Social anxiety is identified by unwarranted feelings of embarrassment and self-consciousness. Unsurprisingly, people who suffer from this problem often isolate themselves.

(iv) Obsessive-compulsive disorder is characterized by repetitive or compulsive behaviors, such as hoarding, arranging objects in specific patterns, and extreme avoidance of germs.

(v) Another manifestation of anxiety, post-traumatic stress disorder ("PTSD"), has received a wealth of attention in the media because soldiers often experience it. Unlike generalized anxiety disorder or panic disorders, which inherently focus on the future, this problem is heavily focused on the past. Often a traumatic experience gives rise to nightmares and related, intensely upsetting memories.

(vi) Lastly, are specific phobias – the experience of anxiety symptoms brought on by certain situations or objects.

As mentioned in the introduction, anxiety is the most common mental health disorder in the United States. According to the Anxiety and Depression Association of America, 40 million adults age 18 or older, or about 18.1 percent of the population, is affected by anxiety every year [1]. Although the United States has the highest rate of anxiety in the world, the disorder is prevalent elsewhere. Interestingly, there does not seem to be a correlation between anxiety and industrialization: rates are very high in France, Colombia, and Lebanon. China and Nigeria, meanwhile, have relatively low rates. Moderate evidence suggests that culture and context impact how often the problem arises. Poverty correlates with higher rates of generalized anxiety disorder, for instance.

Recent research indicates that life experiences, including stressful environments and incidents, particularly in childhood, can "activate" the disorder (Ghinassi, 2010). Studies have shown that the development of anxiety can be mitigated, however, by positive protective factors. Chief among these are parents who are warm and sensitive to the feelings of a child, and who impart upon the child an internal "locus of control" – a feeling that the child has control over his or her life. Although childhood experiences seem to be foundational, anxiety disorders can arise at any age in a person's life. The average age of onset for generalized anxiety disorder, for instance, is thirty-one. As mentioned in the introduction, it is estimated that the total annual cost of anxiety runs in the neighborhood of $47 billion annually.

One of the reasons that anxiety rates are soaring in the United States could be the fact that the problem is widely under-treated (U.S. Department of Health and Human Services, 2018). One reason for this is stigma: Many people with anxiety are reluctant to seek treatment because they believe others (family members, neighbors, etc.) will judge them poorly if they learn they suffer from anxiety. As with so many aspects of anxiety, the perception of stigma varies greatly by age, ethnicity, religious, and other cultural lines.

In addition to stigma, recent studies have shown that in many areas of the United States, there is a workforce shortage in child psychiatry and in other behavioral health practitioners (Health Resources and Services Administration/National Center for Health Workforce Analysis, 2015). The problem of access is particularly acute in rural areas: A recent study found that 65 percent of non-metropolitan counties do not have a single psychologist, and 47 percent of non-metropolitan areas do not have a single psychologist (Andrilla, et al., 2018). This problem is likely to worsen. The U.S. Department of Health and Human Services has projected that by the year 2025 there will be shortages of between 6,080 and 15,400 psychiatrists; between 8,220 and 57,490 clinical, counseling, and school psychologists; and as many as 26,930 mental health counselors (Health Resources and Services Administration/National Center for Health Workforce Analysis, 2015). Closely tied to the access problem is the cost of mental health care: Many people with anxiety cannot afford treatment.

3.3.3 *Technological Contexts*

3.3.3.1 E-Mental Health Services

Alongside CBT and drugs, several new technologies have been developed in the past twenty years that have helped anxiety sufferers. In the medical world, many of these technologies are referred to generally as "e-Mental Health Services." Since the early 2000s, online services have helped connect patients to therapists online, for instance. Today, several companies provide remote talk therapy sessions carried out over smartphone apps. Similarly, there are a number of services that have made it possible for trained practitioners to administer CBT remotely. Two such services are Joyable and Talkspace. Joyable delivers an eight-week CBT program administered by a trained practitioner, and Talkspace connects users to licensed mental health professionals.[4]

Recent studies have shown that online mental health interventions can be as effective as traditional in-person therapy for treating both depression and anxiety. In one study, for instance, the recovery rates of individuals treated with online CBT for panic disorder and agoraphobia were comparable to people treated in-person. Based on a thirty-month follow-up study for the treatment of social phobia, the long-term effects of CBT delivered over the internet was comparable to CBT carried out over the internet (Mucic, Milty, Parish, and Yellowlees, 2016).

Sometimes, e-Mental Health Services can be even more effective than traditional care. As mentioned earlier, the stigma that some patients associate with visiting a clinician can discourage them from seeking help. Because patients can access e-Mental Health Services from their homes, this barrier disappears (Shoemaker and Hilty, 2016). Recent studies reveal that LGBTQ+ youth, for example, prefer to seek mental health care online (Dreyfuss, 2019). As discussed later in this chapter, the privacy of user data could either reinforce or erode this perception of anonymity.

In addition to linking patients to traditional mental health providers, many apps facilitate complementary services and treatments that may be helpful. These include thousands of apps and online services related to yoga, mindfulness, eating disorders, tracking mental health conditions, and general stress reduction (Mucic,

4 Joyable was aquired by a company called AbleTo in early 2019 [7].

Milty, Parish, and Yellowlees, 2016). A website called "Psyberguide" provides a helpful catalog of these services, along with descriptions and ratings. The website is maintained by Dr. Stephen Schueller, an associate professor of psychological science at the University of California at Irvine [8].

3.3.3.2 Social Networking

Social media marks another nexus between anxiety and technology. At least in theory, an online social network could help anxiety sufferers learn more about their problems and potentially to connect with others who are navigating this complex and challenging disorder. This could help to alleviate feelings of isolation and helpfully establish new social support systems for sufferers.

An emerging body of research has shown that mainstream social networks such as Facebook and Twitter can contribute to anxiety (e.g. Hoge, Bickham, and Cantor, 2017).[5] The chief symptoms of this disorder are anxiety symptoms experienced by someone who is unable to check their social media notifications for even a short time [9]. Separately, the use of Facebook and Twitter has been linked to symptoms of depression. As of this writing, this body of research is still developing, and it is unknown how significant or widespread these problems are, however (Pantic, 2014).

Beyond the most widely visited social networks, a number of online communities exist for people who suffer from anxiety. Health Unlocked, one such service based in London, administers a collection of chat forums where patients can connect, share advice and encouragement with one another online. Interviewed for this book chapter, a person with knowledge of the company's services described it as "a complement to clinical treatment" that "breaks down the isolation" and possibly provides access to "helpful information you wouldn't always find from a doctor." According to the individual interviewed, the service is free, and the company generates revenue by selling anonymized and aggregated data to partners, including pharmaceutical companies.

3.3.3.3 Therapy Chatbots

Therapy chatbots mark another nexus between mental health and technology. The development of such apps could be traced back to the 1950s, when Alan Turing, an English mathematician, considered whether a computer could simulate a human conversation. To analyze the question, Turing developed a thought experiment that involved two people and a machine designed to mimic a person. One of the two human participants, whom Turing called the "interrogator," types questions to a subject located in a different room. The subject responds through typed messages. The interrogator must then guess whether the subject is the other human or the

5 Notably, the American Medical Association has not yet recognized this disorder.

machine. Turing used this hypothetical setup to show that, in principle, there is nothing to stop a cleverly programmed computer from fooling the interrogator. Turing's work solidified his place as the grandfather of modern AI.

Turing's work also inspired generations of researchers to build chatbots. The first, a chatbot named "Eliza" and developed in 1966, simulated a psychotherapist. Although the system could not comprehend what was typed to it, Eliza was able to simulate human-like understanding through simple pattern matching. In 1972, a chatbot named "Parry" cleverly fooled many human interrogators by simulating a person suffering from paranoid schizophrenia. In 1992, a chatbot "therapist" named "Dr. Sbaitso" was developed for MS-DOS-based computers. This "doctor" was notable because it was one of the first chatbots that were widely available to the public. Ultimately, a limitation of the early chatbots was the fact that their behavior was scripted through rules. Given a certain input, they would always produce a pre-programmed output. Programming all of the possible conversations that a person might wish to have with a machine would, in theory, require providing the machine with an internal model of the universe.[6]

Since the late 2000s, chatbots or conversational agents have grown more sophisticated thanks to a new approach called "machine learning" ("ML"). In contrast to rule-based systems like Eliza, machine learning is a process by which a computer can identify and match patterns in massive sets of data. Provide an ML-based chatbot with enough examples of typical two-sided human conversations, and over time, the software will learn, through statistics and probability, what a good response to a new question it has never seen should look like. Many people saw the technology on display for the first time when IBM's Watson system defeated the Jeopardy Champion, Ken Jennings, before a national audience in 2011. For many of us, examples closer to home include personal assistants built into our phones and smart speakers. Apple's *Siri*, Google's *Assistant*, Amazon's *Alexa*, and Microsoft's *Cortana* have (for better or worse) integrated themselves into billions of people's daily routines.

Against this backdrop, a new generation of therapy chatbots has recently been developed and provided to the public (Hernandez, 2018). The first such service, Woebot, is the focus of this study. Tess, a chatbot developed by San Francisco-based X2AI, also delivers CBT interventions, along with similar techniques, including mindfulness therapy, acceptance and commitment therapy, self-compassion therapy, and interpersonal psychotherapy (Fulmer et al., 2018; Gionet, 2018; Green et al., 2019; Joerin, Rauws, and Ackerman, 2019; Stephens et al., 2019) [14]. The service works entirely through a text-like exchange. Wysa, a startup based in London and Bangalore, similarly delivers "CBT, mindfulness techniques, and other techniques via in-app text changes" (Wallach, 2018). When a patient uses Wysa for the first time,

6 "But as those projects unfolded, researchers hit a major problem: there were simply too many rules that needed to be encoded for a system to do anything useful. This jacked up costs and significantly slowed ongoing efforts" (Pantic, 2014).

the app asks a series of questions designed to help it understand what sorts of problems the user is grappling with. Some chatbot designers are moving beyond text in order to better diagnose patients. AiME (Chin, 2018), a therapy chatbot developed by a team of researchers at UCLA, aims to detect risks of depression, anxiety, and addiction based on several minutes of video footage of a user's face (Condliffe, 2017; Garg and Glick, 2018; McCaney, 2019; Morris, Kouddous, Kshirsagar, and Schueller, 2018; Rieland, 2018; Rosso, 2018). To capture video and audio, the app requests access to the microphone and camera on a user's device.

Early evidence, while limited, suggests that these tools are effective. A peer-reviewed study shows that Tess can significantly reduce symptoms of anxiety and depression, for instance. Youper, another entrant in the therapy chatbot industry, claims that more than 80 percent of its users "experience a reduction in negative moods after just one conversation." Studies show that Wysa has promise in reducing anxiety symptoms, particularly in assisting children [10].

Because therapy chatbots need to collect private information from users in order to converse with them, these apps also carry privacy risks. These risks may seem especially serious today, as the technology industry is facing a widespread reckoning with user privacy. The privacy problem has played out in the form of countless user data leaks, hacks, and unauthorized disclosures by large technology companies – most notably, Facebook. The privacy issue is explored more deeply later in this chapter.

3.3.4 *The Legal and Regulatory Landscape*

The emerging therapy chatbot industry is taking form against a complicated patchwork of law and regulations. This policy framework significantly influences how these technologies are developed, funded, and provided. It is important to note that the areas highlighted here are simply the most visible and may not provide a complete picture of the laws and regulations relevant to every therapy chatbot, however.

3.3.4.1 Privacy Laws

The Health Insurance Portability and Accountability Act of 1996 (HIPAA) forbids healthcare providers such as hospitals from disclosing specific types of patient data. These include patient names, zip codes, and dates of treatment.[7] A number of other privacy laws enacted at the state and federal levels impose civil liabilities for wrongful disclosure of such data by health-care providers.[8] Interestingly, HIPAA rules pertain only to so-called covered entities, which include health-care providers

[7] 18 USC 1836 et seq.
[8] 45 C.F.R. 164.514(e) (2013).

(e.g., doctors, clinics, psychologists), health plans (e.g., health insurance companies, HMOs), and health clearinghouses (entities that process health information into standard formats).

Therapy chatbots appear to operate outside the purview of HIPAA by billing themselves as "wellness apps" rather than new forms of traditional psychotherapy. This distinction seems murky, however, especially in light of the fact that patients are encouraged to share the same kinds of information with these apps as they might traditionally share with a therapist. John Torous, the chair of the American Psychiatric Association's smartphone app evaluation group, has said that the "gap" in HIPAA coverage raises privacy concerns (De Salvo and Samules, 2016; Nutt, 2017).[9] A recent government report on this coverage gap made the same conclusion, stating, "As the electronic sharing and storage of health information increases, and as individuals become more engaged in sharing personal health information online, organizations that are not regulated by HIPAA, the FTC, or state law may collect, share, or use health information about individuals in ways that may put such data at risk of being shared improperly" (Department of Health and Human Services, 2016).

Depending on its geographic reach, a therapy chatbot could also be subject to the requirements of the EU's General Data Protection Regulation (GDPR). The GDPR ensures that EU citizens are able to access their personal data, as well as information about how their data is processed. It also provides individuals the right to request that their personal data is deleted promptly upon request. The regulation also requires that companies collecting personal data design their products around user privacy. This requirement could include encrypting all personal data, making sure such data isn't transferred unnecessarily and ensuring that encryption and decryption of data aren't conducted on remote servers.

3.3.4.2 The FDA

The Food and Drug Administration ("FDA") has had the authority to oversee the safety of medical devices since the 1930s. It does so by requiring device manufacturers to demonstrate the safety of their products. (If they cannot do so, the devices may not be made available for sale.) Traditionally, the FDA's definition of "medical device" offered a fairly predictable and clear indication of what sorts of products might receive oversight. The recent rise of smartphones has presented a new and challenging question, however: Can a smartphone running an app constitute a medical device?

Under the FDA Act's broad definition of "medical device," the agency has the authority to regulate medical software before it is released to the public. Although the FDA has declined to oversee most types of mobile health apps carefully, it has published guidance documents that leave open the possibility that it could regulate

[9] Snowdy, Christopher E., Erica Z. Shoemaker, Steven Chan, and Donald M. Hilty. "Social Media and Clinical Practice: What Stays the Same, What Changes, and How to Plan Ahead?." In *e-Mental Health*, pp. 151–170. Springer, Cham, 2016.

mental health apps. The FDA has said it intends to exercise enforcement discretion over apps that (i) help patients (i.e., users) self-manage their disease or conditions without providing specific treatment or treatment suggestions; (ii) provide patients with simple tools to organize and track their health information; (iii) provide easy access to information related to patients' health conditions or treatments; (iv) help patients document, show, or communicate potential medical conditions to health-care providers; (v) automate simple tasks for health-care providers. The twenty-first century Cures Act (CURES) excludes from FDA oversight apps "for maintaining or encouraging a healthy lifestyle and is unrelated to the diagnosis, cure, mitigation, prevention, or treatment of a disease or condition."[10] By contrast, according to an expert at Woebot, the FDA might be more motivated in the future to regulate technologies that make clear claims regarding a particular clinical indication.

Some legal commentators are troubled by the FDA's current approach, in light of the potential risks that patients may face when using psychotherapy apps that don't work in accordance with accepted clinical procedures. Specifically, on the subject of CBT, Theodore Lee has commented, "untreated or poorly treated conditions can lead to adverse outcomes for the patient or others. The lack of conformity with established CBT principles for most CBT-based apps suggests that patients may not be getting adequate treatment" (Lee, 2018). Despite these concerns, however, the FDA appears reluctant to regulate mobile mental health apps, and Congressional action like the CURES Act has reinforced this hands-off stance by removing many such apps from FDA purview.

3.3.4.3 The FTC

The Federal Trade Commission is charged to "protect consumers against unfair or deceptive acts or practices in commerce." The agency accomplishes this in a variety of ways, including legal enforcement and providing education. Although the FTC has not initiated legal action against any manufacturers of mental health apps, it recently filed a complaint against a "brain training" app called Luminosity that claimed to provide cognitive benefits. Specifically, the app promised to "protect against . . . age-related conditions such as mild cognitive impairment, dementia, and Alzheimer's disease; and will reduce cognitive impairment associated with . . . post-traumatic stress disorder, traumatic brain injury, attention deficit hyperactivity disorder, Turner syndrome, stroke, and other health conditions."[11] The FTC claimed that this language was deceptive. Under a settlement agreement, Luminosity paid $2 million and was enjoined from future

[10] CURES Act, Section 3060 (page 1130).

[11] Complaint at 5, F.T.C. v. Lumos Labs, Inc. d/b/a Lumosity, No. 3:16-cv-00001 (N.D. Cal. January 4, 2016), ECF No. 1, www.ftc.gov/system/files/documents/cases/160105lumoslabscmpt.pdf [https://perma.cc/5ME3-A3Y9].

deceptive conduct.[12] The suit serves as a cautionary tale to any company that cannot substantiate the benefits they claim to provide.

3.3.4.4 The VA and DARPA

Interestingly, the US Department of Veterans Affairs ("VA") has developed and delivered e-Mental Health tools to soldiers as well as the public. As Davor Mucic and Donald Milty explain in their book e-Mental Health,

> Once again, the military may be in the lead for providing Internet-based care options, with foci of remote screening and assessment, post-deployment adjustment, suicide prevention and management, and delivery of training/education. Many personnel prefer to receive care at home – particularly those with anxiety, PTSD, and phobia – in addition to those who prefer to avoid the stigma of entering a mental health facility (Mucic, Milty, Parish, and Yellowlees, 2016).

The VA has developed and made available several apps for treating PTSD and other forms of anxiety. These include PTSD coach, an app that provides users with the ability to track and monitor PTSD symptoms; CBT-i, an app designed to deploy CBT to treat insomnia; ACT Go, which delivers acceptance and commitment therapy; and Moving Forward, an app designed to help reduce stress. All of these apps are provided to the public at no charge.

DARPA, the branch of the US military that focuses on developing new technologies, has also been involved in developing therapy chatbots. In 2014, the agency funded a study of "Ellie," a chatbot therapist developed by researchers at the University of California's Institute for Creative Technologies (Gratch, 2014).

3.3.4.5 Intellectual Property

Intellectual property protection is also relevant to chatbot therapy apps. Patent protection is designed to encourage investments into developing new technologies by offering inventors an exclusivity window of twenty years. To receive patent protection, an invention must be new, non-obvious, and useful. Importantly, it also must qualify as patentable subject matter. For companies seeking to patent chatbot therapy software, this requirement could present some challenges. Although software has traditionally enjoyed robust patent protection since the late 1990s,

[12] Stipulated Final Judgment and Order for Permanent Injunction and Other Equitable Relief at 5–9, F.T.C. v. Lumos Labs, Inc. d/b/a Lumosity, No. 3:16-cv-00001 (N.D. Cal. January 8, 2016), ECF No. 10, www.ftc.gov/system/files/documents/cases/160105lumoslabsstip.pdf [https://perma.cc/7JZL-GK7Y]. These qualifications to the settlement are not atypical of FTC enforcement actions in digital health. See, e.g., Stipulated Final Judgment and Order for Permanent Injunction and Other Equitable Relief against Defendants Kristi Zuhlke Kimball and New Consumer Solutions LLC at 8–9, No. 1:15-cv-01614 (N.D. Ill. April 30, 2015), ECF No. 27, www.ftc.gov/system/files/documents/cases/new_consumer_solutions_5-1-15.pdf [https://perma.cc/UJQ8-V3LV].

a Supreme Court ruling from 2014 appeared to narrow this form of protection to include only software that does not constitute an abstract idea and that includes an inventive concept. The Court's lack of specificity over the meaning of these terms has called into question the validity of many software patents since the ruling.

Despite these uncertainties about patenting algorithms, however, there still appear to be opportunities for patenting in the realm of chatbot therapy apps. Ginger.io, a company that provides a therapy chatbot service, has received eleven patents for, among other things, the modeling of psychological states (e.g., moods, conditions) based on what a user has expressed to their app, and for providing therapeutic interventions such as CBT to users based on those models. IBM, which created the widely known "Watson" AI system, has also received a number of patents in this space. The potential for acquiring patents may explain why academics who have sought to commercialize therapy chatbots have left their universities: Universities often require their employees to assign intellectual property they develop to their employers.

Trade secrecy, meanwhile, seeks to encourage investments in innovation by a different means: providing a cause of action that can be asserted against anyone who wrongfully misappropriates valuable and secret information. Trade secret protection is provided through state and federal statutes. Because valuable software systems and data can often be kept secret through tools like encryption and other security measures, trade secret protection has played an important role in many industries that rely upon data.

3.3.4.6 Public–Private Partnerships

Public–private partnerships are yet another place where law and policy have affected the mental health app industry. In 2018, state and county mental health officials in California worked closely with two Silicon Valley companies, Mindstrong and 7Cups, to evaluate the efficacy of mental health apps for patients of the public mental health system (Carey, 2019). Mindstrong's app excels in identifying patterns in user behavior that could signal the onset of certain types of psychological episodes. 7Cups, meanwhile, connects patients with trained "listeners" who can connect them to trained therapists.

As of this writing, press reports indicate that the effort has faced challenges related to recruitment and informed consent relating to the disclosure of user data. Commenting to the *New York Times*, Dr. John Torous, director of the division of digital psychiatry at the Beth Israel Deaconess Medical Center in Boston stated, "If we're excited about the potential of data, we should be equally worried about the risks, and those seem to be evolving faster than the scientific benefit . . . There may be guarantees the companies make about not sharing data, but if the company is sold to another company, that data goes with it," he said. "A lot of apps have that clause buried in 13 pages in mouse print" (Carey, 2019).

3.4 GOALS, OBJECTIVES, AND HISTORY

The Woebot story began in 2016 when Alison Darcy, a Stanford University clinical research psychologist, began exploring the potential of a therapy chatbot to help people with common mental health disorders. At the time, Dr. Darcy was working alongside Andrew Ng, an eminent expert in the field of artificial intelligence. Dr. Darcy became convinced that a well-designed chatbot could truly make a difference in the lives of people who suffer from anxiety and depression – so convinced, in fact, that she decided to leave academia to build a commercial product full-time.

The science behind Woebot is based largely on cognitive-behavioral therapy. As Darcy explained in a recent interview with Wired, "CBT asks people to recast their negative thoughts in a more objective light. Patients are encouraged to talk about their emotional responses to life events, and then stop to identify the psychological traps that cause their stress, anxiety, and depression" (Molteni, 2017). Woebot delivers CBT in the form of tightly scripted conversations, which are usually triggered when users describe problems they are experiencing. In response to a user who tells the system they are anxious, for instance, Woebot might tell the user about common distorted patterns of thinking in people who experience anxiety. The system then might walk the user through a common CBT exercise, such as writing down a recent anxious thought and searching for cognitive distortions in it.

Dr. Darcy and the team she assembled believed that Woebot couldn't succeed if users didn't enjoy using it and returning to it. The threshold challenge for her and her team thus became a question: "How do you make CBT in a way that people want to use every day?" Dr. Darcy and her team found answers to this question in an unlikely place: the world of gaming. "As a field, gaming has developed some of the most sophisticated engagement methodologies you can find," she explained. Although gaming and therapy might seem like disconnected fields on the surface, Dr. Darcy and her team saw a meaningful connection: "A game places you in a suspended reality, and therapy is also a suspended reality. For example we typically want someone to ask themselves, "what if you didn't have to think in a particular way"? In a sense, "you get to try out, and experience a different identity." One technique that seems to reflect Woebot's gaming DNA are quizzes: after teaching a user a new idea, the system often presents a short quiz designed to test the user's understanding.

During the development process, which took about nine months (Molteni, 2017), Dr. Darcy and her colleagues asked a team of writers and therapists to help make Woebot's conversational abilities sound as natural as possible [10]. According to the company, this work was successful. "People started calling it by name," Dr. Darcy explained. She emphasized, however, that Woebot is not designed to fool users into thinking it is a human. Instead, it is very transparent – humorously so, at times – that its entire personality is nothing more than artifice. Interestingly, Dr. Darcy believes that a human user's awareness that Woebot is not a human could lead to be more candid conversations.

A peer-reviewed study conducted by researchers at Stanford and Dr. Darcy concluded that Woebot was "a feasible, engaging, and effective way to deliver CBT." The study compared the outcomes for two groups of individuals recruited from a university setting who agreed to either engage with Woebot or receive information about mental health from the National Institute of Mental Health's website. The study reported as follows: "The study confirmed that after 2 weeks, those in the Woebot group experienced a significant reduction in depression" (Fitzpatrick, Darcy, and Vierhile, 2017).

3.5 ATTRIBUTES: THE CHARACTERISTICS OF INFORMATION SHARED

Woebot collects a wide variety of data from users. Nearly all of this information is unstructured text collected through conversational prompts presented to users in the Woebot app, which is available for iOS and Android operating systems (Molteni, 2017). Importantly, as Dr. Darcy explains, the system absorbs "only as much as you divulge to it." Woebot could, but does not necessarily, record a user's name, the problems the user wishes to address – for example, anxiety, depression, loneliness – and specific thoughts the user has had associated with those problems – that is, "I'm not popular enough" and "I'm worried I'll fail an upcoming test."

To appreciate the variety of data that can be collected from users, consider the following exchange. (This is a real exchange that I carried out with Woebot for this book chapter.)

Woebot: Howdy Mike, so nice to hear from you. How are you feeling today?

User: Anxious.

Woebot: Are you experiencing these feelings right now?

User: Yes, now.

Woebot: I see. Let's get ready to identify & write your negative automatic thoughts in this moment . . .

User: OK, I'm worried that I might develop a serious illness because I'm feeling a bit unwell.

Woebot: btw, I've remembered your most frequent distortions in thinking. Would you say that "All or Nothing" was in the thought?

User: Yes, actually.

Woebot: Now it's time to rewrite your thought without any distortions. Give it a go!

User: Feeling a bit unwell does not mean that I have, or will have, a serious illness.

This short dialog shows how Woebot uses its memory of a user's name and a cognitive distortion the user has experienced to deliver a CBT technique. The exchange also illustrates why a patient-driven modality like CBT is so well suited to a chatbot interface. As Dr. Darcy explained in an earlier interview with Wired, "A good CBT therapist should facilitate someone else's process, not become a part of it" (Molteni, 2017). According to Woebot, the service engaged in two million conversations per week in early 2019 (Nutt, 2017).

According to Dr. Darcy, the system retains records of all of the chats it has with users and stores them on a secure server. The company then de-identifies and aggregates these records to draw new insights from them. This underscores an important point: Woebot does not use machine learning techniques to generate its written responses to users. Instead, it uses ML to initiate partially scripted exchanges with users. Commenting for a recent magazine interview, Darcy explained, "Woebot uses machine learning to direct the right content or methods to that person in that moment. However, it is true that we do this in a highly controlled way" (Lee, 2018).

The company has already found interesting insights in its pool of data. "Some of the things we're learned have surprised us in the aggregate," Dr. Darcy explains. "There are things you just don't can't see in a traditional setting with one data point. We have been surprised, for instance, to see how many people experience loneliness. Some younger users report feeling lonely while they are in social settings. We've also learned from people reaching out in the middle of the night that they have postpartum depression." Dr. Darcy and her team have also been struck by the remarkable similarity in what users write. "It's not just that people say similar kinds of things – they say *the exact same thing*," she says. Woebot's data scientists apply insights like these to improving the topics that Woebot focuses on, and how the software interacts with users. In this way, the more that each user interacts with the system, the more helpful the system can become to all users.

3.6 GOVERNANCE

Woebot Labs is a privately held corporation founded by Dr. Alison Darcy in 2017. The company's headquarters are in San Francisco. According to reports provided by PrivCo, a service that provides research data on privacy companies, Woebot received $8 million from venture capital investors in March, 2018. In exchange for this "Series A" investment, the investors received equity in the company. The company's website lists the CEO (Alison Darcy), the Chief Clinical Officer (Athena Robinson), the Chairman of the Board of Directors (Andrew Ng), and the Chief Technology Officer (Casey Sackett) (Knight, 2017). Decisions relating to Woebot and the user data that underlies it are entirely made within the hierarchical structure of the corporation. Corporate decisions may be constrained to some extent by the company's contractual relationship with its source of VC capital. Although the contract is not public, such deals often grant the shareholders significant power over key corporate decisions, such as the sale of the company.

Beyond the formal corporate structure, professional standards, and codes of conduct constrain the behavior of Woebot's leadership. The CEO, for instance, is a clinical research psychologist and adjunct faculty member of Stanford School of Medicine. The company's CCO is a licensed clinical psychologist and an adjunct clinical associate professor in psychiatry and behavioral sciences at Stanford School of Medicine. Thus, the two most important decision-makers at the company are familiar with and must adhere in varying respects to codes of conduct and ethical standards promulgated by Stanford University. These require a psychologist to take reasonable precautions to protect patient confidentiality. Moreover, as a clinical psychologist, the CCO must adhere to similar codes and standards promulgated by the American Psychological Association and the state of California. However, whether Woebot is regarded as a therapeutic intervention and whether users of a therapy chatbot might be "patients" under a particular rule could be debated.

The company's privacy policy offers a view of how user data is treated [11]. Importantly, the service is available in two forms: through a stand-alone app and through Facebook's Messenger chat service. Woebot's privacy policy states, "Conversations with Woebot within Facebook Messenger are subject to the Facebook privacy policy. Facebook can see that you are talking to Woebot, and they can see the content of the conversations." Users seeking greater privacy than this will likely opt for Woebot's standalone app, which is available on iOS and Android, the two most widely used mobile operating systems. Without Facebook acting as an intermediary, Woebot alone can control the flow of user data.

To help explain this information flow, the company helpfully provides a chart on its website that divides user data into different categories and explains the company's purpose for collecting and processing it. The categories of user data include: "Personal information (including first name), password, referral code for participation in special programs, and email address," "Financial and billing information," and "Conversation data," which the company explains includes "Information, participation data, text, graphics, video, messages, responses to treatment and satisfaction surveys, or other materials generated through your interactions with Woebot." Under a section of the policy titled, "Where does Woebot obtain my personal data from," the policy states, "Most of the personal data we process is obtained from you when, through the application you: register for a Woebot account and exchange messages with Woebot."

The policy then defines what the company may do with this data. Under a section of the policy titled "Use of De-identified and Aggregated Information," the policy states that user data may be used to "create de-identigied and aggregated information," for "analyses we create." Such analyses would presumably include the types of internal studies of user interactions with the system described by Darcy earlier in this chapter.

Woebot does not make user data directly available to any users. As explained earlier in this chapter, the company takes precautions against unauthorized data access by storing user data on a secure server. The company's privacy policy states that the company may share it (with some restrictions) with certain third parties, however. According to the policy, these parties include "service providers who provide technical and support services to help us provide an improve the product and its services." The policy also explains that the company may share personal data with third parties for a variety of legal reasons, including compliance with applicable law, law enforcement or national security requests, subpoenas and the like. The policy also explains that the company reserves the right to share user data with insurance companies, financial institutions, or in connection with a corporate reorganization, merger, or acquisition. Finally, it states that user data may be shared with third parties in connection with "Special Programs." The term "Special Program" is not defined in the policy, but the document states that relevant third parties under this provision may include "your employer, certification authorities, or other medical and academic partners who conduct the study."

On the whole, Woebot's governance of user data shows the unique potential that chatbots may have to aggregate health data and, in turn, address the mental health crisis. By allowing users to receive help through a smartphone app, the service removes the sense of embarrassment that some people may feel about visiting a therapist in person. This, along with the company's treatment of user data, affords potential users with a sense that their conversations will be kept private. To benefit from the service, users must converse with Woebot. With each such conversation, the designers of Woebot have more data with which they can improve the service for others. And, because Woebot can talk to many users at the same time, the service can connect with more people than the current population of mental health workers is able to.

3.7 CHALLENGES

Because therapy chatbots have been available to the public for just a short time, a clear picture of the challenges Woebot and its competitors might face hasn't yet developed. It is possible, however, to discuss challenges that the company and experts in the industry perceive.

Although many bodies of law and regulation are relevant to therapy chatbots, one of the most significant relates to user privacy. Privacy is critical to Woebot for several reasons. First, the product solicits or otherwise prompts users to share information they consider private related to mental health conditions. Interestingly, a 2018 public blog post written by Dr. Darcy suggests that decisions about user data will be guided by long-standing rules and norms from the worlds of medicine and science: "First and foremost, this company was established by psychologists, which means we are subject to an ethical code of conduct. For us, this is so obvious that it seems self-evident."

The economic potential for mental health data seems significant. As an expert on medical ethics for this book chapter explained, insurance companies have an enormous interest in obtaining this data. "The question that policymakers should focus on," she said, "is whether they should have access to it. Should people with preexisting conditions revealed by their data still receive coverage? Can an insurer require you to sign up for one of these apps and use them?" These questions led the expert to opine that new laws limiting the data that insurers may receive and act upon should be enacted.

In addition to insurers are advertisers. In the 2010s, a common business model for online services is targeted advertising – the practice of directing advertisements to users based upon what they might like to buy. Online services usually accomplish this by collecting and processing data about their users and building up profiles that reflect users' probable likes, dislikes, interests, and so forth. For a fee paid by retailers, they direct ads to users. This business model has been phenomenally lucrative to ad sellers, helpful to ad buyers, and it has helped fuel countless avenues of important research that stands to benefit the public. Privacy advocates have long argued, however, that this practice can be harmful when users do not have a clear view of what information has been collected about them, with whom this information has been shared, and the purposes for which it is has been shared (Wu, 2017). These perspectives gained support when, in 2018, press reports revealed that user data collected by Facebook had been shared with an organization called Cambridge Analytica for the purpose of political advertising. The news stories garnered enough of the public's attention to blossom into a scandal that, over time, has brought privacy to the forefront of public policy discussions about technology.

Woebot's creators are keenly aware of how these developments might harm existing users and discourage potential users. Since the product was launched in 2017, Woebot has been unequivocal in their pledge not to monetize user data for third-party advertising (Molteni, 2017). Interviewed for this book chapter, Dr. Darcy explained that advertising runs counter to the company's core mission: "What we're best at," she explained,

> is this ability to challenge distorted thinking. And one of the most commonplace distorted thoughts is "I'm not X enough." Almost everybody has that core distortion, and it's something the ad industry has fed off of. It is the belief that allows ads to be effective. The idea that we would sell our data for advertising goes against everything the company stands for.

The post goes on to explain that selling data to advertisers would "instantly undermine" the trust users have placed in Woebot. "Our investment has been in symptom change outcomes – not in data gathering. If it were the latter, we would have built our product to orient around gathering as much data as possible" [12].

Consistently, the company has been a champion of GDPR. As Dr. Darcy explained, "We supported GDPR, and last May we did a lot of work towards complying with it. [The GDPR] shifts technology companies toward providing data ownership at the individual level, and we go for that level of privacy because we believe in it." Dr. Darcy added that, because leaders within Woebot come from human subjects research backgrounds, they are familiar with obtaining "seriously painstaking informed consent." She added, "Since the company launched in 2017, all user data is limited to the minimum amount required for the service to function. Data is not linked to users in an identifiable way" [13].

Interestingly, Woebot isn't the only mental health firm in favor of robust privacy. Another CEO interviewed for this article suggested that HIPAA should be extended to cover mental health data collected by corporations. "[I]f we can get a policy that says digital biomarkers are protected health information, then companies like Facebook and Google which could collect this stuff in the past suddenly couldn't do that anymore. You'd need to treat the data in a manner consistent with HIPAA."

Another problem that could undermine public confidence in therapy chatbots is lack of demonstrated efficacy. As discussed earlier, Woebot and other services like it are not required to obtain FDA clearance because of the FDA's hands-off approach. (As mentioned, if the FDA decides to be more involved in the future, it will likely focus on technologies that make clear claims regarding particular clinical indications – so-called digital therapeutics.) For now, though, consumers have no guarantee that these apps will deliver the results they promise. Additionally, a mental health app that is poorly designed could theoretically harm someone struggling with a mental health disorder.

Regulation isn't the only way to address this problem, but it might be the most effective. Peer-reviewed studies like the one cited earlier, for instance, could help consumers believe that an app works, but consumers are unlikely to search for and read scientific literature. Psyberguide, also discussed earlier in this chapter, helpfully provides a review system [8]. Ultimately, though, it cannot block a deficient app from being available to the public. Companies that administer app stores, such as Apple and Google, do have this kind of gatekeeping power. Experts interviewed for this article suggested that app stores are not the best solution, however. As the CEO of a Silicon Valley mental health startup commented, "You wouldn't want Walgreens to put a stamp of approval on drugs, so why would you want Apple to be making decisions about the efficacy and safety of mental health interventions?"

Dr. Darcy suggests that more regulation could be helpful in this area: "I would love to see more regulation, honestly, because the fact is, there hasn't been any. If health and wellness apps are quickly adopted but lack any support for efficacy, that threatens the public's confidence." Of course, a lengthy FDA review process would seem to run counter to the fluid, ongoing process of product improvement that therapy chatbots are based on. To balance the need for regulation with the realities of innovation, Dr. Darcy suggests a new approval process that focuses on companies rather than products – a process that is already in play at the FDA. "I love the idea of shifting away from approving products to approving companies. Allowing them the freedom to innovate quickly. The government might say, 'you have to show us how your company operates, how your QA systems are carried out, and, and so forth.'"

3.8 CONCLUSION

The emerging body of scientific literature on therapy chatbots suggests that these services could help large numbers of people reduce their levels of anxiety and depression. This possibility seems important for all of the reasons that these mental health disorders are so harmful: Anxiety can drain the enjoyment from life, interfere with personal relationships, as well as their productivity. Moreover, the problem only seems to be growing more widespread.

Therapy chatbots also may offer some unique advantages to traditional therapy. They can serve millions of people in a cost-effective way, for example. Because they can be accessed within one's home, they don't involve the stigma that some people associate with seeking mental health care. They can be accessed by people who cannot easily travel to a clinic. Finally, although these tools are not designed to replace traditional mental health treatment, they could be a cost-effective supplemental form of help for many. These technologies are still new, however, and some in the field of psychology believe their full potential remains an unknown. As one expert recently stated in a newspaper interview, "These things can work well on a superficial level with superficial conversations, but are they effective tools, do they change outcomes, and do they deliver more efficient care? It's still early" (Nutt, 2017).

Ultimately, the success of therapy chatbots may not only depend on how well they can be engineered but how effectively they can manage pools of private user data. As discussed in the introduction to this chapter, chatbots suggest a promising new technique for aggregating and making use of large sets of mental health. By conditioning access to the benefits of the existing pool – for example, knowledge – on new interactions – for example, typed exchanges – they effectively establish an incentive that might not otherwise exist. By delivering aggregated knowledge through an interactive system that is tightly scripted – rather than, say, a database – chatbots can effectively obscure private user data. This privacy is reinforced by other measures the company has taken, such as encryption.

As effective as this approach seems, the Knowledge Commons Framework shows why privacy remains an important area of work for the company. In light of the stigma that some people feel regarding mental health disorders, there is a need for users to feel that their data will not be disclosed. The degree of privacy the law ensures, meanwhile, is relatively low. HIPAA doesn't appear to cover chatbots billed as wellness apps, and the FDA has not sought to regulate data security in these types of apps tightly. Meanwhile, high-profile hacks and disclosures at companies like

Facebook have made the public aware that companies have an enormous financial impetus to use private data to make money. As a result, the app's creators and other companies like it must rely on public messaging. This has taken a variety of forms, including pledges not to use user data for advertising, corporate advocacy in favor of more robust privacy laws, and frank statements to the press that professional codes of conduct limit the behavior of corporate leaders. Ultimately, changes to the law combined with ancillary efforts like these may lead to a future where therapy chatbots can help people who suffer from anxiety and reveal new insights about the disorder itself.

LINKS

[1] https://adaa.org/about-adaa/press-room/facts-statistics
[2] www.apa.org/monitor/2016/06/numbers
[3] www.nhs.uk/Conditions/stress-anxiety-depression/Pages/benefits-of-talking-therapy.aspx
[4] https://adaa.org/finding-help/transcranial-magnetic-stimulation
[5] https://adaa.org/finding-help/treatment/complementary-alternative-treatment
[6] https://nccih.nih.gov/health/tips/stress
[7] www.ableto.com/news/ableto-acquires-joyable-2019/
[8] https://psyberguide.org
[9] https://adaa.org/social-media-obsession
[10] www.youtube.com/watch?v=AE966uRo9es
[11] https://woebot.io/privacy
[12] https://woebot.io/blog/why-well-never-sell-your-data-to-advertisers/
[13] https://woebot.io/blog/what-is-gdpr/
[14] www.x2ai.com/outcomes

REFERENCES

Andrilla, C. Holly A., Davis G. Patterson, Lisa A. Garberson, Cynthia Coulthard, and Eric H. Larson. "Geographic Variation in the Supply of Selected Behavioral Health Providers." *American Journal of Preventive Medicine* 54, no. 6 (2018): S199–S207.

Carey, Benedict. "California tests a digital 'fire alarm' for mental distress." *The New York Times*, June 17, 2019. www.nytimes.com/2019/06/17/health/mindstrong-mental-health-app.html

Chin, Monica. "This AI therapist is helping me get over my ex." *Mashable*, February 22, 2018. https://mashable.com/2018/02/22/worlds-first-ai-therapist/

Condliffe, Jamie. "How machine learning may help tackle depression." *MIT Technology Review*, April 5, 2017. www.technologyreview.com/s/604075/how-machine-learning-may-help-tackle-depression/

De Salvo, Karen B. and Jocelyn Samuels. "Examining oversight of the privacy & security of health data collected by entities not regulated by HIPPA." *Health IT Buzz*, July 19, 2016. www.healthit.gov/buzz-blog/privacy-and-security-of-ehrs/examining-oversight-privacy-security-health-data-collected-entities-not-regulated-hipaa.

Department of Health and Human Services. Examining oversight of the privacy & security of health data collected by entities not regulated by HIPPA." 2016. www.healthit.gov/sites/default/files/non-covered_entities_report_june_17_2016.pdf

Dobbs, David. "The smartphone psychiatrist." *The Atlantic*, July/August 2017. www.theatlantic.com/magazine/archive/2017/07/the-smartphone-psychiatrist/528726/

Dreyfuss, Emily. "LGBTQ+ youth prefer to seek mental health help digitally." *Wired*, June 11, 2019. www.wired.com/story/lgbtq-mental-health-digital-outreach/

DuPont, Robert L., Dorothy P. Rice, Leonard S. Miller, Sarah S. Shiraki, Clayton R. Rowland, and Henrick J. Harwood. "Economic Costs of Anxiety Disorders." *Anxiety* 2, no. 4 (1996): 167–172.

Fitzpatrick, Kathleen Kara, Alison Darcy, and Molly Vierhile. "Delivering Cognitive Behavior Therapy to Young Adults with Symptoms of Depression and Anxiety Using a Fully Automated Conversational Agent (Woebot): A Randomized Controlled Trial." *JMIR mental health* 4, no. 2 (2017): e19.

Frischmann, Brett M., Michael J. Madison, and Katherine J. Strandburg, eds. *Governing Knowledge Commons*. New York: Oxford University Press, 2014.

Fulmer, Russell, Angela Joerin, Breanna Gentile, Lysanne Lakerink, and Michiel Rauws. "Using Psychological Artificial Intelligence (Tess) to Relieve Symptoms of Depression and Anxiety: Randomized Controlled Trial." *JMIR mental health* 5, no. 4 (2018): e64.

Garg, Parie and Sam Glick. "AI's potential to diagnose and treat mental illness." *Harvard Business Review*, October 22, 2018. https://hbr.org/2018/10/ais-potential-to-diagnose-and-treat-mental-illness

Ghinassi, Cheryl Winning. *Anxiety*. Biographies of Disease Series. Santa Barbara, CA: Greenwood Publishing Group, 2010.

Gionet, Kylie. "Meet Tess: the mental health chatbot that thinks like a therapist." *The Gaurdian*, April 25, 2018. www.theguardian.com/society/2018/apr/25/meet-tess-the-mental-health-chatbot-that-thinks-like-a-therapist

Gratch, Jonathan. "The computer will see you now." *The Economist*, August 20, 2014. www.economist.com/science-and-technology/2014/08/20/the-computer-will-see-you-now

Green, Eric P., Nicholas Pearson, Sathyanath Rajasekharan, Michiel Rauws, Angela Joerin, Edith Kwobah, Christine Musyimi, Chaya Bhat, Rachel M. Jones, and Yihuan Lai. "Expanding Access to Depression Treatment in Kenya Through Automated Psychological Support: Protocol for a Single-Case Experimental Design Pilot Study." *JMIR research protocols* 8, no. 4 (2019): e11800.

Health Resources and Services Administration/National Center for Health Workforce Analysis; Substance Abuse and Mental Health Services Administration/Office of Policy, Planning, and Innovation. 2015. National Projections of Supply and Demand for Behavioral Health Practitioners: 2013–2025. Rockville, Maryland.

Hilty, Donald M. and Davor Mucic. "Technology, Health, and Contemporary Practice: How Does E-Mental Health Fit and What Does It Offer?" In *e-Mental Health*, Davor Mucic and Donald M. Hilty, eds., Cham: Springer, 2016, 3–27.

Hernandez, Daniela. "Meet the chabots providing mental health care." *The Wall Street Journal*, August 9, 2018. www.wsj.com/articles/meet-the-chatbots-providing-mental-healthcare-1533828373

Hoge, Elizabeth, David Bickham, and Joanne Cantor. "Digital Media, Anxiety, and Depression in Children." *Pediatrics* 140, no. Supplement 2 (2017): S76–S80.

Horwitz, Allan V. *Anxiety: A Short History*. Baltimore, MD: JHU Press, 2013.

Joerin, Angela, Michiel Rauws, and Mary Lou Ackerman. "Psychological Artificial Intelligence Service, Tess: Delivering On-demand Support to Patients and Their Caregivers: Technical Report." *Cureus* 11, no. 1 (2019): e3972.

Kleisiaris, Christos F., Chrisanthos Sfakianakis, and Ioanna V. Papathanasiou. "Health care practices in ancient Greece: The Hippocratic ideal." *Journal of Medical Ethics and History of Medicine* 7 (2014): 6.

Knight, Will. "Andrew Ng has a chatbot that can help with depression." *Technology Review*, October 18, 2017. www.technologyreview.com/s/609142/andrew-ng-has-a-chatbot-that-can-help-with-depression/

Lee, Debra. "Alison Darcy." *New Learning Times*, July 9, 2018. https://newlearningtimes.com/cms/article/5417/alison-darcy

Lee, Theodore T. "Recommendations for Regulating Software-Based Medical Treatments: Learning from Therapies for Psychiatric Conditions." *Food & Drug LJ* 73 (2018): 66.

Mathotaarachchi, Sulantha, Tharick A. Pascoal, Monica Shin, Andrea L. Benedet, Min Su Kang, Thomas Beaudry, Vladimir S. Fonov, Serge Gauthier, Pedro Rosa-Neto, and Alzheimer's Disease Neuroimaging Initiative. "Identifying Incipient Dementia Individuals Using Machine Learning and Amyloid Imaging." *Neurobiology of aging* 59 (2017): 80–90.

McCaney, Kevin. " AI programs can help in early detection of mental health issues." *Government CIO Media and Research*, January 24, 2019. www.governmentciomedia.com/ai-programs-can-help-early-detection-mental-health-issues

Molteni, Megan. "The chatbot therapist will see you now." *Wired*, June 7, 2017. www.wired.com/2017/06/facebook-messenger-woebot-chatbot-therapist/

Morris, Robert R., Kareem Kouddous, Rohan Kshirsagar, and Stephen M. Schueller. "Towards an Artificially Empathic Conversational Agent for Mental Health Applications: System Design and User Perceptions." *Journal of Medical Internet Research* 20, no. 6 (2018): e10148.

Mucic, Davor, Donald M. Hilty, Michelle B. Parish, and Peter M. Yellowlees. "Web- and Internet-Based Services: Education, Support, Self-Care, and Formal Treatment Approaches." In *e-Mental Health*, Davor Mucic and Donald M. Hilty, eds., Cham: Springer, 2016, 173–192.

Nutt, Amy Ellis. "'The Woebot will see you now' – the rise of chatbot therapy." *Washington Post*, December 3, 2017. www.washingtonpost.com/news/to-your-health/wp/2017/12/03/the-woebot-will-see-you-now-the-rise-of-chatbot-therapy/

Ostrom, Elinor. *Governing the Commons: The Evolution of Institutions for Collective Action*. New York: Cambridge University Press, 1990.

Pantic, Igor. "Online Social Networking and Mental Health." *Cyberpsychology, Behavior, and Social Networking* 17, no. 10 (2014): 652–657.

Rachman, Stanley J. *Anxiety*. London: Psychology Press, 2020.

Rieland, Randy. "Can artificial intelligence detect depression in a person's voice?" *Smithsonian Magazine*, November 5, 2018. www.smithsonianmag.com/innovation/can-artificial-intelligence-detect-depression-in-persons-voice-180970702/

Rosso, Cami. "Is the robot psychologist the next big AI app?" *Psychology Today*, October 17, 2018. www.psychologytoday.com/intl/blog/the-future-brain/201810/is-the-robot-psychologist-the-next-big-ai-app

Shoemaker, Erica Z. and Donald M. Hilty. "e-Mental Health Improces Access to Care, Facilitates Early Intervention, and Provides Evidence-Based Treatments at a Distance." In *e-Mental Health*, Davor Mucic and Donald M. Hilty, eds., Cham: Springer, 2016, 43–57.

Stephens, Taylor N., Angela Joerin, Michiel Rauws, and Lloyd N. Werk. "Feasibility of Pediatric Obesity and Prediabetes Treatment Support through Tess, the AI Behavioral Coaching Chatbot." *Translational Behavioral Medicine* 9, no. 3 (2019): 440–447.

U.S. Department of Health and Human Services. "The U.S. health workforce chartbook: part IV: behavioral and allied health." September 2018. https://bhw.hrsa.gov/sites/default/files/bhw/health-workforce-analysis/research/hrsa-us-health-workforce-chartbook-part-4-behavioral-and-allied-health.pdf

Wallach, Eric. "An interview with Jo Aggarwal, co-inventor of Wysa." *The Politic*, March 28, 2018. http://thepolitic.org/an-interview-with-jo-aggarwal-co-inventor-of-wysa/

Wu, Tim. *The Attention Merchants: The Epic Scramble to Get Inside Our Heads*. New York: Vintage, 2017.

4

Privacy in Practice

A Socio-technical Integration Research (STIR) Study of Rules-in-Use within Institutional Research

Kyle M. L. Jones[1] *and Chase McCoy*[2]

4.1 INTRODUCTION

The ubiquity of information systems on university campuses for supporting university work has led to an undeniable increase in the quantity of institutional data. Higher education institutions have taken note of the trove of data to which they now have access, arguing that they have a responsibility to use data in service to their administrative and educational missions and to act upon accountability pressures from external constituents to use data to identify actionable insights directed toward institutional improvement (Prinsloo and Slade, 2014). In response to this institutional data influx and to address mounting external pressures, learning analytics (Johnson, Smith, Willis, Levine, and Haywood, 2011) and other data-based research and practitioner communities have emerged, while existing communities, such as institutional research, are transforming their practices to account for the evolving data environment (Zilvinskis, Willis, and Borden, 2017).

Within this landscape, significant new privacy issues are emerging as a result of changing data use practices and the sociopolitical pressures on higher education institutions to surface, analyze, and act on data. One of the questions associated with

We would like to thank Erik Fisher, Ira Bennett, Jamey Wetmore, Rider Foley, and all the participants at the 5th Annual Winter School on Responsible Innovation and Social Studies of Emerging Technologies at Arizona State University. Many of the ideas that motivated this project were seeded from constructive conversations at the Winter School. We would also like to thank the participants at the Fairness and Equity in Learning Analytics Systems (FairLAK) workshop hosted at the 2019 Learning Analytics and Knowledge conference, as attendee feedback informed the evolution of this chapter. Please note that parts of this chapter were originally presented in the following paper: Jones, K. M. and McCoy, C. (2019, March). "Ethics in Praxis: Socio-Technical Integration Research in Learning Analytics." In *Companion Proceedings of the 9th International Learning Analytics & Knowledge Conference*.

[1] Assistant Professor, School of Informatics and Computing, Department of Library and Information Science at Indiana University-Indianapolis (IUPUI). Ph.D., University of Wisconsin-Madison iSchool; M.L.I.S., Dominican University; B.A., Elmhurst College.

[2] Ph.D. Candidate, Luddy School of Informatics, Computing, and Engineering, Department of Library and Information Science at Indiana University-Bloomington. M.L.S., Indiana University-Bloomington; B.A., University of Illinois Urbana-Champaign.

these issues concerns how higher education actors are handling private data, especially student data, in praxis given the increasing sensitivity of the data (Slade and Prinsloo, 2013). However, the existing rules and norms that govern the privacy practices of institutional researchers and other data practitioners are often unable to account for the nuances of data privacy in praxis (Fuller, 2017b; Zeide, 2016), which has led to informal and implicit institutional policies about student data privacy (Fuller, 2017b).

Understanding the rules and norms that shape the practices of institutional researchers and other data practitioners in regard to student data privacy within higher education could be researched using descriptive methods, which attempt to illustrate what is actually being done in this space. But, we argue that it is also important for practitioners to become reflexive about their practice while they are in the midst of using sensitive data in order to make responsive practical and ethical modulations.

To achieve this, we conducted a socio-technical integration research (STIR) (Fisher, 2012). STIR provides structured opportunities for research participants to integrate perspectives and methods from the social sciences and humanities. The STIR method targets small teams or groups of participants, often scientific laboratory researchers. We adopted this method to STIR a single institutional researcher over an extended period of time. The participant's responsibilities entailed, among other things, conducting statistical analyses on important administrative metrics, such as retention, recruitment, and enrollment for their university's administration. Drawing on Crawford and Ostrom's (1995) institutional grammar, we assessed the rules, norms, and strategies that governed the participant's practices as they related to data privacy.[3] This theoretical join of STIR and institutional grammar helped us to answer the general research question: What rules-in-use govern the participant's privacy practices, and how might STIR lead to modulations in those practices? In summary, the findings reveal that the participant was encouraged to reflect on the conditions of her context and her agency to make modulations of her own work and consider whether existing rules, norms, and strategies are justifiable. These reflections, in turn, led to active modulations where her practices were modified to more explicitly consider privacy or, at the least, brought about ideas for future privacy-focused initiatives (e.g., data management strategies and documentation processes).

4.2 DATA ANALYTICS IN HIGHER EDUCATION AND CHALLENGES TO CONTEXTUAL INTEGRITY

4.2.1 *The Value of Analytics*

The advent of new technologies and analytical techniques are enabling the proliferation of data and information within higher education institutions.

[3] To be clear, "institutional grammar" has no explicit conceptual or theoretical ties to colleges and universities as institutions. Unless situated in discussions around the grammar of institutions, our reference to "institutions" concerns higher education.

Goldstein and Katz (2005, 11) explain that "the challenge [to colleges and universities] is no longer the lack of access to timely information"; it is the ability to make actionable decisions based on available information. In the early aughts, universities began to develop capacity for what was then called "academic analytics." Like business intelligence, academic analytics is the use of various technological systems and applications to analyze accessible institutional data in support of decision-making.

Much of the capacity-building done in support of academic analytics has led to additional analytic practices to serve various ends, in part due to function creep. Most prominent among these practices is the learning analytics movement. Since 2010, institutions have methodically worked to make data about students once "unseen, unnoticed, and therefore unactionable" to be visible and analyzable (Bienkowski, Feng, and Means, 2012, ix). Defined, learning analytics is "the interpretation of a wide range of data produced by and gathered on behalf of students in order to assess academic progress, predict future performance, and spot potential issues" (Johnson et al., 2011, 28). A driving goal of learning analytics is to "tailor educational opportunities to each student's level of need and ability" (Johnson et al., 2011, 28), but learning analytics is *not* just about learners: it is also about the learning context and can be used to "assess curricula, programs, and institutions" (Johnson et al., 2011, p. 28). To a lesser extent than learning analytics, institutions have also begun using their information infrastructures to mine and analyze data about faculty performance and productivity (see Flaherty, 2016; Patel, 2016).

Why are higher education institutions pursuing analytics (academic, learning, faculty, or otherwise)? Campbell, DeBlois, and Oblinger (2007, 42) present analytics as a sort of salve for higher education, writing that "academic analytics is emerging as a new tool that can address what seem like intractable challenges." As in other contexts, institutional actors and higher education pundits have applied powerful metaphors to express – and influence – the role of data mining at the university level (Stark and Hoffman, 2019). Some argue that the data and information institutions can aggregate and analyze is akin to valuable natural resources, like oil and gold, that they have social, political, and economic value (see Mayer-Schönberger and Cukier, 2014; Watters, 2013). Proponents of analytics argue that the insightful information they create can help institutions defend themselves against mounting accountability pressures and provide useful insights regarding resource usage in languishing economic times (Prinsloo and Slade, 2014).

4.2.2 *Competing Interests*

The turn toward data analytics in higher education raises particular questions about the effects caused by an increasingly data-driven, technocratic institution (Slade and Prinsloo, 2013). Maturing institutional data infrastructures enable the administrative surveillance of researcher productivity, instructional methods, and the day-to-day life of students, which in turn allow for granular reforms of programs, practices, and people – all in the name of institutional effectiveness (Selwyn, 2014; Williamson, 2018). Reflecting on this point, Johnson (2016, 27) argues:

> Data systems . . . are too often assumed to be value-neutral representations of fact that produce justice and social welfare as an inevitable by-product of efficiency and openness. Rarely are questions raised about how they affect the position of individuals and groups in society. But data systems both arbitrate among competing claims to material and moral goods and shape how much control one has over one's life.

It could be that data analytics privilege bureaucratic and politically expedient outcomes in ways that suppress what is otherwise "educationally desirable" (Slade and Prinsloo, 2013), including developing just educational systems that support student autonomy and well-being (Rubel and Jones, 2016). Important questions emerge: Who has the power to wield institutional data, to what ends are analytics directed, and whose interests are served (or ignored)? Kitchin (2014, 165) reminds us that "there is a fine balance between using data in emancipatory and empowering ways, and using data for one's own ends and to the detriment of others, or in ways contrary to the wishes of those the data represent."

Government actors, institutional administrators, parents and guardians, and, among others, companies who develop and participate in educational analytics all have varying interests in maximizing value from analyzable data (Ferguson, 2012; Rubel and Jones, 2016). Such stated benefits include increases in academic success for students, but analytics also enable others to gain financial, social, and reputational advantages.

Consider the following examples of plausible conflicts of interests. Administrators want to decrease time-to-degree measures and increase graduation rates. One method may be to use analytics to direct students to enroll in academic programs or courses for which they meet the threshold for predicted success, say 75 percent. Students share the same goals, but forcing them down an academic path not of their choosing will not benefit them if they find their future careers to be dull and uninteresting. Where faculty are concerned, analytics may enable tenure and promotion committees to do peer-institution comparisons of research output and impact, which help them to make quicker recommendations, in addition to strategically build a core faculty according to standardized metrics. However, these analytics are decontextualized and limited; tenure and promotion candidates may not be provided the opportunity to tell a complete story about their body of work. These competing interests highlight the fact that data and information are not neutral artifacts, but instead they are "cooked" with the motivations of those who wield data and analytic tools (Bowker, 2013).

4.2.3 *The Appropriate Flow of Information*

When the *appropriate flow* of information changes, and those changes run counter to normative expectations, privacy is put at risk within a given context (Nissenbaum,

2010). With higher education analytics, the creation of new information flows – many of which contain identifiable data – and the alteration of existing flows to support analytic practices have raised privacy concerns, primarily but not exclusively regarding students (Pardo and Siemens, 2014; Rubel and Jones, 2016). The problem with higher education analytics is that all of these parts are affected in some way by emerging analytic infrastructures, related practices, and changes in who is able to access and use data – which are indubitably affected by shifting politics and administrators' neoliberal interests (Heath, 2014). Some existing informational norms are, therefore, uncapable of providing clear direction in this era of analytics. As a result, institutional actors may find themselves making sensitive, and often critical, data privacy decisions based on their own personal values and ethical judgement. For the purposes of this chapter, we focus on institutional researchers whose very role dictates that they access, manage, and analyze an array of data to inform institutional practices.

4.3 A SOCIO-TECHNICAL INTEGRATION RESEARCH STUDY OF AN INSTITUTIONAL RESEARCHER

4.3.1 *Downstream Effects, Impacting Midstream Practice*

There is a need to better understand how higher education's information workers, like institutional researchers, make sense of their moral practices as they implement data analytics into important decision-making strategies. Instead of looking at downstream effects and then shining the proverbial light after the fact, there is a need to look at – and influence – the design of ethically sensitive data technologies and practices closer upstream. These efforts are *crucial* for identifying problems before they are baked into socio-technical data analytics systems and individuals are made into and considered as data (Jones and McCoy, 2018). We argue that the socio-technical integration research (STIR) method can lead to positive upstream engagement and useful modulations at the midstream level.

STIR enables research practitioners – laboratory scientists, engineers, technologists, and information professionals – to consider perspectives from the humanities. STIR projects pair practitioners with embedded social scientists who together work to "unpack the social and ethical dimensions of research and innovation in real time and to document and analyse the results" (Fisher, 2010, 76). These partnerships enable researchers to study the practices of their research practitioner partners, while engaging them in conversations that explore the societal and ethical dimensions of their work. Surfacing these issues provides the conditions necessary for research practitioners to reconsider their efforts and make midstream modulations that reduce downstream harms.

4.3.2 *Socio-Technical Awareness*

During their time together, the STIR researcher takes the opportunity to move the practitioner toward "reflexive awareness," or an attentiveness to "the nested processes, structures, interactions, and interdependencies, both immediate and more removed, within which they operate" (Fisher, Mahajan, and Mitcham, 2006, 492). Such awareness provides the conditions necessary for the practitioner to consider one's socio-political position, usage of resources, ethical reasoning, among other things, which can give rise to "goal-directed" (Fisher, Mahajan, and Mitcham, 2006, 492) modulations that directly impact current practices. To build toward this opportunity for change, the researcher structures discussion protocols around these basic questions, which are asked in relation to a specific practice:

1. What are you doing?
2. Why are you doing it?
3. How could you do it differently?
4. Who might care?

The first question establishes the particulars of a practice (e.g., cleaning a laboratory table with disinfectant or developing an algorithm), while the second prompts the practitioner to take up the underlying justification(s) for the action. Question three begins to nudge the practitioner toward reflexivity by providing the intellectual time and space to consider alternative ways of doing and other justificatory reasons. The fourth and final question stimulates the practitioner to reflect on the present and proposed altered practice by considering relevant stakeholders and downstream effects thereon.

4.3.3 *Modulations in Practice*

There are three stages of identifiable modulations: de facto, reflexive, and deliberate. With de facto modulations, research data indicates that socio-technical integration occurs, but the research participant does not actively reflect on the integration because there is no incentive to do so. Reflexive modulations by participants arise because of heightened awareness of socio-technical considerations brought about by working with the researcher. In these cases, participants explicitly notice how social influences (e.g., actors, politics, values, resources, etc.) interact with a given practice. At the deliberate modulation stage, participants begin to act on their reflexive modulations. They take stock of their heightened awareness of the socio-technical milieu to plan strategies, curate resources, and make changes in their practices. Such changes may simply make their current practice more efficient and effective, and this would be a first-order deliberate modulation. But if the participant makes changes to alter the goals, objectives, and assumptions of the project due to enhanced social sensitivity, then these changes would be second-order deliberate modulations. In the remainder of this chapter, we discuss our work using STIR to study an institutional research practitioner and the participant's privacy practices in praxis.

4.3.4 *Joining STIR with Institutional Grammar*

We integrated the STIR method (Fisher, Mahajan, and Mitcham, 2006; Fisher and Shuurbiers, 2013) and Crawford and Ostrom's (1995) institutional grammar for identifying rules-in-use as expanded to address information privacy concerns (Sanfilippo, Frischmann, and Strandburg, 2018). The STIR approach was used to probe the research participant into considering and acknowledging the implicit socio-technical characteristics that guided the participant's practice and those within the participant's office, and with the intention that these have been made explicit that they would lead to identifiable modulations in the participant's privacy practices. Institutional grammar's rules-in-use were used to assess rules such as policies and laws, norms that govern privacy practices in institutional research, and strategies that shape the privacy practices of institutional researchers.

4.3.5 *Study Design*

The study's participant was a single institutional researcher at a mid-sized public university. The participant's institutional research responsibilities entail, among other things, conducting statistical analyses on important administrative metrics, such as retention, recruitment, and enrollment, and providing this information to their institution's administration. Over four months, we conducted twelve semi-structured in-person and virtual interviews with the participant. Furthermore, during the interviews, the participant often shared data artifacts, such as an ongoing project on enrollment projections and trends, while discussing the practices associated with their everyday work. While studying one participant is a unique sample size, the STIR method has traditionally been used with small teams of scientific laboratory workers. Studying just one institutional researcher is adequate given the often solo nature of this type of professional's work. Moreover, working with one individual allowed us to develop an intimate rapport and gain access to sensitive information shared by the participant, which may have been held back if we had also been working with her peers.

We developed an interview protocol to guide the participant to reflect on her privacy practices and those of her staff within the office of institutional research. The interviews sought to elicit from the participant reflections upon four decision components: the institutional research activities that they engage in (opportunities); the reasons for and against their practices (considerations); possible alternative approaches to their activities and reasons that might lead to acting on those alternatives (alternatives); and the possible outcomes if such outcome were acted upon (outcomes) (Flipse, van der Sanden, and Osseweijer, 2013) to identify the rules-in-use, values, goals, and other socio-technical variables that shaped the practitioner's privacy practice.

4.3.6 *Data Analysis Procedures*

We digitally recorded all interviews, using the audio to create transcriptions for coding purposes. We imported transcripts into MAXQDA, a qualitative data analysis application, and then coded interviews based on a two-stage approach. First, Crawford and Ostrom's (1995) institutional grammar approach was used to identify the rules-in-use that governed the practitioner's institutional research privacy practices. These codes assessed the rules, norms, and strategies, and each of these rules-in -use's associated attributes, aims, conditions, deontics, and consequences associated with the Governing Knowledge Commons (GKC) framework devised by Sanfilippo, Frischmann, and Strandburg (2018). At the same time as these items were coded, we coded for the level at which a particular rule-in-use existed: individual, office, institution, external to the institution. Second, the interviews were then coded based on the STIR approach to identify the four socio-technical decision components, followed by codes for identifying the various socio-technical modulations that emerged throughout the interview process. What follows is relevant background information on institutional researchers and the findings we uncovered from our GKC-informed STIR.

4.4 THE ROLE OF INSTITUTIONAL RESEARCHERS IN HIGHER EDUCATION'S ANALYTIC PRACTICES

4.4.1 *Higher Education Intelligences*

Institutional research is a branch of educational research that concentrates on improving "understanding, planning, and operating of institutions of postsecondary education" (Peterson, 1999, 84). The role of institutional researchers is then to provide information to institutional administrators to aid in the improvement of planning, policy generation, and effective decision-making. Volkwien, Liu, and Woodell (2012, 23) suggest that the institutional researcher is engaged in three areas of study, which they call the "golden triangle of institutional research":

1. institutional reporting and administrative policy analysis;
2. strategic planning, enrollment, and financial management;
3. outcomes assessment, program review, accountability, accreditation, and institutional effectiveness.

Furthermore, institutional researchers are called upon to not only provide information to facilitate improvement in these areas, but to actively engage in information sharing practices that contribute to organizational learning and, in turn, improve institutional effectiveness (Borden and Kezar, 2012).

Effective institutional research practices require that the institutional researcher engage three types of intelligences as they relate to their institution and higher education in general: technical and analytical; issues; and contextual and cultural (Terenzini, 1999). Given the diversity of these intelligences, institutional researchers have to balance various, and often competing, demands from administrators internal to their institutions, and from their external constituents, including state and federal policy makers, and their local communities (Volkwein, 1999). One such balancing concerns what Volkwien (1999, 13) calls, "enrollment pressures." Institutions are "asked to simultaneously admit more students (for financial health and access) and become more selective (to bolster academic standards and performance measures)." For this reason, he likens the institutional researcher to Janus, the two-faced Roman God of "doors and gateways" in that they have to look inward toward internal improvement, while contemporaneously facing outward to ensure that they are attuned to external accountability demands.

4.4.2 *Information and Knowledge Managers*

In addition to appraising the demands of variegated internal and external actors, Serban (2002) emphasizes the institutional researcher's role regarding managing the flow of institutional data and information throughout their institutions. It is for this reason that the institutional researcher should also be understood as their institution's knowledge manager, whereby they are responsible for the "processes that underlie the knowledge management framework – creation, capturing, and sharing of knowledge – that serve both internal and external purposes and audiences" (Serban, 2002, 105). Understanding and addressing the complexity of the flow of institutional information and data throughout institutions of higher education is necessary given growing interest in advanced analytic practices.

Where once there was a time when institutional researchers served as their institution's "one source of truth," this new environment is leading to situations where "decision makers at all levels are establishing their own data collection processes and analytics" (Swing and Ross, 2016, 5). Zilvinskis, Willis, and Borden (2017, 12) argue that broad interest in analytics across campus units and offices creates a new situation where institutional researchers are playing a different role, writing: "[w]orking on learning analytics projects requires IR staff to engage with colleagues who tend to use information in operational and individualized contexts rather than the more strategic and aggregate uses to which they are accustomed." This is so because institutional research offices are no longer the primary source of data, information, and analytic insights; each academic unit and office increasingly uses highly contextual data to serve their information needs. For instance, advisors are adopting analytic systems to analyze student movement through curricula, and information technology offices are developing their own metrics and data dashboards to evaluate system usage and services. Swing and Ross (2016) contend that because data flows are becoming more complex and analytics more widespread, institutional researchers should become more actively engaged in managing and shaping of policies regarding the flow and use of institutional information and data.

4.4.3 *Governing Sensitive Institutional Data and Information*

Among professional institutional research associations and in the research literature, there have been ongoing conversations about principles, rules, and national and institutional policies that do or should govern uses of institutional information (Shiltz, 1992). Much of this work concerns privacy as it relates to security, confidentiality, and appropriate use. And since student data and information is of chief importance in institutional research, policy conversations tend to revolve around students and less about faculty and staff.

On a national level, institutional research practices are bound by the Family Educational Rights and Privacy Act (FERPA). The law dictates that educational institutions who receive federal funding must protect and hold in confidence student data and information considered a part of a student's identifiable educational record. Institutional actors have the right to gain access to such records when they have a legitimate educational interest in doing so. However, Fuller (2017a) argues that institutional researchers are often unaware or undertrained regarding FERPA. According to a survey of 232 institutional researchers, 53 percent self-taught themselves about FERPA, while 22.5 percent had received no training. Lacking in knowledge of FERPA and its relation to data privacy matters should be a matter of concern, given that data breaches and other FERPA violations have led to numerous institutions being litigated in recent years (Fuller, 2017b). Knowledge of and training with regard to FERPA is especially important given that the law's definitions and requirements are imprecise and/or able to be bent based on an institution's interpretations (Zeide, 2016).

Information sharing and information flow practices are also guided by professional ethics, institutional policies, and personal values (Fuller, 2017b). Regarding professional ethics, the Association for Institutional Research (2013) outlines how institutional researchers should handle privacy issues in their Code of Ethics. However, the code is scant on this issue and merely states that institutional researchers should balance privacy risks and confidentiality against the potential benefits that the information can provide to the institution. Additionally, institutional researchers' practices are supposed to be informed by internal institutional policies on data privacy. However, Fuller (2017b) claims that many institutions do not have formal written policies.

4.4.4 *Ethical Murkiness*

The ambiguity in federal law, the "squishiness" of codes of ethics, and possibly the lack of guiding institutional information policy leads institutional researchers into a murky, ethical gray area. Researchers acknowledge that educational data analytics – a social *and* technological practice – raises significant ethical concerns (see Slade and Prinsloo, 2013). If data analytics produced by institutional researchers and others are to be considered trustworthy and legitimate, then they must attend to the ethical issues, the so-called "critical barriers" that will determine success and failure of data-based analytic initiatives (Gašević, Dawson, and Jovanović, 2016, 2). Higher education analytics are "moral practice[s]" (Slade and Prinsloo, 2013, 1519) that must account for actual and potential harms brought about data and information access, analysis, and use (Pardo and Siemens, 2014).

4.5 GOVERNANCE IN PRACTICE: STIR FINDINGS

4.5.1 *Attributes*

The findings below highlight how various information resources, policies, institutional actors, and various – and sometimes divergent – goals and objectives influence and frame the work done by the institutional researcher who participated in our socio-technical integration research (STIR). But briefly, it is important to highlight how these attributes make up the contextual background of the participant.

The participant's resources are data-based and informational. She relied on datasets in various forms to complete her responsibilities, and she primarily used a centralized data warehouse to access and export data to her local computer for statistical analysis and data visualization purposes. Some but not all data sets were shared on a local network in the office of institutional research with specific user permissions set to limit access and protect sensitive data. Notably, the office's information infrastructure was described differently in terms of its data security protections when compared to other offices on campus. The datasets were comprised of identifiable and de-identified student data, in addition to "raw" and aggregate data provided by other institutional offices, including among others human resources and admissions.

The participant's office was, as expected, comprised of a staff of roughly twenty individuals. The makeup of the staff included administrators, data analysts, institutional researchers, and part-time graduate assistants. It would not be accurate to think that this office worked in a silo; they often collaborated with institutional administration to provide them actionable information and worked with other offices on campus when specific projects needed access to and analysis of institutional data. The work the institutional research office did was shaped and limited at times by the political interests of those to whom they reported data findings, as well as policy set by the institution's office of information technology.

The goals and values of the institutional research and her office were not made explicit during interviews. However, such things were made clear upon examining the office's documentation. The office strives to provide actionable information to support decision-making throughout the campus, as well as support the institution's wider goals around student success and the effective operation of the campus. It is notable that the office explicitly aims to provide access to a data infrastructure and related tools, signaling that its staff wishes to be enablers of data – not gatekeepers – and help institutional colleagues leverage data in innovative ways.

4.5.2 *Existing Rules-in-Use*

The analysis of the conversations with the participant uncovered the rules-in-use (norms, rules, and strategies) that govern her work practices with institutional data. Furthermore, the analysis found that addressing the levels at which rules-in-use occur is important for understanding how rules-in-use emerge and differ in practice. For this analysis, we found rules-in-use at the following levels: individual, office, institution, and external-to-the-institution. The level of the rules-in-use impacted their scope and determined what and how they were governed. Understanding rules-in-use and the levels at which they occur will be important for our to-be-discussed STIR findings, where we explore the participant's reflections upon and her modulations of her privacy practices and, in turn, the rules-in-use that govern her practice.

The participant's privacy practices are governed by a variety of rules, most of which occur at the external-to-the-institution, institution, and office levels. Regarding the rules external to the institution, her and her colleagues are required to follow the appropriate FERPA guidelines. At the university level, university rules require that the participant and her colleagues are compliant with rules related to data sharing and use, such as ensuring that data consumers have the proper data use training and have signed the institution's data use agreement in order to receive and share data. At the office level, the participant described rules primarily related to working with the university's institutional review board (IRB) prior to conducting research and ensuring that she and her colleagues are up to date with institutional and federal privacy policies.

Regarding the norms, these predominantly occur at the institution and office levels. At the institution level, the norms revolve around data use for institutional improvement. According to the participant, the institutional norm is that data should be shared and made available to those seeking to improve the educational mission of the institution to develop useful insights. As the participant stated, "I think it's been a policy [at the university] that we share information and we don't try to silo things." Given this, it is expected that her office collaborates with and supports other offices across the campus. The office level norms that guide the participant and her office's practices relate primarily to protocols for how to share data with those external to their office and how student data should be de-identified in their institutional research products, such as in reports, dashboards, and data sets.

The strategies that govern the participant's privacy practices primarily occur at the office and individual levels. These relate to spatial privacy practices and the appropriate use of student data. Spatial privacy practices refer to how the participant and her colleagues consider and modify their work and office spaces to ensure that student data are kept secure. Regarding office level strategies for appropriate data use, the participant stated that they assist data consumers to develop their business use cases when requesting access to institutional data. In addition, her office collaborates with other campus offices when they have questions about data access and use rules and norms.

Based on the analysis of the rules-in-use occurring at the office and individual levels an interesting trend emerged. The office and individual rules-in-use that the participant and her colleagues developed were in response to instances when the institution failed to adequately govern the participant's privacy practices. In some instances, the office and individual's rules-in-use explicitly contradicted that of the institution, but in other situations individual rules-in-use at the office and individual levels were developed in response to gaps at the institutional and federal levels. These contradictions and gaps will be further explained in the following section, where we discuss the findings of the STIR analysis.

4.5.3 *Rethinking Rules-in-Use with Socio-Technical Integration Research*

Conversations with the participant probed to examine the socio-technical conditions of her work regarding data practices and privacy. These probing questions enabled the participant to reflect on her workaday routines, but also to nudge the participant to examine the criteria (e.g., values, principles, procedures) that inform decisions a part of her routines. As we describe below, the participant was acutely knowledgeable of privacy issues, related processes and procedures, and had even developed unique privacy-protecting strategies.

The participant was keenly aware of the fact that data to which she had access, especially student data, were sensitive and needed to be kept secure. She expressed a personal ethos of responsibility, suggesting several times that data handling actions needed care and attention to potential downstream privacy effects. When asked why she felt this normative responsibility, she replied, "Why is it so important to protect student data in the way that we are? Because we're here for the students because we want to make sure that we're not creating any kind of violation, that we're not violating this trust that they have." Notably, she suggests that her ethos is one to which her institutional research peers subscribe as well. Additionally, the motivation for protecting the privacy of those she analyzes in data is due to a sense of obligation to uphold the trust data subjects have in her, but also the institution, to use data appropriately. If trust was something that could be violated, we asked, then what would be the consequences? To this probing question, she suggested that 1) students would not be willing participants in research projects and 2) her office would "lose access to some of the data that we need to be able to do our jobs" due to non-compliance with existing policies.

Before beginning her analytical work, the participant claimed that she strategically worked with her institution's institutional review board (IRB), using it as a means to discuss and protect data privacy. "We tend to err on the side of caution," she said, "and at least talk to IRB about every single project that we do .... We want to at the very least make IRB aware of [the project] and get some sort of approval." Pursuing an "ethical consultation" with IRB, to the participant, would help her understand if her work was "consistent with good ethical research practices," in compliance with federal rules, and in alignment with what the institution expects regarding access to student data. The IRB could help her limit downstream harms, such as the following she expressed in a conversation:

> It is easy to see how that sort of access to data could be abused, um, should it get into the wrong hands. People could theoretically be linking, you know, survey responses with income data from the [Free Application for Federal Student Aid (FAFSA)] or things like that if it's not used properly.

After working with the IRB, the participant described the process for gaining access to data. Institutional policy limited who within the institution could gain access to different sources of data. Depending on the source of the data, the participant would have to consult with a dedicated data steward (e.g., the registrar for enrollment data, the bursar for financial data, or a library administrator for library data). Conversations with the stewards required her to "build a business use case to justify" data access and use. The participant emphasized that the creation of the "business use case" was a collaborative process, and she stated that finding the necessary justification would not be as easy at other institutions where data sharing was more restrictive and there was less value placed on analytics based on combinable data from across various offices.

Before conversations gained significant traction, the participant would have to prove that she had successfully passed the institution's FERPA training and consented to its data use agreement; both processes informed the participant of her legal and institutional responsibilities. Since her office also serves as a source of institutional data and information, the participant also asked for proof of the same compliance credentials from those with whom she worked within the institution. Notably, she questioned if others thoughtfully considered the compliance measures like she did, saying, "I would hope that everybody reads that information and takes it seriously; I don't have any kind of assurance." When she provides a data set, she makes the data requester "promise" that data will not be shared unless carefully outlined and approved ahead of time, detail how the data will be used, and share their data deletion strategies, all in order to make sure that institutional policy compliance is assured. When data requests proved difficult to determine access and use privileges, she consulted with other data stewards to seek their interpretations. The participant did not detail requirements that guided these types of conversations and blindly trusted that all data stewards would be just as rigorous in their analysis of data use requests.

About her office's data privacy practices, she revealed a significant detail concerning the physical layout of her own office and that of her colleagues. The conversation unfolded in this way:

RESEARCHER: You were saying that each analyst I think has a door, right? It's not in a cubicle. And you were saying your monitors are faced away from the wall.

PARTICIPANT: We're all kind of positioned in a way that nobody just walking by can just take a look and peek at your machine.

RESEARCHER: So how did that come about? It's an interesting decision to make.

PARTICIPANT: We were just very sensitive about the fact that we had student-level data in our records on our computer at any given time, and we just wanted to be cognizant of the fact that somebody could just come in just happen to accidentally peep over and take a look at something that they weren't supposed to be looking at. We are responsible for data security for this information . . . . It is something that I think we do need to be conscious about.

When her office hires student workers who do not have the benefit of a secure office, students are made aware of the fact that their work may involve sensitive data and that they should situate their computer screens to limit others from looking over their shoulders. The participant noted that her office's privacy-protecting strategies were not as stringent as those in other offices, such as financial aid, whose employees "keep the windows drawn" and do not allow unaccompanied visitors.

Regarding digital data privacy practices, the participant expressed two strategies. First, another employee in the office was in charge of maintaining scoped data pulls from administrative systems (e.g., the student information system) and subsequently checking the veracity of the data. Having a point person for this data practice reduced inaccurate data and limited access to data unnecessary for informing analytic projects (i.e., they followed data minimization principles). Second, any analytics created by the office abided by their own rule that for data including a sample size of five or less, the reportable number changes to an asterisk. For instance, if a data dashboard includes aggregate data demonstrating that three Hawaiian/Pacific Islander students reflected a certain behavior or outcome, then the number would be masked to reduce reidentification risks. The participant emphasized that this rule went beyond less stringent requirements set by FERPA and guidance by the registrar's office.

When the participant described her privacy practices – or a lack thereof in some cases – we prompted her to discuss alternative ways of thinking, doing, and valuing. The purpose of this strategy was to provide intellectual space and time to consider how outcomes of her privacy practices could be different and to reconsider the stimuli motivating standard practices. Responses to this strategy ranged from affirmative alternative designs (e.g., "I could do this . . . ") to negative responses (e.g., "There is no other possibility . . . ") due to existing conditions. The following highlights two instances where the participant outlined possible alternatives and outcomes.

An ongoing frustrating experience for the participant concerned her relationship with the institution's office of information technology (OIT). Part of her position's responsibility covered creating internal use and publicly available data dashboards, which required permission from an internal review panel *and* OIT. She expressed that even in cases where the internal review panel gives permission, OIT removes the dashboard – but they often fail to tell the participant that they had done so. Consequently, she "has to play ball" with OIT even if their decision would align with the internal review panel in the first place; if she does not, she loses her completed work.

The purpose for OIT rules is to protect data and the privacy of data subjects. But, the participant argued that these rules were too restrictive and unconstructive:

> [OIT] kind of feels like everybody outside of [OIT] is the crazy grandmother who's going to be signing up for Nigerian banking schemes, and they're going to click on every link and wantonly do all kinds of stuff to make the databases vulnerable . . . . I do have a degree of empathy. I just kind of wish they would go about it in a way that they don't treat anybody outside of [OIT] like they're an idiot.

We confirmed with the participant that the issue boils down to a lack of trust between OIT and the office of institutional research, among others, and asked what she could do to get a different result. Even though she expressed skepticism that OIT would change its behavior and views, she noted that communications between her office could be more strategic. For instance, any issues with OIT decisions should be communicated from administrators from the office of institutional research, and not staffers. Additionally, attempts to "make nice" with OIT are preferable and probably more efficacious in the long run than battling OIT's decisions. These alternatives were not optimal, but the participant perceived they could prove to be better than existing practices.

Another instance of alternative practices and outcomes concerned the development of new policy. The participant's status as an administrator, not just an analyst, meant that she had policy-making privileges. If she desired and felt it would be useful, she could develop standardized data use practices with related compliance measures to guide her work and that of her peers within the office of institutional research. When the conversation shifted to this possibility, the response was negative. Her argument against forcing new policy was as follows (note: names changed to protect those referenced):

> Well, because we have, like I said, Jane has got a very vested interest in, you know, FERPA and a lot of experience with that. Um, Danica was one of the data stewards for institutional research-level data. You know, we have some expertise in this office, you know, Jared and Kristin manage all of the survey information. Jonathan deals a lot with [human resource] data. We have a lot of expertise in a lot of different data sources and we want to consult everybody and also make sure that we're on the same page. That's just kinda the culture of the office. I think also that Susan [a peer administrator] has established that we're a collaborative group and we want to make sure that we have buy-in from everyone before moving forward with that kind of thing.

Considering the alternative enabled the participant to take stock of a potential outcome, which even though it was denied still proved useful. Thinking through the possibilities enabled her to consider the expertise of her peers (e.g., Jane and FERPA), knowledge of institutional policy and procedure (e.g., Danica as a data steward), location of various data and who knew of such data (e.g., Jonathan and HR data), and the norms and expectations around collaboration (e.g., as developed with Susan's leadership).

4.5.4 *Modulating Practice*

With the participant made more aware of the socio-technical dimensions of her work due to the STIR conversations, she began to think through different strategies for navigating rules-in-use regarding her data practices and data privacy. Analysis of the findings suggest that the participant engaged in a greater number of reflexive deliberations than deliberate modulations. In what follows, we report on the participant's most clearly articulated reflexive deliberation regarding foregrounding privacy and a series of deliberate, second-order modulations.

Towards the end of the interview sessions, the participant began to reflect on the topics covered, issues discussed, and useful takeaways. Not all of these contemplations led to weighty considerations, but one significant reflexive deliberation concerned a new approach to her thinking on privacy. When asked to consider what, if anything, had been influential about her time with the researchers, she answered in detail:

> Just to be constantly cognizant about who we're sharing data with, what relevant policies exists, what are the complications with being able to share information and things like that? Just being cognizant. A lot of times I do try to be cognizant about what are the FERPA implications, what are the [institutional] data sharing policy implications. Um, admittedly I always need refreshers. I feel like I, I've done several trainings on them, but they're, they're so detailed that I've always constantly needing refreshers and I usually err on the side of caution. Um, but to just be constantly cognizant about that when I'm sharing information, I think, is a good step .... These conversations have again, kind of pushed it more to the forefront.

The simple statement of "being cognizant" reveals a heightened awareness in the participant's mind about the important of privacy in her daily practices. It also demonstrates that she recognizes that privacy entails a variety of different rules-in-use, not just following institutional policy (though noted). This reflexive deliberation suggests that "being cognizant" takes focus and awareness, yet the common tasks and pressures – not to forget institutional politics – of the job intervene. To be cognizant involves pursuing strategies, such as vetting individuals requesting sensitive data and more carefully navigating information sharing expectations. Moreover, having privacy in the forefront of her mind, she believes, will enable her to think more carefully about the downstream consequences of sharing sensitive data. Finally, this deliberation also gave rise to a recognition that committing to ongoing professional education about her privacy responsibilities and the policies that govern her practices would better assist her in her work.

Based on the conversations with the participant, three types of deliberate modulations emerged: documentation of office data sharing and security practices; collaboration with data consumers on campus to help them use institutional data properly; and creation of a campus group to determine appropriate data sharing practices. Notably, these modulations reflect an "action arena" in the Governing Knowledge Commons (GKC) framework (Sanfilippo, Frischmann, and Strandburg, 2018). These modulations will be addressed shortly, but it should be noted first that all of the participant's modulations are considered second-order deliberate modulations, as opposed to first-order.

First-order modulations focus on actual changes in the STIR participant's practices, whereas second-order are modulations where the participant alters her project's goals, objectives, and assumptions to such a degree that they "come to challenge their own established routines of thought and practice, and also crucially, the various external forces which shape these" (Wynne, 2011, p. 794). In the case of this study's deliberate modulations, by the end of the study the participant had yet to make actual changes in their practices, rather they reflected upon the need for substantial changes in their *future* practices, and in some cases, set the stage for first-order modulations to occur.

The first second-order deliberate modulation that the participant reflected upon focuses on creating opportunities for her and her staff to document the implicit strategies and norms that guide their practices, such as spatial privacy practices and the norms that guide how they share data with campus data consumers. As the participant stated, documentation had not been an integral part of her office's culture: "I think being a little bit more intentional about documenting policies for how we share data and things like that would probably be a good idea for our office and something that we haven't really thought too much about."

The participant reflected upon how the conversations led her to start a conversation with her supervisor about creating documentation opportunities, which could include setting aside dedicated office time during the week, such as "documentation Fridays," focusing on documentation strategies as a team during a staff retreat or during office meetings, or by encouraging staff to document their practices concurrently as they work. The participant reflected that documenting office practices would help to reify and make explicit her office's rules and norms, and to help justify their practices to others within the institution:

> We should be able to justify what we're doing. We've always done it that way is not a good excuse for doing anything. So, we should be able to justify what we're doing and we should be able to document it for our own purposes as well as to better explain to people how we're doing something.

For the second of the second-order deliberate modulations, the participant reflected upon the need for her and her staff to actively work with data consumers on campus to inform them about proper institutional data use in ways that align with campus and federal-level rules and norms. As the findings suggest, the campus requires data consumers to adhere to rules in regards to having appropriate FERPA training and data use agreements signed. However, the participant stated the need for ensuring that the campus' existing rules and norms are followed by working with data consumers to ensure that they understand proper data storage practices and protect institutional data they receive:

> [Our conversations have] gotten me to think a little bit more intentionally about making sure that people have use agreements about making sure that people understand data appropriately. Making sure that people are understanding data security and how they keep their information a little bit better and just being a little bit more thoughtful in those kinds of conversations.

The final second-order deliberate modulation addresses the need for creating a campus-level initiative focused on developing standardized data sharing best practices. As addressed in the previous section, throughout the conversations the participant reflected upon the lack of campus-level rules and norms governing data sharing practices. Given this, the various offices on campus with data sharing responsibilities, including her own, have created their own rules and norms governing how data should be shared.

Historically, campus offices had limited interactions with one another regarding campus data sharing practices; data analysis had not been central to their respective work. But with it becoming so and the pressures increasing to make data-informed decisions, the participant recognized the need for developing consistent practices and policies across campus. "We've never really gotten together a group of people," she said, "and just kind of discussed it out here, discussed things with the exception of like a handful of large-scale projects, um, that are about to be released." There was a need, the participant expressed, for creating a campus group to discuss standardized data sharing practices on the campus, and that it was "not something that I had really thought to do before." She and her supervisor were planning to meet to discuss how they might go about creating this campus group.

4.6 A CONCLUDING DISCUSSION

The socio-technical milieu within higher education is drastically influencing data and information practices, according to the literature. With various analytics initiatives emerging and institutional actors trying to determine the right sources and types of data as inputs, it should be expected that the rules-in-use, especially policies, governing cutting-edge practices are not clear-cut and standardized. Moreover, as these actors take on new data-driven roles and responsibilities, especially within institutional research, it will take time for useful strategies to form and norms to settle.

We see in the data, the STIR of a single institutional researcher, some evidence of changes in information flow, reactions to it, and ways of thinking and doing to reestablish privacy-protecting rules-in-use. A single participant does not make for generalizable results about changes in higher education writ large. However, using STIR to address rules-in-use about privacy has led to notable insights and a potentially valuable research agenda.

The norms, strategies, and rules that govern interactions with sensitive data and information are often taken for granted. They may drive workaday practices, but they rarely give rise to reflexive or deliberative moments about alternative ways of doing. Additionally, rules as they exist as policies are to many individuals simply things one follows – not things one seeks to create or change. But with STIR, and as made evident in the findings, we see that there is an opportunity to make rules-in-use worthy of deliberation, as something that when given the space and time to consider can become something to rethink and reconsider. As the findings suggest, the act of naming and describing what structures privacy practices creates the circumstances necessary to then evaluate rules-in-use, solidify and support those that are successful, fill gaps where they exist, and plan for improvements.

Within the context of higher education and in other contexts where data analytics are gaining interest and momentum, it is an opportune time – if not a necessary responsibility – to investigate data practices. The consequences of predictive analytics, algorithms, black-boxed technological systems, and the data on which they all rely are getting serious scholarly consideration. But, looking downstream is only one way of approaching these issues. Instead, looking upstream at seemingly boring and benign practices, and prodding those actors to reflect on their practices, can produce significant insights for the actors-cum-research participants that lead to altered or new practices more attuned to the socio-technical mélange and its implications. Applying the STIR method to address informational privacy rules-in-use, ethics, or otherwise can advance research in this important area.

REFERENCES

Association for Institutional Research. "Code of Ethics and Professional Practice." Last modified May 2, 2013. www.airweb.org/ir-data-professional-overview/code-of-ethics-and-professional-practice.

Bienkowski, Marie, Mingyu Feng, and Barbara Means. *Enhancing Teaching and Learning Through Educational Data Mining and Learning Analytics: An Issue Brief*. Washington: U.S. Department of Education, 2012. http://tech.ed.gov/wp-content/uploads/2014/03/edm-la-brief.pdf.

Borden, Victor M. H. and Adrianna Kezar. "Institutional Research and Collaborative Organizational Learning." In *The Handbook of Institutional Research*, Richard D. Howard, Gerald W. McLaughlin, and William E. Knight, eds. San Francisco: John Wiley & Sons, 2012, 86–106.

Bowker, Geoffrey. C. "Data Flakes: An Afterword to 'Raw Data' is an Oxymoron." In *"Raw data" is an Oxymoron*, Lisa Gitelman, ed. Cambridge: MIT Press, 2013, 167–171.

Campbell, John, Peter DeBlois, and Diana Oblinger. "Academic Analytics: A New Tool for a New Era." *EDUCAUSE Review* 42, no. 4 (2007): 40–57. www.educause.edu/ero/article/academic-analytics-new-tool-new-era.

Crawford, Sue E. S. and Elinor Ostrom. "A Grammar of Institutions." *American Political Science* 89, no. 3 (1995): 582–600. https://doi.org/10.2307/2082975

Ferguson, Rebecca. "Learning Analytics: Drivers, Developments and Challenges." *International Journal of Technology Enhanced Learning* 4, no. 5/6 (2012): 304–317. https://doi.org/10.1504/IJTEL.2012.051816.

Fisher, Erik. "Causing a STIR." *International Innovation* (2012): 76–79. https://sciencepolicy.colorado.edu/news/fisher.pdf.

Fisher, Erik, Roop L. Mahajan, and Carl Mitcham. "Midstream Modulation of Technology: Governance from Within." *Bulletin of Science, Technology & Society* 26, no. 6 (2006): 485–496. https://doi.org/10.1177/0270467606295402.

Fisher, Erik and Daan Schuurbiers. "Socio-Technical Integration Research: Collaborative Inquiry at the Midstream of Research and Development." In *Early engagement and New Technologies: Opening up the Laboratory*, Neelke Doorn, Daan Schuurbiers, Ibo van de Poel, Michael E. Gorman, eds. Dordrecht: Springer, 2013, 97–110.

Flaherty, Colleen. "Academic 'Moneyball.'" *Inside Higher Ed*, December 20, 2016. www.insidehighered.com/news/2016/12/20/mit-professors-push-data-based-model-they-say-more-predictive-academics-future.

Flipse, Steven M., Maarten C. A. van der Sanden, and Patricia Osseweijer. "Midstream Modulation in Biotechnology Industry: Redefining what is 'Part Of The Job' of Researchers in Industry." *Science and Engineering Ethics* 19, no. 3 (2013): 1141–1164. https://doi.org/10.1007/s11948-012–9411-6.

Fuller, Matthew. "An Update on the Family Educational Rights and Privacy Act." *New Directions for Institutional Research* 2016, no. 172 (2017a): 25–36. https://doi.org/10.1002/ir.20201.

Fuller, Matthew. "The Practices, Policies, and Legal Boundaries Framework in Assessment and Institutional Research." *New Directions for Institutional Research* 2016, no. 172 (2017b): 9–23. https://doi.org/10.1002/ir.20200.

Gašević, Dragan, Shane Dawson, and Jelena Jovanović. "Ethics and Privacy as Enablers of Learning Analytics." *Journal of Learning Analytics* 3, no. 1 (2016): 1–4. https://doi.org/10.18608/jla.2016.31.1.

Goldstein, Phil and Richard Katz. *Academic Analytics: The Uses of Management Information and Technology in Higher Education*. Louisville: EDUCAUSE, 2005. https://net.educause.edu/ir/library/pdf/ers0508/rs/ers0508w.pdf.

Heath, Jennifer. "Contemporary Privacy Theory Contributions to Learning Analytics." *Journal of Learning Analytics* 1, no. 1 (2014): 140–149. https://doi.org/10.18608/jla.2014.11.8.

Johnson, Jeffrey. "The Question of Information Justice." *Communications of the ACM* 59, no. 3 (2016): 27–29. https://doi.org/10.1145/2879878.

Johnson, Larry, Rachel S. Smith, H. Willis, Alan Levine, and Keene Haywood. *The 2011 Horizon Report*. Austin: The New Media Consortium, 2011. https://library.educause.edu/-/media/files/library/2011/2/hr2011-pdf.pdf.

Jones, Kyle M. L. and Chase McCoy. "Reconsidering Data in Learning Analytics: Opportunities for Critical Research." *Learning, Media and Technology* 44, no. 1 (2018): 52–63. https://doi.org/10.1080/17439884.2018.1556216.

Kitchin, Rob. *The Data Revolution: Big Data, Open Data, Data Infrastructures, and their Consequences*. Los Angeles: SAGE Publications, 2014.

Mayer-Schönberger, Viktor and Kenneth Cukier. *Learning with Big Data: The Future of Education*. New York: Houghton Mifflin Harcourt, 2014.

Nissenbaum, Helen. *Privacy in Context: Technology, Policy, and the Integrity of Social Life*. Stanford: Stanford University Press, 2010.

Oudshoorn, Nelly and Trevor Pinch. *How Users Matter: The Co-Construction of Users and Technology*. Cambridge: MIT Press, 2003.

Pardo, Abelardo and George Siemens. "Ethical and Privacy Principles for Learning Analytics." *British Journal of Educational Technology* 45, no. 3 (2014): 438–450. https://doi.org/10.1111/bjet.12152.

Patel, Vimal. "Productivity Metrics: What is the Best Way to Assess Faculty Activity?" *The Chronicle of Higher Education*, February 29, 2016. www.chronicle.com/article/Productivity-Metrics/235436.

Peterson, Marvin W. "The Role of Institutional Research: From Improvement to Redesign." *New Directions for Institutional Research* 1999, no. 104 (1999): 83–103. https://doi.org/10.1002/ir.10408.

Prinsloo, Paul and Sharon Slade. "Student Data Privacy and Institutional Accountability in an Age of Surveillance." In *Using Data to Improve Higher Education: Research, Policy and Practice*, Maria Eliophotou Menon, Dawn Geronimo Terkla, and Paul Gibbs, eds. Rotterdam: Sense Publishers, 2014, 197–214.

Rubel, Alan and Kyle M. L. Jones. "Student Privacy in Learning Analytics: An Information Ethics Perspective." *The Information Society* 32, no. 2 (2016): 143–159. https://doi.org/10.1080/01972243.2016.1130502.

Sanfilippo, Madelyn, Brett Frischmann, and Katherine Strandburg. "Privacy as Commons: Case Evaluation Through the Governing Knowledge Commons Framework." *Journal of Information Policy* 8, no. 2018 (2018): 116–166. https://doi.org/0.5325/jinfopoli.8.2018.0116.

Selwyn, Neil. "Data Entry: Towards the Critical Study of Digital Data and Education." *Learning, Media and Technology* 40, no. 1 (2014): 64–82. https://doi.org/10.1080/17439884.2014.921628.

Serban, Andreea M. "Knowledge Management: The 'Fifth Face' of Institutional Research." *New Directions for Institutional Research* 2002, no. 113 (2002): 105–112. https://doi.org/10.1002/ir.40.

Shiltz, M. "Ethics and Standards and Institutional Research." *New Directions for Institutional Research* 73 (1992): 3–9.

Slade, Sharon and Paul Prinsloo. "Learning Analytics: Ethical Issues and Dilemmas." *American Behavioral Scientist* 57, no. 10 (2013): 1510–1529. https://doi.org/10.1177/0002764213479366.

Stark, Luke and Anna Lauren Hoffmann. "Data is the New What? Popular Metaphors & Professional Ethics in Emerging Data Culture." *Journal of Cultural Analytics* (May 2, 2019). https://doi.org/10.22148/16.036.

Swing, Randy L. and Leah Ewing Ross. *Statement of Aspirational Practice for Institutional Research*. Tallahassee: Association for Institutional Research, 2016. www.airweb.org/aspirationalstatement.

Terenzini, Patrick T. "On the Nature of Institutional Research and the Knowledge and Skills it Requires." *New Directions for Institutional Research* 1999, no. 104 (1999): 21–29. https://doi.org/10.1002/ir.10402.

van Dijk, José and Thomas Poell. "Understanding Social Media Logic." *Media and Communication* 1, no. 1 (2013): 2–14. https://doi.org/10.17645/mac.v1i1.70.

Volkwein, J. Fredericks. "The Four Faces of Institutional Research." *New Directions for Institutional Research* 1999, no. 104 (1999): 9–19. https://doi.org/10.1002/ir.10401.

Volkwein, J. Fredericks, Ying Liu, and James Woodell. "The Structure and Function of Institutional Research Offices." In *The Handbook of Institutional Research*, Richard D. Howard, Gerald W. MacLaughlin, and William E. Knight, eds. San Francisco: John Wiley & Sons, 2012, 22–39.

Watters, Audrey. "Student Data is the New Oil: Moocs, Metaphor, and Money." Last modified October 17, 2013. http://hackeducation.com/2013/10/17/student-data-is-the-new-oil.

Williamson, Ben. "The Hidden Architecture of Higher Education: Building a Big Data Infrastructure for the 'Smarter University.'" International Journal of Educational Technology in Higher Education 15, no. 12 (2018): 1–26. https://doi.org/10.1186/s41239-018–0094-1.

Wynne, Brian. "Lab Work Goes Social, and Vice Versa: Strategising Public Engagement Processes." *Science and Engineering Ethics* 17, no. 4 (2011): 791–800. https://doi.org/10.1007/s11948-011–9316-9.

Zeide, Elana. "Student Privacy Principles for the Age Of Big Data: Moving Beyond FERPA and FIPPS." *Drexel Law Review* 8, no. 2 (2016): 339–394. http://drexel.edu/law/lawreview/issues/Archives/v8-2/zeide/.

Zilvinskis, John, James Willis III, and Victor M. H. Borden. "An Overview of Learning Analytics." *New Directions for Higher Education* 2017, no. 179 (2017): 9–17. https://doi.org/10.1002/he.20239.

5

Public Facebook Groups for Political Activism

Madelyn Rose Sanfilippo[1] *and Katherine J. Strandburg*[2]

5.1 INTRODUCTION

The rise of social media has raised questions about the vitality of privacy values and concerns about threats to privacy (Marwick and boyd, 2014). As online communities have flourished, debate over appropriate information flows among users, as well as to platforms, service providers, and surveillance networks, has grown (Ellison et al., 2011; Marwick and boyd, 2014). Facebook has received considerable scholarly attention (e.g. Acquisti and Gross, 2006; Hargittai, 2010) in this debate. Social media use has become pervasive not only in economic and social interactions (Kaplan and Haenlein, 2010) but also in politics and political organizing (Gonzalez-Bailon and Wang, 2016; Nam, 2012). The convergence of politics with social media use amplifies the privacy concerns traditionally associated with political organizing (Breuer, 2016; Nam, 2012), particularly when marginalized groups and minority politics are involved (Stacheli, 1996).

Despite the importance of these issues, there has been little empirical exploration of how privacy governs political activism and organizing in online environments. This project explores how privacy concerns shape political organizing on Facebook, through detailed case studies of how groups associated with March for Science, Day Without Immigrants ("DWI"), and Women's March govern information flows. Each of these groups emerged from distributed grassroots efforts, gaining critical

We thank participants at PLSC, the 2nd Annual CI Symposium, and the Workshop on the Growing Influence of Social Media in Global Politics and Society for their valuable feedback. We also thank NYU's Information Law Institute, which supported Madelyn as a fellow while this research was conducted, and the Microsoft Corporation for its generous support of the ILI Fellows program. This chapter draws, in part, on research published: Sanfilippo, Madelyn Rose, and Katherine J. Strandburg. "Privacy governing knowledge in public Facebook groups for political activism." *Information, Communication & Society* (2019): 1–18.

[1] Assistant Professor, School of Information Sciences, University of Illinois at Urbana-Champaign; Affiliate Scholar, The Vincent and Elinor Ostrom Workshop in Political Theory and Policy Analysis, Indiana University, Bloomington. Ph.D., Indiana University, Bloomington; M.I.S., Indiana University, Bloomington; B.S., University of Wisconsin-Madison.

[2] Katherine J. Strandburg is the Alfred Engelberg Professor of Law and Director of the Information Law Institute at New York University.

visibility and participation because of their use of social media both to organize demonstrations and events and to share political knowledge ideas. This comparative case study employs an empirical framework that we developed in earlier work (e.g. Sanfilippo, Frischmann, and Strandburg, 2018), in which we synthesized contextual integrity analysis (Nissenbaum, 2009) with the Governing Knowledge Commons (GKC) framework (e.g. Madison, Frischmann, and Strandburg, 2014) for institutional analysis of commons governance of knowledge (e.g. Ostrom, 2011).

The specific activist movements we have studied – the March for Science, the DWI, and the Women's March – are recent examples through which we can explore how privacy governs both the organization of activism, particularly in an age of social media and surveillance, and the sharing of knowledge in public Facebook groups. All three movements grew quickly in scale and structure following the 2016 presidential election, leading up to demonstrations in early 2017 through extensive use of social media and under the attention of traditional media.

The January 21, 2017, Women's March on Washington, along with the 672 other satellite marches that took place on all seven continents, drew between three and five million people (e.g. Boothroyd et al., 2017; Wallace and Parlapiano, 2017). While the Women's March focused on women's issues, it became a venue for expressing solidarity and concern relative to many other human rights issues (Boothroyd et al., 2017; Fisher, Dow, and Ray, 2017). This movement originated with a single individual on Facebook proposing a march on Washington, DC, and eventually evolved into a sustained organization advocating and informing regarding gender and equality issues in a historical moment when opposition to misogyny and sexual violence is historically prevalent (Fisher, Dow, and Ray, 2017; Moss and Madrell, 2017). While historically, many movements have petered out after large-scale demonstrations, the Women's March organization has continued to organize events and information campaigns, including the Women's Convention and a second annual Women's March in 2018. It has also grown in public support, as the #MeToo movement has intersected with it. The national movement also has been criticized, however, by some who see it as less inclusive of women of color than some of the local efforts have been (Boothroyd et al., 2017; Rose-Redwood and Rose-Redwood, 2017).

The April 22, 2017, March for Science drew on many existing advocacy networks, piggy-backing on and transforming an annual Earth Day observance in response to a post-truth era in which the legitimacy of science and objectivity are questioned; 1,070,000 people are estimated to have attended worldwide (Milman, 2017). While movement was not initiated on Facebook, it employed Facebook to muster pro-science support and respond to perceptions of manipulation of scientific information and "fake news" (e.g. Reardon et al., 2017). Like the Women's March movement, the March for Science movement has maintained visibility after the March and continues to respond to anti-science, anti-fact rhetoric in politics, media, and social networks.

Unlike the Women's March, however, it did not coalesce into a formal organization.

The February 16, 2017, DWI was different from the other two movements we studied in that it did not focus on a large-scale march in Washington, DC. DWI was primarily intended to illustrate the importance of immigrants to the economy, as well as to advocate for immigration reform. It also expressed opposition to the proposed border wall and to racial profiling (Robbins & Correall, 2017). Demonstrations were held in thirty cities across the United States, while individuals who did not march expressed solidarity through other forms of protest and boycotts. Some restaurants and businesses also closed to express their support (Stein, 2017). The DWI movement was organized through more distributed networks of immigrants and their supporters, working in various ways to advocate and make their influence felt through a day in which they did not participate in the economy (e.g. Blitzer, 2017). Facebook's network structure was employed by the movement to allow groups to connect, learn from one another, and share information (e.g. Hamann and Morganson, 2017).

These three cases are particularly fruitful to compare because they were similar in many respects, but differed in significant ways relevant to privacy. All three movements emerged in response to the rhetoric and political positions, or actions, of President Donald Trump and were active during the same period. Yet the historical legacy of each movement also shaped each response in a distinctive way. The Day with Immigrants and Women's March movements stemmed from historically entrenched marginalization and inequalities based on ethnicity and gender, respectively – and from a concern that society was beginning to move backward on these issues. The March for Science, on the other hand, was a response to a relatively more recent and emerging concern about disintegrating societal respect for and trust in science.

Social media also played an enormous role in facilitating interactions between organizers and publicizing each of these movements and their events. These cases, addressing distinct issues, while operating in similar contexts and on the same timescales, thus allow for the exploration of privacy, as it plays out through governance of personal information flows, for both political organizing and Facebook sub-communities. Privacy practices and concerns differed between the cases, depending on factors such as the nature of the group, the political issues it confronts, and its relationships to other organizations or movements.

In order to better understand what these cases can reveal about privacy as governance of personal information flow, in the context of political activism and for organizations coordinating through Facebook, we employ the Governing Knowledge Commons framework, which we have recently adapted for the study of privacy (Sanfilippo, Frischmann, and Strandburg, 2018).

5.2 RESEARCH DESIGN

This case study focuses on six March for Science groups (Austin, TX; New Jersey; New York, NY; Princeton, NJ; Seattle, WA; and Washington, DC), seven Women's March groups (Ann Arbor, MI; Atlanta, GA; Global, which represented all international events; Madison, WI; New York, NY; Princeton NJ; Washington, DC), and eight DWI groups (Baltimore, MD; Elkhart, IN; Greenville, NC; Nashville, TN; Students; VA; WA; Washington, DC). In addition to analysis of 4,352 posts from the DWI, 294,201 from the March for Science, and 196,358 from the Women's March, we conducted interviews with decision-makers from these twenty-one groups, structured by the questions within the GKC framework, and distributed surveys to their members. Our textual analysis placed particular emphasis on public Facebook discussions of privacy, information flows, and institutional legitimacy and development. We also used network analysis to interrogate the relationships between national and satellite groups within each movement, between groups associated with different movements, and between each movement and external organization.

Additional details about our methods, and these cases, can be found in two companion journal articles, analyzing aspects of participatory privacy (Sanfilippo and Strandburg under review) and how privacy in knowledge resources governs online political movements (Sanfilippo and Strandburg, 2019).

5.3 BACKGROUND ENVIRONMENTS FOR THE CASE STUDIES

5.3.1 *Day Without Immigrants*

Participants, including members and followers, and non-member discussants within various DWI Facebook groups provided a rich depiction of the background context in which they were organizing, emphasizing how both supportive participants and their opposition saw the movement as fitting into a larger narrative of social and political dimensions, including recognition of how the movement related to the 2016 presidential election. Discussion, and embedded arguments, focused on what was perceived to have changed under President Trump; while many recognized the historical path, "The immigration system is broken and for most of the Central America and South America countries the only way to come here is a stupid lottery created 50 years ago," others recognized the rhetorical changes in the national dialogue as leading to something different, for example contesting that "Donald Trump was talking about . . . CRIMINAL illegal immigrants." Action was perceived to be required in order to fight against both the historical trend and the current threats. As one organizer explained, "Gracias. Injustice under Trump is not only seen more, but more severe. It is an important time to act and I need to be a part, for myself and for others."

The DWI movement thus emerged from a background environment in which many supporters, as potential participants, had serious concerns about potentially dire consequences for themselves or their family members if they were identified in a public forum. President Trump's anti-immigrant campaign rhetoric and promises heightened fears of discrimination and racial violence for many immigrants, especially Latinos, whether documented or undocumented, as well as fears of mass deportation for undocumented immigrants, including hundreds of thousands of DACA recipients and millions of DREAMERS (Kocher, 2017).

One consequence of the heightened vulnerability of undocumented immigrants was that many of their documented friends and relatives felt a similarly heightened responsibility, despite their own fears of discrimination and retaliation, to take up visible roles in the movement, since such roles were perceived as too dangerous for the undocumented.

5.3.2 *Women's March*

The Women's March was galvanized by President Trump's election in a contest that most expected Hillary Clinton, the nation's first female presidential candidate, to win. Many women experienced Trump's win over Clinton, despite her substantial expertise and government experience and his complete lack of either, as a wake-up call. Women's outrage over Trump's election was heightened by his record of disrespectful behavior and comments, including those recorded on the infamous Access Hollywood tape, and the numerous sexual harassment and assault allegations that emerged shortly before the election.

The background environment included the long-standing movement for women's rights. Equality and respect, as both objectives and core values of the historic women's movement, shaped Women's March institutions in fundamental ways. Specific values emphasized centered on inclusion and privacy, as concerns about safety, in the wake of sexual harassment and assault allegations against President Trump and recent history of #gamergate, made concerns about targeting individuals serious (Moss and Madrell, 2017).

5.3.3 *March for Science*

Unlike the other two movements, the March for Science did not grow out of a historical political movement responding to discrimination or hostility. Rather, it was a response to a fear that science was in danger of losing the nearly universal status and acceptance that it has enjoyed in modern times. An anti-science strain had been emerging in US politics for a few years, particularly within the Republican Party, particularly in relation to issues such as energy and climate change (Selepak, 2018). The 2016 campaign, culminating in President Trump's election, crystallized and heightened scientists' fears that facts, objectivity, and scientific evidence were being supplanted in public discourse and decision-making by reliance on experience, personalization of information in favor of beliefs over facts, and conspiracy theories. These threats to scientific values were accompanied by more practical concerns about the possibilities of funding cuts, disruption of accepted scientific standards for peer review and allocation of funding, and corruption of the output of government-supported scientific endeavors.

Reflecting its emergence out of concerns for *loss* of historical status, the March for Science drew from the outset directly on the support and resources of large and established scientific professional organizations. In this respect, it differed notably from both the Women's March and DWI. In deciding whether to become involved in the political arena by organizing a March for Science, scientific organizations and individual participants confronted the question of whether participating, as *scientists*, in a movement that responded directly to the election of a particular president would violate scientific norms of objectivity that had ordinarily been understood to include political nonpartisanship. Some members of the scientific community viewed participation as a means of opposing an already dangerous politicization of science, while others feared that employing the tools of political advocacy on behalf of science would contribute to its further politicization.

5.4 ATTRIBUTES

5.4.1 *Community Members*

5.4.1.1 Membership

In the most expansive sense, community members could include everyone who supported the movement in any way at all, including expressing agreement with its aims, providing financial support, attending a national or satellite march, RSVPing on EventBrite, joining an associated Facebook group, attending offline events or meetings, or serving as an organizer for one of the events. Beyond even the most inclusive definition of community "members" taking part in the movement, each of the movements we studied had the potential – and the goal – to impact outsiders. In a broad sense, each of these movements had the potential to affect society at large. More specifically, potentially impacted outsiders encompassed all women, immigrants, and scientists who did not participate, including some who remained outside because they were concerned about the consequences of participation.

Our discussion of "members" of a particular group or march will ordinarily refer to individuals who joined one of the Facebook groups studied. Membership in these public Facebook groups was not representative of all members or supporters. This is most emphatically the case for the DWI movement because privacy concerns were a serious barrier to publicly affiliating with the movement on Facebook. To give us further insights into community membership, we have supplemented the detailed

TABLE 5.1 *Attendance versus expectations*

Movement	Day Without Immigrants	March for Science	Women's March
Attendance	3940	206000	1578500
EventBrite RSVPs	1278	172000	798800
Facebook RSVPs	621	61500	402026

picture available from our main sources with estimates of march attendance and numbers of EventBrite RSVPs for our case study groups, as well as data about all organizations affiliated with the national groups and geographic co-location data for national and all satellite marches.

Table 5.1 shows the numerical relationships between estimated attendance, EventBrite RSVPs, and Facebook group members for the groups included in our study. For each movement, we compare projected attendance based on different platforms with estimated aggregate attendance at the 2017, or first wave of, national and satellite marches. (We do not consider follow-up marches in this study.)

For all three movements, the number of march attendees was larger than the number of EventBrite RSVPs, which was yet larger than the expected numbers based on responses within the associated Facebook groups. As a fraction of attendees, DWI supporters were the least likely to register in advance, either by RSVPing through EventBrite or by participating in a Facebook group, including by formally joining or by responding to event invitations. Though there are various possible explanations for this trend, it seems plausible that this failure to register in advance reflects greater concern within DWI about leaving persistent, personally identified, public trails of their involvement in the movement.

The preference for EventBrite over Facebook across all three movements also reflects privacy concerns, since EventBrite RSVPs are not public, do not link to vast amounts of personal information, and can be made effectively anonymous. As one key organizer from the New York City Women's March explained:

> We needed to have a way of developing unique registrations, but at the same time, we're dealing with people involved in activism, and we want people to know that their information is secure, right? So, that's one reason we started using EventBrite, just to get the numbers. Now, the thing is, you don't have to put your real name in there. You don't even have to put in a real email address. You can put in an address, you know, that's a temporary one. People make those all the time . . . but, you know, it was a way for us to keep track.

Participation in all three movements was open to the public at nearly every level of involvement. Anyone could (and was encouraged to) attend the marches. All three national marches, as well as the satellite groups that we studied, maintained public

Facebook groups. Anyone could join these groups, yet membership was not required to participate in public discussions and there were few limits placed on discussion contributions. Though membership in the public Facebook groups associated with the various national and satellite marches was generally open to anyone, privacy concerns created significant barriers to membership in the Facebook groups associated with DWI, as discussed in greater detail later.

The openness of these public Facebook groups meant that not only supporters but also individuals who were hostile to a group's goals and objectives could join. This openness to dissenters sometimes resulted in contentious – or even troll-like – exchanges. Maintaining this openness, despite the dissension it invited, was considered important by many groups not only as a means to inform and engage the broader public but also as a way to signal willingness to engage in reasonable debate. In particular, discussions within the Facebook groups of various DWI movement groups emphasized the hope that openness would help to legitimize the planned marches in the eyes of the public.

5.4.1.2 Community Demographics

The demographic makeup of each movement largely aligned with objectives. Thus, Women's March organizers and other participants were overwhelmingly female – and, as some impacted outsiders critiqued, overwhelmingly white (Fisher, Dow, and Ray, 2017; Rose-Redwood and Rose-Redwood, 2017). Many DWI group demographics roughly reflected the demographics of the undocumented population, though organizers specifically were more often those with more legal security, such as DACA recipients, Green Card holders, and legally documented relatives. Furthermore, a minority of satellite groups within this movement more broadly reflected the demographics of recent immigrants, rather than reflecting the undocumented population. Moreover, participants in both of these movements included family members and other supporters who did not fit the mold.

The March for Science was supported by numerous scientific organizations and many participants were research scientists and medical professionals. However, participants, including many organizers, also included many K-12 educators, students, university administrators, and corporate R&D staff. Families turned out for the affiliated Earth Day events, capitalizing on the openness of their designs and appealing to the assertions that trust in the objectivity of science should be learned early and believed pervasively. Moreover, while STEM fields have continuing, and historical, gender diversity problems, various March for Science groups were not only more gender-balanced but organized by women.

Moreover, some satellite marches, such as the Atlanta March for Social Justice and Women, intentionally defined themselves differently and in more inclusive ways, to better reflect the diversity of stakeholders in their local communities. As one co-organizer of the Atlanta event explained:

> We are a non-profit organization and we organized the March for Social Justice, which coincided with the Women's March all over, to represent all marginalized communities and to stand up for our rights and opportunities in the face of opposition. We wanted to stand together, for women, for our LGBTQIA friends, for people of color, for my fellow Muslim Americans and all religions, for ... autonomy over our bodies and safety, for voting rights, for things we deserve and expect, but are held back and repressed, for victims of sexual violence who aren't believed. For immigrants, of all statuses ... I am involved because I want to stand up for myself and my community, not just by marching, but by making the demonstration and ongoing activism as impactful as possible.

In contrast to efforts by this satellite march to be inclusive in organization and participation, DWI movement groups were almost intentionally obfuscating in their design; many of these groups were composed, at least with respect to public affiliation, primarily of the friends, documented significant others, and children of undocumented immigrants, rather than by undocumented individuals – the most seriously impacted stakeholders. The absence of these individuals from publicly acknowledged membership did not necessarily preclude their participation or the reflection of their preferences, but rather mediated it for safety. As one organizer explained:

> My mom and my aunt took me to a protest when I was a kid and from then on, I knew this was important and I wanted to help. I was born here, but people in my family are undocumented. ... How can you just watch bias or discrimination and not do something, you know? So in this case, my aunt had been discussing this with other activists around immigration, but wasn't going to go on social media, but I could and did, and then it could get around to lots of other people.

This individual was thus simultaneously in the roles of organizer-group member and proxy for family members, in order to protect the privacy of those family members.

5.4.1.3 Outside Groups

In addition to their individual members and organizers, these movements were supported in various ways and to greater and lesser degrees by pre-existing organizations. The Women's March and March for Science each were affiliated with a large number of outside organizations, including thirty-nine organizations that interacted with both. The DWI movement, by contrast, had very few connections with outside organizations. Only one organization, the AFL-CIO, supports both DWI and the Women's March. DWI shares no external affiliates with the March for Science.

These external affiliations reflect the dramatically different roles that outside organizations played in different movements. At one extreme, many March for Science events were not only supported by but also directly organized by pre-existing organizations – professional, academic, and advocacy-oriented. At the other extreme, the DWI movement intentionally eschewed most public affiliations with advocacy groups, even when receiving other kinds of support from such groups. The Women's March was positioned at a relative middle ground with respect to the influence of outside organizations. Interestingly, the Women's March also institutionalized itself, formalizing an organization that was much more lasting and stronger than either of the other movements.

5.4.2 *Resources*

Across all three movements, information resources were developed, aggregated, and shared to inform members, other participants, impacted individuals, and the general public about the movements' objectives and events, as well as to share human interest stories and news coverage of their activities, and provide information resources for impacted populations. By using public Facebook pages, groups from all three movements made these shared information resources open resources, leveraging the visibility Facebook, and other social media platforms, provided to cultivate their own knowledge resources for use by affected individuals beyond participating stakeholders.

Prioritization of choice and opportunity shaped not only each group's online information sharing practices, as described with respect to the mailing lists and organizational partnerships, but also the information resources constructed (Kitch, 2018). Facebook and social media were most visibly central to the Women's March, perhaps partly because of the role social media played in the group's origins, but also because social media were seen as legitimate forums for personal information and sharing by participants in this movement. Facebook was not, however, considered to be perfect for this or any movement. Other tools and channels, such as EventBrite, were deemed necessary both to allow organizers to better anticipate numbers of demonstrators and to ensure that feminists and supporters who did not participate in Facebook could be adequately up to date on important information.

Facebook also had a significant impact on these activist movements because of the way it affected dialogue, by increasing disinhibition and opening groups to criticism, rather than simply insulating them. Interestingly, the smaller the group, the less it appears to attract critical posts, even when a small satellite was organized in a place where one would expect little ideological alignment between the movement and the populace at large. This was especially the case for small DWI groups, but also seemed to be true for smaller Women's March satellites. Furthermore, some groups defused opposition by describing their membership in more socially acceptable terms; for example, groups organized by students and "DREAMERS" were perceived to be "sort of good that kids care about STEM" and "the kind of immigrants we want" (Facebook posts). "Asian and well-educated" immigration groups were also complimented, even by individuals who publicly stated their opposition to the DWI movement overall. In contrast, plenty of opposition was expressed relative to "Mexican, undocumented" groups. Obvious stereotypes played out in this environment, particularly relative to the perceived legitimacy of action arenas and resources, as individuals were open about their fears and prejudices in the mediated environment. In the words of one Facebook post, "Like you would even say that if this wasn't fb!"

In the course of their activities, these groups handled large amounts of personal information. Some of this information was in the obvious form of contact information for members of the Facebook groups and those who RSVP'd using their real identities on EventBrite. But other personal information emerged less obviously, from discussions in the Facebook groups as individuals debated issues and told personal stories, or in photos taken at demonstrations. All of these forms of personal information were absolutely central resources for these movements, enabling coordination, publicity, public engagement, and more for these groups.

5.4.2.1 Contact Information

Norms about how to generate and secure RSVP lists and contact information reflected at least a partial consensus across movements about how to handle this form of personal information in online political organizing. Groups in all three movements used both public Facebook pages and EventBrite RSVPs, to developing lists of those who intended to participate in the marches. EventBrite was considered to be more accurate than Facebook, as well as more private, though neither provided complete lists of attendees. As an organizer of the NYC Women's March explained, "I really recommend that to people if they're doing their own event. Have multiple channels, even if they're different, have multiple channels. Because we had people registered through Facebook, and I think it was only 50,000. [laughter] And over 200,000 in EventBrite alone."

Yet while their basic approaches to gathering information resources were superficially similar, the movements diverged in important ways in their assessments of appropriate flow of these information resources. The DWI movement eschewed affiliations with outside groups in order to create a barrier to information flow about the identities of those who were involved with the movement. The Women's March was affiliated with a large number of outside organizations, but groups often did not share member lists or contact information with those organizations.

The New York City Women's March group, for example, did not share contact information or other personally identifiable information about members, attendees, or subscribers with outside organizations, no matter how closely interests and objectives overlapped. Nor did it accept similar information from such organizations. Instead of sharing contact information, the new group pursued its shared objectives with outside affiliates by publicizing events and information relating to its partner organizations, so that the group's members could find out about other organizations and events reflecting their interests. They went so far as to delete the contact information and email list it had generated for the 2017 march, so as to prevent anyone under any circumstances from obtaining that information. As one key organizer explained,

> we needed to have a way of developing unique registrations, but at the same time, we're dealing with people involved in activism, and we want people to know that their information is secure, right? So, that's one reason we started using EventBrite, just to get the numbers. Now, the thing is, you don't have to put your real name in there. You don't even have to put in a real email address. You can put in an address, you know, that's a temporary one. People make those all the time . . . but, you know, it was a way for us to keep track. We were still, you know, knowing some people would put their real name in there, we wanted to establish a list for when the march was over. We had an opt-in process, after the march, for people wanted to continue to receive email from us and then we destroyed the original database.

To work around the difficulties imposed by the decision to delete the lists, subscribers to the list had to opt-in to be contacted for future events.

Both of these approaches were in stark contrast to the easy exchange of contact information that occurred between science and technology organizations and March for Science groups. For these groups, the appropriateness of sharing contact information with affiliate organizations was established by the identification of these affiliates as reputable professional organizations. One Women's March organizer, who was also involved, to a lesser degree, in organizing a March for Science satellite march, identified a source of this difference in perspective between the March for Science and the other movements, stating "it's an issue of trust in the powers that be. People who have been historically discriminated against don't trust the status quo in the same way that scientists who are respected professionals might. It's completely different."

5.4.2.2 Stories, Narratives, and Other Forms of Personal Information

All of these movements also accumulated personal information in the form of stories and other personal details and each dealt with such information differently. The desire to use personal stories as a way of appealing to the public was common to all three movements, but levels of comfort in linking those humanizing stories to real identities differed greatly. The March for Science encouraged publicly identifiable scientists to share their personal stories and commitment to the movement. One March for Science organizer explained that "it was best when we could get famous faculty to buy-in and talk, not just demonstrations and things for kids, but in a way that was more political, because it got attention and was . . . I guess, more credible." However, very real fears about employability were expressed by junior scientists, making privacy a core organizing value. In contrast to leveraging privacy by obscurity, as within the Women's March, or privacy by proxy, as within the DWI movement, participants within the March for Science used established figures and institutions as shields, providing privacy to graduate students, for example, who served in key organizational roles.

DWI groups, at the other end of the spectrum, were more uniformly averse to sharing personal stories in ways that identified the status of particular individuals. Posts on public Facebook groups devoted to the movement illustrate direct admonitions against individuals who shared the stories of their friends, as well as metadata revealing deleted posts preceding these discussions as evidence of moderation to control information flows regarding immigration status. Furthermore, comments posted provide general warnings to be careful with information about immigration statuses, along with extensive discussions revealing support for this specific aversion to sharing among discussants and members of these groups.

Facebook discussions and interviews, relative to the DWI movement, included many expressions of fear and concern about what ICE and law enforcement might do with the personal information of any undocumented members who were publicly associated with the movement. These fears strongly affected the willingness of DWI supporters to formally affiliate with the movement on Facebook, as participants in the groups, or even to maintain Facebook accounts. As a result, while Facebook was often used to publicize demonstrations and share resources, other, less permanent and public tools, such as encrypted messaging apps promoted by Cosecha or Snapchat, were employed for organizing and connecting undocumented individuals to the movement. Even Snapchat was often avoided, because of its relationship to Facebook.

Women's March groups varied in their approaches to sharing personal stories. Rather than avoiding documentation of personal information or identities, as with immigrants and their advocates, the Women's March sought safety in numbers and privacy through obscurity, tightly controlling images documenting the events and contact lists, as much as possible. Because the #MeToo movement unfolded during the course of interviews for this study, a number of interviewees mentioned the impact that the movement was having on women's willingness to share their stories, yet worried about the potential consequences of being able to connect stories shared online with real world identities. For example, one Women's March interviewee noted that "we didn't really have strict rules about people disclosing personal information, sensitive stories or anything, but I'm getting worried about it, still moderating the group, with #MeToo, because I'll feel responsible when some weirdo decides to target someone because of what they've posted in our group, like the physical threat is real." These comments evoke similar concerns to those expressed by members of the DWI movement relative to threats of deportation or problems from legal authorities that might arise if the immigration status of anyone associated with the movement could be gleaned from its Facebook groups.

Most groups addressed concerns about inappropriate personal information flows primarily using rules and norms about sharing using the group's Facebook pages and other, now traditional, communications technologies, such as email. Additionally, however, interviewees from a number of DWI groups reported receiving lessons from organizations such as Cosecha, to help them understand how to appropriately use privacy-enhancing technologies, such as encrypted messaging or Slack channels, rather than more visible platforms like public Facebook groups.

5.4.2.3 Photos and Other Visual Resources

One arena of particular concern related to the identifiability of those who attended events from photographs taken or posted that captured participation in political demonstrations. While most groups, across all three movements, gladly accepted photographs of themselves that individuals shared with the group, some struggled with how to manage photographs of others that had been taken or shared without their consent. As one March for Science organizer explained:

> You sort of expect to be seen when you go to a protest in a public place, but there is a sense of safety in a crowd. You're not the only one, but you can be singled out in a picture, and that becomes more complicated … especially when it's suddenly online forever. We get that this is a real career risk.

In addition to privacy concerns, sharing of photographs and other information resources sometimes raised questions about intellectual property and ownership, as one organizer of a Women's March satellite explained:

> You've got volunteers creating graphics for logos and banners and things … tee-shirts …. And those people aren't savvy enough to negotiate the rights to that stuff, so then you have weird rights issues that come up. Umm … there's navigating that whole nightmare, then, umm … and something we're still navigating, is that we had a whole group of photographers taking pictures. Umm … and we were lucky, in that our lead, the leader of the photographers got written agreement with the group of photographers that we had, to get the rights for use of those images collected.

Groups also worried about how to ensure that photographs of their events and marches were preserved. Many followed the early example provided by the NYC Women's March, in securing the photos on their own machines or servers, rather than entrusting them to social media alone. The NYC Women's March began this practice in hopes of developing an archive of such images.

5.4.2.4 Information Quality and Fake News

Organizers also worried about ensuring the reliability and quality of the information that were shared on their groups' Facebook pages. As one March for Science organizer explained, "It's not unfounded to be concerned that facts and science are undermined anytime any influential person says, 'Oh, fake news,' it's actually happening." Many organizers expressed concern about establishing trust in the resources they developed and shared on behalf of their groups. To address these concerns, groups not only doubled checked FAQs, to ensure that the correct and most up to date information was being shared, but also made efforts to provide quality control regarding news stories and links shared by participants within Facebook groups.

These information quality concerns extended in some ways to personal information. Organizers were concerned not only about the obvious things, such as obtaining correct contact information and ascertaining RSVP quality, but also about ensuring that lies weren't being spread through their platforms via personal stories. As one DWI organizer explained:

> Fake information is a problem, but honestly . . . if people take 5, 10 minutes of time to really look into a story or recheck the facts . . . it's not any longer than a few google clicks away to verify. There have been . . . I have seen some fake news about some woman who got deported, like, making fun of her . . . it turned out it was fake news. What ended up happening? Nothing really happened. It's a thing, it looks sensational, but it's usually obvious if it's really if you look up the story and only find one fringe article . . . I kind of double check all my stuff before I post it . . . you've got to be careful, that's the problem with . . . but a hoax will die out or blow up really quickly . . . you can update or repost to keep things prominent, to folks everywhere, all the time.

Many groups, across movements, documented their processes of vetting stories, including news stories, that were shared within the group's Facebook discussions. For example, a DWI post reflected a norm of vetting through careful reading, "Thanks for sharing this. I will wait to comment until I have a chance to read all of this!" while a March for Science post reflected a norm of confirming sources, "[T]his looks great, but we will get more sources before we add it."

Organizers across all three movements emphasized that it often took only a little work to verify information veracity.

5.4.3 *Goals and Objectives*

The objectives underlying the movements are tied strongly to the exogenous influences associated with their formation, as well as to historical interests shaping their contexts. These objectives reflect common values such as equality, transparency, truth, and fairness, as well as interests unique to each group. The general goal of each of these three movements, though details are specific to each movement and group, is, in part, to resist Trump's agenda in favor of more progressive policies and changes. All groups also shared the objective of informing the public about their focal issues. Groups uniformly placed high value on knowledge production and, as described in the previous section, on maintaining the veracity and quality of the group's information resources.

All of the movements were confronted by entrenched political opposition. Sometimes there were subareas within a movement's objectives where consensus with at least some opposition actors could be reached. For example, children of immigrants were viewed relatively favorably and DACA was a more acceptable issue to address than amnesty. As one Facebook user stated "Yes the people who have crossed the border without a choice are the children they bring, are they criminals too?" Supporters and many who originally identified as the opposition agreed that children had no choice and thus this was seen to be a legitimate objective.

Sometimes, however, opposition led to counter-movements, or even harassment and threats. While some Women's Marches saw anti-abortion, or more specifically, anti-Planned Parenthood, counter-protesters, DWI groups experienced the most visible detractors, with bigoted and hateful language directed toward them, as well as threats made toward exposing individuals to scrutiny over their own statuses. Even the well-sourced resources and campaigns developed by the March for Science was subjected to the same hostility to objectivity that the movement emerged to address. When intelligent public information campaigns were disseminated, comments were posted decrying them as propaganda; for example "Drinking the left wing koolaid made by the C.linton N.ews N.etwork."

The national March for Science group developed and disseminated a relatively clear set of top-down objectives, while the Women's March and DWI movements presented patchworks of objectives even at the national level. Regardless of the degree of consistency at the national level, satellite groups unavoidably augmented and modified national objectives to reflect local contexts.

Many March for Science satellite groups were defined more specifically by goals and objectives determined in the local context. For example, the backgrounds of the individuals determining the agenda and specifying the goals varied from group to group. For example, one group might be organized by the American Association for the Advancement of Science (AAAS) members, while another was organized by high school science teachers. Differences between groups within the March for Science movement could be sufficiently stark to provoke some prospective participants to eschew the closest group in favor of a geographically inconvenient alternative. For example, an organizer for the March for Science Austin reported:

> [I]t didn't really seem like I was going to be able to get to DC right around the beginning of the semester, and the Stand up for Science event on my campus, while technically a satellite march, seemed to have some influences that I didn't agree with ... I figured if I was, umm, going all the way to Austin, I may as well make sure it was something I wanted to be a part in.

This interviewee joined and helped to organize a satellite group located hours away because of dissatisfaction with the fact that the local satellite group was focused too much on public health and improving trust in biomedical resources, rather than encompassing broader issues such as climate change or general esteem for science.

The Women's March had a strong national presence, but many individual satellite groups were very well organized and developed their own values and goals very independently, with only the loosest of coordination with the national group. DWI groups were the most grassroots in nature, yet shared information, practices, and institutions horizontally to great effect, illustrating the strength of the network in developing something to a large scale, despite the fact that some satellite demonstrations did not even occur on the same date as the national event. For example, while most demonstrations took place on February 16, 2017, Milwaukee had its demonstrations three days prior. Organizers of individual satellite marches and walk-outs emphasized the importance of solidarity in objectives, as much as in actions, throughout interviews. One organizer explained group-to-group interaction, as a process of assimilation that did not involve any top-down pressure or aggregation, but rather depended on coordinated interactions between many individuals:

> Yeah, well we do things a lot, but also with other lists and groups, that I follow, a lot. One of them, it's called ... I'm going to look it up real quick, hold on ... anyways, it's One Texas Resistance, that's close to the border, you know what I mean? People here feel pressure, people here connect, but to connect to people there, through social media, is powerful. Share words, show solidarity, share pictures ... it's a good thing ... And the fact that I have an education and the knowledge to spread the word, that's what I'm trying to make a difference on, get it all out there. The fact that I have this information, I want to spread it to more people.

Satellite groups often wanted to learn from one another and leverage national numbers to attract attention to their causes, while serving their own specific communities.

Tensions and dissension about goals and objectives sometimes led satellite groups to differentiate themselves from the national group. Even provocations by outsiders might lead to productive discussions about how the scope of a group's objectives could be narrowed in a way that was acceptable to at least some detractors. For example, a post stating "Immigrants are great! But illegal aliens should not be here. I wish the two wouldn't be used to mean the same thing" triggered a discussion that led one local movement to focus on demands for immigration reform, consideration for families, and respectful dialogue, rather than including calls for amnesty. This approach made that satellite group a relative outlier within the larger movement.

Even the language used to frame problems and objectives was sometimes contested. For example, posts in various DWI Facebook groups related to whether the objectives, and underlying problems, were about illegal or undocumented individuals, "aliens" or "criminals." Extreme objectors posted things like:

> Ok so you don't like "illegal". We will just start calling them what they really are. Criminals..I am a "legal" US citizen, but if I break the laws in our country I am .. wait for it . . . A Criminal

In response to these debates, very different agreements and discussions evolved within different local groups across the country as outside stakeholders contested the legitimacy of the groups and groups responded.

Other provocations re-shaped demonstrations. For example:

> If all of the undocumented students don't show up to school on one day
>
> Then you've got a real good list of all the undocumented students to be reported to ICE or whatever
>
> Doesn't it seem counterintuitive saying "hey I'm an illegal" during this presidency?

In response to this post, this group designed a more inclusive demonstration, with friends and supporters obfuscating the status of their undocumented classmates.

5.5 GOVERNANCE

5.5.1 *Institutions*

Polycentric institutional arrangements defined governance within these cases. Within legal and regulatory institutions regarding freedoms of association and expression, Facebook and other platforms, including EventBrite, Twitter, Slack, and Snapchat provide overarching infrastructure in which individual groups created their own institutions, which alternately abide, work around, or contradict the constraints placed upon them within the nested structure.

Governance mechanisms within these movements were distinctive, yet membership rules, resource contribution, and knowledge sharing expectations had many similarities. For example, very broadly, the membership norm was to have low barriers to entry, without expectations to contribute information or actively organize. Yet there was a clear norm that attendees should publicize and share event details and information resources that were generated by the more active participants.

Across all three movements, there was little explicit discussion of rules within Facebook groups or on other public platforms. Nonetheless, normative expectations about civility in dialogue were often specified (e.g. "yes, i'm sorry it is a little condescending, please edit that out if you could or i'll delete it when i get back :) your heart is in the right place but no human is superior than another human"). Norms of authority were reflected in requests to provide references or sources in order to back up claims (e.g. "I didn't see that. Where did you read that? I'm not saying it isn't true, but") or assist other members (e.g. "can you share those details") were ubiquitous.

The logic, as well as the process, of decision-making in these groups was often non-transparent, despite the groups' ostensibly open nature. For groups at the national level, as well as satellites in large cities such as NYC or Seattle, the lack of transparency sometimes stemmed from the fact that such large groups became dysfunctional when too many people were involved in organizing and decision-making. For smaller satellites, lack of transparency often emerged simply because one or two individuals alone acted as the driving forces of these groups. Furthermore, because much of the decision-making process in these groups occurred off of the public Facebook groups, the best sense of how governance was handled comes from the Facebook group FAQs and from interviews. Moderation of discussion in the Facebook groups was an apparent form of governance. And, of course, governance is also formalized in the technological infrastructure and configurations of platforms.

Informal norms and strategies, relative to how people interacted and what was acceptable information to share, were emerged in an ad hoc fashion and by example, rather than from thoughtful strategic planning. Thus, there were many levels of institutionalization and few internal objections to governance designs for these groups. Overall, responses to our survey suggest that the governance was perceived to be legitimate, though there was sometimes disagreement about particular choices.

Privacy, as governance of personal information flow, was often not discussed publicly, even when privacy was a primary focus of many FAQs, discussions amongst organizers, and provided the logic behind numerous decisions. It is notable that interviewees cited their movements' privacy values very confidently, even when they had not discussed them explicitly with others in the group; "I'm not sure . . . I . . . as we have talked, this idea has come to me, but it's not something we decided on . . . I think we are informal and local, loose connections to other immigrant groups, because it provides privacy and keeps people safe."

Some specific rules-in-use about personal information were discussed prominently, however, including those against oversharing in light of threats associated with disclosure outside of the group (e.g. "Everybody: Don't share immigration statuses. Privacy settings don't hide comments. It's a public group"). Questions about appropriateness were common in the Facebook postings, for example "should we really post pictures? there is no expectation of privacy at a public event" (Facebook post). Beyond privacy-related rules-in-use reflected in the posted discussions, heavy moderation was easily evident on the public Facebook pages of some groups. For example, of 4,352 posts associated with the seven DWI groups that we studied, only 3,946 still have readable text, indicating that 406 have been deleted. Timestamp and post ID, without a post, are downloadable metadata through the API, and in some cases it is possible to infer what the post may have discussed, by looking at responses that are still visible on the page. This illustrates both a privacy threat and an instance in which polycentric governance is competitive, rather than complimentary. While many of the deletions by organizers moderating these pages were intended to remove inappropriate flows of personal information that had been shared, as enforcement of rules governing DWI groups, overarching platform level governance by Facebook undermined this effort, to an extent, by maintaining context and metadata.

There were very real concerns expressed by movement members about surveillance and about what Facebook would do with the data it had amassed about individual participants and groups overall. While this concern was most prominently expressed in relation to DWI groups, members of groups across all three movements echoed the concern. As one organizer explained:

> I think Facebook makes a lot of decisions that don't make people happy, that may not ... well affect people, about their privacy, but most of that is not special to us. What is different, what is important and maybe a problem, is how Facebook works with law enforcement, with ICE. I don't know, really, what happens ... I don't think they have to tell us, but people talk and people are afraid.

Many individuals, across all three movements, expressed doubts about the legitimacy of Facebook's role in making decisions about their groups' information. Furthermore, there was entrenched distrust that Facebook would adhere to what was stated in policies; "We agree to Facebook when we use it, but they don't always do what they say and it changes" (March for Science participant, survey response). Nonetheless, most felt it was necessary to sacrifice in order to benefit from Facebook's social capabilities. They did not see any alternative.

While rules and expectations about conduct within groups were often implicit, aside from rules about sharing information and admonitions to mind norms about civil conversations, there was active enforcement of content and civility standards through moderation. These practices were frustrating to some good-faith participants, who did not understand the implicit expectations, yet faced explicit consequences in moderation. Moderation more often manifested when group organizers simply deleted posts that didn't reflect community standards but, occasionally, organizers would articulate expectations and give participants an opportunity to edit their posts, with deletion serving as a last resort. Beyond censorship, there were no other real consequences or sanctions for violations and conflicts between members or members and outsiders were resolved on an ad hoc basis or through excision by moderators, rather than through any formal or consistent procedure.

5.5.2 *Actors in Governance*

Actors involved in governance, regardless of movement or satellite group, were not always key stakeholder groups and did not include all members in any case. Yet interactions between groups and the permeability of boundaries were often relatively open, allowing for interested and committed individuals to be as involved as they wanted to. DWI groups were relatively the most different than other groups, in terms of having most key organizing roles filled by advocates and family members, rather than undocumented individuals themselves, as least in terms of how these groups documented and presented themselves to outsiders in order to protect impacted individuals' privacy. As one DWI organizer, for a student-led satellite group, explained:

> There are a lot of immigrants within the community. Stamford, as a city, is made up of over 30% immigrants, or non-citizens, so really like a third of people here were born outside of the United States and so we were trying to show that. We were also trying to get rid of peoples' fear, particularly those of students, so that ... there was a lot of confusion.

The organizers, in some cases relatives of immigrants, were themselves simply "civically engaged" and wanted to ensure that their families and classmates were welcome in the community. Other DWI groups were organized by DREAMERS, as well as friends and relatives, and made decisions independent of, yet representing, the impacted communities. In contrast, most Women's Marches were organized by women.

March for Science decision-makers often included a combination of scientists, science educators, and STEM students, along with other STEM advocates. As one March for Science organizer explained:

> it seemed that a lot of science faculty were eager to attend, and some of them to speak or do demos for kids or something, but they didn't have time or experience to organize. Also, some of them were concerned about whether that was really professional for them. For me, I work in communications for the university, I didn't have the same concerns and I had the time. It was important to me, in terms of my kids and a world I wanted to live in. I started our local movement, but had a lot of really great students, from biology and chemistry, even engineering, who wanted to help and did a great job.

This movement was in many cases more collaborative.

Actors involved in governance often expressed their desire to be inclusive, yet also their fears of being influenced by those with contrary values, particularly given concurrent activism by "white supremacists and Neo-Nazis." Boundaries were open, but actively policed, in order to avoid co-option. It was also particularly interesting to see who the groups, or the interacting public, attempted to exclude, given that they were working within open, public Facebook groups. Stakeholder groups wanted to engage the public, but not necessarily everyone in their own networks. As one organizer of a DWI satellite group responded, when asked about establishing boundaries:

> Well, sort of. We do not want our employers involved. We do not share with police or immigration officers ... we prefer those we fear not to be too close, though I think they say keep enemies close ... I do not think they are all enemies, but there is fear.

In this sense, members within groups often leveraged their control, as enabled by Facebook, over who specific posts would be shared with, based on whether they were friends and family, or colleagues, driven by concerns about repercussions from nested oversight.

Decision-makers in all groups were often those who felt personally invested and frustrated with current politics, becoming involved through social media and interpersonal interactions and relationships. Actors who engaged in organizing in most cases were in small, close knit groups, yet at the national level and in some of the largest satellites, large groups coordinated. Smaller satellites were often organized by 1 to 25 individuals, in contrast to the roughly 1000-member group that organized the national Women's March. Overall, decision-makers were generally perceived to be legitimate in organizing, though criticism remained about the non-representative nature of many of the Women's March groups, in particular.

5.6 PATTERNS AND OUTCOMES

The public support, across all three movements, illustrated the relative successes, in terms of shaping debate, yet varied dramatically in terms of the consequences. While the March for Science supporters and organizers faced relatively little opposition, the Women's March has faced audible criticism and the DWI movement has documented numerous repercussions, documented within media coverage in the form of the number of individuals who lost their jobs for failing to report to work during the demonstrations.

Benefits to members and others are relatively difficult to ascertain at this point in time, though many have discussed attitudinal changes relative to gender discrimination, manifesting in #MeToo and accountability for aggressors and perpetrators of sexual harassment and assault as being tied to the Women's March movement. However, the attention gained by all three movements is important, as they demonstrated more widespread support than anticipated. Their creative outputs, in the forms of informative campaigns and knowledge resources about their positions, also persist and are being broadly disseminated, establishing social interactions from both the resources themselves and sustained from interactions at demonstrations. Many of the interactions that emerge from the communities' activities are perceived to be a wonderful benefit toward larger community building by active participants. As one Women's March satellite organizer explained, "I showed up to the meeting alone. I met some great ladies, most of whom I'm still in contact with .... It's wonderful."

Perceptions of success by many members, stakeholders, and the media, were contested, however, by ideological opposition, particularly around the legitimacy of the groups as grassroots, rather than mouthpieces of existing organizations, like Planned Parenthood, and in accepting the attendance numbers as fact.

5.7 IMPLICATIONS

5.7.1 *Privacy Values in Public Facebook Groups*

Despite the obvious impact of privacy values and practices on political demonstrations and movements, the most innovative applications of privacy as governance within these communities shaped the use of public Facebook groups, often in ways specific to ideological or sensitive uses of this technology. Four distinct privacy values emerge, shaping public Facebook groups as commons arrangements: privacy through obscurity; privacy and chilling effects; privacy through autonomy; and participatory privacy.

Privacy was, in many instances, sought through obscurity. Various groups and individuals emphasized the anonymity provided to them by the crowds in demonstrations and the relative safety they felt within the sheer number of supporters, often beyond the expectations of organizers and the media in advance of events. Governance structures around photographs and publicity particularly emphasized this preference, minimizing the ability to single out participants publicly, to the best of their abilities. Large groups also emphasized privacy through obscurity in their configurations of Facebook groups and common patterns of engagement, allowing public numbers, without identities, within RSVP design and through the use of "following" rather than "joining" mechanisms.

Privacy concerns also generated chilling effects, regarding participation patterns. This was closely coupled to fear of repercussions, rather than inappropriate flows alone, with many informants for this research conflating these two problems. Comparing immigration advocacy groups to the Women's March, there were differences in not documenting or "lurking" participation for the immigrants' groups, in comparison to subtle behavioral shifts, or deleting documentation, for the women's groups. While merely symptoms of the more primary surveillance harms and possible repercussions, they represent distinct burdens and tradeoffs surrounding participation (Brennan-Marquez & Susser, work in progress). In this sense, privacy dramatically shaped participation, in addition to resources and governance.

Participatory privacy – including anonymous and pseudonymous participation, as well as non-identifiable participation in a crowd – presented a related set of strategies yet was independent of chilling effects and drew on diversity of modes of interaction. Specifically, the use of multiple platforms and institutional designs that obfuscated identification of sensitive attributes associated with stakeholders in the communities provided a means of participatory privacy, whether though encrypted channels for organization of immigration groups or proxy participants, as well as the use of existing organizational infrastructure, by March for Science groups, to protect junior scientists' careers. Central to Facebook specifically, choices made by individual participants to utilize the least publicly transparent modes of interaction with public groups illustrate nuance to participatory privacy. Following, rather than joining, a group allowed individuals to include information from the groups in their newsfeeds and notifications, without anyone else knowing they were followers. Similarly, liking a group without joining it supported sharing the interest only with friends, rather than with the general public.

Privacy was also attained by many through autonomy. A commons arrangement, in which individuals and collectives had control over flows, rather than accepting other decision-makers' choices around appropriateness or imposed flows, provided acceptable outcomes regarding personal information. Groups made choices to use multiple channels and delete contact resources, in order to contradict default practices or designs of platforms and prevent privacy harms imposed by platforms, law enforcement, or political opposition. These creative choices and work-arounds reflected a desire to overcome the structural and institutional efforts by online platforms, like Facebook, to undermine social norms about appropriate information flows (e.g. Strandburg, 2004, 2006) and were relatively successful at providing privacy to participants and stakeholders.

5.7.2 *Commons Governance for Grassroots Political Organizing*

The GKC provided a useful lens through which to explore how grassroots political organizing in public online spaces functions through commons governance, including privacy as governance. Not only were numerous norms and strategies revealed, as evidence of dependence on lower levels of institutionalization in complex and diverse contexts, but also the polycentric nature of governance arrangements was made visible.

Specifically, not only did individual movements have unique needs, which generated arrangement patterns, but individual groups illustrated creative ways of interacting with platforms like Facebook in their efforts to appropriately structure their communities. Differences in choices about platforms, as well as what arrangements of tools and configurations within those platforms, illustrated experimentation and context specificity, as well as distinct limitations of Facebook. While Facebook allows groups to control events, those created by individuals cannot be shared with other accounts, from an administrative standpoint, leading to inconveniences, as well as lack of functionality, for example, depending on the scope and development patterns for each group. Another example of a flaw for organizing related to what groups had access to, which varied by scope; larger groups did not have access to full lists of respondents to verify against EventBrite RSVPs, though Facebook has access to who might attend. Furthermore, many unique arrangements were designed to protect privacy, through the use of less public channels.

5.7.3 *Emerging Best Practices*

While the scale and frame of this study do not lend themselves toward best generalizable principles for online organizing, a number of privacy practices can be identified from these groups as emerging best practices, reflecting a grounded approach toward description, rather than prescription. Specific privacy institutions are shared within and across movements, with respect to how to handle personally identifiable stories, contact information, event photographs, and discussion moderation.

First, and most broadly accepted, it appears to be a key to success to use multiple platforms, particularly for predicting turnout through RSVP functions and in generating and protecting email lists or other contact information. This allows groups to reach more diverse communities with shared interests, as well as to triangulate. While groups had different expectations around what to do with those forms of information, it was considered best practice to have multiple platforms and not entrust everything to a single platform.

Second, photographs should be archived off of public platforms, regardless of whether they are deemed appropriate to also be hosted on commercial public platforms. Private servers, rather than cloud services, were more often trusted, though some did depend on secure cloud back up. Many groups also backed up contact lists, though there was not a clear consensus on how to do this, and notable exceptions actually deleted all of this information, as well.

Third, in organizing around contentious political issues within public online spaces, moderation has been deemed absolutely critical, even if the extent of moderation and the underlying rationales are different. While some groups were concerned about removing hate speech or fake information, others were concerned about detraction from their carefully constructed messages; whatever the reason, some control over the content is important in pursuing specific goals and maintain civil spaces.

Fourth, efforts were made in diverse groups to protect the personal stories and prevent identifiability of vulnerable members. Even though scientists perceived as public intellectuals were encouraged to disclose personal stories, junior scientists were protected in ways that were similar to individuals' immigration statuses and women in vulnerable situations, often associated with sexual harassment or domestic violence.

Author note

This chapter is derived in part from an article published in *Information, Communication & Society* 2019, copyright Taylor & Francis, available online: www.tandfonline.com/10.1080/1369118X.2019.1668458

References

Acquisti, Alessandro and Ralph Gross. "Imagined Communities: Awareness, Information Sharing, and Privacy on the Facebook." In Danezis G. and Golle P. eds., *International Workshop on Privacy Enhancing Technologies*, Lecture

Notes in Computer Science, vol. 4258. Berlin, Heidelberg: Springer, 2006, 36–58. https://doi.org/10.1007/11957454_3

Blitzer, Jonathan. "After an Immigration Raid, a City's Students Vanish." *The New Yorker* (2017), March 23, www.newyorker.com/news/news-desk/after-an-immigration-raid-a-citys-students-vanish

Boothroyd, Sydney, Rachelle Bowen, Alicia Cattermole, Kenda Chang-Swanson, Hanna Daltrop, Sasha Dwyer, Anna Gunn et al. "(Re) producing Feminine Bodies: Emergent Spaces through Contestation in the Women's March on Washington." *Gender, Place & Culture* 24, no. 5 (2017): 711–721.

Brennan-Marquez, Kiel and Daniel Susser. Privacy and Chilling Effects. (Work in progress).

Breuer, Anita. "The Role of Social Media in Mobilizing Political Protest." In Sayre, Edward A. and Tarik M. Yousef, eds. *Young Generation Awakening: Economics, Society, and Policy on the Eve of the Arab Spring*. New York: Oxford University Press, 2016, 110–131.

Ellison, Nicole B., Jessica Vitak, Charles Steinfield, Rebecca Gray, and Cliff Lampe. "Negotiating Privacy Concerns and Social Capital Needs in a Social Media Environment." In Trepte, Sabine and Reinecke, Leonard, eds., *Privacy Online*, Berlin, Heidelberg: Springer, 2011, 19–32.

Fisher, Dana R., Dawn M. Dow, and Rashawn Ray. "Intersectionality Takes it to the Streets: Mobilizing Across Diverse Interests for the Women's March." *Science Advances* 3, no. 9 (2017): eaao1390.

Frischmann, Brett M., Michael J. Madison, and Katherine J. Strandburg, eds. *Governing Knowledge Commons*. New York: Oxford University Press, 2014.

González-Bailón, Sandra and Ning Wang. "Networked Discontent: The Anatomy of Protest Campaigns in Social Media." *Social Networks* 44 (2016): 95–104.

boyd, danah and Eszter Hargittai. "Facebook Privacy Settings: Who Cares?." *First Monday* 15, no. 8 (2010). https://doi.org/10.5210/fm.v15i8.3086

Hamann, Edmund T. and Cara Morgenson. "Dispatches from Flyover Country: Four Appraisals of Impacts of Trump's Immigration Policy on Families, Schools, and Communities." *Anthropology & Education Quarterly* 48, no. 4 (2017): 393–402.

Kaplan, Andreas M. and Michael Haenlein. "Users of the World, Unite! The Challenges and Opportunities of Social Media." *Business Horizons* 53, no. 1 (2010): 59–68.

Kitch, C. "'A Living Archive of Modern Protest': Memory-making in the Women's March." *Popular Communication* 16, no. 2 (2018): 119–127.

Kocher, Austin. "The New Resistance: Immigrant Rights Mobilization in an Era of Trump." *Journal of Latin American Geography* 16, no. 2 (2017): 165–171.

Madison, Michael J., Brett M. Frischmann, and Katherine J. Strandburg. "Constructing Commons in the Cultural Environment." *Cornell L. Rev.* 95 (2009): 657.

Marwick, Alice E. and Danah boyd. "Networked Privacy: How Teenagers Negotiate Context in Social Media." *New Media & Society* 16, no. 7 (2014): 1051–1067.

Milman, Oliver. "March for Science Puts Earth Day Focus on Global Opposition to Trump." *The Guardian* (April 22, 2017), www.theguardian.com/environment/2017/apr/22/march-for-science-earth-day-climate-change-trump

Moss, Pamela and Avril Maddrell. "Emergent and Divergent Spaces in the Women's March: The Challenges of Intersectionality and Inclusion." *Gender, Place & Culture* 24, no. 5 (2017): 613–620.

Nam, Taewoo. "Dual Effects of the Internet on Political Activism: Reinforcing and Mobilizing." *Government Information Quarterly* 29 (2012): S90–S97.

Nissenbaum, Helen. *Privacy in Context: Technology, Policy, and the Integrity of Social Life*. Stanford, CA: Stanford University Press, 2009.

Ostrom, Elinor. "Background on the Institutional Analysis and Development Framework." *Policy Studies Journal* 39, no. 1 (2011): 7–27.

Reardon, Sara, Nicky Phillips, Alison Abbott, Barbara Casassus, Ewen Callaway, Alexandra Witze, Corie Lok, and Emiliano Rodriguez Mega. "What Happened at March for Science Events Around the World." *Nature News* 544, no. 7651 (2017): 404.

Robbins, Liz and Annie Correal. "On a 'Day Without Immigrants' Workers Show Their Presence by Staying Home." *The New York Times* (February 16, 2017). www.nytimes.com/2017/02/16/nyregion/day-without-immigrants-boycott-trump-policy.html

Rose-Redwood, CindyAnn and Reuben Rose-Redwood. "'It Definitely Felt Very White': Race, Gender, and the Performative Politics of Assembly at the Women's March in Victoria, British Columbia." *Gender, Place & Culture* 24, no. 5 (2017): 645–654.

Sanfilippo, Madelyn Rose and Katherine J. Strandburg. "Privacy Governing Knowledge in Public Facebook Groups for Political Activism." *Information, Communication & Society* (2019): 1–18. 10.1080/1369118X.2019.1668458

Sanfilippo, M., Frischmann, B., and Strandburg, K. "Privacy as Commons: Case Evaluation Through the Governing Knowledge Commons Framework." *Journal of Information Policy* 8 (2018): 116–166.

Selepak, Andrew G. "Exploring Anti-Science Attitudes among Political and Christian Conservatives through an Examination of American Universities on Twitter." *Cogent Social Sciences* 4, no. 1 (2018): 1462134.

Stacheli, Lynn A. "Publicity, Privacy, and Women's Political Action." *Environment and Planning D: Society and Space* 14, no. 5 (1996): 601–619.

Stein, Perry. "Day Without Immigrants' Aims to Show Importance of Migrants." *The Washington Post* (February 16, 2017).

Strandburg, Katherine J. "Privacy, Rationality, and Temptation: A Theory of Willpower Norms." *Rutgers L. Rev.* 57 (2004): 1235.

Strandburg, Katherine J. "Social Norms, Self Control, and Privacy in the Online World." In Katherine J. Strandburg and Daniela Stan Raicu, eds., *Privacy and Technologies of Identity*, Boston, MA: Springer 2006, 31–53.

Wallace, Tim and Alicia Parlapiano. "Crowd Scientists Say Women's March in Washington had 3 Times as Many People as Trump's Inauguration." *New York*

Times 22 (2017). www.nytimes.com/interactive/2017/01/22/us/politics/womens-march-trump-crowd-estimates.html

Weible, Christopher M., Paul A. Sabatier, Hank C. Jenkins-Smith, Daniel Nohrstedt, Adam Douglas Henry, and Peter DeLeon. "A Quarter Century of the Advocacy Coalition Framework: An Introduction to the Special Issue." *Policy Studies Journal* 39, no. 3 (2011): 349–360.

PART II

Privacy as Governance of Participation and Boundaries

6

The Republic of Letters and the Origins of Scientific Knowledge Commons

Michael J. Madison

6.1 INTRODUCTION

Science in the twenty-first century is public and open, both by design and by ambition. Declaring that the production and distribution of scientific research should be freely circulated and accessible does not make it so, of course. Claims of proprietary right and exclusivity magnify the complexities of coordinating multiple researchers, research enterprises, and associated disciplinary conditions and technology tools (Royal Society (Great Britain), Science Policy Centre, and Royal Society (Great Britain) 2012; National Academies of Sciences, Engineering, and Medicine (U.S.) et al. 2018). To understand what may be called ecological relationships among practices of openness and practices of exclusivity in a particular scientific setting, a commons governance rubric may be used to collect for analysis actors, resources, and rules that govern the production of scientific knowledge. The rubric used here is the knowledge commons research framework, sometimes abbreviated "GKC" after the title of the initial collection of case studies describing and applying it (Frischmann, Madison, and Strandburg 2014b). Chapter 1 of this volume lays out the knowledge commons framework in detail.

In brief, knowledge commons refers to governance of shared knowledge and information resources by members of a community. It focuses on institutional design rather than pooled resources as such (Frischmann, Madison, and Strandburg 2014b). This chapter advances application of the knowledge commons research framework by calling attention to additional dimensions of commons governance in scientific enterprises, dimensions that define and apply distinctions between publicness, on the one hand, and privacy and private and personal interest, on the other hand. As its central case, the chapter turns the clock back to the origins of modern scientific research and communications, in the Republic of Letters of the late sixteenth, seventeenth, and early eighteenth centuries.

The goal here is partly to apply the knowledge commons framework carefully to the Republic of Letters, a historical case that has previously been assumed to represent a significant commons institution, and partly to use that careful application to explore dimensions of that commons institution that are better regarded as its private-facing elements rather than its more celebrated public-facing elements. The Republic of Letters (in Latin, *Respublica literaria*) is the name given, then and today, to a large, distributed network of researchers and correspondents centered in Europe, which developed and advanced a sophisticated and robust system of knowledge exchange via letters and printed publications. The Republic of Letters is usually identified as the bridge between medieval and Renaissance scientific investigations and a system of research and communications that is recognizably modern, if only in its rough outline (Darnton 2003; van Miert 2016). That "Republican" system of communications, coupled with the related emergence of formal scientific institutions such as academies and journals, merged into the Scientific Revolution and the Enlightenment and eventually into modern scientific disciplines, research universities, and the present so-called Republic of Science (Polanyi 1962).

The suggestion here is that this parade of seeming progress was accompanied by important development of and dependence on public sharing of private, personal interests and resources. That suggestion complements typical accounts of scientific research and communications that locate their critical value and virtue principally in their publicness. That public character comes to the fore whether science is understood to contribute to collective identity and self-determination, or to economic well-being, or both (Merton 1942; Stokes 2011). The role of privacy is acknowledged; Bruno Latour's work highlights the significance of private spaces, such as laboratories and libraries, in the day to day activity of scientists (Latour and Woolgar 1986). Scholars have described the transition between the private and the public sometimes as a story of complementary practice, and sometimes, as in the well-documented history of Louis Pasteur's work, as a story of conflict between private and public-facing aspects of scientific research (Geison 2014).

The knowledge commons framework applied here offers a way to integrate these points of view. Not all research universities, research institutes, or corporate research and development organizations operate in the same way. Institutional settings vary; patterns of scientific research evolve. Normative practices develop and change, suggesting that norms may be violated as well as followed. Understanding the attributes and influences of particular institutional settings can lead to understanding different patterns of knowledge production and dissemination. The knowledge commons framework provides a fruitful way to tease out that understanding on a case by case basis.

In sum, the Republic of Letters is a case of enormous historical interest in its own right, with both economic historians and historians of science continuing long-standing efforts to grasp its scope and its significance (Grafton 2008; Mokyr 2017). The case also offers lessons in the interweaving of publicness and privacy in commons governance that may be useful, even critical, in understanding and guiding the evolution of modern science.

The chapter begins briefly in Section 6.2 with an introduction to open science, a contemporary rhetorical and institutional construct that highlights both new opportunities and continuing dilemmas associated with scientific research. Its purpose is to prefigure the review of the Republic of Letters in commons terms by illustrating the modern relevance of the historical case study. Section 6.3 describes and examines the Republic of Letters. Its purpose is not to dig anew into the dynamics of the Republic but instead to analyze the Republic of Letters via the knowledge commons framework. The chapter relies on a critical parsing of the diverse body of secondary literature surrounding the Republic of Letters, rather than on revisiting primary sources. This section contrasts the knowledge commons analysis briefly with other analyses that do not adopt a commons governance perspective (or a governance perspective of any sort) or that apply a commons label but without doing so in a systematic way. Section 6.4 highlights attributes of the Republic of Letters that are properly characterized as personal or private resources and interests, suggesting connections among different types of information and knowledge resources in the Republic's knowledge-sharing ecology. Section 6.5 suggests some implications and applications of the case study to modern open science.

6.2 MODERN OPEN SCIENCE AS SCIENTIFIC KNOWLEDGE COMMONS

The Republic of Letters is a critical knowledge commons case precisely because many of the challenges and dilemmas to which the Republic responded correspond to challenges and dilemmas that confront modern scientific research.

In the early twenty-first century, researchers around the world have undertaken social movements and related organizational and bureaucratic efforts to advance the concept of "open science." These efforts are motivated by the idea that broad public dissemination of scientific research results, to both expert and non-expert audiences, is the best way to advance the public interest through science. That proposition has its roots in the Republic of Letters. Open science represents a novel vision that is timely in light of the confluence of emerging social, economic, and technology conditions. That confluence resembles in broad outline the circumstances that held at the outset of the Republic of Letters.

6.2.1 *Open Science Described*

In the twenty-first century, the emerging conditions that constitute open science are high speed computer networks, data storage and data processing capabilities, virtual communications, multi-disciplinary and trans-disciplinary research teams, heterogeneous funding sources, and the power of commercial scientific publishers. A recent report of the National Academies described open science and its foundations as follows:

> Openness and sharing of information are fundamental to the progress of science and to the effective functioning of the research enterprise. The advent of scientific journals in the 17th century helped power the Scientific Revolution by allowing researchers to communicate across time and space, using the technologies of that era to generate reliable knowledge more quickly and efficiently. Harnessing today's stunning, ongoing advances in information technologies, the global research enterprise and its stakeholders are moving toward a new open science ecosystem. Open science aims to ensure the free availability and usability of scholarly publications, the data that result from scholarly research, and the methodologies, including code or algorithms, that were used to generate those data (National Academies of Sciences, Engineering, and Medicine (U.S.) et al. 2018).

An analogous Royal Society report outlining strategies to advance open science expressed similar optimism. It used language cautioning policymakers to realize novel opportunities without sacrificing the integrity of scientific communities as self-policing enterprises, without losing sight of the importance of scientific understanding by non-scientists, and without undermining legitimate interests in private action and privacy of research subjects and results:

> Successful exploitation of these powerful new approaches will come from six changes: (1) a shift away from a research culture where data is viewed as a private preserve; (2) expanding the criteria used to evaluate research to give credit for useful data communication and novel ways of collaborating; (3) the development of common standards for communicating data; (4) mandating intelligent openness for data relevant to published scientific papers; (5) strengthening the cohort of data scientists needed to manage and support the use of digital data (which will also be crucial to the success of private sector data analysis and the government's Open Data strategy); and (6) the development and use of new software tools to automate and simplify the creation and exploitation of datasets. The means to make these changes are available. But their realisation needs an effective commitment to their use from scientists, their institutions and those who fund and support science (Royal Society (Great Britain), Science Policy Centre, and Royal Society (Great Britain) 2012).

6.2.2 *Open Science Dilemmas and Commons Strategies*

Both reports from which these quotations are taken, and the advocates and organizers of open science efforts generally, describe social dilemmas that are recognizable to commons governance researchers. The important questions are not "how and why do researchers produce scientific knowledge?," but instead how the multiple components of "science" and "scientific knowledge" come to be pooled in the first place, how they are shared with various constituencies, and how those constituencies draw on those pooled resources. Scientific expertise, research tools, research results, and data themselves each constitute important commons opportunities (Borgman 2015).

Specifically, in open science, how do (and should) individual researchers both protect important personal interests in reputation, priority, integrity and accuracy, and autonomy, while yielding information to the body of knowledge that constitutes both their scientific discipline(s) and the storehouse of society's knowledge generally? How do scientific research results produced by one researcher come to be accepted as knowledge by others, and then acted on, both in the development of further knowledge (or, possibly, different knowledge) and in the development of useful applications? How does one researcher know whether to shape results in the direction of industrial or commercial application, or to guide results in the direction of broader sharing with the field (usually, open or public)? The directional arrow need not proceed from "basic" insights to "applied" know how and devices. The directional arrow may run in the opposite direction, or it may run in multiple directions at once (Stokes 2011; Frischmann 2012). The resulting insight is that open science is a challenge of managing an ecology of knowledge and information resources, rather than a challenge of managing a production line. Simply labelling everything "open" is a starting point, rather than a conclusion.

Proceeding from that starting point is a matter of empirics and pragmatics, as much as if not more than ideology (David, den Besten, and Schroeder 2008). Pragmatically, contemporary open science, or scientific knowledge production, likely does and should operate as commons, meaning structured production and dissemination of shared knowledge by members of overlapping communities. While a detailed investigation of open science as knowledge commons must await additional research, for now it is important to observe that those modern themes – publicness and openness; community; accuracy, integrity, and trust in pooled resources; and privacy and private interests in the accumulation of knowledge – also informed the emergence of the Republic of Letters, centuries ago. The next sections address the Republic of Letters as knowledge commons and consider whether the lessons of history might help inform modern scientific practice.

6.3 THE REPUBLIC OF LETTERS AND THE ORIGINS OF SCIENTIFIC KNOWLEDGE COMMONS

The Republic of Letters is an aggrandizing, idealizing label given to a network of correspondents and correspondence that was the first recognizably modern scholarly and scientific research enterprise, in its emphasis on public distribution of and reasoned debate concerning information collected in and about the world (Grafton 2009). An adage attributed to the Dutch Renaissance humanist Desiderius Erasmus Roterodamus (Erasmus) (1466–1536) distilled in a single phrase the noble spirit and ambition of the enterprise: "All the property of friends is held in common" (quoted in (Grafton 2009)).[1] In short: knowledge, shared with sociability among colleagues. In the languages of the time, it was the *Respublica literaria* (Latin, from *Res Publica Litterarum*) and the *République des lettres* (French).

As an intellectual enterprise, the Republic of Letters constituted a lengthy postscript to the late Renaissance and precursor to the Enlightenment and eventually to modern science (Fumaroli 1988, 2018). Across Europe and eventually in North America and Southeast Asia (Hindley 2013), thousands of experimentalists, observationalists, natural philosophers, and collectors – men of letters, *philosophes*, *savants*, a self-identified intellectual aristocracy operating outside the formal boundaries of nation, state, and church – documented their studies in letters and distributed them in far flung correspondence networks. The "Letters" of the title refers not to postal correspondence, however, but to the literary character of the public exchange, conducted not only through letters but also through books, pamphlets, and other printed publications. The first scholarly journals were established during this period, in France (the *Journal des sçavans*, later renamed the *Journal des savans* and then the *Journal des savants*) and in England (the *Philosophical Transactions of the Royal Society*).

The product of this intellectual exchange was a large, distributed self-governing collective of early scientists and philosophers, bound to one another informally but normatively by a well-understood, if imperfectly enforced, system of rules and guidelines. Written correspondence was linked to in-person visits and conversation and eventually to the formation of early learned societies, scientific academies, salons, and scholarly journals. The informal and formal versions of all of these are typically clustered by historians under the same "republican" label, as a cluster of institutions and practices in which mostly autonomous individuals aligned themselves and their efforts relative to one another. With the rise of national interests, early steps toward the formation of modern academic disciplines, and re-institutionalization of research in precursors to modern universities and research institutes, the Republic of Letters as such came to an end. Its shared values gave rise to what Michael Polanyi labeled the still-ongoing Republic of Science.

The era of the Republic of Letters had no fixed beginning or end. Historians commonly point to the mid-sixteenth century as an approximate start date, identifying Erasmus himself as a pivotal figure in the transition from the Renaissance to the Republic, and point to the mid-eighteenth century and the end of the *Ancien Régime* as the time of transition away from the Republic toward what we know as the Enlightenment. Voltaire and others combined the outward- or public-facing spirit of the Republic with powerful interests in social progress (Mokyr 2017). The journal, as the printed legacy of the Republic of Letters, was supplemented by the signature intellectual ambition of the Enlightenment, the *Encyclopedie*.

[1] Eden translated the adage, which Erasmus adapted from Pythagoras, as "friends hold all things in common." (Eden 2001).

6.3.1 *The Republic of Letters as a Knowledge Institution*

The name "Republic of Letters" first came into broad circulation via publication in Amsterdam of the journal *Nouvelles de la République des Lettres* by the French philosopher and critic Pierre Bayle, beginning in 1684. Use of the title was unremarked, implying both its currency and a collective understanding regarding its existence. (References to a Republic of Letters go back as far as the early 1400s, and the idea of a *Res Publica* extends at least as far back as Plato (Maclean 2008).) Some scholars periodize the Republic of Letters, emphasizing efforts in natural philosophy (science) in the seventeenth century, and a turn to philosophy in the eighteenth century, leading to the Enlightenment (Goldgar 1995; van Miert 2016). The historian Peter Gay drew a sharp distinction between the Republic of Letters and the Enlightenment, interpreting the former as essentially backward-looking and unimportant and the latter as forward-looking and critical to progress (Gay 1966). Others see fewer clear divisions (Brockliss 2002).

The Republic witnessed the contributions of a large number of celebrated philosophers, critics, natural philosophers, astronomers, chemists, physicians, mathematicians, botanists, geographers, historians, theologians, and many others, to use a number of modern disciplinary categories, including Newton, Hooke, and Leibniz; Huygens and Linnaeus; Locke, Hobbes, Hume, Descartes, Vico, Le Clerc, and Benjamin Franklin. Of course, the Republic included thousands of men, and some women, with local and regional identities, whose intellectual legacies are far less notable than the thousands of letters they left behind (Brockliss 2002).

That abbreviated summary offers only a brief entrée into a complex subject: How and why did the Republic of Letters originate, operate, and end (Goodman 1996; Darnton 2003; David 2008; Grafton 2008; Fumaroli 2018)? If, as historians and economists generally agree, the Republic of Letters constituted and created an infrastructure for scientific knowledge production and intellectual communication, in what respects – if any – can it be counted a success? This chapter identifies some leading lines of scholarly thought on those questions. They are, also, questions to which the knowledge commons research framework offers some additional and perhaps novel responses.

Preliminarily, the premise of the inquiry – that the Republic of Letters involved collective or collaborative governance of one or more knowledge resources, which can be usefully assessed via the knowledge commons framework – deserves attention. Was the Republic of Letters an institution in the sense that the knowledge commons framework is best directed to institutional cases, for use in eventual comparative institutional analysis?

I argue that it is, given the definition of institution offered by the economist and Nobelist Douglass North: the rules of the game of a society devised by humans and shaping human behavior (North 1990). To similar if not identical effect is the concept of the institution developed in modern sociology: institutions as stable behavioral patterns that reflect the coordinated behavior of individuals and organizations, where the relations define the actors rather than the other way around (DiMaggio and Powell 1983; Powell 1990; Padgett and Powell 2017).

The difference between the two definitions, the former focusing more on rules that guide or determine patterned behavior and the latter focusing on rules that reflect patterned behavior, is not determinative here. What matters is that the Republic of Letters was an institution in either sense, in that it produced and relied on a well-understood set of human-created informal norms to determine outcomes among a group of people who significantly self-identified with the enterprise in its own time. The Republic of Letters was not a small community, nor was it clearly or precisely bounded in terms of membership, in terms of time, or in terms of place. It was, to use Anthony Grafton's phrase, a "strange imaginary land" (Grafton 2008), but it was no less real to its citizens than a modern state. The Republic of Letters was an "imagined community" of the sort described by Benedict Anderson (Anderson 1983; Darnton 2003). Ostrom and others speak credibly of knowledge and modern science as subjects of commons governance; it is appropriate to adopt the same framework for a critical moment in scientific history. The economic historian Joel Mokyr draws the same conclusion, aligning the Republic of Letters with Ostrom's view of knowledge as a commons (Mokyr 2017, 2011–2012). In his work that proposition is essentially a final judgment. Here, it is a starting point.

6.3.2 *Resources, Actors, and Dilemmas in the Republic of Letters*

Histories of the Republic of Letters often adopt the vocabulary of modern knowledge practice: the Republic engaged scientists in the construction of modern science (Daston 1991), building on the sixteenth century and early seventeenth century discoveries of the Scientific Revolution, beginning in the sixteenth century (Westfall 1977). Yet the word "scientist" was not coined until the 1830s, by William Whewell. Retrospective application risks imposing a more discipline-specific and rigorously methodological character on citizens of the Republic than was actually the case. The knowledge commons framework begins with investigations into the actors, resources, and dilemmas associated with a governance enterprise. In the case of the Republic of Letters, a central, common theme is their heterogeneity.

6.3.2.1 Actors

The central actors in most commons systems are the producers and consumers of shared resources. In this instance, the principal players in the Republic of Letters, citizens and republicans, were the educated elite, the intellectuals and scholar participants and correspondents themselves. With thousands of contributors and a broad range of substantive knowledge in circulation, it is impossible to describe a standard or canonical actor. They were, on the whole, independent of the sort of institutional association that characterizes modern researchers, who are typically employed in universities, research institutes, or industrial enterprises. Exceptional cases, such as Newton's chair at Cambridge, are well known. In addition to their stand-alone status, they were typically characterized by intellectual catholicity. One of the points of the Republic of Letters was that it sustained intellectual discourse across the full breath of emerging knowledge. Admission to this company of scholars required investment in basic intellectual tools and signing on, by participation, to the Republic's code of conduct. Letters composed in line with the accepted style – gracious introduction, brief polite personal commentary, description of observations, and perhaps an enclosed table, or drawing, or other supplement (Atkinson 1999) – obliged a recipient to reciprocate. Personal visits framed by comparable rituals of civility likewise offered entrée to the Republic. Anthony Grafton wrote:

> [T]hen as now, scholar did not rhyme with dollar. But they looked for learning, for humanity, for generosity, and they rewarded those who possessed these qualities. Any young man, and more than a few young women, could pay the price of admission. Just master Latin – and, ideally, Greek, Hebrew, and Arabic; become proficient at what now seem the unconnected skills of mathematics and astronomy, history and geography, physics and music; turn up at the door of any recognized scholar from John Locke in London to Giambattista Vico in Naples, bearing a letter from a senior scholar, and greet your host in acceptable Latin or French – and you were assured of everything a learned man or woman could want: a warm and civilized welcome, a cup of chocolate (or, later, coffee); and an hour or two of ceremonious conversation on the latest editions of the classics and the most recent sightings of the rings of Saturn (Grafton 2008).

Grafton's direct reference to status without wealth means that a second group of actors also played critical roles: patrons. Social elites, lords and noblemen, who did have wealth and status but not expertise, were largely responsible for retaining and supporting the citizens of the Republic on behalf of their families and estates. Scholars were compensated with both money and credit; reputation was a critical part of the Republic's circulating currency (Biagioli 1989, 1990; David 2008). The patronage system was central but not universal. Some participants in the Republic of Letters supported themselves by professional practice (physicians, often) and some by other, independent means, such as printing (including, in colonial America, Benjamin Franklin).

A third class of actors emerged as the Republic evolved and took on organizational trappings: the founders, convenors, and coordinators of learned societies, academies, salons, and journals. These formalized some face to face interaction among citizens of the Republic and also structured selection and dissemination of scholarly correspondence to (potentially) wider audiences. Some societies and academies, hosting face to face presentations and conversations, had state sponsorship, such as the Royal Society (England), founded in 1660, and the French Academy of Sciences (*Académie des sciences*), founded in 1666. Some did not, such as the Academy of Sciences Leopoldina (*Deutsche Akademie der Naturforscher Leopoldina*, originally the *Academia Naturae Curiosorum*) (Germany), founded in 1652. Journals emerged during the same era but often had autonomous or semi-autonomous origins before, in some instances, merging with society or academy hosts. (In their appearance and content, early journals were more like printed pamphlets of letters than modern-seeming collections of research articles.) The journal of the Royal Society, *Philosophical Transactions*, was established in 1665 as a separate venture of the Society's secretary, Henry Oldenburg, and only later became an official publication of the Royal Society. A third organizational form, the salon, existed side by side with these two and was especially hospitable to women, particularly in French cities (Goodman 1996).

6.3.2.2 Resources

Commons analysis often speaks of managing a single, shared, or pooled resource, holding open the possibility that the resource may be divided physically, culturally, or analytically into resource units that may be contributed to or extracted from the resource, or at least consumed. A fishery has fish; a forest has trees; a patent pool has patents. Knowledge commons studies to date suggest that knowledge commons involve multiple pooled knowledge and information resources, usually intangible and immaterial, but often with links to or overlaps with material objects and systems.

In the Republic of Letters, that complex pattern holds. The logical place to start is the physical letters themselves, transported relatively safely and securely via the system of mail delivery emerging via Continent-wide expansion and consolidation of private, regional systems and courier services (Mokyr 2011–2012), improved transportation networks (roads and seas), and – the Thirty Years' War aside (1618–1648) – relative safety for travelers (Merton 1938). This physical infrastructure of correspondence networks converged with the invention of movable type in the latter part of the fifteenth century and the emergence of a class of printers and publishers. The co-evolution of the material and immaterial aspects of the Republic of Letters as communications network aligns with the co-evolution of material (instruments) and immaterial (methodological and epistemological) aspects of scientific research itself, a topic revisited later.

The technological and organizational infrastructure of printing and publishing converged with commercial interests in the adoption of both the earliest patent statute (the English Statute of Monopolies, 1624) and, more important here, the earliest copyright statute (the English Statute of Anne, 1710). The latter gave early, formal meaning in law to a key attribute of the Republic of Letters. Copyright law documented the concept of piracy as misappropriation of a form, such as a printed work, in which knowledge and information were communicated (Johns 2009). Knowledge itself, by contrast, was currency to be shared. Law formalized a boundary between what was proprietary (and propriety) and what was piracy, or impoliteness, that was defining appropriate conduct within the Republic of Letters itself. Knowledge was to be shared; printed matter could be owned.

The central shared resource in the Republic of Letters was knowledge itself, and especially the beginnings of what today we would characterize as scientific knowledge (Daston 1991; Darnton 2003; David 2008; Grafton 2009). Yet this pooled resource should be treated carefully, so that dilemmas and governance solutions can be mapped in some detail. The practices of the Republic of Letters reflected and reinforced sets of shared beliefs, values, and commitments as much as the content of what, today, we call science.

The polymathic character of many of the citizens of the Republic and the multidimensional character of the letters they shared – possibly blending descriptions of specimens, collections of objects, or observations; the results of experiments; interpretations of historical events, geography, or chronology, and more – suggest that what was pooled as a knowledge resource was not, in the first place, the content of early scientific disciplines, even if individual contributions constituted forms and products of early science. The information shared and then disseminated was a form of shared infrastructure relative to the later development of the intellectual content of scientific fields. In its own time, the primary function of the Republic of Letters was not solely to generate a resource or set of resources consisting of propositional knowledge.

Implicit in the Republic, instead, were several layers of shared knowledge of other sorts, epistemological and methodological, mapping in certain respects onto the distinction between codified knowledge (knowledge of) and tacit knowledge (knowledge how) later drawn by Michael Polanyi (Polanyi 1966). There is an overlap at this point between matters of knowledge and matters of trust: the citizens of the Republic had to manage both the contents of shared communications and also the social and cultural skills needed to critically assess knowledge supplied by distant and possibly unknown sources. The resources at stake should be characterized as both. Drawing out their nuances most effectively involves borrowing briefly from two other scholarly fields, and drawing some preliminary links between the character of the knowledge resources and the character of relevant social dilemmas.

One source is communications theory. Developing governance mechanisms through the Republic of Letters required practical and conceptual mechanisms for accuracy and verifiability and for sharing information about practices and results, including both successes and failures. Practically, information had to be communicated accurately and reliably. A shared syntax of scientific communications had to be developed, in the following sense: "is this a recognizable scientific communication?" A shared semantics of scientific communication had to be developed, in the following sense: "do I understand the scientific content of this communication?"

A shared pragmatics of scientific communication had to be developed, in the following sense: "Given that I understand the scientific content of this communication, do I understand how to act on it appropriately?" The questions go to cognition. Participants in the Republic of Letters had to establish ways of learning by which information communicated by a distant correspondent would be incorporated into a body of knowledge that could and would be acted upon in mostly consistent ways by recipients. "Science" as a practice had to be developed and sustained from individual thought and behavior, much in the same way that "law" as a practice had to be developed and sustained (Shapiro 1972). That summary highlights the role of the individual and hints at the importance of dilemmas associated with aggregating individual practices into a shared knowledge resource.

A second source is the domain of Science and Technology Studies (STS) research that focuses on social epistemology in the history and philosophy of science. The questions go to patterns of social life as they bear on cognition. Relevant perspectives include those suggested by Robert Merton on the role of priority in advancing science as a collective or communal activity (Merton 1957), Thomas Kuhn on the collective constitution of shared scientific paradigms (Kuhn 2012), and Bruno Latour and Steve Woolgar on the construction of scientific facts via processes that represent laboratory practice in text and other forms (Latour and Woolgar 1986). In distinct but overlapping ways, these scholars bring out techniques by which scientists identify as scientists and identify their work as contributing to a shared enterprise. Scientific knowledge is simultaneously individual and collective (Spender 1996). Research on organizational design and organizational learning bring similar questions to bear on formal workspaces (Brown and Duguid 2000; Hutchins 2000).

Applying both sources to the Republic of Letters yields the conclusion that citizens of the Republic shared several distinct knowledge resources, in addition to scientific knowledge itself: First, the idea that knowledge of the world could be obtained via observation, analysis, and systematic study. Second, the idea that this knowledge could be recorded and codified in forms that were intelligible to those who did not generate those observations first-hand. Third, the idea that knowledge of the world could be increased and improved via dialogue with fellow citizens. Fourth, the idea that there existed virtue and value associated with publicizing scholarly information, both in the sense that citizens of the Republic subscribed to the belief that public dissemination of knowledge was useful instrumentally in order to sort good knowledge (accurate, or true) from bad, and also in the sense that the citizens shared a commitment to intellectual and scholarly sociability itself. Both senses were expressed in letters, codifying and reinforcing the existence of that knowledge pool as a tacit resource, that is, as a matter of shared, distributed cognition (Greif and Mokyr 2016).

In sum, the purposes of the Republic of Letters were at least two-fold: one was to produce a shared knowledge base that civil society could draw on as part of social, cultural, and political progress; a second was to produce the communalism that has been the hallmark of scientific practice ever since.

6.3.2.3 Dilemmas

The foregoing summary of actors and resources suggests directly that the standard framing of a shared resource as a "tragic commons" social dilemma, in which individual interests of choice-oriented, self-regarding individual actors dominate collective welfare, is insufficient and perhaps altogether inapt in this instance.

For example, it is possible to summarize the relevant dilemma in brief as follows: As the Scientific Revolution developed in the fifteenth and early sixteenth centuries, European societies lacked conceptual and material systems for accumulating and distributing technological innovation and scientific knowledge. An epistemology of facts, progress, and secular knowledge grounded in experience, so-called Baconian science or the scientific method, was still in formation following publication of the *Novum Organum* in 1620. Individual means and motivations for sharing knowledge were diverse (at best) and limited (at worst). Institutions for authenticating, documenting, distributing, and collecting scientific knowledge were scattered and splintered, between medieval universities and the beneficiaries of noble patronage, particularly in Renaissance Italy, and in some respects (printing and publishing, and learned societies, and peer assessment) were non-existent. In time, but comprehensively, the Republic of Letters addressed each of these challenges.

Yet that summary is too simple. The knowledge setting at hand may represent multiple, overlapping dilemmas, with different attributes and different possible solutions, rather than a single problem. A more nuanced review of social or collective dilemmas in the Republic of Letters context is the following.

As to the individual scholars and their production of knowledge, one social dilemma had to do with the integrity of the intellectual content itself. How would experiments and observations at any scale be acknowledged as parts of a program of Baconian science (Greif and Mokyr 2016)? The concept of assessing the relationship between nature and an examination of nature, which we know as the problem of objectivity, was in development. Methods for describing that relationship in codified form, in text and image, were in development. Peer review did not exist, as we understand its modern form (Baldwin 2017, 2018), even if learned societies and journals implemented early versions of assessment and refereeing systems (Zuckerman and Merton 1971). The dilemma posed both a question of assessing the work of a single scholar, and more importantly a question of how to aggregate that scholar's demeanor relative to his own work into a collective resource: trust in knowledge, or trust in science. How would conflicts and disputes over different interpretations be resolved, and the results synthesized into knowledge?

Deeper dilemmas operated as well. The concept of knowledge as good in itself, culturally, had to be developed. The citizens' shared commitment to the public character of scholarly society, also a knowledge resource, was undoubtedly constructed from a vast and therefore heterogeneous population of contributors. That had motivational dimensions as well as the epistemological implications just mentioned. In a distributed, open network such as this one, the problem of motivation typically is not that everyone is selfish, but rather than many people are selfish, many people are not, and most people exhibit a mix of self-regarding and other-regarding behaviors (Benkler 2017). Diversity is demonstrated not only from individual to individual but also from place to place and from time to time. Local and regional practices diverged even with respect to similar scholarly questions; how was it possible to speak of "the" Republic of Letters, a trans-national practice, rather than practices in London, or Paris, or Amsterdam (Daston 1991)?

At both levels, with respect to the knowledge in production and circulation and with respect to the cluster of values that was needed to sustain its circulation, the essence of the resource, as a belief system or set of shared values expressed in a system of material practice, was a classic public good, in economic terms: something that is non-rival, non-depletable, and non-excludable. The relevant social dilemma was and is how a shared commitment to producing that knowledge, to the progress of knowledge, to its publicness, and to community could be constructed and sustained out of such a fabric of diverse sources.

At an even deeper level of behavior, there was the dilemma of individual or personal investment in developing expertise and conducting research when returns to those investments were uncertain. The patronage relationship solved this problem for many citizens of the Republic. The emerging economy of reputation and status associated with participation in the Republic also contributed to a solution for many. There was no "tragic" risk of overconsumption or depletion. There were risks of undersupply (insufficient commitment) and/or defection or corruption. Participants might not follow through on expectations of reciprocal participation, or might supply the literary network with material not produced in good faith, or might convert shared knowledge or knowledge subject to a duty to share to personal or private benefit.

As to the patrons, the dilemma is framed best in principal/agent terms. The Republic of Letters patronage system evolved out of patronage relationships in the Italian Renaissance (David 2008), but the codified products of the patronage relationships acquired a new, public, shared dimension. It is fair to begin by assuming that patrons, as principals, were motivated to invest in the first place primarily by the prospect of securing returns for themselves, paying artists and engineers, as agents, to produce works to benefit the patron himself. If, as the Republic of Letters evolved, the agents (now constituted as a broad class of scholar intellectuals) shared their works publicly, beyond the patron/scholar setting, the prospect of the patron's benefit might have been reduced. Perhaps not; on a case by case basis, one would need to explore the extent to which public sharing of the knowledge diminished the patron's ability to retain a valuable benefit. At a system level, however, a critical dilemma appears to be the willingness of patrons to invest in the circulation of knowledge that did not clearly benefit them.

As to the founders and convenors of academies, societies, and journals, social dilemmas were at least two-fold. One dilemma can be recognized as a version of the "underproduction" dilemma that characterizes some modern theorizing about intellectual property. Organizing and operating a formal enterprise such as a learned society requires both an initial capital investment and continuing expenditures of time, labor, expertise, and money. That value or its equivalent has to come from somewhere, including underwriting from the state, philanthropy, and subscription and other fees. A second dilemma resembled one of the challenges of contemporary open science: volume. The amount of information and the number of letters and other printed publications made available through the Republic of Letters created a problem of super-abundance not only for those who would try to keep up with the flow of knowledge but also for those who would curate it and organize it via journals and other publications (Blair 2010).

A separate but related dilemma was associated with the fact that the products of many of these organizations had few, if any, industrial applications. In the language of modern science, this was basic rather than applied science (Stokes 2011). Notable for their absence from the account in this chapter are craft guilds and questions of technology development, largely because the presumption of publicness that defined the Republic of Letters was reversed, elsewhere; craft innovation was presumptively secret (Long 1991).

Formal intellectual property law appeared in this history, briefly, and its role was largely to shape the boundary between circulation of knowledge inside the Republic of Letters (which was excluded from the emerging exclusivity associated with early patents and copyrights) and circulation of knowledge outside of it, and partly to guide transitions from one world to the other. For technical advances with industrial application, in practice that role required policing the distinction between basic knowledge and craft or industrial knowledge, and, with respect to the latter, the line between secrecy and publicity. As applied to printed matter, that meant rewarding the enterprises that circulated and re-circulated formal versions of scientific literature. The social dilemma here, in sum, was that the most visible and durable material embodiments of the Republic of Letters (academies, societies, and journals) provided forms of intellectual infrastructure, as to which the expected value and demand for the resource was diffuse and emergent and therefore difficult to aggregate for purposes of pricing in a market economy (Frischmann 2012).

6.3.2.4 Arenas, Rules, and Social Norms

The description earlier of the Republic of Letters as an imagined construct implies that defining "arenas" of interaction for knowledge commons purposes is difficult. But it is not impossible. Material environments could be located in homes, offices, shops, libraries, laboratories, observatories, coffeehouses, salons, and academy and society meeting places. The shared commitment to the circulation of knowledge could be located only in the minds of participants, as reflected in their writings and their conversations. In a sense, all of Europe was the setting for the Republic of Letters, along with epistolary connections in North America and Asia, bearing in mind the fact that it was all but invisible to those without the credentials and training that qualified them to participate.

Far more important here than material settings were the social norms that defined expected and right conduct and distinguished it from the bad. Norms in the Republic of Letters were widely documented and circulated. In what respects were they idealized and in what respects were they observed regularly in practice? In what respects were norms disciplinary, in fact?

6.3.2.5 Ideals

The literature of the Republic of Letters itself, and historians' accounts, agrees in providing rich descriptions of the duties of scholars in the Republic and the benefits to be obtained by participating in it. The values and practices of the Republic of Letters were strongly associated with the empiricism for which Francis Bacon advocated. Some scholars have treated the Republic of Letters via intellectual history as a movement motivated by idealism, prompted by and advancing Bacon's work (Eamon 1996).

Both to participants themselves and in histories of the era, participation was conditioned on observing a set of distinct, overlapping norms: (i) civility and cordiality through regular and reciprocal contact and collaboration (politeness and "taste" in Robert Darnton's account (Darnton 2003)); (ii) a commitment to the production of knowledge via empiricism and freedom of expression; (iii) evaluation by intellectual merit rather than rank or birth, and public reason; and (iv) religious and national tolerance and collaboration and participation across national boundaries.

6.3.2.6 Practice

The practiced Republic of Letters matched the idealized Republic of Letters to a significant degree. Historians agree that norms of civility and publicness and transnationalism were honored more in the observance than the breach; how else would the Republic of Letters have lasted as long as it did or generated as much material and as many institutions as it did, over such a large territory? The historian Lorraine Daston referred to the Republic of Letters as relying on technologies of trust and proximity (Daston 1994) – where trust referred to the credibility typically accorded to free and independent gentlemen, and proximity referred to personal ties expressed via both face-to-face interaction and the letters that embodied it.

Thus, the new academies typically welcomed foreign or "corresponding" members, and scientific correspondence and the transnational community carried on notwithstanding the disruptions of the Thirty Years' War (Daston 1991; Goldgar 1995; Goodman 1996; van Miert 2016). The disputatious and contentious character of scholarly dialogue in the preceding era, with scholastic commitments to theoretical truths competing with one another, was replaced by a system of trust in proper scholarly behavior (Dear 1992; Daston 1994). This marked the beginning of an epistemic shift. A participant who conducted himself civilly and honestly in reporting the results of Baconian investigations was accorded respect, and the work subjected to correspondence and critique within the norms of the collective. But the work was accepted because of who the producer was, rather than because of the mode of its production. The point was the person, not the object.

In a large, norm-governed, heterogeneous setting, bad behavior was hardly unheard of. Trust and proximity have been contrasted with distrust and distance (Porter 1996); in systems defined by the latter, credibility and objectivity are founded on the work itself rather than on the person. In the Republic of Letters, less of the former and more of the latter must have been part of the mix at times. Resentments and prejudices, and the absence of civil behavior and the exercise of public reason, led to well-known public disputes over priority and over credit (between Newton and Hooke, for example, and later between Newton and Leibniz). Less sensational cases typically turned on violations of civility norms, including failures of discourse (absence of language of credit or respect), and accusations of plagiarism (Grafton 2008). The resulting discipline took various forms: judgments of scientific priority, validity, and even, via conclusions as to reputation, to exclusion from the community (Daston 1991; David 2008).

Other norm-based judgments are easier to see once the polycentric or pluralistic character of the Republic of Letters is highlighted. The informal transnational collective had its regional and local constituents and, in academies, societies, and journals, its formal organizational complements. Ideals and practices were operating at multiple scales and in multiple places simultaneously. Karen Knorr-Cetina focuses on this multiplicity in describing scientific research as "epistemic culture" (Knorr-Cetina 1999). So, the Republic of Letters represented science, and science was represented in the Republic of Letters. What was not scientific did not make its way into the Republic of Letters in the first place or was subjected to its reason-based disciplinary system. The multitudinous character of the work of scholars meant that scholars channeled some of their work into the idealized, imagined community of the Republic, where it became part of social worlds of disputation and reasoned analysis by others (Newton, on physics) and they channeled some of their work elsewhere, where it would be received and interpreted according to different, older standards (Newton, on alchemy) (David 2008).

External forces of other sorts interfered with participants' idealism, managing the pragmatic boundaries of the Republic from the outside rather than from within.

National and religious tolerance was managed in part by scholars' voluntarily moderating the content of their correspondence, and both periods of war and linguistic shifts – in particular, from Latin to French as the default language of scholars – at times depressed the volume and character of publicly-circulated works. Peter Gay directly contrasted the nobility of the ideals of the Republic of Letters with the claim that in practice, an oligarchy of landed gentry and Ancien Régime patrons rather than authors mostly directly controlled the flow and content of their letters (Gay 1966). That argument is most directly addressed to seventeenth-century practices and to works in the arts, literature, and culture rather than natural philosophy and science, but it gets to an important theme in the knowledge commons framework: If commons governance is the observed solution to one or more social dilemmas associated with a knowledge resource, is that (or was that) governance solution successful?

6.3.3 *Outcomes and assessment*

Evaluating the Republic of Letters in comparative institutional terms is difficult for two special reasons. One is the fact that the Republic of Letters emerged and evolved over time. It was not chosen purposely in all respects as a governance solution to one or more social dilemmas. Two is that systems of exclusivity governed via market exchange and systems of state supply largely did not exist in anything approaching their modern forms during the time periods in question. In fact, the opposite is true. The end of the Republic of Letters, both in the sense of its transition into the Enlightenment and in the sense of its purpose or value, is often described in terms of the rise of nationalism and state support for scientific institutions (Burke 2012), on the one hand, and more robust scientific and industrial specialization, on the other hand, leading to greater investment in recognizably modern scientific organizations (research universities, scientific articles, peer review) and to accelerated economic growth (Mokyr 2017).

The most accurate way to describe the relative success and impact of the Republic of Letters as knowledge commons governance is that the Republic became and sustained itself, until it did not, and that the practices and values of the Republic of Letters evolved later, mostly productively, in ways that allow us to recognize their descendants today. That judgment is not to suggest that the Republic of Letters had an inertia of its own, independent of the energy of its citizens. Rather, the description of actors, norms, and practices elicited by the knowledge commons framework implies that it was a network of individuals comprising a collective or community, imprecisely defined (Strathern 1996; Margócsy 2017). Because of its relative openness, the Republic of Letters may be characterized institutionally as a community of practice (Brown and Duguid 1991; Wenger 2010). Its distributed form suggests combining those views via a final amendment: the Republic of Letters was a successful network of practice (Duguid 2005). The network label highlights its fragility; calling the Republic of Letters a community highlights its robustness.

The knowledge commons framework adds nuance to this summary, for clarity. Each added layer of analysis contributes additional perspective but not a comprehensive or final evaluation.

6.3.3.1 The Production of Knowledge

The best place to begin is by treating knowledge as an intrinsic good. Characterized in material terms, the Republic of Letters left a significant legacy of knowledge-generating institutions and practices, and intellectual content. Many of the academies, learned societies, and journals established during that era have survived to the present day, although in modified form, and remain leading institutions of scientific collaboration and communications. Thousands of letters survive.

Characterized in immaterial terms, as to the tacit aspects of the Republic of Letters, its values and practices likewise endure. Public circulation of scientific research results, critique of the work using objective criteria based on merit rather than status, and the exercise of public debate and reasoned analysis by communities of trained experts remain central normative ideals of modern science. That remains the case, and it remains part of the legacy of the Republic of Letters, even if modern science and scientists do not always live up to those ideals, and even if, as the earlier review of twenty-first century open science illustrated, new threats and challenges to those ideals are often present. But the central dilemmas addressed by the Republic of Letters, consisting of developing the conceptual as well as technical tools needed to aggregate individual scientific knowledge into something called "science," remain the subjects of vigorous investigation.

The propositional and codified dimensions of the knowledge produced during the Republic of Letters are more difficult to assess. The influence of some of its citizens on the development of science was enormous and enduring, Newton being perhaps the easiest case. The influence of many others was either significantly smaller or less enduring, or both. Of these, some are well-known to historians of science (Grafton 2008), others are known principally as exemplars of the types of individuals who were active participants of the time (Brockliss 2002). Still others occupy both camps, particularly the women of the Republic of Letters (Pal 2012).

6.3.3.2 The Production of Value

Knowledge, particularly scientific knowledge, also has instrumental and functional value. Joel Mokyr's examination of the Republic of Letters as a knowledge commons has approached the topic primarily from the standpoint of economics. He argued that the Republic of Letters created an engine of knowledge production that contributed significantly to economic growth in the eighteenth and nineteenth centuries, primarily via what today we would refer to as spillover effects (Mokyr 2011–2012, 2017). Mokyr called the Republic of Letters "one of the taproots of

European technological change" and sustainable economic growth (a link that he cements via the phrase a "culture of growth"), in its influence on the Enlightenment and later on the Industrial Revolution. Anthony Grafton, too, analogized the Republic of Letters to a market for ideas rather than a community or collective of knowledge or knowledge producers (Grafton 2008). His reading is not motivated by economic understanding, like Mokyr, but it shares Mokyr's interest in the sources and impacts of the circulation of knowledge.

6.3.3.3 The Production of Community and Identity

Rather than prioritizing the production and dissemination of knowledge itself, focusing on communal identity and interest is an additional, distinct mode of assessing commons governance in this case. The Republic of Letters unambiguously articulated a scientific collective and unambiguously articulated the concept of the practitioner operating within and identifying with a scientific collective. That is so even if, in both respects, the precise contours of the collective and the precise definition of the scientific identity were fluid and evolutionary. The practices of the Republic of Letters produced both, over time. In this instance as in others, both the existence of a bounded network of practitioners and the porosity and fluidity of those boundaries are among its essential attributes (Strathern 1996). Similar analyses of community governance and the production of scientific or technical identity in knowledge commons settings have been undertaken with respect to modern technology, including the practice of citizen science in the Galaxy Zoo astrophysics project (Madison 2014) and governance of open source computer software collectives (Kelty 2008; Schweik and English 2012). Christopher Kelty's concept of the "recursive public," a phrase that denotes a distributed collective that constitutes its own identity via public practice of norm-bound technical skills, seems particularly apt with respect to the Republic of Letters.

The historian of science Mario Biagioli offered economies of prestige and reputation as significant motivators of the practices of both patrons in the Republic, who benefitted from public imputation of the accomplishments of "their" scientists, and citizens of the Republic, whose stature derived in part from their association with wealthy and high status patrons (Biagioli 1989, 1990). The developing prestige of scientific research was neither sufficient in itself to get the Republic of Letters under way nor to sustain it over time, either in individual or collective settings. But the Republic of Letters validated reputational considerations in the construction of scientific identity and community, as they interacted with resolution of disputes about priority, among other things (Merton 1957; Polanyi 1962).

6.3.3.4 Costs

Costs and harms should be accounted for, along with value and benefit. Norm-driven and community-based governance generally poses risks of internalizing benefits for members and participants, and externalizing harms for others. Power dynamics and hierarchies may distort the workings of the group both within the collective and at the boundary between insiders and outsiders. The porosity of community and network boundaries and the informality of norm-governed systems create risks of opportunism and defection that may be particularly difficult to police, even while they enable a diverse range of positive spillovers. Communities of experts and elites both rely on and perpetuate exclusionary reputation and status economies. Among the challenges associated with contemporary open science is expanding the domain of effective scientific communications so that the character and benefits of open science appropriately includes non-experts (Royal Society (Great Britain), Science Policy Centre, and Royal Society (Great Britain) 2012).

Notably, Peter Gay claimed that the Republic of Letters enabled powerful patrons (in his account, oligarchs) to structure and control the flow of knowledge, particularly cultural knowledge (Gay 1966). That represents a significant cost of the Republic as a norm-driven, collectively managed enterprise, even if it is far from clear that those costs could have been avoided at the time. State-related investment in support for scientific research and communications got its start in and as part of the Republic of Letters, via scientific academies. Formal exclusive rights to be traded in markets, as incentives to invest and engage in knowledge production and dissemination, were just finding their toeholds during the Republic. Informal exclusivities, such as the secrecy practiced by craft guilds, spoke to different knowledge domains. Research universities, the modern equivalents of seventeenth and eighteenth century scientific patrons and similarly situated in ecologies of governance of shared knowledge resources, likewise preach values of community and knowledge sharing, but together with market-based enterprises and the expectations of modern patent law, universities exercise significant practical control over the flow of research and research results. And universities in the time of the Republic of Letters had not yet matured into research-based enterprises (Madison, Frischmann, and Strandburg 2009).

The fact that citizenship in the Republic of Letters was comparatively open, informal, and merit-based should not obscure the fact that participation was weighted heavily in favor of men, in favor of educated men at a time when education was accessible only to the few, and in favor of men with the means and opportunity to engage in study, reflection, preparation of correspondence, and participation in in-person meetings and visits. That characterization is not intended to diminish the contributions of the Republic of Letters in any respect other than to note that the institutional arrangement of actors, capabilities, and practices in an expertise-based field such as science was, and remains, contingent. The account earlier emphasized the breadth and heterogeneity of scientific interest within in the Republic of Letters. This brief account of demographics and material resources suggests a corresponding level of homogeneity. Which contributed and in which respects to the Republic's overall system of values and practices is open for debate. That debate continues.

Modern practices of citizen science and substitution of "peer produced" industrial goods for firm-based production prompt examination of essentially identical questions of who participates and how, and with what results (Benkler 2017).

6.4 THE PRIVATE ORIGINS OF THE REPUBLIC OF LETTERS

"Privacy" grounded in information about a person appears not to be part of the Republic of Letters as knowledge commons governance. One might examine scientists' letters themselves for indications that some of their contents were to be marked off as "private" and others as "public" or shareable, but on the whole, that sort of evidence is not present (Atkinson 1999). The style and content of the material products of the Republic of Letters is highly consistent with the era's emphasis on politeness and civility. While the letters themselves were far more conversational in style and character than modern propositional scientific articles, the contents were stylized and ritualized to align with the normative ambitions of the age.

Yet privacy interests and practices in material forms played key parts in the construction of the Republic of Letters. Letters themselves were sealed to protect their contents from disclosure other than to their intended recipients. But in the context of the Republic, letters were not intended to transmit intimate or possibly objectionable or unformed thoughts, as modern letter writing sometimes does. Letters to periodicals were intended to be adapted for publication. Writers of letters to other individuals expected their contents to become part of the circulating corpus of scientific knowledge. The physical spaces of private activity played the sorts of roles in the Republic of Letters that their counterpart spaces play today. Scientists conducted observations and prepared letters and manuscripts in private laboratories, libraries, and personal studies.

The most significant private resource developed and shared in the Republic of Letters was immaterial: the habit of personal and private thought and reflection that formed the practice of public reason and the style of objective disagreement and disputation for which the Republic of Letters was celebrated. The private resource in question was epistemological and conceptual, rather than material. It began in the mind of individual citizens of the Republic. It was materialized through the letters themselves. Via the circulation of print, what was necessarily an individual's capacity for reasoned analysis became a collectively managed, shared resource. What we would today call private scientific thought, the Baconian style and strategy, became a public good. The Republic of Letters emerged from the minds as well as the hands of its individual practitioners.

The pivotal character in this development, explaining both the problem and his understanding of the solution, was Immanuel Kant. The challenge was freedom itself, as in humankind's release from its self-incurred immaturity, "the inability to use one's own understanding without the guidance of another" (Kant 1996). Kant identified enlightenment with the process of thinking for oneself, employing and relying on one's own intellectual capacities in determining what to believe and how to act. In the essay "What is Enlightenment?," published in 1785, Kant described what he described as the distinction between "public" reason and "private" reason (Kant 1996). The "private" use of reason, in Kant's framing, consisted of the activities and contributions of individuals acting in their capacities as agents or officers of the state, or the military service, or the church. To protect the interests of the community of which the individual was a part, the state could, Kant believed, legitimately restrain the exercise of that "private" faculty. By contrast, the "public" use of reason was the capacity of individuals to think for themselves, without being bound by accepted historical authorities, inherited learning, or patterns of thought – or, in short, enlightenment. As to individuals using those faculties, the state could not legitimately censor "public" communications.

But enlightenment itself required community, and a community of a particularly new sort: a universal community, one not defined by institutional hierarchy, role, and domination, circumscribed locally or territorially. When Kant wrote that "the public should enlighten itself," he anticipated a community with open participation. And when he wrote, "[b]y the public's use of one's reason I understand the use which a person makes of it as a scholar before the reading public," thinking for themselves, communicating in their own names, and engaging in dialogue with other learned men, as their peers, Kant had in mind the Republic of Letters (Chartier 1991).

In sum, Kant suggested that the practices of the Republic of Letters evidenced the conversion of what in modern terms would be considered private thought into a collectively produced public resource, a resource defined philosophically and epistemologically rather than materially. And that public resource was itself both a critical contribution to and product of the Republic of Letters. It was the power to reason independently, with others.

The link between Kant's work and the Republic of Letters was highlighted when Kant's argument became the foundation for Habermas's concept of the "public sphere": a kind of publicness that Habermas argued came into being at the end of the seventeenth and beginning of the eighteenth centuries in Europe (Habermas 1989) and that was specifically associated with the emergence of public science with respect to both scholarship and industrial application (Stewart 1992; Jacob 1997; Mokyr 2017). Habermas defined the public sphere as private individuals coming together to make a public use of their reason via periodicals and the medium of print, and via salons and other social organizations. Habermas argued that until the era of the Republic of Letters, a conception of publicness as reasoned debate open to all literally did not exist – even if it was limited to learned society rather than to "the public" as a whole. Outside of the institutions of the state and the church, individuals did not have the political freedom, the conceptual tools, or the material devices to engage in reasoned analysis of their worlds (the Baconian point), to believe that they could and should share that analysis with others (the Kantian point), or to be able to actively take steps to construct the boundaries and links that developed between private thought and behavior and a construct of the public (Habermas' conclusion).

Private thought and reflection independent of the legacy institutions of state and society, or what Kant framed as "public" reason, therefore both supplied and was the product of the shared immaterial and material knowledge of the Republic of Letters. Private reflection was infrastructure, in the sense that it enabled virtually all of what followed via public circulation of scientific material, but private reflection, as infrastructure, was also the product of public circulation of scientific material. This is the sense in which the Republic of Letters constituted itself, as an identity, as a collective, and as a set of practices. It is also the sense in which private thought and reflection contributed and constituted a key Republic of Letters resource (Kuchar and Dekker 2021).

A brief schematic description of the respective roles of the private and the public in practice, moving up and down the register of personal and collaborative or shared activity, makes the point more concrete. The description evokes the earlier reference to how communications theory itself may explain certain features of the social dilemmas present.

To begin with, a citizen of the Republic had to learn and adopt an epistemological stance for himself relative to empiricism (his ability to learn new things about the world, for himself) and relative to the communitarian norms of the collective (his duty to share his work with friends, as colleagues and peers). This would be an act of learning, in which collective, shared knowledge would become personalized and privatized in the mind, and the act of the individual. Those acts would be combined with the related acts of interpreting and applying for himself related propositional knowledge and tacit or uncodified knowledge about particular scientific work. Conversing with a visitor or reading a letter from a correspondent, this citizen would form judgments about the character and reputation of the person, the character of the person's correspondents, the nature of the questions being considered, the state of related work being done by others, and what steps to take next.

These judgments would, in turn, form the basis of that citizen's own next acts and correspondence (Goldgar 1995), combining his private reaction to and reflection on what he had learned with his own collecting, observing, experimenting, and interpreting. The documented version, in public circulation, would prompt the next round of reaction, reflection, documentation, and circulation of material by others.

Material objects thus served critical roles in scaling the knowledge collective of the Republic of Letters up from the individual to the group, and then back down again. Those documents were books, letters, and their derivatives, such as news, extracts, and abstracts, which appeared in journals. Narratives were often accompanied by attachments and appendices in the form of drawings, diagrams, and tables (van Miert 2013). This latter category of material is particularly interesting in the context of the circulation and expansion of private reflection into public infrastructure. Bruno Latour refers to these printed representations of immaterial knowledge "things" as "immutable mobiles," because they simultaneously document and simplify individual engagement with nature as they circulate, permitting the exercise of faculties of collective acceptance and skepticism (Latour 1986). This is an important cognitive add-on to standard arguments about the significance of print to the development of science. The printed letter form served as both the medium of personal knowledge codification and transmission – the technological mechanism that documented solitary reflection and communicated trustworthiness in the person to the recipient and to the collective, so important to the Republic of Letters – as well as the means by which science eventually became objective and durable at scale, independent of the person.

6.5 MODERN IMPLICATIONS

The study of the Republic of Letters as knowledge commons reveals three noteworthy modern implications. The first has to do with the character and utility of the knowledge commons framework itself. This case study suggests some noteworthy strengths and weaknesses. The second has to do with the Republic of Letters and its early scientific community as knowledge commons governance. Careful examination of the Republic and its shared resources link certain existing lines of research more closely that they may have been linked previously, indicating some new directions for further examination of scientific practice. The third has to do with open science.

6.5.1 *The Future of the Knowledge Commons Framework*

The knowledge commons framework has been described from the beginning as a research device, a heuristic akin to Ostrom's IAD framework for collecting data in a structured and systematic way (Madison, Frischmann, and Strandburg 2010). Theorizing and modeling of knowledge commons have been deferred, and the framework is not intended to be used as a set of rules or guidelines for constructing viable or successful knowledge commons governance.

Nevertheless, given the conceptual affinities between the knowledge commons framework and the IAD framework (Ostrom 1990), it has been difficult for many to avoid the instinct that Ostrom's guidelines for successful commons practice ought to inform application of the knowledge commons framework. Noteworthy among those guidelines are the ideas that successful commons requires a well-bounded community with a clear consumption pattern relative to the resource at hand, and that the community ought to have well-managed systems for monitoring consumption and for disciplining inappropriate behavior. The knowledge commons framework itself directs researchers to identify and evaluate systems of boundary management, resource monitoring, and discipline.

For legal scholars drawn to Ostrom's vision in knowledge-based settings, the instinct to define the scope of commons governance with relative specificity are echoed in research on social norms and property management, which indicates that community self-governance is likely to be effective (welfare-maximizing, in economic terms) only in small, close-knit, relatively homogenous collectives (Darling and Perzanowski 2017; Oliar and Sprigman 2008).

Against that background, the Republic of Letters disappoints. It did not constitute a well-bounded membership community, it had few shared mechanisms for monitoring resource production and consumption, and its disciplinary practices relied as much or more on implicit appeals to the shared values of civility and publicness as on explicit dispute resolution processes. The open-endedness of the Republic of Letters explains, in part, the appeal of metaphors drawn from exclusivity-based market exchange (the Republic of Letters as a market of and for ideas (Grafton 2008)), anachronistic though that metaphor obviously is. The anachronism is telling: the Republic of Letters emerged at a time when state institutions for knowledge production were primitive, and market-based alternatives, such as patents and copyrights, were just starting to displace guild practice.

Yet the assumption that precise boundaries are necessary to effective commons governance may be mistaken. The search for boundaries and boundedness is necessary and appropriate, because only via the search can researchers determine the relevance of the results across different cases and contexts. Earlier work applying the knowledge commons framework suggested the utility of the framework to atypical cases of knowledge commons (Frischmann, Madison, and Strandburg 2014a). Those cases indicate that knowledge commons governance may flourish even in the absence of features that might, in other settings, be deemed essentially necessary, such as firm boundaries, and systems for monitoring and disciplining resource over-consumption. The case of the Republic of Letters affirms that finding, and in doing so it affirms the core insight motivating knowledge commons research: governance systems for shared resources are best understood via nuanced understanding of the social dilemmas to which they relate. Earlier, the chapter explained the insufficiency of the "tragedy of the commons" metaphor to describe social dilemmas concerning knowledge and information resources. Relevant social dilemmas for knowledge commons tend to collect around ideas of collaborative participation and contribution, as well as or as alternatives to production.

The knowledge commons framework has not, however, emphasized sufficiently the roles that shared conceptual infrastructures can play in knowledge commons, as they do in the Republic of Letters. Many infrastructural resources are governed as commons, not in the sense that Ostrom's work documented commons governance that solved tragic commons dilemmas, but in the sense that the legal scholar Carol Rose described shared material resources, such as roads, as "the more the merrier" settings, where the social benefits of shared access multiply as more and more people use the resource. Maximizing social value in that setting justifies governance via commons mechanisms (Rose 1986; Frischmann 2012). The Republic of Letters should be characterized as both having relied on shared infrastructural resources, particularly the epistemological developments described in the last section, and having produced shared infrastructural resources, in the form of scientific community as a social fact.

6.5.2 *The Future of the Republic and the Organization of Science*

The institutional evolution of scientific research and scientific communities continued after the end of the Republic of Letters and continues today. The evolution of organizational pathways signified by and in some respects initiated during the Republic of Letters is well-known. Learned societies and academic journals coevolved with research universities and scientific specializations through the eighteenth and nineteenth centuries. Funding mechanisms took on a more complex and diverse character, as patronage systems and private sponsorship even inside universities were eventually displaced by formal state support (outside the United States) and by blends of state support and philanthropy (in the United States). The practice of scientific research in the later nineteenth century distinguished between basic and applied research, the former practiced largely in universities and research institutes, and the latter practiced in industrial research and development organizations. Norms of civility were gradually displaced by ever-more-formal systems of peer review as a mechanism for ensuring trust and objectivity in scientific results.

The knowledge commons framework should remain a useful tool for diagnosing problems and institutional solutions with respect to the evolution of social dilemmas in different aspects of scientific research, and in particular questions of what is "inside" self-governed scientific communities and what is "outside," possibly governed differently. The research university is one particularly fruitful case (Madison, Frischmann, and Strandburg 2009). It offers a powerful illustration of polycentricity and the interweaving of multiple governance systems at different organizational levels, for different purposes.

Evolution of shared values and conceptual frameworks has proceeded differently, and some would say has proceeded with less variation over time and across institutional settings. Robert Merton and Michael Polanyi each proffered essentially universal accounts of the norms of open, objective, and communitarian scientific research (Merton 1942; Polanyi 1962). Constructivist accounts of science, by scholars including Thomas Kuhn, Bruno Latour, and Etienne Wenger focused instead on the variability of social and material conditions underlying scientific production (Latour and Woolgar 1986; Wenger 2010; Kuhn 2012). Latour in particular was sensitive to the social and material implications of the changing epistemological foundations of scientific research that the Republic of Letters embodied. Wenger shifted the analytic lens from an idealized community of openness to a pragmatic community of shared practice. One implication of this study is that researchers using the knowledge commons framework should excavate shared knowledge resources down to the level of the mind of the individual researcher. The work of Kuhn, Latour, and Wenger offers different ways to link the results of that excavation to the specifics of scientific practice. Science may be normatively public, but the idea of the private is embodied in multiple models of scientific behavior. Further research may disclose others, in the new light of knowledge commons.

6.5.3 *Open Science Reconsidered*

A final implication of the study of the Republic of Letters builds on that note about the changing embodiments of public and private interests in scientific knowledge commons. Open science, the modern combination of technologies, funding strategies, and publication systems in which the chapter situated its interest in the Republic of Letters, is likewise concerned with appropriate blends of public and private interests. An implication of the present work is that the contemporary meanings and significance of those terms may differ from their importance historically. The practical embodiments operate at both explicit and tacit layers and polycentric organizational and institutional settings.

To modern ears, the interwoven ideas of public and private often connote sectoral settings. Public interest is identified with the state, and with the intuition that the institutions of the state are designed to enact and support the interests of the public as a whole, as a collective. Private interest and private actors are non-state-related. They draw their foundations and legitimacy from law, either as entities or as individuals, but law codifies their capacity for acting as they wish, for their own benefit or for others'. The modern concept of privacy enforces a set of norms that partly protects the second group of interests (private actors) from overreaching by the first (the state, and the collective) and that partly protects members of the second group from overreaching by other members.

As applied to modern knowledge and information production, that syntax is often translated concretely into a set of specific concerns relevant to governance questions. Those questions include the extent to which knowledge and information resources should be governed as private resources or private goods: patents, or copyrights. Open means public, and public means open, and idealized. Private means the market, and privacy as such means personal. Each governance strategy, whether public or private, may be understood in relation to corresponding social dilemmas.

The implications of the study of the Republic of Letters, drawing on the summary earlier of Kant's writing about science and public and private uses of reason, is that this syntax and the accompanying concepts and practices are, like the material conditions of scientific practice, porous and changeable. The immaterial goals and values of science may change with the organizational settings of science but not necessarily at the same pace or in the same direction. The question for open science today is in part the boundary between presumptively open scientific research shared in the research setting, and presumptively private scientific research disclosed via systems of exclusive right – technology transfer practices, encoding patent law and market expectations. Can open science move that boundary more in the direction of public and open access and impact? In part that is a question of materiality and organizational design. The Republic of Letters suggests that it is also a question of immateriality and the syntax of shared values.

The Republic of Letters operated as a set of norms pulling scientific knowledge out of the mind, the library, and the laboratory and into a shared collective setting. Kant (and later Habermas) called this practice the "public" use of reason. Patent law, today, is the counterpart institution, "pulling" scientific research out of the university laboratory and into the marketplace (Frischmann 2009). The "pull" is from the construct that today we call public to the construct that today we call private. These are different governance systems relating to overlapping but distinct social dilemmas.

Fully modernizing the material and conceptual apparatus of scientific research to achieve the hoped-for benefits of open science suggests recasting at least some of those public and private constructs. One possible pathway forward is recalibrating the conceptual foundations of the major organizations of scientific research – research universities themselves – as to both the social dilemmas they embody and the governance strategies they advance. As universities have matured over the last 100 years, and especially since World War II, they have gotten ever more enmeshed in the rhetoric and practice of intellectual property as a governance solution to one set of university-related social dilemmas – to wit, how to maximize the social benefit associated with university-based scientific research funded by the public sector?

That boundary between public and private, in short, is defined today by a governance solution (intellectual property) to a social dilemma (public access to scientific research results). That solution has become the very thing that some argue needs to be displaced, going forward, to realize the ambitions of open science (Madison 2019). A governance strategy that addressed one social dilemma has generated another social dilemma. The system is, in a word, dynamic. The implication of the present study is not that open science justifies a return to the conceptual framework observed beneath the Republic of Letters, let alone to Kant, or Habermas. Instead, the implication is this: the way forward need not depend on the terms on which the social dilemmas of research science have proceeded historically. The concepts of publicness, private interest, and privacy are tools with which the resources, collectives, and rules of governance may be both stabilized and reconstituted in new material settings. One scholar describing the potential for economic impact associated with twenty-first century science refers to the enterprise as the "new invisible college," explicitly invoking a metaphor for scientific collaboration that may have predated the Republic of Letters (Wagner 2008). In open science, analysis and advocacy should focus on the character of relevant governance relationships and on boundary construction and boundary management – what is inside and what is outside; how different governance institutions are linked to one another; what (and who) is infrastructure and what is application – rather than solely on the science itself, as an object. Governance may produce publicness and privateness, not simply manage them.

6.6 CONCLUSION

This chapter has extended the knowledge commons research framework to an early historical case of scientific research: the Republic of Letters, an extended communications network of scientists that flourished across Europe in the sixteenth, seventeenth, and eighteenth centuries. The defining character of the Republic was its normative emphasis on public dissemination of scientific knowledge via both formal and informal communications networks, including circulation of books and letters, the production of early scientific journals, and face to face conversation.

The chapter draws particular attention to the role of private interests and private research in the production of the Republic's shared publicness and collective of scientific knowledge. The Republic of Letters was characterized by early forms of the personal and private reason at the level of and in the mind of the individual scientist, which had to be shared via communications and communication networks to form the publicly shared epistemological infrastructure of modern science. The chapter links those practices to Kantian philosophy, which explains the significance of shared private contributions and private reason in the context of community-based scientific knowledge governance.

The concept of private reason as a shareable knowledge resource in knowledge commons terms is new. For modern scientific knowledge production, which is concerned in many respects with the concept of open science, the chapter suggests that attention to openness must always be tempered by the fact that openness may depend on critical if sometimes concealed personal and private resources.

REFERENCES

Anderson, Benedict R. O'G. 1983. *Imagined Communities: Reflections on the Origin and Spread of Nationalism*. London: Verso.

Atkinson, Dwight. 1999. *Scientific Discourse in Sociohistorical Context: The Philosophical Transactions of the Royal Society of London, 1675–1975*. Rhetoric, Knowledge, and Society. Mahwah, NJ: L. Erlbaum Associates.

Baldwin, Melinda. 2017. "In Referees We Trust?" *Physics Today* 70 (2): 44–49. https://doi.org/10.1063/PT.3.3463.

2018. "Scientific Autonomy, Public Accountability, and the Rise of 'Peer Review' in the Cold War United States." *Isis* 109 (3): 538–558. https://doi.org/10.1086/700070.

Benkler, Yochai. 2017. "Law, Innovation, and Collaboration in Networked Economy and Society." *Annual Review of Law and Social Science* 13 (1): 231–250. https://doi.org/10.1146/annurev-lawsocsci-110316-113340.

Biagioli, Mario. 1989. "The Social Status of Italian Mathematicians, 1450–1600." *History of Science* 27 (1): 41–95. https://doi.org/10.1177/007327538902700102.

1990. "Galileo's System of Patronage." *History of Science* 28 (1): 1–62. https://doi.org/10.1177/007327539002800101.

Blair, Ann. 2010. *Too Much to Know: Managing Scholarly Information before the Modern Age*. New Haven: Yale University Press.

Borgman, Christine L. 2015. *Big Data, Little Data, No Data: Scholarship in the Networked World*. Cambridge, MA: MIT Press.

Brockliss, L. W. B. 2002. *Calvet's Web: Enlightenment and the Republic of Letters in Eighteenth-Century France*. Oxford: Oxford University Press.

Brown, John Seely and Paul Duguid. 1991. "Organizational Learning and Communities-of-Practice: Toward a Unified View of Working, Learning, and Innovation." *Organization Science* 2 (1): 40–57. https://doi.org/10.1287/orsc.2.1.40.

2000. *The Social Life of Information*. Boston: Harvard Business School Press.

Burke, Peter. 2012. "The Republic of Letters as a Communication System." *Media History* 18 (3–4): 395–407. https://doi.org/10.1080/13688804.2012.721956.

Chartier, Roger. 1991. *The Cultural Origins of the French Revolution*. Translated by Lydia G. Cochrane. Durham: Duke University Press.

Darling, Kate and Aaron Perzanowski, eds. 2017. *Creativity without Law: Challenging the Assumptions of Intellectual Property*. New York: NYU Press.

Darnton, Robert. 2003. *George Washington's False Teeth: An Unconventional Guide to the Eighteenth Century*. New York: W. W. Norton & Co.

Daston, Lorraine. 1991. "The Ideal and Reality of the Republic of Letters in the Enlightenment." *Science in Context* 4 (2): 367–386. https://doi.org/10.1017/S0269889700001010.

1994. "Baconian Facts, Academic Civility, and the Prehistory of Objectivity." In *Rethinking Objectivity*, edited by Allan Megill, 37–64. Durham: Duke University Press.

David, Paul. 2008. "The Historical Origins of 'Open Science': An Essay on Patronage, Reputation and Common Agency Contracting in the Scientific Revolution." *Capitalism and Society* 3 (February): 5–5. https://doi.org/10.2202/1932–0213.1040.

David, Paul, Matthijs den Besten, and Ralph Schroeder. 2008. "Will E-Science Be Open Science?" SIEPR Discussion Paper No. 08–10. https://siepr.stanford.edu/research/publications/will-e-science-be-open-science.

Dear, Peter. 1992. "From Truth to Disinterestedness in the Seventeenth Century." *Social Studies of Science* 22 (4): 619–631.

DiMaggio, Paul and Walter W. Powell. 1983. "'The Iron Cage Revisited': Institutional Isomorphism and Collective Rationality in Organizational Fields." *American Sociological Review* 48: 147–160.

Duguid, Paul. 2005. "'The Art of Knowing': Social and Tacit Dimensions of Knowledge and the Limits of the Community of Practice." *The Information Society* 21 (2): 109–118. https://doi.org/10.1080/01972240590925311.

Eamon, William. 1996. *Science and the Secrets of Nature: Books of Secrets in Medieval and Early Modern Culture*. Princeton: Princeton University Press.

Eden, Kathy. 2001. *Friends Hold All Things in Common: Tradition, Intellectual Property, and the Adages of Erasmus*. New Haven: Yale University Press.

Frischmann, Brett M. 2009. "The Pull of Patents." *Fordham Law Review* 77 (5): 2143–2167.

2012. *Infrastructure: The Social Value of Shared Resources*. New York: Oxford University Press.

Frischmann, Brett M., Michael J. Madison, and Katherine J. Strandburg. 2014a. "Governing Knowledge Commons." In *Governing Knowledge Commons*, edited by Brett

M. Frischmann, Michael J. Madison, and Katherine J. Strandburg, 1–43. New York: Oxford University Press.

Frischmann, Brett M., Michael J. Madison, and Katherine J. Strandburg, eds. 2014b. *Governing Knowledge Commons*. Oxford; New York: Oxford University Press.

Fumaroli, Marc. 1988. "The Republic of Letters." *Diogenes* 36 (143): 129–152. https://doi.org/10.1177/039219218803614307.

2018. *The Republic of Letters*. Translated by Lara Vergnaud. New Haven: Yale University Press.

Gay, Peter. 1966. *The Enlightenment: An Interpretation. Volume 2: The Science of Freedom*. New York: W W Norton & Co.

Geison, Gerald L. 2014. *Private Science of Louis Pasteur*. Princeton: Princeton University Press.

Goldgar, Anne. 1995. *Impolite Learning: Conduct and Community in the Republic of Letters, 1680–1750*. New Haven: Yale University Press.

Goodman, Dena. 1996. *The Republic of Letters: A Cultural History of the French Enlightenment*. Ithaca: Cornell University Press.

Grafton, Anthony. 2008. "A Sketch Map of a Lost Continent: The Republic of Letters." *Republics of Letters* 1 (1). https://arcade.stanford.edu/rofl/sketch-map-lost-continent-republic-letters.

2009. *Worlds Made by Words: Scholarship and Community in the Modern West*. Cambridge: Harvard University Press.

Greif, Avner and Joel Mokyr. 2016. "Cognitive Rules, Institutions, and Economic Growth: Douglass North and Beyond." *Journal of Institutional Economics* 13 (1): 25–52. https://doi.org/10.1017/S1744137416000370.

Habermas, Jürgen. 1989 [1962]. *The Structural Transformation of the Public Sphere: An Inquiry into a Category of Bourgeois Society*. Translated by Thomas Burger. Cambridge: The MIT Press.

Hindley, Meredith. 2013. "Mapping the Republic of Letters." *Humanities* 34 (6). www.neh.gov/humanities/2013/novemberdecember/feature/mapping-the-republic-letters.

Hutchins, Edwin. 2000. *Cognition in the Wild*. Cambridge: The MIT Press.

Jacob, Margaret C. 1997. *Scientific Culture and the Making of the Industrial West*. New York: Oxford University Press.

Johns, Adrian. 2009. *Piracy: The Intellectual Property Wars from Gutenberg to Gates*. Chicago: University of Chicago Press.

Kant, Immanuel. 1996 [1784]. "What Is Enlightenment?" In *What Is Enlightenment? Eighteenth-Century Answers and Twentieth Century Questions*, edited by James Schmidt. 58–64. Berkeley: University of California Press.

Kelty, Christopher M. 2008. *Two Bits: The Cultural Significance of Free Software*. Experimental Futures. Durham: Duke University Press.

Knorr-Cetina, K. 1999. *Epistemic Cultures: How the Sciences Make Knowledge*. Cambridge: Harvard University Press.

Kuchar, Pavel and Erwin Dekker. Forthcoming. "Governing Markets as Knowledge Commons: Introduction." In *Governing Markets as Knowledge Commons*. Cambridge: Cambridge University Press.

Kuhn, Thomas S. 2012 [1962]. *The Structure of Scientific Revolutions*. 4th ed. Chicago, IL: University of Chicago Press.

Latour, Bruno. 1986. "Visualization and Cognition: Thinking with Eyes and Hands." In *Knowledge and Society: Studies in the Sociology of Culture Past and Present:*

A *Research Annual*, edited by Elizabeth Long and Henrika Kuklick, 6:1–49. Greenwich, CT: JAI Press.

Latour, Bruno and Steve Woolgar. 1986. *Laboratory Life: The Construction of Scientific Facts*. Princeton: Princeton University Press.

Long, Pamela O. 1991. "Invention, Authorship, 'Intellectual Property,' and the Origin of Patents: Notes toward a Conceptual History." *Technology and Culture* 32 (4): 846–84. https://doi.org/10.2307/3106154.

Maclean, Ian. 2008. "The Medical Republic of Letters before the Thirty Years War." *Intellectual History Review* 18 (1): 15–30. https://doi.org/10.1080/17496970701819327.

Madison, Michael J. 2014. "Commons at the Intersection of Peer Production, Citizen Science, and Big Data: Galaxy Zoo." In *Governing Knowledge Commons*, edited by Brett M. Frischmann, Michael J. Madison, and Katherine J. Strandburg, 209–254. New York: Oxford University Press.

2019. "Data Governance and the Emerging University." In *Research Handbook on Intellectual Property and Technology Transfer*, edited by Jacob H. Rooksby, 364–390. Cheltenham, UK: Edward Elgar Publishers.

Madison, Michael J., Brett M. Frischmann, and Katherine J. Strandburg. 2009. "The University as Constructed Cultural Commons." *Washington University Journal of Law and Policy* 30: 365–403.

2010. "Constructing Commons in the Cultural Environment." *Cornell Law Review* 95 (4): 657–709.

Margócsy, Dániel. 2017. "A Long History of Breakdowns: A Historiographical Review." *Social Studies of Science* 47 (3): 307–325. https://doi.org/10.1177/0306312717706559.

Merton, Robert K. 1938. "Science and the Social Order." *Philosophy of Science* 5 (3): 321–337.

Merton, Robert K. 1942. "Science and Technology in a Democratic Order." *Journal of Legal and Political Sociology* 1: 115–126.

1957. "Priorities in Scientific Discovery: A Chapter in the Sociology of Science." *American Sociological Review* 22 (6): 635–659.

Miert, Dirk van, ed. 2013. *Communicating Observations in Early Modern Letters (1500–1675): Epistolography and Epistemology in the Age of the Scientific Revolution*. London: Warburg Institute.

Miert, Dirk van. 2016. "What Was the Republic of Letters? A Brief Introduction to a Long History." *Groniek*, 204 (5): 269–287. https://ugp.rug.nl/groniek/article/view/27601.

Mokyr, Joel. 2011–2012. "The Commons of Knowledge: A Historical Perspective." *The Annual Proceedings of the Wealth and Well-Being of Nations* IV: 16.

2017. *A Culture of Growth: The Origins of the Modern Economy*. Princeton: Princeton University Press.

National Academies of Sciences, Engineering, and Medicine (U.S.), National Academies of Sciences, Engineering, and Medicine (U.S.), National Academies of Sciences, Engineering, and Medicine (U.S.), and National Academies of Sciences, Engineering, and Medicine (U.S.), eds. 2018. *Open Science by Design: Realizing a Vision for 21st Century Research*. A Consensus Study Report. Washington, DC: The National Academies Press.

North, Douglass C. 1990. *Institutions, Institutional Change, and Economic Performance*. Cambridge: Cambridge University Press.

Oliar, Dotan and Christopher Sprigman. 2008. "There's No Free Laugh (Anymore): The Emergence of Intellectual Property Norms and the Transformation of Stand-up Comedy." *Virginia Law Review* 94 (8): 1787–1867.

Ostrom, Elinor. 1990. *Governing the Commons: The Evolution of Institutions for Collective Action*. Cambridge: Cambridge University Press.

Padgett, John Frederick and Walter W Powell. 2017. *The Emergence of Organizations and Markets*. http://dx.doi.org/10.23943/princeton/9780691148670.001.0001.

Pal, Carol. 2012. *Republic of Women: Rethinking the Republic of Letters in the Seventeenth Century*. Cambridge: Cambridge University Press.

Polanyi, Michael. 1962. "The Republic of Science: Its Political and Economic Theory." *Minerva* 1 (1): 54–73.

Polanyi, Michael. 1966. *The Tacit Dimension*. Chicago: University of Chicago Press.

Porter, Theodore M. 1996. *Trust in Numbers: The Pursuit of Objectivity in Science and Public Life*. Princeton: Princeton University Press.

Powell, Walter W. 1990. "Neither Market nor Hierarchy: Network Forms of Organization." *Research in Organizational Behavior* 12: 295–336.

Rose, Carol M. 1986. "The Comedy of the Commons: Commerce, Custom, and Inherently Public Property." *University of Chicago Law Review* 53 (3): 711–781.

Royal Society (Great Britain), Science Policy Centre, and Royal Society (Great Britain). 2012. *Science as an Open Enterprise*. https://royalsociety.org/~/media/royal_society_content/policy/projects/sape/2012-06-20-saoe.pdf.

Schweik, Charles M. and Robert C. English. 2012. *Internet Success: A Study of Open-Source Software Commons*. Cambridge: The MIT Press.

Shapiro, Martin. 1972. "Toward a Theory of Stare Decisis." *Journal of Legal Studies* 1 (1): 125–34.

Spender, J. C. 1996. "Making Knowledge the Basis of a Dynamic Theory of the Firm." *Strategic Management Journal* 17 (S2): 45–62. https://doi.org/10.1002/smj.4250171106.

Stewart, Larry. 1992. *The Rise of Public Science: Rhetoric, Technology, and Natural Philosophy in Newtonian Britain, 1660–1750*. Cambridge: Cambridge University Press.

Stokes, Donald E. 2011. *Pasteur's Quadrant: Basic Science and Technological Innovation*. Washington, DC: Brookings Institution Press.

Strathern, Marilyn. 1996. "Cutting the Network." *The Journal of the Royal Anthropological Institute* 2 (3): 517–35.

Wagner, Caroline S. 2008. *The New Invisible College: Science for Development*. Washington, DC: Brookings Institution Press.

Wenger, Etienne. 2010. "Communities of Practice and Social Learning Systems: The Career of a Concept." In *Social Learning Systems and Communities of Practice*, edited by Chris Blackmore, 179–98. London: Springer London. https://doi.org/10.1007/978-1-84996-133-2_11.

Westfall, Richard S. 1977. *The Construction of Modern Science: Mechanisms and Mechanics*. Cambridge: Cambridge University Press.

Zuckerman, Harriet and Robert K. Merton. 1971. "Patterns of Evaluation in Science: Institutionalisation, Structure and Functions of the Referee System." *Minerva* 9 (1): 66–100. https://doi.org/10.1007/BF01553188.

7

Privacy and Knowledge Production Across Contexts

Brett M. Frischmann,[1] *Katherine Haenschen,*[2] *and Ari Ezra Waldman*[3]

In his seminal article, *The Sociology of Secrecy and of Secret Societies*, Georg Simmel (1906) argued that secrecy is a "universal sociological form" defined by hiding something in certain contexts (p. 463). Although secrecy can constitute a barrier between people, separating those who know the secret from those who don't, secrecy within a social space binds people together; secrecy in this context "determines the reciprocal relations of those who possess the secret in common" (p. 470). Those relations are often governed by rules that protect the secret, whether that is a Masonic rite, a pledge at an Alcoholics Anonymous meeting, a provision in a contract, or a norm developed over time. In other words, far from stifling conversation, social interaction, and sharing, formal and informal rules about secrecy, privacy, and information dissemination actually allow social groups to share information among their members, contributing to social solidarity, cohesion, and even knowledge production.

This chapter begins where Simmel and many other social and legal scholars left off. In contrast to many traditional theories of privacy (Westin 1967; Inness 1992; Rosen 2000), we argue, as one of us has argued before, that privacy rules and norms are essential to social interaction and generativity (Waldman 2018). Through primary source research, we suggest that the rules and norms governing information privacy in three knowledge creation contexts – Chatham House, Gordon Research Conferences ("GRC"), and the Broadband Internet Technical Advisory Group ("BITAG") – are

1 Charles Widger Endowed University Professor in Law, Business and Economics, Villanova University, Charles Widger School of Law; Affiliated Faculty, The Vincent and Elinor Ostrom Workshop in Political Theory and Policy Analysis, Indiana University Bloomington; Affiliate Scholar, Center for Internet and Society, Stanford Law School; Affiliate of the Princeton Dialogues on AI and Ethics, Princeton University; Trustee, Nexa Center for Internet & Society, Politecnico di Torino. J.D. Georgetown University Law Center; M.S., Columbia University; B.A., Columbia University.

2 Assistant Professor, Department of Communication Studies and Political Science, Northeastern University. Ph.D., University of Texas at Austin; M.A., University of Chicago; B.A., Columbia University.

3 Professor of Law and Founding Director, Innovation Center for Law and Technology, New York Law School; Microsoft Visiting Professor of Information Technology Policy, Princeton University, Center for Information Technology Policy; Affiliate Fellow, Yale Law School Information Society Project. Ph.D., sociology, Columbia University; J.D., Harvard Law School; A.B., Harvard College.

necessary to develop the kind of trust that is essential for sharing ideas, secrets, and other information. More specifically, when it is part of institutional structures governing knowledge commons, privacy fosters knowledge through a systematic social process. Privacy rules have *expressive effects* that embed confidentiality norms in the background of institutional participation, which in turn create a sense of *community* among participants that can both bring in new members and threaten *sanctions* for misbehavior. Knowledge production, therefore, depends on privacy.

7.1 COMMONS, KNOWLEDGE PRODUCTION, AND PRIVACY

This chapter builds on some of our previous work. Madison, Frischmann, and Strandburg (2010a, 2010b) and Frischmann, Madison, and Strandburg (2014), for example, describe the knowledge commons framework. *Commons*, they note, refers to an institutional arrangement governing resources, whatever they may be, among a group of people. In addition to being both a form of governance and a social construct, the "basic characteristic that distinguishes commons from noncommons is institutionalized sharing of resources among members of a community" (Madison, Frischmann, and Strandburg 2010b, 841). That is, the goal of commons governance is to devise a way to share resources despite endogenous (e.g., diminishing resources) and exogenous (e.g., political pressure) obstacles.

Knowledge, one of the resources governed within the commons, is a broad term, encompassing the "various cultural, intellectual, scientific, and social resources (and resource systems) that we inherit, use, experience, interact with, change, and pass on to future generations" (Frischmann, Madison, and Strandburg 2014, 2–3). Whether these are norms of interaction, cultural artifacts, or art, knowledge refers to the full range of socially constructed pieces of information constituting human social experience. Knowledge *production*, then, is the social process in which information is shared and added to our collective consciousness. Knowledge production can be the development of new ideas for research, new cultural or artistic contributions, new processes or systems, and so on. Together, *knowledge commons* captures the "institutionalized community governance of the sharing and, in some cases, creation, of information," broadly defined (p. 3).

Privacy is part of that community governance and we argue that it plays a critical role in knowledge production (Sanfilippo, Frischmann, and Strandburg 2018). Understanding what we mean by *privacy*, then, is critical. There is a long tradition of social scientists, lawyers, philosophers, economists, and other scholars trying to develop a singular definition of privacy (Warren and Brandeis 1890; White 1951; Blaustein 1964; Westin 1967; Gerety 1977; Gavison 1980; Bok 1983; Reiman 1984; Innes 1992; Rosen 2000). There is also a growing group of researchers eschewing that approach (Solove 2002; Nissenbaum 2009) and recognizing how privacy can be generative (Richards 2015; Waldman 2018). But many scholars have defined privacy in terms of separating, hiding, or staking out autonomy from society (Waldman 2018,

13–33). We resist that conceptualization. In previous work, Waldman defined privacy as a social structure governing information sharing (p. 67). Similarly, Sanfilippo, Frischmann, and Strandburg (2018) conceptualize "privacy as information flow rules-in-use constructed within a commons governance arrangement." It may sound strange to talk about privacy from a social perspective. But privacy presumes that we exist in both formal and information relationships with others; privacy only matters when we share within those relationships. When making sharing decisions, we rely on and develop expectations about what should happen with our information based on the contexts in which we share, thus integrating privacy into our lives relative to other people. As Post (1989) has noted, privacy norms "rest[] not upon a perceived opposition between persons and social life, but rather upon their interdependence" (p. 959). Privacy, then, is socially situated; it is about the social relationships governing disclosure between and among individuals.

Those relationships are based on trust, or lack thereof. Trust is a "resource of social capital between or among two or more persons concerning the expectations that others will behave according to expected norms" (Waldman 2018, 51). Social capital is the advantages and benefits that accrue to individuals in a community by virtue of their connected status (Putnam 1997). For example, teams of coworkers can be more productive by learning from each other and relying on each team member's particular expertise. Scholars, physicians, lawyers, compliance professionals, technologists, and other elite professionals can learn from each other at workshops and conferences. Unionized workers can exercise greater leverage over their working conditions and contract terms than isolated laborers. Different countries can realize economic, political, military, and cultural benefits from cooperation. In all of these examples, social capital refers to the good things that develop out of our interactions with others.

Trust is one of those good things, and an essential part of the social structure created by privacy governance. Trust is the "favorable expectation regarding other people's actions and intentions," or the belief that others will behave in predictable manners according to accepted contextual norms (Möllering 2001, 404). In the information context, those norms are usually confidentiality and discretion. For example, if we ask a friend to hold our spare set of keys, we trust she will not break in and steal from us. When an individual speaks with relative strangers in a support group like Alcoholics Anonymous, she trusts that they will not divulge her secrets. Trust, therefore, includes a willingness to accept some risk and vulnerability toward others and steps in to grease the wheels of social activity in the absence of perfect knowledge. We cannot know for certain that our neighbor will not abuse her key privileges or that our fellow support group members will keep our confidences.

Trust, like other norms of social life, can develop hierarchically from above or organically from below. For example, legal rules can influence norms of behavior through the law's expressive power (Citron 2009; Hellman 2000). Fiduciary laws, medical malpractice law, and legally enforced canons of ethics are just three of the myriad rules and private ordering schemes that support trust norms. Private ordering can achieve the same end, like when organizations establish rules of conduct, prohibit harassment, and create privacy protocols. From below, experience or explicit or implicit social cues develop trust. Experience gives us more data from which to judge the trustworthiness of others: keeping a friend's confidences for ten years gives them a stronger basis for trust than doing so for a single day. Explicit ("This is between us") and implicit cues (physically turning away from a crowd, huddling down, whispering) can also generate expectations of trust (Goffman 1966). As can reciprocity, that is, mutual sharing, which establishes mutual vulnerability (Buchan, Croson, and Dawes 2002) and helps generate mutual feelings of cooperation and altruism (Fukuyama 2001). Cues also allow us to trust strangers. For example, two people who share a stigmatizing social identity often create an instant bond of trust based on a shared set of narratives and experiences (Williams 2001). And we are more willing to interact with others the more embedded they are in a familiar social network, even if we don't know them (Granovetter 1985). As Niklas Luhmann (1979) has stated, trust begins where knowledge ends. As such, trust allows us to interact with and rely on others.

7.2 CASE STUDIES

In this way, privacy governance contributes to knowledge production in institutional contexts by greasing the wheels of disclosure and social interaction. Privacy rules define the terms and expectations of information sharing and express the norms of trust for a given community. That community then internalizes those privacy rules and expectations of trust to ensure ongoing compliance by bringing in new members to an environment where privacy is a social fact (Durkheim 1895/1982) and leveraging the threat of formal and informal sanctions for breaches. That social process helps develop new ideas, new knowledge, and new culture.

To illustrate this process and its role in knowledge creation, we rely on primary source research, including interviews with leaders and participants, to describe three different information sharing contexts that have associational rules and norms that govern disclosure.[4] First, Chatham House has an eponymous non-attribution rule widely used in meetings to facilitate open dialogue. The rule restricts the dissemination of identity and affiliation information, but does not govern what participants can do with the content of communications. Second, GRCs follow a well-known set of nondisclosure and nonuse rules designed to enable researchers to come together and present their cutting-edge data without fear of being scooped. Third, the BITAG has adopted privacy and intellectual property rules that allow their expert participants to come together, hash out their ideas and points of contention, and develop

[4] In line with past GKC case studies, we conducted semi-structured interviews using the GKC framework to organize questions. In this chapter, we report on the privacy rules directly focused on appropriate information flows within and beyond the community and context.

technical advisory reports for industry and government. In all three of these case studies, privacy governance builds the trust necessary for knowledge production.

7.2.1 *Chatham House*

British and American delegates to the Paris Peace Conference after World War I originally conceived of what would become Chatham House as a community of cross-Atlantic experts "to study international problems with a view to preventing future wars." Then called the British Institute of Foreign Affairs, the think tank moved to Chatham House in 1923 and received its official Royal Charter in 1926. To this day, it remains a locus of expert discussions and global problem solving in foreign affairs, economic progress, and sustainability (Chatham House, History). Despite its participation in many of the most important worldwide debates in the last century, the community is primarily known for one thing: the Chatham House Rule.

The Chatham House Rule ("Rule") is a simple rule of non-attribution used far beyond the confines of the Chatham House itself. The Rule reads as follows:

> When a meeting, or part thereof, is held under the Chatham House Rule, participants are free to use the information received, but neither the identity nor the affiliation of the speaker(s), nor that of any other participant, may be revealed (Chatham House, About, Chatham House Rule).

The Rule allows "people to speak as individuals, and to express views that may not be those of their organizations." Therefore, the Rule "encourages free discussion" (Chatham House Rule FAQ) and knowledge production by establishing dissemination rules and norms of a given context, creating a sense of community around those rules, and threatening sanctions for violators. And the Rule can be modified in any given circumstance to fit the needs of a particular environment, thus providing the flexibility needed for knowledge production in different settings (Burnett Interview).

Keith Burnett, the Director of Communications and Publications at Chatham House, explains that the Rule sets the terms for information flow. Any event, meeting, or discussion governed by the Rule would either begin with an acknowledgment that the Rule applies – "This meeting is governed by Chatham House Rule" – or participants "would know in the invitation" to the event. Laying out the ground rule at the beginning has several important effects, according to Burnett. First, it lets meeting participants set their expectations for the shelf life, if any, of their statements during the event. Burnett noted, for example, that "whoever is running the meeting could take away some information and use it" to write a report or address some ongoing problem. Participants come into the meeting knowing this and can calibrate their participation accordingly. Second, the Rule encourages free flow of ideas by protecting participants from any negative effects of open sharing. The Rule is "there to help people share information that they learn in the meeting" without having to "worry about attribution" and any retribution that can result. Third, it prioritizes ideas and solutions over people and egos. Chatham House was established to solve important and vexing problems of international affairs, so sharing ideas is essential: "the idea is to free people up [to speak], free people up to feel that the ideas are more important than the individuals sharing them." Finally, putting everyone on the same page with respect to information use immediately creates a sense of mutual trust among participants; there is, at least, an initial expectation that participants will behave according to the norms set out by the Rule (Waldman 2018; 52–54). Chatham House itself makes this connection between the Rule and trust, noting that "the rigorous implementation of the Rule is crucial to its effectiveness and for Chatham House's reputation as a trusted venue for open and free dialogue" (Chatham House Rule FAQ).

The Chatham House Rule, then, reflects the contextual nature of information flow. Like the American sociologist Erving Goffman (1959), who explained that differences in social behavior and information disclosure often depend on the rules and expectations associated with different contexts, the Chatham House Rule creates contexts conducive to free discussion. Goffman suggested that social life can be divided into "front" and "back" stages, like a play, with different forms of social interaction happening in each. In front, like in the dining room of a fancy restaurant, servers interact with patrons formally, conversation is restricted to business, and behaviors are constrained by strict rules. In back, like in a kitchen out of view of paying customers, servers can let their hair down, curse, talk about their lives, and behave more informally among their colleagues. There are many front and back stages: work/home, professional/social interactions, when the kids are awake/after bedtime, and so forth. Each context maintains different rules and expectations, which permit or constrain social behavior accordingly. As Julie Cohen (2000) has noted, this account of social behavior is not really about hiding from others; rather, it is about establishing the parameters of social space in ways that make continued interaction possible. That is precisely what the Chatham House Rule does, as well. It establishes the parameters of information flow in a meeting governed by the Rule, allowing participants to act more informally, engage more freely, and, hopefully, work more effectively to achieve the meeting's goal. As Burnett notes, the Rule clarifies what is and is not permissible: "the whole purpose of the Rule," Burnett notes, "is to share ideas without identifying the speaker, the source of the information, so if you do anything to identify that person, directly or indirectly, you should avoid it."

Although one has to apply, anyone can join Chatham House in London (Chatham House Individual Membership). For Chatham House events and meetings held under the Chatham House Rule, it is the expressive power of the Rule that creates a sense of community among participants. A meeting governed by the Chatham House Rule immediately binds all participants together in a secret-keeping endeavor (Simmel 1906). This creates a sense of trust among the members of the group that they are all present for the same purpose, on the same terms (Waldman 2018, 52–54). Although Chatham House is a "global community" and that "academics come from all over" to participate, Burnett suggests that the Rule, and the information flow it facilitates, is what matters. That is, it doesn't matter who says what, "the whole point is to come and share knowledge – we share ours, you share yours," and the Rule creates the space for that to happen (Burnett Interview). This is also part of the ethos of meetings run under the Rule, which allows participants new to Chatham House or the Rule to integrate into the community norms rather quickly.

The threat of sanctions also plays that role. Chatham House explains that although its Rule is "not legally binding, Chatham House will take disciplinary action against a member or guest who breaks the Rule," which can mean "exclusion from all institute activities" (Chatham House Rule FAQ). Participants in Chatham House events governed by the Rule also mutually reinforce the Rule. The FAQs and Burnett both note that individuals ask other members if a given example of sharing – on social media or to other people – is permissible, with the overarching response focused on sharing without any kind of attribution. In this way, formal and informal sanction from the governing structure, as well as reinforcing work from other participants, work to ensure the Rule, and the meetings it governs, will achieve their goals.

This discussion suggests that the Chatham House Rule may be an effective form of privacy governance that fosters knowledge production within specific groups. By setting the parameters of information flow, it creates a sense of trust among participants, allowing them to rely on the confidentiality and discretion of a community built around the Rule.

7.2.2 *Gordon Research Conferences*

Like the Chatham House Rule, the Gordon Research Conference is a replicable institutional structure where privacy governance can foster knowledge production. The GRC was started in 1931, when the chemist Neil Gordon brought together scientists to network and share research results at Johns Hopkins University. Since then, the GRCs have grown worldwide, having attracted more than 30,000 participants annually to 300 conferences across the world (Gordon Research Conferences, History of GRC). They are well-regarded, invite-only, and attract what one participant called "the best people" (Sanfilippo Interview). Like Chatham House, GRC integrates a simple privacy rule into institutional governance; unlike Chatham House, its rule is strict confidentiality, not nonattribution. Like most knowledge commons, GRCs depend on other governance strategies beyond the privacy rule. For example, to maintain a close-knit community, each GRC is kept small and focused on a narrow topic at the frontier of the field. Secluded locations are preferred because seclusion is seen as something that helps structure the community, create a forum where people can get together and build relationships and trust, and avoid distractions.

The GRC No Publication Policy ("Policy"), sometimes referred to as the "off-the-record policy," states, in relevant part: "To encourage open communication, each member of a conference agrees that any information presented at a Gordon Research Conference ... is a private communication ... and is presented with the restriction that such information is not for public use." The Policy prohibits audio or video recording and photography. It also prohibits participants from preparing any form of publication based on the conference proceedings. The Policy covers any form of information sharing, including through social media, and covers formal presentations, poster sessions, and even informal discussions and conversations among participants. Yet the Policy is not an absolute prohibition; it vests authority in the individual making a presentation to consent to quotation, publication, recording, or other deviations from the rule: "[Y]ou [must] have the explicit written permission of the person you're planning to quote. So, it's allowable, but it's kind of locked down" (Grannas Interview).

The primary purpose of the Policy is to give participants the confidence that they can share their latest, in-progress research without fear of others taking their ideas and publishing them first (Grannas Interview). Amanda Grannas, Associate Vice Provost for Research and Professor in the Department of Chemistry at Villanova University, explained how at the GRCs, she and other participants presented early stage research, data, and hypotheses without fear of being "scooped" by other participants. Her post-doc advisor had encouraged her to attend her first GRC to present work in progress to receive feedback and network with others. For Grannas, this experience stood in stark contrast to the American Chemical Society national meeting routinely attended by 12,000–15,000 people, where she would not present early work because the risk of being scooped was real. Grannas had been warned and knew of people whose ideas had been taken at the conference. During our interview, she praised GRCs for being a trusted community and forum and emphasized how important it was to be able to present pre-publication research in an environment where the rules facilitated free and constructive feedback on in-progress works.

Therefore, the GRC's No Publication Policy contributes to knowledge production through a social process similar to that of the Chatham House Rule: a clearly defined rule sets participant expectations, building trust through community and the threat of sanctions. And those expectations are communicated to participants clearly and repeatedly up front. According to Grannas, acceptance letters to GRCs state "congratulations, ... here are all kinds of expectations .... It's expected that you're not sharing this information, you're not quoting any of this, you can't refer to anything." The Policy is also on the GRC webpage and conference chairs state the rules at the beginning of the event. "When the group comes together for the first time, there is a welcome from the chair and ... they sa[y] explicitly that you can have a great time at Gordon" and even have a Gordon hashtag on Twitter, "but do not talk about hearing a great talk, . . . do not take a picture of a slide and tweet it or put it on Facebook." There is, then, a real sense in which "what happens at Gordon, stays at Gordon" (Grannas Interview).

The confidentiality policy reinforces a sense of community by relying on participants to enforce it and, as noted earlier, by creating a network of secret-keepers (Simmel 1906), thus creating the trust necessary for open discussion. The GRC Policy "facilitates community" by permitting open "coordination, collaboration, and direction of research" (Sanfilippo Interview). The Policy, in other words, solves a problem particularly salient to academic researchers: "how to facilitate discussion without worrying about people stealing your ideas" (Id.).

When veterans see new participants, "the chain keeps going and norms and rules are passed on" (Grannas Interview). Sometimes this happens explicitly. One participant recalled hearing presenters say, for example, "In the spirit of the GRC, I'm showing you unpublished research," which implies a duty to maintain the speaker's confidentiality (Sanfilippo Interview). Otherwise, participants "learn [the norms] just by observing the practice" (Id.). Participants recognize that GRCs include a relatively "small number of people" where "everybody knows everybody, except for new people coming in and we want to do right by them" (Grannas Interview). GRCs include social events for networking purposes, including group meals, mentorship opportunities, and other "non-sciencey" meet-ups (Id.). These not only promote additional knowledge production but also serve to pass on appropriate expectations of social behavior to the next generation of scholars. Invited attendees are encouraged to bring guests who can participate in daily social activities, but to preserve confidentiality, "guests are not permitted to attend the conference lectures, or poster sessions." (Gordon Research Conferences, Policies; Grannas Interview). As Grannas noted, the GRC has become "more family friendly. They very much lock it down that guests cannot attend the science. Only the scientists are there. And I think that is kind of leading towards the privacy issue. It's easy for someone that isn't as familiar with the expectations to start tweeting about, oh this cool thing that I'm sitting at with my wife or my husband at this thing."

Also like Chatham House, GRCs mostly rely on participants to enforce privacy governance. Participants who notice someone flouting the Policy may "contact the chair and say, 'look, this happened, I don't know what you want to do, but maybe this person shouldn't come back to one of these" (Id.). More commonly, though, the pressure to adhere to GRC confidentiality norms is social and informal. According to Grannas, there is a "level of accountability that, I think, the small nature of the group [provides]. . . . [T]he fact that you're going into it with very explicit goals, it would be very antithetical to then take an idea and go off and scoop or do whatever nefarious thing you're going to do." Violators are "blackballed" in the scientific community if they record, tweet, or scoop. "We would take care of it," Grannas noted, if it actually happened.

Notably, the GRC Policy is different from the Chatham House Rule. The former is a confidentiality requirement, whereas the latter permits disclosure of the substance of discussions just without names and attribution. Although both are privacy governance structures, they serve both overlapping and distinct purposes. The goal of the Chatham House Rule was, from the beginning, to foster open conversation to solve a pressing problem in world affairs. The discussion would inform the meeting's chair, who would likely take what she had learned and incorporate it into public facing reports, recommendations to policymakers, or proposals for peace. The GRC No Publication Policy also fosters conversation and sharing ideas by creating the space necessary for researchers to trust they won't be scooped. Indeed, its expansion over the last few decades is a testament to its success at creating that kind of environment. But the goal of the GRCs is to help participants, not the outside world, learn and receive feedback on their own research projects. As such, different rules regarding dissemination make sense. Both rules, however, leverage the same social process by which privacy governance fosters knowledge production.

7.2.3 *Broadband Internet Technical Advisory Group*

The Broadband Internet Technical Advisory Group (BITAG) was created to bring together technical experts on a voluntary basis to discuss and develop consensus advisory reports on technical operation of the Internet. Here, there is no risk of being scooped, as there is at GRCs. Like the original Chatham House meetings, BITAG members come together to produce a public-facing document. But the need for privacy governance to create open and frank conversation remains; stakeholders and participants come from different sectors, business, and backgrounds, and they are trying to solve potentially contentious technical problems. To do that, members must be free to share inchoate or developing ideas (Richards 2015) and offer suggestions that their employers might oppose. To achieve this goal, BITAG sets out a strict confidentiality rule that leverages the same social process of fostering knowledge production through trust, community, and the threat of sanctions.

The BITAG restricts the dissemination of "all information disclosed by any Participant during any meeting or activity" of the BITAG Technical Working Group or committees ("BITAG information").[5] All such information is considered confidential, and participants agree that they "shall not use any portion of the … information for any purpose except to perform his, her, or its obligation to BITAG" (BITAG Intellectual Property Rights Policy ("IPR Policy") Section 4.1). BITAG also

[5] With the exception of "public information" and "highly confidential information," "all information disclosed by any Participant during any meeting or activity" is classified as BITAG information. See BITAG IPR Policy Sections 4.1, 4.2, and 4.3. Notably, in contrast with the Chatham House rule, public information includes "BITAG and TWG [technical working group] membership rosters" as well as "identities of BITAG's Board, including the identity of Designated Participating Members and their Director Designees, and BITAG's officers and employees." BITAG IPR Policy Section 4.2.

binds itself to not use or disclose confidential information shared during BITAG meetings and working group sessions (Id.). There is some leeway to share information with other BITAG members. Membership in BITAG extends beyond the individuals who participate in meetings to the companies and organizations of which individuals are a part. Thus, for example, if one company's employee attends a BITAG meeting, that employee may disclose BITAG information (but not "highly confidential information"[6]) to other "employees, contractors and agents of" her company, but only if they "agree to maintain the confidentiality of the BITAG Information" (BITAG IPR Policy Section 4).

The BITAG confidentiality rule "helps, especially when there is disagreement" to ensure open and frank discussion. Jason Livingood, Vice President of Technology Policy and Standards at Comcast and a BITAG participant, notes that the point of the rule is to "learn and move forward" together and "talk about things openly." To do that, participants need to know that "there's not going to be any attribution; we're not going to go back to our bosses and say, 'this other guy at this other company said'" something at a BITAG meeting. What's more, BITAG wants to encourage expert participants to speak openly, even if what they say conflicts with their employers' official position. Therefore, the expectation is that conversations "are very private and in particular may surface something about my company's perspective, but I personally disagree with. . . . If someone were to share that, I would be in a lot of hot water professionally" (Id.). In this way, the rule fosters sharing and knowledge production by protecting participants from professional retribution.

To ensure that all participants can operate under the same set of confidentiality expectations, BITAG deploys the same strategy as Chatham House and GRC: event chairs state the rule at the beginning and participants reinforce it over time. At the start of working group sessions, for example, leaders will "go back for the standards . . . [and say,] 'here, just as a reminder, this is how we work, we are not going to tweeting about what we're talking about here to sharing anything we talk about.' Everything is confidential" (Livingood Interview). Throughout the process of working together to achieve some kind of consensus report, "there are reminders, [like,] 'hey, don't share any of this externally. There will be a point in time when we're ready to do that, but it's not right now'" (Id.). This set clear expectations and fosters trust among BITAG working group participants by setting the terms of social

6 An even stricter confidentiality rule applies to "Highly Confidential Information," which "(a) relates to any non-public financial information disclosed by the Member to BITAG and its staff and advisors as part of the membership application process; (b) identifies how any individual TWG Representative voted with respect to a majority opinion in a Report; or (c) is marked by the Member as 'Highly Confidential Information' when disclosing such information to BITAG." BITAG IPR Policy Section 4.3. The first two categories are not surprising or controversial; the last category is open-ended in that it allows Members to attach the label upon disclosure. "BITAG will not use or disclose such Highly Confidential Information to any person except that BITAG may disclose such information to its legal counsel and advisors or to the Board if BITAG legal counsel deems such disclosure necessary to enable BITAG, BITAG staff and the Board to comply with its obligations under the Bylaws, the TWG Governance Manual, these Policies or the Certificate of Incorporation." Id.

interaction and expressing what the organization feel is proper behavior. If participants found out that someone was disclosing the substance of their discussions, members "would be very upset." It would, Livingood noted, "be a real violation of trust."

According to Kaleb Sieh, the Deputy Director and General Counsel of BITAG, Inc., the confidentiality and nondisclosure rules create a community of members: "confidentiality binds the entire organization" because everyone knows that "we only share with people as necessary." BITAG further develops this community sentiment by design, creating working groups and committees that have professional membership requirements. This allows participants to trust that they're getting the best input and advice on their projects (Livingood Interview). Membership rules aim to (i) maintain openness to "both individuals and organizations representing stakeholders from a broad cross-section of the Internet ecosystem" (Seih and Hatfield 2012, 8) while (ii) ensuring technical expertise among the working group participants and (iii) guarding against "forum packing" or other strategic behavior by particular stakeholders. In other words, membership and some associated voting rules aim to maintain the integrity of the community and trust within and from outside the community.

This community takes it upon itself to police and enforce the confidentiality rules, even though there has been little need for enforcement (Livingood Interview). Although individuals and companies can be terminated from BITAG for violating the rules, the most important sanctions are more organic and social: "if they violate the rules, their professional reputation would be shot" (Id.). Individual participants, the scientific experts and engineers, often know (or know of) each other from the broader scientific and technological community or even from other similar working groups or standard setting organizations, such as the Internet Engineering Task Force. While governance rules vary across organizations and contexts, the professional norms and reputations span them (Id.). More importantly, violations of BITAG confidentiality represent breaches in trust (Waldman 2018). As Livingood noted, those who disseminate information are "definitely no longer part of the group. . . . But even other members would make it clear that you can't trust" those who violate the rules. "Not trusting on an individual level is important," and when BITAG members can't trust someone, they are ostracized from the community, even if they're not formally expelled.

7.3 COMPARATIVE ANALYSIS

These organizations and their rules are not identical. Chatham House and BITAG have always been structured to produce outward-facing reports on contentious issues; GRCs provide scholarly feedback to participants only. GRCs and BITAG use strict confidentiality rules; Chatham House created a rule that encourages sharing without attribution. The Chatham House Rule is leveraged by working groups, discussions, and meetings across the world that have nothing to do with the original Chatham House, whereas the GRC No Publication Policy applies to its series of scholarly scientific conferences and BITAG's confidentiality rule applies to its meetings alone. GRCs and BITAG depend on strictly managed membership in groups where relationships are expected to last beyond the duration of a specific meeting; Chatham House membership is open, and the Chatham House Rule can but need not be used in conjunction with membership rules. The differences in institutions reflect different social dilemmas faced in pursuit of shared community objectives (Sanfilippo, Frischmann, and Strandburg 2018).

And yet despite these differences, all three institutions leverage privacy governance to foster knowledge production, and they use the same social process to do it. Their rules give meeting participants the confidence to share sensitive information and engage openly and honestly without fear of retribution or premature public dissemination. This reflects the connection between trust and sharing within a community (Waldman 2018; Sanfilippo, Frischmann, and Strandburg 2018). That is, regardless of any variation in their strength and breadth, the rules generate trust among participants that their colleagues will behave according to the privacy norms established by the rules. This allows members to share sensitive information, whether to improve colleagues' scholarship or solve a vexing problem. As secret keepers pursuing a shared set of objectives or common purpose, participants are bound together in a community and, because the secret defines the boundaries of their community, members have an interest in reinforcing the strength of their privacy rules (Simmel 1906). As such, they mutually reinforce the privacy norms that allow the institutions to persist.

None of the organizations rely on legal enforcement of privacy governance rules. Instead, members leverage the value of the community itself and threat of being removed from it to drive conformity with the norm. Chatham House explicitly states in its FAQ that members or guests who break the rule will likely be excluded from all future events. For GRC, violators can be banned from future events, and other members might go so far as to speak to the offending faculty member's university administrators about the action, causing even greater professional harm. For BITAG members, breaching the confidentiality and intellectual property rules could lead to legal action, but our research suggests that has yet to happen. Breaking the rules would greatly upset the other members, potentially leading to expulsion from the community and reputational consequences that extend into other professional communities. In all instances, it is the threat of shame, the perception that others would look down on an individual for violating the privacy norm, that compels this behavior.

In this way, privacy rules foster knowledge production by socially constructing an environment in which trust gives individuals the confidence and safety to share information. Without the Chatham House Rule, the GRC No Publication Policy, and BITAG's confidentiality rule participants would restrict what they say to guard against personal and professional harm. These rules, then, foster open communication, learning, and new ideas.

7.4 CONCLUSIONS

In this Chapter, we have relied on ethnographic interviews of participants and leaders in three organizations – Chatham House, the Gordon Research Conferences, and the Broadband Internet Technical Advisory Group – to suggest that privacy rules contribute to knowledge production. But although the interviews reinforced evidence from the social science literature on the connection between trust and a propensity to disclose information, ethnographic evidence is necessarily limited. Empirical research can add rigor to the theoretical structure developed here. Scholars can survey participants in meetings governed by the Chatham House Rule, the GRC Policy, and the BITAG confidentiality requirement for self-reported perceptions on the role of privacy governance in knowledge production across contexts. Researchers can also move beyond the narrow confines of the three case studies discussed here to analyze privacy governance in more informal social institutions, including among friends and families, among support group members, and even among strangers. Other questions remain, including the role of formal law in fostering knowledge production and the ways in which privacy may interact with conflicting values like openness and transparency.

REFERENCES

Blaustein, Edward J. "Privacy as an Aspect of Human Dignity: An Answer to Dean Prosser." *New York University Law Review* 39, 962–1007 (1964).

Bok, Sissela. *Secrets: On the Ethics of Concealment and Revelation*. New York: Vintage, 1983.

Broadband Internet Technical Advisory Group, Inc., Intellectual Property Rights Policy, Version 2.0, Adopted: June 28, 2012.

Buchan, Nancy R., Rachel T.A. Croson, and Robyn M. Dawes. "Swift Neighbors and Persistent Strangers: A Cross-Cultural Investigation of Trust and Reciprocity in Social Exchange." *American Journal of Sociology* 108, 168–206 (2002).

Burnett, Keith. Interview. By Brett Frischmann. October 9, 2018.

Chatham House Rule FAQ. *Chatham House: The Royal Institute of International Affairs*. www.chathamhouse.org/chatham-house-rule-faq.

Chatham House Individual Membership. *Chatham House: The Royal Institute of International Affairs*. www.chathamhouse.org/membership/individual-membership.

Citron, Danielle Keats. "Law's Expressive Value in Combatting Cyber Gender Harassment." *Michigan Law Review* 108, 373–415 (2009).

Cohen, Julie E. "Examined Lives: Informational Privacy and the Subject as Object." *Stanford Law Review* 52, 1373–1438 (2000).

Durkheim, Émile. *Les règles de la méthode sociologique*. Translated by Halls, W. D. as *The Rules of Sociological Method*. New York: Free Press, [1895]1982.

Frischmann, Brett M., Michael J. Madison, and Katherine J. Strandburg, eds. *Governing Knowledge Commons*. Oxford, UK: Oxford University Press, 2014.

Fukuyama, Francis. "Differing Disciplinary Perspectives on the Origins of Trust." *Boston University Law Review* 81, 479–494 (2001).
Gavison, Ruth. "Privacy and the Limits of Law." *Yale Law Journal* 898, 421–471 (1980).
Gerety, Tom. "Redefining Privacy." *Harvard Civil Rights-Civil Liberties Law Review* 12, 233–296 (1977).
Goffman, Erving. *Behavior in Public Places: Notes on the Social Organization of Gatherings*. New York: Free Press, 1966.
The Presentation of Self in Everyday Life. New York: Doubleday, 1959.
Grannas, Amanda. Interview. By Brett Frischmann. April 6, 2018.
Granovetter, Mark. "Economic Action and Social Structure: The Problem of Embeddedness." *American Journal of Sociology* 91, 481–510 (1985).
Hellman, Deborah. "The Expressive Dimension of Equal Protection." *Minnesota Law Review* 85, 1–70 (2000).
History. *Chatham House: The Royal Institute of International Affairs*. www.chathamhouse.org/about/history.
History of GRC. *Gordon Research Conference*. www.grc.org/about/history-of-grc/.
Inness, Julie. *Privacy, Intimacy, and Isolation*. Oxford, UK: Oxford University Press, 1992.
Livingood, Jason. Interview. By Brett Frischmann. May 14, 2018.
Luhmann, Niklas. *Trust and Power*. New York: John Wiley and Sons, 1979.
Madison, Michael J., Brett M. Frischmann, and Katherine J. Strandburg. "Constructing Commons in the Cultural Environment." *Cornell Law Review* 95, 657–709 (2010a).
"Reply: The Complexity of Commons." *Cornell Law Review* 95, 839–850 (2010b).
Möllering, Guido. "The Nature of Trust: From Georg Simmel to a Theory of Expectation, Interpretation and Suspension." *Sociology* 35, 403–420 (2001).
Nissenbaum, Helen. *Privacy in Context: Technology, Policy, and the Integrity of Social Life*. Palo Alto, CA: Stanford University Press, 2009.
Policies. *Gordon Research Conference*. www.grc.org/about/grc-policies-and-legal-disclaimers/.
Post, Robert. "The Social Foundations of Privacy: Community and Self in the Common Law Tort." *California Law Review* 77, 957–1010 (1989).
Putnam, Robert. "Democracy in America at Century's End." *Democracy's Victory and Crisis*. Ed. Axel Hadenius. Cambridge, UK: Cambridge University Press, 1997.
Reiman, Jeffrey H. "Privacy, Intimacy and Personhood." *Philosophical Dimensions of Privacy*. Ed. Ferdinand David Schoeman. Cambridge, UK: Cambridge University Press, 1984.
Richards, Neil. *Intellectual Privacy: Rethinking Civil Liberties in the Digital Age*. Oxford, UK: Oxford University Press, 2015.
Rosen, Jeffrey. *The Unwanted Gaze: The Destruction of Privacy in America*. New York: Vintage, 2000.
Sanfilippo, Joseph. Interview. By Brett Frischmann. August 2, 2018.
Sanfilippo, Madelyn Rose, Brett M. Frischman, and Katherine J. Strandburg. "Privacy as Commons: Case Evaluation through the Governing Knowledge Commons Framework." *Journal of Information Policy* 8, 116–166 (2018).
Sieh, Kaleb A. Interview. By Brett Frischmann. January 11, 2019.
Sieh, Kaleb August and Hatfield, Dale N., "The Broadband Internet Technical Advisory Group (BITAG) and Its Role in Internet Governance" (March 31, 2012). 2012 *TPRC*. Available at SSRN: https://ssrn.com/abstract=2032233.
Simmel, Georg. "The Sociology of Secrecy and of Secret Societies." *American Journal of Sociology* 11, 441–498 (1906).
Solove, Daniel J. "Conceptualizing Privacy." *California Law Review* 90, 1087–1155 (2002).

Waldman, Ari Ezra. *Privacy As Trust: Information Privacy for an Information Age*. Cambridge, UK: Cambridge University Press, 2018.
Warren, Samuel and Louis D. Brandeis. "The Right to Privacy." *Harvard Law Review* 4, 193–220 (1890).
Westin, Alan. *Privacy and Freedom*. New York: Ig Publishing, 1967.
White, Howard B. "The Right to Privacy." *Social Research* 18, 171–202 (1951).
Williams, Michele. "In Whom We Trust: Group Membership as an Affective Context for Trust Development." *Academy of Management Review* 26, 377–396 (2001).

PART III

Bringing Information Subjects into Commons Governance

8

Governing the Internet of Everything

Scott J. Shackelford[1]

Since the term was first coined in the late 1990s during a presentation about the benefit of radio-frequency identification (RFID) tags in the retail sector, the "Internet of Things" (IoT) has promised a smart, interconnected global digital ecosystem enabling your toaster to text you when your breakfast is ready, and your sweatshirt to give you status updates during your workout. This rise of "smart products" such as internet-enabled refrigerators and self-driving cars holds the promise to revolutionize business and society. But the smart wave will not stop with stuff owing to related trends such as the "Internet of Bodies" now coming into vogue (Atlantic Council, 2017). It seems that, if anything, humanity is headed toward an "Internet of Everything," which is a term that Cisco helped to pioneer (Evans, 2012).

The Internet of Everything (IoE) takes the notion of IoT a step further by including not only the physical infrastructure of smart devices but also its impacts on people, business, and society. Thus, the IoE may be understood as "the intelligent connection of people, process, data and things[,]" whereas IoT is limited to "the network of physical objects accessed through the Internet" (Banafa, 2016). This broader lens is vital for considering the myriad security and privacy implications of smart devices becoming replete throughout society, and our lives. Other ways to conceptualize the problem abound, such as Bruce Schneier's notion of Internet+, or Eric Schmidt's contention that "the Internet will disappear" given the proliferation of smart devices (Giles, 2018). Regardless, the salient point is that our world is getting more connected, if not smarter, but to date governance regimes have struggled to keep pace with this dynamic rate of innovation.

I thank my wonderful colleagues at the Ostrom Workshop for their suggestions and leadership on the many important topics covered herein, particularly Dan Cole and Mike McGinnis.

[1] Chair, Indiana University-Bloomington Cybersecurity Program; Director, Ostrom Workshop Program on Cybersecurity and Internet Governance; Associate Professor, Indiana University Kelley School of Business. An earlier version of this chapter appeared as Scott J. Shackelford, *Governing the Internet of Everything*, Cardozo Arts & Entertainment Law Journal (2019).

Yet it is an open question whether security and privacy protections can or will scale within this dynamic and complex global digital ecosystem, and whether law and policy can keep up with these developments. As Schneier has argued:

> The point is that innovation in the Internet+ world can kill you. We chill innovation in things like drug development, aircraft design, and nuclear power plants because the cost of getting it wrong is too great. We're past the point where we need to discuss regulation versus no-regulation for connected things; we have to discuss smart regulation versus stupid regulation. (Giles, 2018)

The natural question, then, is whether our approach to governing the IoE is, well, smart? This chapter explores what lessons the Institutional Analysis and Development (IAD) and Governing Knowledge Commons (GKC) frameworks hold for promoting security, and privacy, in an IoE, with special treatment regarding the promise and peril of blockchain technology to build trust in such a massively distributed network. Particular attention is paid to governance gaps in this evolving ecosystem, and what state, federal, and international policies are needed to better address security and privacy failings.

The chapter is structured as follows. It begins by offering an introduction to the IoE for the uninitiated, and continues by applying the IAD and GKC frameworks, emphasizing their application for the IoE. The utility of blockchain technology is next explored to help build trust in distributed systems before summarizing implications for managers and policymakers focusing on the intersection between polycentric governance and cyber peace.

8.1 WELCOME TO THE INTERNET OF EVERYTHING

As ever more stuff – not just computers and smartphones, but thermostats and baby monitors, wristwatches, lightbulbs, doorbells, and even devices implanted in our own bodies – are interconnected, the looming cyber threat can easily get lost in the excitement of lower costs and smarter tech. Indeed, smart devices, purchased for their convenience, are increasingly being used by domestic abusers as a means to harass, monitor, and control their victims (Bowles, 2018). Yet, for all the press that the IoT has received, it remains a topic little understood or appreciated by the public. One 2014 survey, for example, found that fully 87% of respondents had never even heard of the "Internet of Things" (Merriman, 2014). Yet managing the growth of the IoE impacts a diverse set of interests: US national and international security; the competitiveness of firms; global sustainable development; trust in democratic processes; and safeguarding civil rights and liberties in the Information Age.

The potential of IoT tech has arguably only been realized since 2010, and is arguably the result of the confluence of at least three factors: (1) the widespread availability of always-on high-speed Internet connectivity in many parts of the world; (2) faster computational capabilities permitting the real-time analysis of Big Data;

and (3) economies of scale lowering the cost of sensors and chips to manufacturers (Shackelford, 2017). However, the rapid rollout of IoT technologies has not been accompanied by any mitigation of the array of technical vulnerabilities across these devices, highlighting a range of governance gaps that may be filled in reference to the Ostrom Design Principles along with the IAD and GKC frameworks.

8.2 APPLYING THE IAD AND GKC FRAMEWORKS TO THE INTERNET OF EVERYTHING

The animating rationale behind the IAD framework was, quite simply, a lack of shared vocabulary to discuss common governance challenges across a wide range of resource domains and issue areas (Cole, 2014). "Scholars adopting ... [the IAD] framework essentially commit to 'a common set of linguistic elements that can be used to analyze a wide diversity of problems,'" including, potentially, cybersecurity and Internet governance. Without such a framework, according to Professor Dan Cole, confusion is common, such as in defining "resource systems" that can include "information, data, or knowledge" in the intellectual property context, with natural resources (Cole, 2014, 51). In the Internet governance context, similar confusion surrounds core terms such as "cyberspace," "information security," and "cybersecurity (Shackelford, 2014). There are also other more specialized issues to consider, such as defining what constitutes "critical infrastructure," and what if any "due diligence" obligations operators have to protect it from cyber attackers. Similarly, the data underlying these systems is subject to a range of sometimes vying legal protections. As Professor Cole argues, "[t]rade names, trade secrets, fiduciary and other privileged communications, evidence submitted under oath, computer code, and many other types of information and flows are all dealt with in various ways in the legal system" (Cole, 2014, 52).

Although created for a different context, the IAD framework can nevertheless improve our understanding of data governance, identify and better understand problems in various institutional arrangements, and aid in prediction under various alternative institutional scenarios (Cole, 2014). Indeed, Professor Ostrom believed that the IAD framework had wide application, which has been born out given that it is among the most popular institutional frameworks used in a variety of studies, particularly those focused on natural commons. The IAD framework is unpacked in Figure 8.1, and its application to IoE governance is analyzed in turn, after which some areas of convergence and divergence with the GKC framework are highlighted.

It can be difficult to exclude users from networks, especially those with valuable trade secrets, given the extent to which they present enticing targets for both external actors and insider threats. With these distinctions in mind, Professor Brett Frischmann, Michael Madison, and Katherine Strandburg have suggested a revised IAD framework for the knowledge commons reproduced in Figure 8.2.

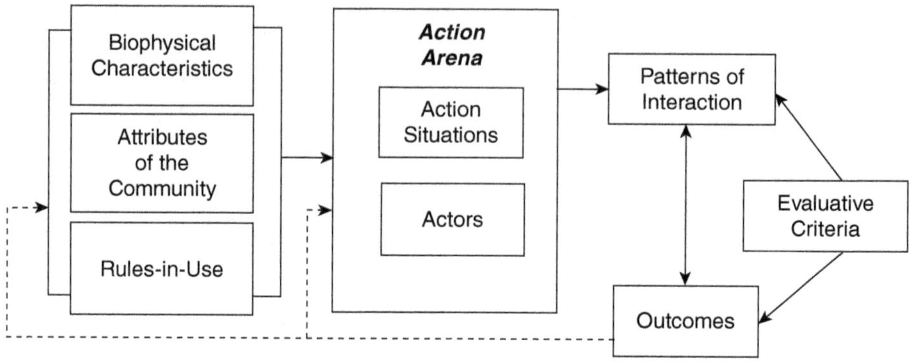

FIGURE 8.1 The Institutional Analysis and Development (IAD) framework

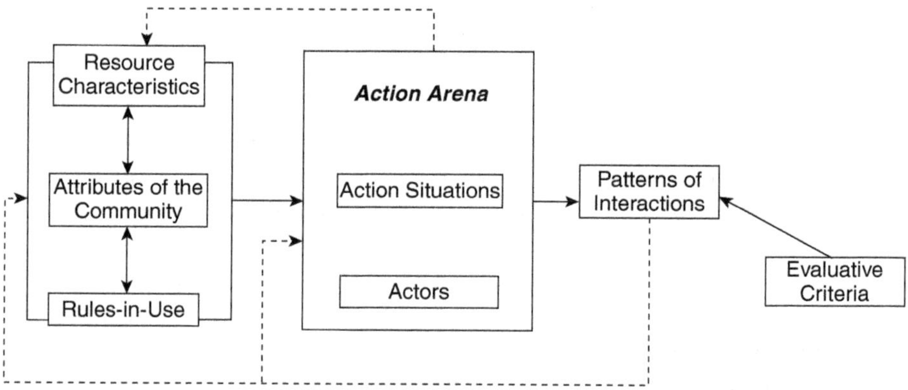

FIGURE 8.2 The Governing Knowledge Commons (GKC) framework

Space constraints prohibit an in-depth analysis of the myriad ways in which the GKC framework might be useful in conceptualizing an array of security and privacy challenges in the IoE, but nevertheless a brief survey is attempted later. In brief, the distinctions with this approach, as compared with the traditional IAD framework, include (1) greater interactions on the left side of the chart underscoring the complex interrelationships in play; (2) the fact that the action area can similarly influence the resource characteristics and community attributes; and (3) that the interaction of rules and outcomes in knowledge commons are often inseparable (Frischmann, Madison and Strandburg, 2014, 19). These insights also resonate in the IoE context, given the tremendous amount of interactions between stakeholders, including IoT device manufacturers, standards-setting bodies, regulators (both national and international), and consumers. Similarly, these interactions are dynamic, given that security compromises in one part of the IoE ecosystem can lay out in a very different context, as seen in the Mirai botnet, in which compromised smart light bulbs and other IoE devices were networked to crash critical Internet services (Botezatu, 2016).

The following subsections dive into various elements of the GKC framework in order to better understand its utility in conceptualizing IoE governance challenges.

8.2.1 *Resource Characteristics and Classifying Goods in Cyberspace*

Digging into the GKC framework, beginning on the left side of Figure 8.2, there are an array of characteristics to consider, including "facilities through which information is accessed" such as the Internet itself, as well as "artifacts … including … computer files" and the "ideas themselves" (Cole, 2014, 10). The "artifacts" category is especially relevant in cybersecurity discussions, given that it includes trade secrets protections, which are closer to a pure private good than a public good and are also the currency of global cybercrime (Shackelford et al., 2015). Internet governance institutions (or "facilities" in this vernacular) can also control the rate at which ideas are diffused, such as through censorship taking subtle (e.g., YouTube's decision to take down Nazi-themed hate speech videos) or extreme (e.g., China's Great Firewall) forms (Beech, 2016).

There is also a related issue to consider: what type of "good" is at issue in the cybersecurity context? In general, goods are placed into four categories, depending on whether they fall on the spectra of exclusion and subtractability (Buck, 1998). Exclusion refers to the relative ease with which goods may be protected. Subtractability evokes the extent to which one's use of a good decreases another's enjoyment of it. If it is easy to exclude others from the use of a good, coupled with a high degree of subtractability, then the type of good is likely to be characterized as "private goods" that are defined by property law and best regulated by the market (Hiller and Shackelford, 2018). Examples in the IoT context are plentiful, from smart speakers to refrigerators. Legal rights, including property rights, to these goods include the right of exclusion discussed above. At the opposite end of the spectrum, where exclusion is difficult and subtractability is low, goods are more likely characterized as "public goods" that might be best managed by governments (Ostrom and Ostrom, 2015). An example is national defense, including, some argue, cybersecurity (Ostrom, 2009). This is an area of some debate, though, given the extensive private sector ownership of critical infrastructure, which makes drawing a clear line between matters of corporate governance and national security difficult.

In its totality, the IoE includes all forms of goods, including private devices and municipal broadband networks, catalyzing a range of positive and negative externalities from network effects to cyberattacks. For example, the IoE includes digital communities as a form of club good, with societies being able to set their own rights of access; a contemporary example is the efforts of Reddit moderators to stop trolls, limit hate speech, and promote a more civil dialogue among users (Roose, 2017). Such communal property rights may either be recognized by the state, or be based on a form of "benign neglect" (Buck, 1998, 5). Indeed, as of this writing, there is an active debate underway in the United States and Europe about the regulation of social-media platforms to limit the spread of terrorist propaganda, junk news, sex trafficking, and hate speech. Such mixed types of goods are more the norm than the exception. As Cole has argued:

> [S]ince the industrial revolution it has become clear that the atmosphere, like waters, forests, and other natural resources, is at best an impure, subtractable, or congestible public good. As such, these resources fall somewhere on the spectrum between public goods, as technically defined, and club or toll goods. It is such impure public goods to which Ostrom assigned the label "common-pool resources". (Cole, 2014, 54)

Naturally, the next question is whether, in fact, cyberspace may be comparable to the atmosphere as an *impure* public good, since *pure* public goods do not present the same sort of governance challenges, such as the well-studied "tragedy of the commons" scenario, which predicts the gradual overexploitation of common pool resources (Feeny et al., 1990). Though cyberspace is unique given that it can, in fact, expand such as through the addition of new networks (Jordan, 1990), increased use also multiplies threat vectors (Deibert, 2012).

Solutions to the tragedy of the commons typically "involve the replacement of open access with restricted access and use via private property, common property, or public property/regulatory regimes" (Frischmann, Madison, and Strandburg, 2014, 54). However, in practice, as Elinor Ostrom and numerous others have shown, self-organization is in fact possible in practice, as is discussed later (Frischmann, 2018). The growth of the IoE could hasten such tragedies if vulnerabilities replete in this ecosystem are allowed to go unaddressed.

8.2.2 *Community Attributes*

The next box element on the left side of the GKC framework, titled "Attributes of the Community," refers to the network of users making use of the given resource (Smith, 2017). In the natural commons context, communities can be macro (at the global scale when considering the impacts of global climate change) or micro, such as with shared access to a forest or lake. Similarly, in the cyber context, communities come in every conceivable scale and format from private pages on Facebook to peer-to-peer communities to the global community of more than four billion global Internet users as of October 2018, not to mention the billions of devices comprising the IoE. Even such a broad conceptualization omits impacted non-user stakeholders and infrastructure, as may be seen in the push to utilize 5G connectivity, AI, and analytics to power a "safe city" revolution, albeit one built on Huawei architecture. The scale of the multifaceted cyber threat facing the public and private sector parallels in complexity the battle to combat the worst effects of global climate change (Cole, 2014; Shackelford, 2016). Such a vast scale stretches the utility of the GKC framework, which is why most efforts have considered subparts, or clubs, within this digital ecosystem.

An array of polycentric theorists, including Professor Ostrom, have extolled the benefits of small, self-organized communities in the context of managing common pool resources (Ostrom, 1999). Anthropological evidence has confirmed the benefits of small-scale governance. However, micro-communities can ignore other interests, as well as the wider impact of their actions, online and offline (Murray, 2007). A polycentric model favoring bottom-up governance but with a role for common standards and baseline rules so as to protect against free riders may be the best-case scenario for IoE governance, as is explored further. Such self-regulation has greater flexibility to adapt to dynamic technologies faster than top-down regulations, which even if enacted, can result in unintended consequences, as seen now in the debates surrounding California's 2018 IoT law. As of January 2020, this law would require "any manufacturer of a device that connects 'directly or indirectly' to the Internet . . . [to] equip it with 'reasonable' security features, designed to prevent unauthorized access, modification, or information disclosure" (Robertson, 2018). Yet, it is not a panacea, as we will see, and there is plentiful evidence that simple rule sets – especially when they are generated in consultation with engaged and empowered communities – can produce better governance outcomes.

8.2.3 *Rules-in-Use*

This component of the GKC framework comprises both community norms along with formal legal rules. One of the driving questions in this area is identifying the appropriate governance level at which to formalize norms into rules, for example, whether that is at a constitutional level, collective-choice level, etc. (Cole, 2014, 56). That is easier said than done in the cybersecurity context, given the wide range of industry norms, standards – such as the National Institute for Standards and Technology Cybersecurity Framework (NIST CSF) – state-level laws, sector-specific federal laws, and international laws regulating everything from banking transactions to prosecuting cybercriminals. Efforts have been made to begin to get a more comprehensive understanding of the various norms and laws in place, such as through the International Telecommunication Union's (ITU)'s Global Cybersecurity Index and the Carnegie Endowment International Cybersecurity Norms Project, but such efforts remain at an early stage of development. A variety of rules may be considered to help address governance gaps, such as position and choice rules that define the rights and responsibilities of actors, such as IoT manufacturers and Internet Service Providers (ISPs), as is shown in Table 8.1 (Ostrom and Crawford, 2005). Given the degree to which core critical infrastructure – such as smart grids and Internet-connected medical devices – are also subsumed within IoT debates, there is a great deal of overlap between potential rule sets from incentivizing

TABLE 8.1 *Types of rules*

Aggregation rules	Determine whether a decision by a single actor or multiple actors is needed prior to acting at a decision point in a process.
Boundary rules	Define: 1. who is eligible to take a position; 2. the process for choosing who is eligible to take a position; 3. how actors can leave positions; 4. whether anyone can hold multiple positions simultaneously; and 5. succession to vacant positions.
Choice rules	Define what actors in positions must, must not, or may do in their position and in particular circumstances.
Information rules	Specify channels of communication among actors, as well as the kinds of information that can be transmitted between positions.
Payoff rules	Assign external rewards or sanctions for particular actions or outcomes.
Position rules	Define positions that actors hold, including as owners of property rights and duties.

the use of cybersecurity standards and frameworks, as is happening in Ohio to hardening supply chains.

Many of these rules have cyber analogues, which emphasize cybersecurity information sharing through public–private partnerships to address common cyber threats, penalize firms and even nations for lax cybersecurity due diligence, and define the duties – including liability – of actors, such as Facebook and Google (Reardon, 2018).

The question of what governance level is most appropriate to set the rules for IoT devices is pressing, with an array of jurisdictions, including California, pressing ahead. For example, aside from its IoT-specific efforts, California's 2018 Consumer Privacy Act is helping to set a new transparency-based standard for US privacy protections. Although not comparable to the EU's new General Data Protection Regulation (GDPR) discussed later, it does include provisions that allow consumers to sue over data breaches, including in the IoT context, and decide when, and how, their data is being gathered and used by companies (Adler, 2018). Whether such state-level action, even in a state with an economic footprint as the size of California, will help foster enhanced cybersecurity due diligence across the broader IoE ecosystem remains to be seen.

8.2.4 *Action Arenas*

The arena is just that, the place where decisions are made, where "collective action succeeds or fails" (Cole, 2014, 59). Such arenas exist at three levels within the GKC framework – constitutional, collective-choice, and operational. Decisions made at each of these governance levels, in turn, impact a range of rules and community attributes, which is an important feature of the framework. Examples of decision-makers in each arena in the cybersecurity context include (1) at the constitutional level, judges deciding the bounds of "reasonable care" and "due diligence" (Shackleford, 2015); (2) federal and state policymakers at the collective-choice (e.g., policy) level, such as the Federal Trade Commission (FTC) policing unfair and deceptive trade practices; and (3) at the operational level, firms, households, and everyone else.

8.2.5 *Evaluation Criteria*

The final component, according to Cole, is "the most neglected and underdeveloped" of the frameworks (Cole, 2014, 62). Elinor Ostrom, for example, offered the following "evaluative criteria" in considering how best to populate it, including "(1) economic efficiency; (2) fiscal equivalence; (3) redistributional equity; (4) accountability; (5) conformance to values of local actors; and (6) sustainability" (Cole, 2014, 62). In the GKC context, these criteria might include "(1) increasing scientific knowledge; (2) sustainability and preservation; (3) participation standards; (4) economic efficiency; (5) equity through fiscal equivalence; and (6) redistributional equity" (Hess and Ostrom, 2007, 62). This lack of rigor might simply be due to the fact that, in the natural commons context, the overriding goal has been "long-run resource sustainability" (Cole, 2014, 62). It is related, in some ways, to the "Outcomes" element missing from the GKC framework but present in the IAD framework, which references predictable outcomes of interactions from social situations, which can include consequences for both resource systems and units. Although such considerations are beyond the findings of the IAD framework, in the cybersecurity context, an end goal to consider is defining and implementing cyber peace.

"Cyber peace," which has also been called "digital peace," is a term that is increasingly used, but it also remains an arena of little consensus. It is clearly more than the "absence of violence" online, which was the starting point for how Professor Johan Galtung described the new field of peace studies he helped create in 1969 (Galtung, 1969). Similarly, Galtung argued that finding universal definitions for "peace" or "violence" was unrealistic, but rather the goal should be landing on an apt "subjectivistic" definition agreed to by the majority (Galtung, 1969, 168). He undertook this effort in a broad, yet dynamic, way recognizing that as society and technology changes, so too should our conceptions of peace and violence. That is why he defined violence as "the cause of the difference between the potential and the actual, between what could have been and what is" (Galtung, 1969, 168).

Cyber peace is defined here not as the absence of conflict, what may be called negative cyber peace. Rather, it is the construction of a network of multilevel regimes that promote global, just, and sustainable cybersecurity by clarifying the rules of the road for companies and countries alike to help reduce the threats of cyber conflict, crime, and espionage to levels comparable to other business and national security risks. To achieve this goal, a new approach to cybersecurity is needed that seeks out best practices from the public and private sectors to build robust, secure systems, and couches cybersecurity within the larger debate on Internet governance. Working together through polycentric partnerships of the kind described later, we can mitigate the risk of cyber war by laying the groundwork for a positive cyber peace that respects human rights, spreads Internet access along with best practices, and strengthens governance mechanisms by fostering multistakeholder collaboration (Galtung, 2012). The question of how best to achieve this end is open to interpretation. As Cole argues, "[f]rom a social welfare perspective, some combination of open- and closed-access is overwhelmingly likely to be more socially efficient than complete open or close-access" (Cole, 2014, 61). Such a polycentric approach is also a necessity in the cyber regime complex, given the prevalence of private and public sector stakeholder controls.

In the cybersecurity context, increasing attention has been paid identifying lessons from the green movement to consider the best-case scenario for a sustainable cyber peace. Indeed, cybersecurity is increasingly integral to discussions of sustainable development – including Internet access – which could inform the evaluative criteria of a sustainable cyber peace in the IoE. Such an approach also accords with the "environmental metaphor for information law and policy" that has been helpful in other efforts (Frischmann, Madison, and Strandburg, 2014, 16).

It is important to recognize the polycentric nature of the IoE to ascertain the huge number of stakeholders – including users – that can and should have a say in contributing to legitimate governance. Indeed, such concerns over "legitimate" Internet governance have been present for decades, especially since the creation of the Internet Corporation for Assigned Names and Numbers (ICANN). Given the pushback against that organization as a relatively top-down artificial construct as compared to the more bottom-up Internet Engineering Task Force (IETF), legitimacy in the IoE should be predicated to the extent possible locally through independent (and potentially air gapped) networks, Internet Service Providers (ISPs), and nested state, federal, and international law. To conceptualize such system, the literature on regime complexes might prove helpful, which is discussed next in the context of blockchain technology.

8.3 IS BLOCKCHAIN THE ANSWER TO THE IOE'S WOES?

Professor Ostrom argued that "[t]rust is the most important resource" (Escotet, 2010). Indeed, the end goal of any governance institution is arguably trust – how to build trust across users to attain a common goal, be it sustainable fishery management or securing the IoE. The GKC framework provides useful insights toward this end. But one technology could also help in this effort, namely blockchain, which, according to Goldman Sachs, could "change 'everything'" (Lachance, 2016). Regardless of the question being asked, some argue that it is the answer to the uninitiated – namely, a blockchain cryptographic distributed ledger (Trust Machine, 2015). Its applications are widespread, from recording property deeds to securing medical devices. As such, its potential is being investigated by a huge range of organizations, including US Defense Advanced Research Projects Agency (DARPA), IBM, Maersk, Disney, and Greece, the latter of which is seeking to leverage blockchain to help enhance social capital by helping to build trust around common governance challenges, such as land titling (Casey and Vigna, 2018). Examples similarly abound regarding how firms use blockchains to enhance cybersecurity. The technology could enable the Internet to become decentralized, pushing back against the type of closed platforms analyzed by Professor Johnathan Zittrain and others (Zittrain, 2008). Already, a number of IoT developers are experimenting with the technology in their devices; indeed, according to one recent survey, blockchain adoption in the IoT industry doubled over the course of 2018 (Zmudzinski, 2019).

Yet formidable hurdles remain before blockchain technology can be effectively leveraged to help promote sustainable development, peace, and security in the IoE. No blockchain, for example, has yet scaled to the extent necessary to search the entire web. There are also concerns over hacking and integrity (such as when a single entity controls more than fifty percent of the processing power), including the fact that innovation is happening so quickly that defenders are put in a difficult position as they try to build resilience into their distributed systems (Villasenor, 2018). But the potential for progress demands further research, including how it could help promote a polycentric cyber peace in the burgeoning IoE.

8.4 POLYCENTRIC IMPLICATIONS

As Professor Cole has maintained, "those looking for *normative* guidance from Ostrom" and the relevant governance frameworks and design principles discussed herein are often left wanting (Cole, 2014, 46). Similar to the big questions in the field of intellectual property, such as defining the optimal duration of a copyright, it stands to reason, then, that the Ostroms' work might tell us relatively little about the goal of defining, and pursuing, cyber peace. An exception to the Ostroms' desire to eschew normative suggestions, though, is polycentric governance, which builds from the notion of subsidiarity in which governance "is a 'co responsibility' of units at central (or national), regional (subnational), and local levels" (Cole, 2014, 47).

For purposes of this study, the polycentric governance framework may be considered to be a multi-level, multi-purpose, multi-functional, and multi-sectoral model that has been championed by numerous scholars, including the Ostroms (Mcginnis, 2011). It suggests that "a single governmental unit" is usually incapable of managing "global collective action problems" such as cyber-attacks (Ostrom, 2009,

35). Instead, a polycentric approach recognizes that diverse organizations working at multiple scales can enhance "flexibility across issues and adaptability over time" (Keohane and Victor, 2011, 15). Such an approach can help foster the emergence of a norm cascade improving the Security of Things (Finnemore and Sikkink, 1998, 895).

Not all polycentric systems are guaranteed to be successful. Disadvantages, for example, can include gridlock and a lack of defined hierarchy (Keohane and Victor, 2011). Yet progress has been made on norm development, including cybersecurity due diligence, discussed later, which will help IoT manufacturers better fend off attacks against foreign nation states. Still, it is important to note that even the Ostroms' commitment to polycentric governance "was contingent, context-specific, and focused on matching the scale of governance to the scale of operations appropriate for the particular production or provision problem under investigation" (Cole, 2014, 47). During field work in Indianapolis, IN, for example, the Ostroms found that, in fact, medium-sized police departments "outperformed both smaller (neighborhood) and larger (municipal-level) units" (Cole, 2014, 47). In the IoE context, as has been noted, the scale could not be greater with billions of people and devices interacting across myriad sectors, settings, and societies. The sheer complexity of such a system, along with the history of Internet governance to date, signals that there can be no single solution or governance forum to foster cyber peace in the IoE. Rather, polycentric principles gleaned from the GKC framework should be incorporated into novel efforts designed to glean the best governance practices across a range of devices, networks, and sectors. These should include creating clubs and industry councils of the kind that the GDPR is now encouraging to identify and spread cybersecurity best practices, leveraging new technologies such as blockchain to help build trust in this massively distributed system, and encouraging norm entrepreneurs like Microsoft and the State of California to experiment with new public–private partnerships informed by the sustainable development movement. Success will be difficult to ascertain as it cannot simply be the end of cyber attacks. Evaluation criteria are largely undefined in the GKC framework, as we have seen, which the community should take as a call to action, as is already happening by members of the Cybersecurity Tech Accord and the Trusted IoT Alliance.

Such efforts may be conceptualized further within the literature on the cyber regime complex. As interests, power, technology, and information diffuse and evolve over time within the IoE, comprehensive regimes are difficult to form. Once formed, they can be unstable. As a result, "rarely does a full-fledged international regime with a set of rules and practices come into being at one period of time and persist intact" (Keohane and Victor, 2011, 9). According to Professor Oran Young, international regimes emerge as a result of "codifying informal rights and rules that have evolved over time through a process of converging expectations or tacit bargaining" (Young, 1997, 10). Consequently, regime complexes, as a form of bottom-up institution building, are becoming relatively more popular in both the climate and Internet governance contexts, which may have some benefits since negotiations for multilateral treaties could divert attention from more practical efforts to create flexible, loosely coupled regimes (Keohane and Victor, 2011). An example of such a cyber regime complex may be found in a work by Professor Joseph S. Nye, Jr., which is reproduced in Figure 8.3.

But there are also the costs of regime complexes to consider. In particular, such networks are susceptible to institutional fragmentation and gridlock. And there are moral considerations about such regime complexes. For example, in the context of climate change, these regimes omit nations that are not major emitters, such as the least developed nations that are the most at risk to the effects of a changing climate. Similar arguments could play out in the IoE context with some consumers only being able to access less secure devices due to jurisdictional difference that could impinge on their privacy. Consequently, the benefits of regime complexes must be critically analyzed. By identifying design rules for the architecture, interfaces, and integration protocols within the IoE, both governance scholars and policymakers may be able to develop novel research designs and interventions to help promote cyber peace.

8.5 CONCLUSION

As Cole has argued, "there are no institutional panaceas for resolving complex social dilemmas" (Cole, 2014, 48). Never has this arguably been truer than when considering the emerging global digital ecosystem here called the IoE. Yet, we ignore the history of governance investigations at our peril, as we look ahead to twenty-first century global collective action problems such as promoting cyber peace in the IoE. Important questions remain about the utility of the Ostrom Design Principles, the IAD, and GKC frameworks in helping us govern the IoE. Even more questions persist about the normative goals in such an enterprise, for example, what cyber peace might look like and how we might be able to get there. That should not put off scholars interested in this endeavor. Rather, it should be seen as a call to action. The stakes could not be higher. Achieving a sustainable level of cybersecurity in the IoE demands novel methodologies, standards, and regimes. The Ostroms' legacy helps to shine a light on the path toward cyber peace.

REFERENCES

Adler, Ben. "California Passes Strict Internet Privacy Law with Implications for The Country." *NPR*. June, 2018.
Ashton, Kevin. "That 'Internet of Things' Thing." RFID Journal, June, 2009.
Banafa, Ahmed. "The Internet of Everything (IOE)." *Open Mind*, August, 2016.

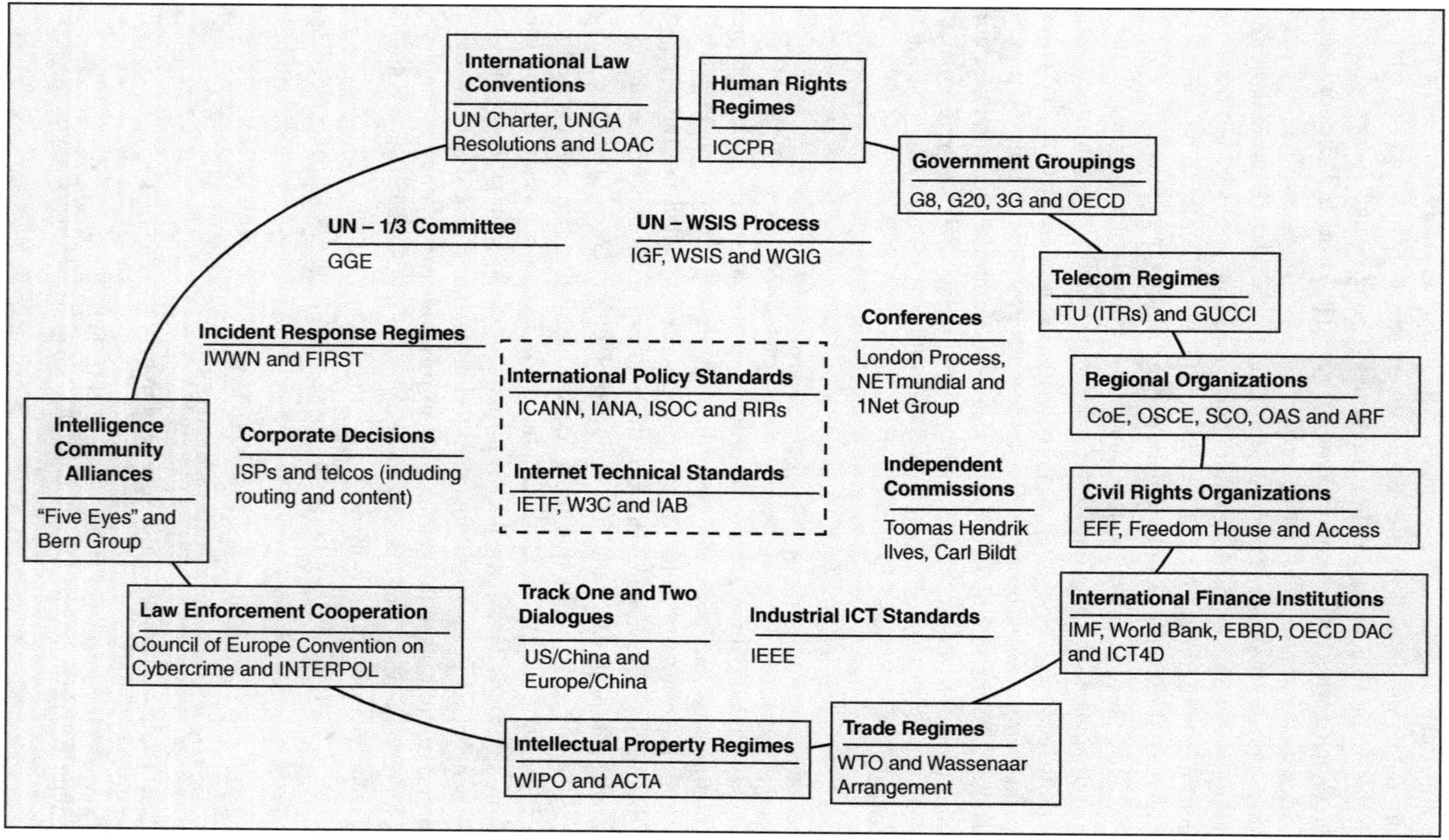

FIGURE 8.3 Cyber regime complex map (Nye, 2014, 8)

Beech, Hannah. "China's Great Firewall is Harming Innovation, Scholars Say." *Time*, June 2016.

Botezatu, Bogdan. "Unprotected IoT Devices Killed the US Internet for Hours." *Bitdefender*, October, 2016.

Bowles, Nellie. "Thermostats, Locks and Lights: Digital Tools of Domestic Abuse." *New York Times*, June, 2018.

Buck, Susan J. *The Global Commons: An Introduction*. New York: Island Press, 1998.

Casey, Michael J. and Vigna, Paul. *The Truth Machine: The Blockchain and the Future of Everything*. New York: St. Martin's Press, 2018.

Cole, Dan. "Learning from Lin: Lessons and Cautions from the Natural Commons for the Knowledge Commons." In *Governing Knowledge Commons*, Edited by Brett M. Frischmann, Michael J. Madison, and Katherine J. Strandburg, 1st ed. Oxford University Press, 2014.

"Cyber Risk Thursday: Internet of Bodies." *Atlantic Council*, September, 2017.

Deibert, Ron. "Distributed Security as Cyber Strategy: Outlining a Comprehensive Approach for Canada in Cyberspace." Canadian Defense and Foreign Affairs Institute, 2012.

Evans, Dave. "The Internet of Everything: How More Relevant and Valuable Connections Will Change the World." *Cisco*, 2012.

Feeny, David, Berkes, Fikret, Mccay, Bomnnie J., and Acheson, James M. "The Tragedy of the Commons: Twenty-Two Years Later." *Human Ecology*, 18 (March 1990): 1–19.

Finnemore, Martha and Sikkink, Kathryn. "International Norm Dynamics and Political Change." *International Organization*, 52 (1998): 887–917.

Frischmann, Brett. "The Tragedy of the Commons, Revisited." *Scientific American*, November, 2018.

Frischmann, Brett M., Madison, Michael J., and Strandburg, Katherine J., eds. *Governing knowledge commons*. Oxford University Press, 2014.

Galtung, Johan. "Peace, Positive and Negative." *In The Encyclopedia of Peace Psychology*. Edited by Daniel J. Christie. Oxford, UK: Wiley-Blackwell, 2012.

Galtung, Johan. "Violence, Peace, and Peace Research." *Peace Research*, 6, 3 (1969): 167–191.

Giles, Martin. "For Safety's Sake, We Must Slow Innovation in Internet-Connected Things." *MIT Technology Review*. September, 2018.

Hiller, Janine and Shackelford, Scott J. "The Firm and Common Pool Resource Theory: Unpacking the Rise of Benefit Corporations." *American Business Law Journal*, 55, 1 (2018): 5–51.

Interview with Nobel Laureate Elinor Ostrom, ESCOTET FOUND., http://escotet.org/2010/11/interview-with-nobel-laureate-elinor-ostrom/ (last visited June 29, 2018).

Keohane, Robert O. and Victor, David G. "The Regime Complex for Climate Change." *Perspectives on Politics*, 9, 1 (2011): 7–23.

Johnson, Gregoray A. "Organizational Structure and Scalar Stress." In *Theory and Explanation in Archeology*, Edited by Colin Renfrew, Michael Rowlands and Barbara A. Segraves-Whallon, Academic Press, Inc., 1982.

Jordan, Tim. *Cyberpower: The Culture and Politics of Cyberspace and the Internet*. London: Routledge Press, 1999.

Lachance, Naomi. "Not Just Bitcoin: Why the Blockchain Is a Seductive Technology to Many Industries." *NPR*, May, 2016.

McGinnis, Michael D. "An Introduction to IAD and the Language of the Ostrom Workshop: A Simple Guide to a Complex Framework." Policy Studies, 39, 1 (2011): 169–183.

Merriman, Chris. "87 Percent of Consumers Haven't Heard of the Internet of Things." *Inquirer*, August, 2014.

Murray, Andrew. *The Regulation of Cyberspace: Control in the Online Environment*. London: Routledge, 2007.

Nye, Joseph S. "The Regime Complex for Managing Global Cyber Activities." *Global Commission on Internet Governance*, 2014.

Ostrom, Vincent and Ostrom, Elinor. "Public Goods and Public Choices." In *Elinor Ostrom and the Bloomington School of Political Economy Vol. 2*, Edited by Daniel H. Cole and Michael McGinnis, Lexington Books, 2015.

Ostrom, Elinor. "Beyond Markets and States: Polycentric Governance of Complex Economic Systems." Nobel Prize Lecture, 2009.

Ostrom, Elinor. "A Polycentric Approach for Coping with Climate Change." *World Bank Policy Research*, 35, 5095 (2009).

Ostrom, Elinor and Hess, Charlotte. "A Framework for Analyzing the Knowledge Commons." *In Understanding Knowledge as a Commons: From Theory to Practice*. Edited by Charlotte Hess and Elinor Ostrom, London: MIT Press, 2007.

Ostrom, Elinor and Crawford, Sue. "Classifying Rules." In *Understanding Institutional Diversity*. Edited by Elinor Ostrom. Princeton, NJ: Princeton University Press, 2005.

Ostrom, Elinor, Burger, Joanna, Field, Christopher B., Norgaard, Richard B., and Policansky, David, "Revisiting the Commons: Local Lessons, Global Challenges." *Science*, April, 1999.

Reardon, Marguerite. "Facebook's FTC Consent Decree Deal: What You Need to Know." *CNet*, August, 2018.

Robertson, Adi. "California Just Became the First State with an Internet of Things Cybersecurity Law." *Verge*. September, 2018.

Roose, Kevin. "Reddit Limits Noxious Content by Giving Trolls Fewer Places to Gather." New York Times, September, 2017.

Shackelford, Scott J., Raymond, Anjanette, Charoen, Danuvasin, Balakrishnan, Rakshana, Dixit, Prakhar, Gjonaj, Julianna, and Kavi, Rachith. "When Toasters Attack: Enhancing the 'Security of Things' through Polycentric Governance." *University of Illinois Law Review*, 2017: 415.

Shackelford, Scott J. "On Climate Change and Cyber Attacks: Leveraging Polycentric Governance to Mitigate Global Collective Action Problems." *Vanderbilt Journal of Entertainment and Technology Law*, 18 (2016): 653–711.

Shackelford, Scott J., Richards, Eric L., Raymond, Anjanette H., and Craig, Amanda N., "Using BITs to Protect Bytes: Promoting Cyber Peace and Safeguarding Trade Secrets through Bilateral Investment Treaties." *American Business Law Journal*, 52 (2015): 1–74.

Shackelford, Scott J., Proia, Andrew, Craig, Amanda, and Martell, Brenton. "Toward a Global Standard of Cybersecurity Care? Exploring the Implications of the 2014 NIST Cybersecurity Framework on Shaping Reasonable National and International Cybersecurity Practices." *Texas International Law Journal*, 50 (2015): 287.

Shackelford, Scott J. *Managing Cyber Attacks in International Law, Business, and Relations: In Search of Cyber Peace*. Washington, DC: Cambridge University Press, 2014.

Smith, Michael. "The Tragedy of the Commons' in the IoT Ecosystem." *Computerworld*, August, 2017.

The Promise of the Blockchain: The Trust Machine, *Economist*, October, 2015.

Villasenor, John. "Blockchain Technology: Five Obstacles to Mainstream Adoption." *Forbes*, June, 2018.

Young, Oran R. "Rights, Rules, and Resources in World Affairs." *In Global Governance: Drawing Insights from the Environmental Experience*. Edited by Oran R. Young. New Haven: MIT Press, 1997.

Zittrain, Jonathan. *The Future of the Internet and How to Stop It*. New Haven: Yale University Press, 2008.

Zmudzinski, Adrian. "Blockchain Adoption in IoT Industry More Than Doubled in 2018: Survey." *Cointelegraph*, January, 2019.

Waltl, Josef. *IP Modularity in Software Products and Software Platform Ecosystems*.

9

Contextual Integrity as a Gauge for Governing Knowledge Commons

Yan Shvartzshnaider,[1] *Madelyn Rose Sanfilippo,*[2] *and Noah Apthorpe*[3]

9.1 INTRODUCTION

This chapter describes our approach to combine the Contextual Integrity (CI) and Governing Knowledge Commons (GKC) frameworks in order to gauge privacy expectations as governance. This GKC-CI approach helps us understand how and why different individuals and communities perceive and respond to information flows in very different ways. Using GKC-CI to understand consumers' (sometimes incongruent) privacy expectations also provides deeper insights into the driving factors behind privacy norm evolution.

The CI framework (Nissenbaum, 2009) structures reasoning about the privacy implications of information flows. The appropriateness of information flows is defined in context, with respect to established norms in terms of their values and functions. Recent research has operationalized CI to capture users' expectations in varied contexts (Apthorpe et al., 2018; Shvartzshnaider et al., 2016), as well to analyze regulation (Selbst, 2013), establish research ethics guidelines (Zimmer, 2018), and conceptualize privacy within commons governance arrangements (Sanfilippo, Frischmann, and Strandburg, 2018).

The GKC framework examines patterns of interactions around knowledge resources within particular settings, labeled as action arenas, by identifying background contexts; resources, actors, and objectives as attributes; aspects of governance; and patterns and outcomes (Frischmann, Madison, and Strandburg, 2014). Governance is further analyzed by identifying strategies, norms, and rules-in-use through an institutional grammar (Crawford and Ostrom, 1995). According to GKC,

[1] Assistant Professor/Faculty Fellow in the Courant Institute of Mathematical Sciences, NYU; Visiting Associate Research Scholar at the Center for Information Technology Policy (CITP), Princeton University.

[2] Assistant Professor, School of Information Sciences, University of Illinois at Urbana-Champaign; Affiliate Scholar, The Vincent and Elinor Ostrom Workshop in Political Theory and Policy Analysis, Indiana University, Bloomington. Ph.D., Indiana University, Bloomington; M.I.S., Indiana University, Bloomington; B.S., University of Wisconsin-Madison.

[3] Assistant Professor, Department of Computer Science, Colgate University; Ph.D., Department of Computer Science, Princeton University; Graduate Student Fellow, Center for Information Technology Policy, Princeton University.

strategies are defined in terms of attributes, aims, and conditions; norms build on strategies through the incorporation of modal language; and rules provide further structure by embedding norms with consequences to sanction non-compliance. For example, a strategy can describe a digital personal assistant that uses audio recordings of users (attributes) in order to provide personalized advertisements (aim) when a user does not pay for an ad-free subscription (condition). If this information flow also included modal language, such as a hedge, like "may" and "could," or a deontic, like "will" and "cannot," it would be a norm. The addition of a consequence, such as a denial of service or financial cost, would make this example a rule. It is also notable that, from this perspective, there are differences between rules-on-the-books, which prescribe, and rules-in-use, which are applied.

GKC and CI are complementary frameworks for understanding privacy as both governing institutions (Sanfilippo, Frischmann, and Strandburg, 2018) and appropriate flows of personal information, respectively. Within the GKC framework, as with the broader intellectual tradition of institutional analysis, an institutional grammar can be applied to deconstruct individual institutions (Crawford and Ostrom, 1995). Table 9.1 illustrates the overlap between these frameworks and how each provides parameter specificity to the other. While the CI framework deconstructs information flows, the GKC framework considers governance structures and constraints regarding actors and their interactions with knowledge resources. Consider the digital personal assistant example from the previous paragraph. Under the institutional grammar (Crawford and Ostrom, 1995), the digital personal assistant, audio recordings, and users are all considered "attributes." The CI framework further divides these elements into sender, information type and subject parameters, respectively. Conversely, the CI framework uses the "transmission principle" parameter to articulate all constraints on information flows, while the GKC framework provides definitions of aims, conditions, modalities, and consequences.

In this work, we use the GKC and CI frameworks to understand the key aspects behind privacy norm formation and evolution. Specifically, we investigate divergences between privacy expectations and technological reality in the IoT domain.

TABLE 9.1 *Conceptual overlap between CI and Institutional Grammar (GKC) parameters*

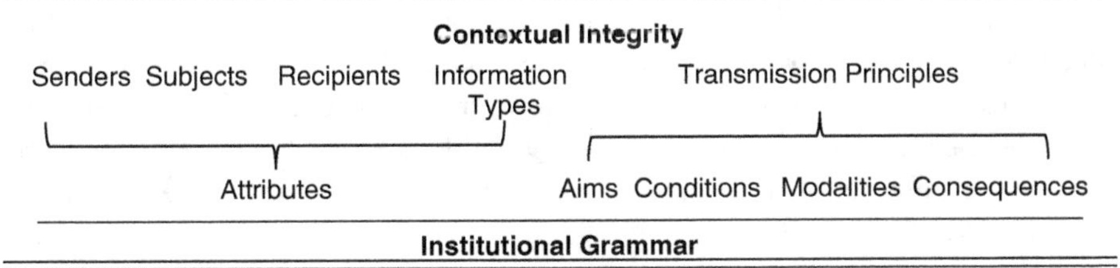

The consumer Internet of things (IoT) adds Internet-connectivity to familiar devices, such as toasters and televisions, resulting in data flows that do not align with existing user expectations about these products. This is further exacerbated by the introduction of new types of devices, such as digital personal assistants, for which relevant norms are only just emerging. We are still figuring out whether the technological practices enabled by these new devices align with or impact our social values. Studying techno-social change in the IoT context involves measuring what people expect of IoT device information flows as well as how these expectations and underlying social norms emerge and change. We want to design and govern technology in ways that adhere to people's expectations of privacy and other important ethical considerations. To do so effectively, we need to understand how techno-social changes in the environment (context) can lead to subtle shifts in information flows. CI is a useful framework for identifying and evaluating such shifts as a gauge for GKC.

We conduct a multi-part survey to investigate the contextual integrity and governance of IoT devices that combines open-ended and structured questions about norm origins, expectations, and participatory social processes with Likert-scale vignette questions (Apthorpe et al., 2018). We then perform a comparative analysis of the results to explore how variations in GKC-CI parameters affect privacy strategies and expectations and to gauge the landscape of governing norms.

9.2 RESEARCH DESIGN

In the first part of the survey, we asked respondents to list the devices they own and how they learn about the privacy properties of these devices (e.g., privacy policies, discussions with legal experts, online forums). We next presented the respondents with scenarios A through D, as described in Table 9.2, each scenario was followed by applied questions based on the GKC framework.

Each scenario focused on different factors that previous research has identified as having an effect on users' expectations and preferences (Apthorpe et al., 2018). Scenario A focused on third-party information sharing practices involving a smart TV that tracks viewing patterns and TV watching habits that are sold to an advertiser. Questions assessed the respondents' specific concerns in this scenario as well as their anticipated reactions. We interpreted these reactions as indicators of respondents' privacy expectations and beliefs as well as their understanding of information flows in context.

The remaining scenarios were built on Scenario A to explore different factors affecting privacy opinions and reactions. Scenario B introduced an additional, exogenous influence: a parallel, cross platform tracking incident that happened to someone else the respondent might know. Questions assessed how experiences with cross-device information flows and surrounding factors alter respondents' expectations and resulting actions. This provides a sense of communities and contexts surrounding use, in order to support future institutionalization of information flows to better align with users' values.

TABLE 9.2 *Survey scenarios with corresponding aspects of the GKC framework*

#	Scenario	GKC Aspects
A	Imagine you're at home watching TV while using your phone to shop for socks on Amazon. Your TV then displays an ad informing you about a great discount on socks at a Walmart close to your neighborhood.	**Background:** normative values **Attributes:** resources **Patterns and Outcomes:** benefits
B	You later hear from your neighbor that a similar thing happened to him. In his case, his wife posted on Facebook about their dream vacation. A few days later he noticed an ad as he was browsing the web from a local cruiser company.	**Background:** normative values **Attributes:** resources, community members, goals and objectives **Governance:** institutions **Patterns and Outcomes:** benefits
C	Companies usually detail their information handling practices in their privacy policies and terms of service. Imagine you do read through the privacy policy for your smart TV. You find a statement saying that the TV could, sometimes, send your information to third parties for analysis to offer you all the top features. The privacy policy also states that you may disable third party sharing; however, this may cause additional subscription charges for some features.	**Governance:** context, institutions, actors **Patterns and Outcomes:** benefits, costs, legitimacy
D	You have an acquaintance who is a software engineer. They tell you that you shouldn't be concerned. It's considered a normal practice for companies to track the habits and activities of their users. This information is then typically sold to third parties. This is how you can get all of these free personalized services!	**Attributes:** community members, goals and objectives **Governance:** institutions, actors **Patterns and Outcomes:** costs, legitimacy

Scenario C focused on privacy policies and whether they mitigate privacy concerns. Specifically, we asked how often respondents read privacy policies and what they learn from them. We also queried whether the practice of information sharing with third parties potentially changes respondents' behavior whether or not the data are anonymized. Finally, we asked whether the respondents would be willing to employ a workaround or disable information sharing for an additional charge – examples of rules-in-use contrasting sharply with rules-on-the-books that otherwise support information flows respondents may deem inappropriate.

Scenario D assessed how exogenous decision-makers influence privacy perceptions and subsequent behavior by providing respondents with an example of expert advice. Questions about this scenario addressed differences in perceptions between stakeholder

TABLE 9.3 *Smart home GKC-CI parameters selected for information flow survey questions*

Sender	Modality	Aim
Google Home	can	if the information is used for advertising
Amazon Echo (Alexa)	might	if the information is used for academic research
Apple HomePod (Siri)	will	if the information is used for developing new device features
Smart watch		
Garmin watch		
Subject & Type		**Condition**
Your personal information		if you have given consent
Your location		if you are notified
Recorded audio		
Recipient		**Consequence**
Its manufacturer		if the information is used to generate summary statistics
A third party		if the information is necessary for the device to function properly
		if the information is used to personalize content

FIGURE 9.1 Example baseline information flow question

groups as well as the legitimacy of expert actors in governance. While Scenario D specifically included a software engineer as the exemplar expert role, a parallel study has assessed perceptions of many additional expert actors (Shvartzshnaider, Sanfilippo, and Apthorpe, under review).

The second section of the survey tested how variations in CI and GKC parameters affect the perceived appropriateness of information flows. We designed this section by combining GKC parameters with an existing CI-based survey method for measuring privacy norms (Apthorpe, 2018).

We first selected GKC-CI parameters relevant to smart home device information collection. These parameters are listed in Table 9.3 and include a variety of timely privacy issues and real device practices.

The questions in this section followed a parallel structure. Respondents were first presented with an information flow description containing a randomly selected combination of sender, subject, information type, recipient, and modal parameters (Figure 9.1). Respondents rated the appropriateness of this flow on a 6-point Likert scale from "very inappropriate" to "very appropriate."

Would the above scenario be more or less appropriate under the following conditions?

	Much more appropriate	Somewhat more appropriate	Equally appropriate	Somewhat less appropriate	Much less appropriate
If you are notified	○	○	○	○	○
If you have given consent	○	○	○	○	○

FIGURE 9.2 Example question with varying condition parameters

This baseline question was followed by a series of matrix-style multiple choice questions with one row for each condition, aim, and consequence parameter (Figure 9.2). Respondents were asked to indicate how each of these parameters would affect the appropriateness of the original information flow on a 5-point Likert scale from "much more appropriate" to "much less appropriate."

This process was repeated three times for each survey participant. Each participant rated three sets of baseline flows with different subject/type/recipient/modal parameters and corresponding matrices for condition/aim/consequence parameters. Null parameters were included as controls for each category.

The survey concluded with a series of standard demographics questions, querying respondents' age, gender, state of residence, education level, and English proficiency. Each of these questions had a "prefer not to disclose" option in case respondents were uncomfortable divulging this information.

We created the survey using Qualtrics. We conducted "cognitive interviews" to test survey before deployment via UserBob, an online usability testing platform. Five UserBob workers were asked to take the survey while recording their screen and providing audio feedback on their thought processes. These workers were paid $1 per minute, and all completed the survey in less than 10 minutes. While the UserBob responses were not included in the results analysis, they confirmed the expected survey length of less than 10 minutes and that the survey did not contain any issues that would inhibit respondents' understanding.

We deployed the survey as a Human Intelligence Task (HIT) on Amazon Mechanical Turk (AMT). The HIT was limited to AMT workers in the United States with a 90–100 percent HIT approval rating. We recruited 300 respondents and paid each $1 for completing the survey.

We began with 300 responses. We then removed 14 responses from individuals who provided incomprehensible answers or non-answers to the free-response questions. We also removed 2 responses from individuals who answered all matrix questions in the same column. This resulted in 284 total responses for analysis.

9.3 GOVERNING APPROPRIATE FLOWS OF PERSONAL INFORMATION FROM CONSUMER IOT

We analyze our survey results from the combined GKC-CI perspective. We use GKC framework to identify the background environment (specific context) of consumer IoT, attributes involved in the action arena of IoT information flows (including goals and objectives), governance rules within consumer IoT contexts, and various patterns and outcomes, including the perceived cost and benefits of IoT information flows. We also use the CI framework with the institutional grammar parameters (aims, conditions, consequences, modalities) as transmission principles to understand what specific aspects of governance have the most significant impact on respondent perceptions.

9.3.1 *Background Environment*

Smart devices are pervasive in Americans' lives and homes. We interact with a wide range of these supposedly smart systems all the time, whether we recognize and consent to them or not, from Automated License Plate Readers (ALPR) technologies tracking drivers' locations (Joh, 2016) to Disney World's MagicBand system (Borkowski et al., 2016) to Alexa in dorm rooms (Manikonda et al., 2018). These devices, which are part of a larger digital networked environment, collect massive amounts of data that surreptitiously capture human behaviors and support overt sociotechnical interactions in public and private spaces.

It is notable that there are very different scales of use and applications of smart devices, with many deployed publicly without public input. In contrast, smart devices in individuals' homes are most often configured by the users themselves with appropriate use negotiated within households. Notable exceptions include the controversial and well-publicized implementations of smart locks and systems in rental housing (e.g., Geeng and Roesner, 2019) and uses of IoT to surveil victims by perpetrators of domestic violence (Tanczer et al., 2018). These consumer IoT devices have wildly different patterns of interactions and governance. They are operated under complex arrangements of legal obligations, cultural conditions, and social norms without clear insight into how to apply these formal and informal constraints.

It is thus important to establish applicable norms and evaluate rules-in-use to support good governance of consumer IoT moving forward. Understanding interactions where users have some control of institutional arrangements involving their devices is helpful toward this end. We therefore focus on consumers' everyday use of smart devices, primarily smartphones, wearables, and in-home smart devices. It is our objective to understand both how users would like information flows associated with these devices to be governed and how their privacy perceptions are formed.

The background context for personal and in-home IoT device use extends beyond individual interactions with smart devices. It includes aggregation of information flows from devices and interactions between them, discussion about the relevant normative values surrounding device use, and governance of information flows. There are distinct challenges in establishing norms, given that there is no default governance for data generated, as knowledge resources, or predictable patterns of information to help form user expectations.

Our survey respondents documented the devices they owned, which aligned with recent consumer surveys of IoT prevalence (e.g., Kumar et al., 2019). About 75 percent of respondents reported owning more than one smart device, with 64 percent owning a smart TV and 55 percent owning a Digital Personal Assistant (such as an Amazon Echo, Google Home, or Apple HomePod). Smartwatches were also very popular. A small percentage of respondents owned smart lightbulbs or other Internet-connected appliances.

As these devices become increasingly popular and interconnected, the contexts in which they are used are increasingly complex and fraught with value tensions, making it important to further study user preferences in order to develop appropriate governance. For example, digital personal assistants don't clearly replace any previous analogous devices or systems. They therefore lack pre-existing norms or underlying values about appropriateness to guide use. In contrast, smart televisions are obviously analogous to traditional televisions and are thereby used in ways largely guided by existing norms. These existing norms have often been shaped by entrenched values but do not always apply to emerging information flows from and to new smart features. The resulting tensions can be resolved by identifying relevant values and establishing appropriate governing institutions around IoT information flows. To do so, it is first important to understand the relevant factors (attributes) so as to clarify how, when, and for what purpose changes in information flows governance are and are not appropriate.

9.3.2 *Attributes*

9.3.2.1 Resources

Resources in the IoT context include both (1) the data generated by devices and (2) knowledge about information flows and governance. The latter also includes characteristics of these devices, including necessary supporting technologies and personal information relevant to the IoT action arena.

The modern home includes a range of devices and appliances with Internet-connectivity. Some of these devices are Internet-connected versions of existing appliances, for example, refrigerators, TVs, thermostats, lightbulbs. Other devices, such as digital assistants (e.g., Amazon Echo and Google Home), are new. These devices produce knowledge by generating and consuming information flows. For example, a smart thermostat uses environmental sensors to collect information about home temperature and communicates this information to cloud servers for remote control and monitoring functionality. Similar information flows across devices are causing the IoT ecosystem to evolve beyond the established social norms. For example, now refrigerators order food, toasters tweet, and personal health monitors detect sleeping and exercise routines. This rapid change in the extent and content of information flows about in-home activities leads to a mismatch between users' expectations and the IoT status quo. Furthermore, mismatches extend beyond privacy to features, as some new "smart" functions are introduced for novelty sake, rather than consumer preferences, such as kitchen appliances that are connected to social media.

Our survey respondents' comments reveal discrepancies between users' privacy perceptions/preferences and how IoT devices are actually used. This provides further insight into the attributes of data resources within this context by illustrating what is considered to be appropriate. For example, some respondents noted that even though they have smart TVs, they disconnect them from the Internet to limit communication between devices. Generally, our survey results highlight the range of confusion about how smart devices work and what information flows they send.

A few respondents implied that they were only learning about IoT cross-device communications through the scenarios described in our survey, describing their surprise (e.g., "How they already know that. How did it get from my phone to the tv? That seems very fishy") or in some cases absolute disbelief ("I see no connection between what I'm doing on the phone and a random TV ad") that such a thing was possible. One respondent specifically summarized this confusion amidst common experiences with new technologies:

> *At first, you are concerned. The lightning fast speed at which Google hits you in the heads* [sic] *for an item you were considering buying makes you believe they are spying on you. They aren't spying, because spying implies watching you without your permission, but in using the service you give them complete permission to use any data you put into search queries, posts, etc, to connect you to items you are shopping for, even if it is just to look around.*
>
> *Social media consumers do not understand that they are NOT the customer. They are the product. The customer is the numerous businesses that pay the platform (Google, Facebook, etc) various rates to get their product in front of customers most likely to pay. Radio did this long before Cable TV who did this long before Social Media companies. It's a practice as old as steam.*

This quotation highlights perceived deception about information collection practices by popular online platforms and IoT devices. Users of IoT devices are shaping their expectations and practices amidst a lack of transparency about privacy and problematic notions of informed consent (e.g., Okoyomon et al., 2019). This respondent also touches on the inextricable links between the two knowledge

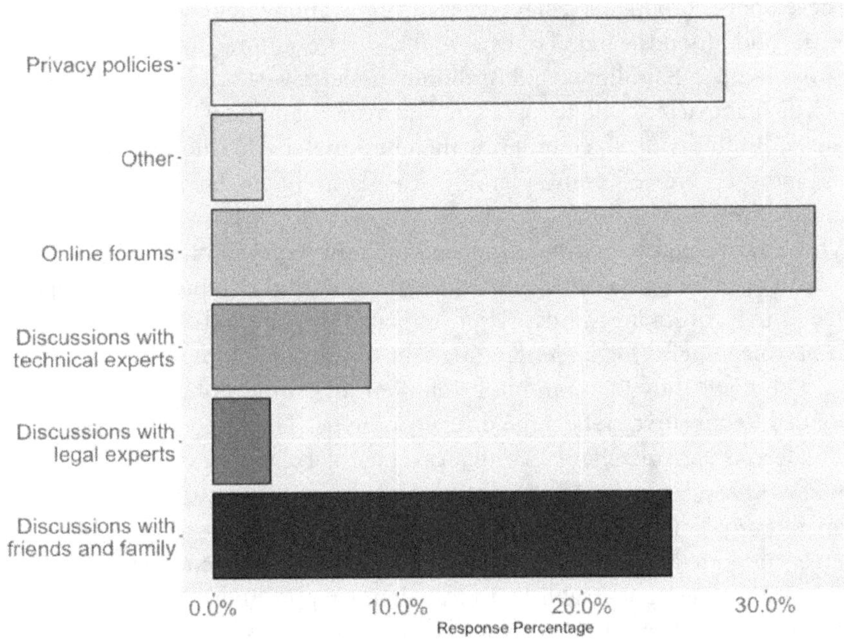

FIGURE 9.3 Where respondents learn about the privacy implications of IoT devices

resources; when users have poor, confusing, or limited explanations of information flows, they fail to understand that they are a resource and that their data is a product.

As Figure 9.3 illustrates, respondents learn about IoT information flows and privacy from a variety of different sources. Online forums represent the most prevalent source of privacy information, yet only just over 30 percent of respondents turn to online forums of IoT users with privacy questions. Privacy policies and discussions with friends and family were also common sources of privacy information, but even these were only consulted by 28 percent and 25 percent of respondents, respectively. Respondents turned to technical and legal experts for privacy information even less frequently, with only 9 percent and 3 percent of respondents reporting these sources, respectively. Overall, there was no single source of privacy information consulted by a majority of respondents.

9.3.2.2 Community Members

Community members, through the lens of the GKC framework, include those who participate and have roles within the action arena, often as users, contributors, participants, and decision-makers. The action arena also includes a variety of additional actors who shape these participants' and users' expectations and preferences, including lawyers and privacy scholars; technologists, including engineers and developers; corporate social media campaigns; anonymous discussants in online forums; and friends and family, which we examine in a related study (Shvartzshnaider, Sanfilippo, and Apthorpe, under review). It is important to consider who is impacted, who has a say in governance, and how the general public is impacted. In this context, community members include IoT device owners, developers, and users, as well as users' family, friends, and neighbors in an increasingly connected world.

While the respondents who depend on online communities and forums for privacy information are a small subset, those communities represent an important source of IoT governance in use. User-generated workarounds and privacy discussions are meaningful for understanding and establishing appropriate information flows. Users are thus the community-of-interest in this context, and those who responded to our survey reflect the diversity of users. The respondents were 62 percent male and 37 percent female with an average age of 34.5 years. 53 percent of the respondents had a Bachelor's degree or higher. 38 percent of respondents self-reported annual incomes of <$40,000, 43 percent reported incomes of <$80,000, 8 percent reported incomes of <$100,000, and 10 percent reported income of > $100,000. We have not established clear demographic indicators for the overall community of IoT users, in this sense, beyond ownership and a skew toward a younger population. However, it is also possible that tech savviness is overrepresented among users.

9.3.2.3 Goals and Objectives

Goals and objectives, associated with particular stakeholders, are grounded in history, context, and values. It is important to identify the specific obstacles and challenges that governance seeks to overcome, as well as the underlying values it seeks to institutionalize.

In our studies, the respondents identified multiple governance objectives and dilemmas associated with information flows to and from IoT devices, including control over data collection and use, third parties, and autonomy in decision-making. Interests among respondents were split between those who valued cross-device information flows and those who felt increased interoperability and/or communication between devices was problematic. Additionally, there were a few respondents who agreed with some of the perceived interests of device manufacturers that value monetization of user data; these respondents appreciated their ability to utilize "free services" in exchange for behavioral data collection. Furthermore, there are additional tensions between the objectives of manufacturers and developers and the interests of users, as evidenced by the split in trust in the expertise of a technical expert in judging appropriateness of information flows. These results show fragmentation in perception of both governance and acceptance of the status quo for information flows around IoT devices.

9.3.3 *Governance*

Through the lens of the GKC framework, including the institutional grammar, we gain insight into different aspects of governance. We can capture how the main decision-making actors, individual institutions, and the norms governing individual information flows emerge and change over time, as well as how these norms might be enforced. Results also indicate that privacy, as appropriate flows of personal information, governs interactions with and uses of IoT devices. For example, we see evidence that anonymization, as a condition modifying the information type and its association with a specific subject within an information flow, does not serve as meaningful governance from the perspective of respondents. Fifty-five percent of respondents stated that they would not change their behavior, or support cross-device communication, just because data was anonymized. It is not immediately clear, from responses to that question alone, what leads to divergence on this interpretation of anonymization or any other perceptions about specific information flows. However, it echoes theorization about CI that incomplete transmission principles are not helpful in understanding information flows (e.g., Bhatia and Breaux, 2018), extending this idea to governance; the condition of anonymity is not a stand-alone transmission principle.

This aligns with our approach combining the GKC and CI frameworks to gauge the explicit and implicit norms that govern information flows within a given context. The CI framework captures norms using five essential parameters of information flows. Four of the parameters capture the actors and information type involved in an information flow. The fifth parameter, transmission principle, constrains information flows. The transmission principle serves as a bridging link between the CI and GKC frameworks. Figure 9.4 shows the average score for perceived appropriateness for an information flow without qualifying it with the transmission principle. We remind the reader that the respondents were first presented with information flow descriptions using sender, subject, information type, recipient, and modal parameters. They rated the appropriateness of these flows on a 6-point Likert scale from "very inappropriate" (-2) to "very appropriate" (+2).

For the GKC framework questions in the first part of the survey, 73 percent of respondents reported that they would change their behaviors in response to third-party sharing. Specific actions they would take are illustrated in Figure 9.6. Figure 9.4 shows that respondents view a "manufacturer" recipient less negatively than a generic third party. Additionally, not stating a recipient all together has a lesser negative effect on information flow acceptability than a generic "third party" recipient. We can speculate that when the recipient is omitted, the respondents mentally substitute a recipient that fits their internal privacy model, as shown in previous research (Martin and Nissenbaum, 2016).

We further gauge the effect on user perceptions of aims, conditions, modalities, and consequences as components of transmission principles. Figure 9.5 illustrates

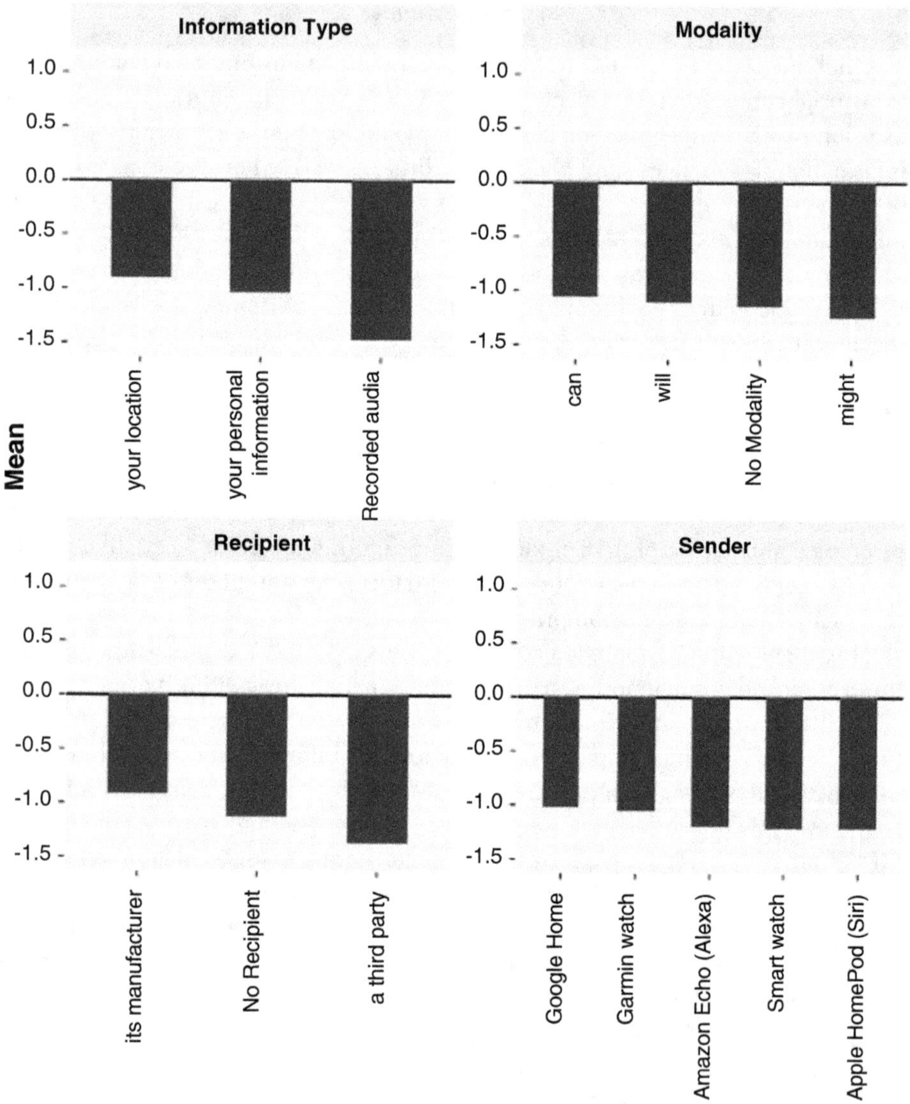

FIGURE 9.4 Average perceptions of information flows by parameter
This figure illustrates the average participant opinion of information flows controlled to specific examples of information type and subject, modalities, recipients, and senders.

changes in average perceptions based on the addition of specific aims, conditions, and consequences to the description of an information flow. We see that stating a condition (such as asking for consent, upon notification or keeping the data anonymous) has a positive effect on the perception of appropriateness. Conversely, we see that not stating an aim correlates with positive perception,

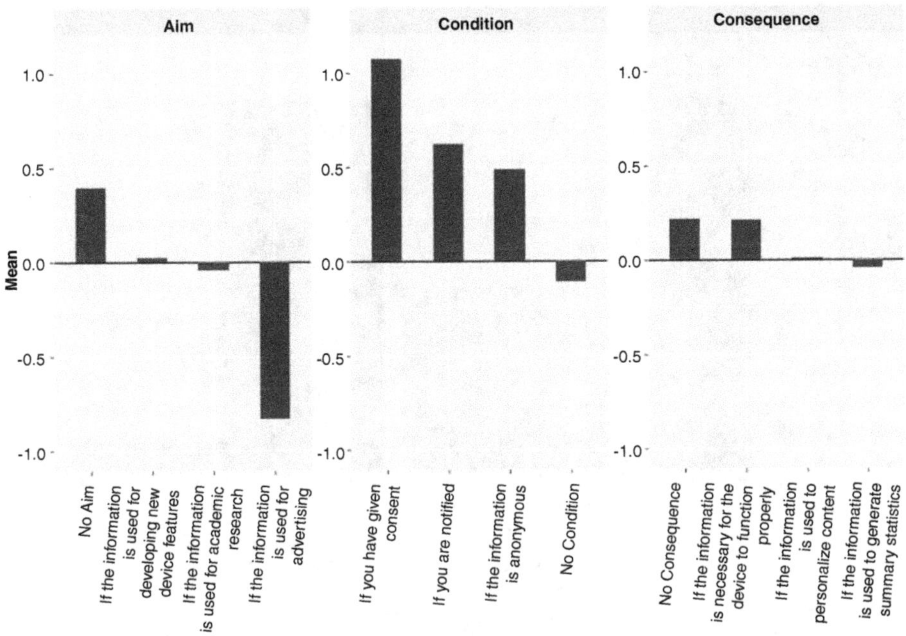

FIGURE 9.5 The impact of specific parameters in changing respondent perceptions of information flows. This figure indicates the average change in perceptions in response to specific examples for each parameter. It does not indicate initial perceptions, in contrast to Figure 9.4.

while the respondents seemed on average neutral towards "for developing new features" and "for academic research" aims, they show negative attitude towards the "for advertising purposes" aim. When it comes to consequences, the results show that the respondents view not stating a consequence as equal, on average, to when the information "is necessary for the device to function properly." However, respondents viewed information flows with the consequence "to personalize content" slightly positively, while viewing information flows with the consequence of "[generating] summary statistics" correlates with slightly negative perception.

Respondents also identified a number of additional approaches that they might take in order to better control flows of their personal information and details of their behaviors between devices. In addition to browsing anonymously and disconnecting their smart TV from the Internet, various respondents suggested:

- *"Use a VPN"*
- *"Wouldn't buy the TV in the first place"*
- *"It's just getting worse and worse. I'll almost certainly return it."*
- *"Research and see if there is a way to not have my info collected."*

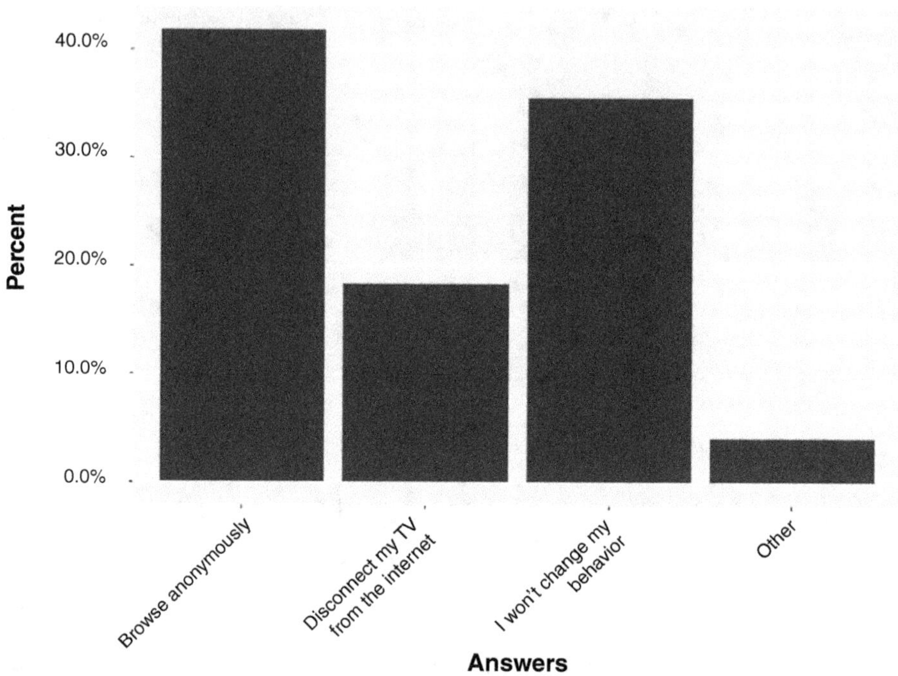

FIGURE 9.6 User actions in response to third-party sharing scenarios

- *"Be much more careful about my browsing/viewing habits."*
- *"Circumvent the tracking"*
- *"Try to find a way to circumvent it without paying"*
- *"Sell it and get a plain TV"*
- *"Block access to my information"*
- *"Delete cookies"*
- *"Disable features"*

When they perceived information flows to be inappropriate, many respondents favored rules-in-use that would circumvent inadequate exogenous governance. While many respondents favored opportunities to opt out of inappropriate flows, a small sub-population developed their own approaches to enact their privacy preferences as additional layers of governance in use. Often these work-arounds subverted or obfuscated default information flows.

9.3.3.1 Rules-in-Use and Privacy Policies

Few respondents found the rules-on-books described in privacy policies to be useful for understanding information flows associated with IoT devices. Many respondents described how they found privacy policies lengthy and confusing. For example, when asked what they learn from reading privacy policies, one respondent explained:

> *That they* [sic] *hard to read! Seriously though, they are tough to interpret. I know they try and protect some of my information, but also share a bunch. If I want to use their services, I have to live that* [sic].

One of the 62 respondents who reported that they read privacy policies "always" or "most of the time" further elaborated:

> *I've learned from privacy policies that a lot of times these company [sic] are taking possession of the data they collect from our habits. They have the rights to use the information as they pleased, assuming the service we're using from them is advertised as 'free' I've learned that sometimes they reserve the right to call it their property now because we had agreed to use their service in exchange for the various data they collect.*

The information users learn from reading a privacy policy can undermine their trust in the governance imposed by IoT device manufacturers. The above comment also touches on issues of data ownership and rights to impact or control information flows. Privacy policies define rules-on-the-books about these issues, which some respondents perceive to be imposed governance. However, as noted by another respondent, the policies do not apply consistently to all devices or device manufacturers:

> *That companies can be pretty loose with data; that some sell data; that others don't go into specifics about how your data is protected; and there are some that genuinely seem to care about privacy.*

This comment emphasizes an important point. For some respondents, practices prescribed in privacy policies affect how they perceive each respective company. In cases where privacy policy governance of information flows aligns with social norms, companies are perceived to care about privacy. Respondents also identify these companies as more trustworthy. In contrast, privacy policies that are vague about information flows or describe information flows that respondents perceive to be egregious or excessive, such as selling user data to many third parties, indicate to respondents that associated companies do not care about user privacy.

Relative to these inappropriate and non-user centered information flows and policies, respondents also described rules-in-use and work-arounds that emerged in order to compensate for undesirable rules-on-the-books. Over 80 percent of respondents indicated that they would pursue work-arounds, with many pursuing alternate strategies even if it took an hour to configure (31 percent) or regardless of difficulty (32 percent).

A few respondents recognized that privacy policies sometimes offer ways to minimize or evade tracking, such as outlining opportunities to opt out, as well as defining the consequences of those choices. When asked "What do you learn from privacy policies?," one respondent elaborated:

> *Occasionally, there are ways to minimize tracking. Some of the ways the data is used. What things are needed for an app or device.*

In this sense, privacy policies disclose and justify information flows, often discouraging users from opting-out through institutionalized mechanisms, such as options to disable recommendations or location services, by highlighting the features they enable or the consequences of being left out. However, despite institutionalized mechanisms to evade tracking, opt out options are sometimes insufficient to protect privacy (Martin, 2012). Furthermore, many respondents don't actually read privacy policies and therefore may not be aware of them. Thus, individuals also develop their own approaches and share them informally among friends and online communities, as shown in Figure 9.1.

Through the lens of the GKC framework, privacy policies serve as a source for rules-on-the-books. These rules govern the flow of information into and out of IoT companies. From respondents' comments, we see that privacy policies play an important role in shaping their expectations for better for worse. On one side, the respondents turn to privacy policies because they want to learn "what [companies] do and how they may use information they receive." On the other side, respondents echoed the general public frustration of not being able to "to learn anything because [privacy policies] are purposefully wordy and difficult to understand." Companies that outline clear information governance policy help inform users' expectations about their practices, while those companies that offer ambiguous, lengthy, hard to understand policies force users to rely on their existing (mostly negative) perceptions of company practices and/or turn to other sources (family, experts) for information.

Finally, the respondents discuss several options for dealing with the gap between rules-on-the-books and their expectations. First, they could adjust their expectations ("these smart devices know too much about me," "be more careful about what I do searches on"). They could also find legal ways to disable practices that do not align with their expectations, such as paying to remove ads or changing settings ("I trust them but I still don't like it and want to disable"). In addition, they could opt out from the service completely ("Sell it and get a plain TV").

9.3.4 *Patterns and Outcomes*

Our survey reveals a significant fragmentation within the community of IoT users relative to current governance practices, indicating irresolution in the action arena. As we piece together data on who IoT users are and how they are shaping appropriate flows of personal information from and between their smart devices, certain patterns and outcomes become evident. Table 9.4 illustrates how respondents' preferences about third party sharing, professed concerns about privacy, and device ownership

TABLE 9.4 *Average perceptions of information flow appropriateness gauged by respondent subpopulations. For each subcommunity we calculate the number of respondents and the average perception score across information flows including consequence, condition, and aim.*

	Embrace Tech (own >2 devices)	Don't embrace tech	Concerned about third party sharing	Not concerned about third party sharing
Unconcerned	0.53 (n=48)	0.5 (n=35)	0.5 (n=52)	0.6 (n=31)
Concerned	0.06 (n=94)	0.05 (n=92)	0.05 (n=171)	0.7 (n=15)

shape their average perceptions of governance outcomes around IoT. We assessed the extent to which respondents embraced technology based on the number of devices they own.

Table 9.4 divides the respondents of our survey into subcommunites based on the opinions of various IoT practices elicited from the first part of the survey. Some respondents largely have embraced IoT technology[4] and are not concerned about privacy issues.[5] Others, while embracing the technology, are concerned about privacy issues. Concerns about third party sharing or a lack of embrace of smart technology yield very different opinions, on average. We cluster these subcommunities into three groups, in order to gauge their perceptions.

When gauging the respondents' perceptions, we note that those who are unconcerned about the privacy implications of cross platform sharing, regardless of other values associated with information governance, have on average favorable views of information flows. Additionally, those respondents who express general concern about the privacy implications, but are not concerned about third party sharing, have similar perceptions on average. These subpopulations of our respondents are the most likely to belong to group 1, who perceive current governance of IoT information flows to be positive, on average. In contrast, those who are concerned about privacy and either don't embrace smart technologies or express concerns about third party sharing are most likely to belong to group 3, who are slightly dissatisfied with current governance outcomes on average. Finally, group 2 is generally concerned about privacy but embraces smart devices with average perceptions slightly above neutral.

We now highlight the open-ended comments from respondents belonging to each group, that put their opinions in context, in an effort to better understand fragmentation and what underlying beliefs and preferences lead to divergent normative

4 Respondents indicated to own more than two smart devices.

5 Respondents in Group 1 indicated that they weren't concerned with the privacy implications of the survey Scenario A.

patterns. While individual comments are not representative, they illuminate individuals' rationales underlying perceptions associated with groups.[6]

9.3.4.1 Group 1: Positive Perceptions

This group includes respondents that positively perceive information sharing practices and tend to emphasize both user consent and preferences for personalization on average. As one user specified:

> *Because I knew what I was getting myself into when using these types of products. How else should companies market to me? We could go back to the old days when there was no personalization at all, when ads were completely dumb and never actually spoke to your needs. But, how is that better? People worry about privacy, but they should only really be concerned with security, which is not the same thing. Keep my financial info secure, keep certain embarrassing stuff under wraps to the public, sure, but we share so much of our lives openly that it seems silly to scoff at ad personalization. I do, however, get annoyed when it doesn't seem personalized ENOUGH, because then it's akin to the uncanny valley for CGI ... in those moments, I'm frustrated that the personalization isn't stronger, such as when I continually see ads for stuff I've already bought.*

Some participants in this group also expressed a firm belief that linking devices that share data would have to be deliberate on the part of users. These users would implicitly consent to information flows, in contrast to respondents with neutral and negative perceptions. In this sense, discoverability, or the ability of smart devices to recognize and communicate with one another, was not acknowledged as a smart feature. For example:

> *For the devices to work like that I must have linked them in some way. That deliberate action would have been my consent to allow these devices to exchange data.*

9.3.4.2 Group 2: Neutral Perceptions

Respondents in this group have a relatively neutral perception of information flows on average. While participants in this group seem to recognize the issues related to discoverability between devices, they don't view them as a privacy violation. As one participant explained their thought process:

> *I feel like at this point everything is somehow connected. There have been many times where I browse the internet and then on my Facebook profile I see adds for the very*

[6] Each group was identified by their average perceptions of appropriateness, rather than by similarity in open-ended responses.

> *thing that I was looking for. I know that it is an effort to target me and things that I might like, I don't think my privacy is being compromised.*

They accept data flows between devices, relative to their user behavior, as standard practice and seem to perceive personalized advertising as independent of their privacy values. However, other members of this group raised concerns about the risks of specific information recipients:

> *I trust them because I think they just want to advertise to me better, I'd only be concerned if the information was being sold to criminals or hackers.*

In this sense, those with neutral perceptions of IoT information flows view credible commercial entities to be legitimate recipients. Sales and advertising are valid objectives, which various individuals within this moderate group saw as compatible with their privacy interests. In contrast, "criminals or hackers" were not seen to be acceptable recipients; future research should assess the differences in perceptions between these recipients and others.

In addition to concerns about some lesser-known third-party recipients, the past history of particular major manufacturers and commercial actors who have been careless or whose security has been compromised was also considered. Some respondents firmly believed that recent history with respect to breaches was unlikely to repeat, consistent with a recent study (Zou et al., 2018). One respondent explained their trust that violations of privacy would not recur:

> *because it seems that a lot of companies have gotten into trouble over the years and hopefully they're taking extra precautions these days.*

In other words, there is a belief that the companies would learn from past events and govern data in a way that was acceptable to them. This group was largely defined by acceptance of major manufacturers as trustworthy enough, without particular enthusiasm. Some of these users appeared to consider these flows in primarily the context of economic transactions.

9.3.4.3 Group 3: Negative Perceptions

Finally, those with negative perceptions of information flows and governance did not share the overall trust in companies to govern user data in accordance with social expectations. In particular, this group held negative perceptions of information flows between devices. Many of these respondents described these cross-platform flows as invasive:

> *It seems invasive and annoying. I also worry that my devices are exchanging information which each other that I didn't specifically agree to divulge. And who knows where else this information is going! All for what? To try and sell me garbage that I don't need and won't actually buy.*

The underlying problem was often with information being used out of context:

If it was just on the browser that I was using to search for socks, it wouldn't be as creepy. It's the fact that multiple platforms are being used in conjunction to analyze what I am doing for targeted advertising that I find invasive.

This sizeable community perceives current information flow practice and governance relative to IoT as violating their expectations.

Some respondents explained how IoT information flows also undermine their trust in other contexts because governance is non-transparent:

> *This seems like an invasion of privacy and makes me wonder what kinds of information it is collecting, storing, or otherwise utilizing for purposes not formally disclosed. Additionally, some devices are shared among families and friends when they visit. I find it to be a violation of my right to privacy to have data related to my phone searches and activities show up across multiple devices that are not used by only one person.*

This is only exacerbated by the industry's continued downplaying of the significance of data sharing.

This group of users was most unified and verbose in explaining their frustration with current governance and information flows in practice. They more often distrusted the technology industry and practitioners, such as in the software engineer scenario on our survey. In addition to not valuing personalization, some emphasized the problematic lack of control and uncertainty about data destinations beyond initial third-party recipients:

> *. . . who knows what happens to this data in the end? Will these third parties sell my info to other third parties? Of course they will. Is all this "free" stuff worth it? There's always a price, you know.*

Some respondents emphasized that current outcomes are egregious and that companies and regulators are falling short in governing user data:

> *I don't believe that it's something people should roll over about. When do we consider it out of hand? It's better to nip these kind of things in the bud. As a computer science major, having one persons opinion on the matter is not going to sway my opinion entirely. I wouldn't just get one opinion from a single doctor of my life was on the line would I?*

These respondents, in particular, emphasize that they want to play a more active role in governing their personal information flows.

Our results demonstrate the tensions that users experience when thinking of privacy in the IoT context. Through the scenarios addressing GKC concepts in the survey, we can observe divergence in interests and concerns of various respondents. Some welcome the new innovations and believe companies have their interest at heart. Others are more concerned, however, and often admit that they feel that there is little they can do to protect their information. This reflects technological acceptance models in the larger population (e.g., Valdez and Ziefle, 2019). By gauging their perceived appropriateness of specific information flows, we can examine additional dimensions of governance using the language of the institutional grammar.

9.4 IMPLICATIONS

9.4.1 *Conceptual and Methodological*

As home environments evolve with the introduction of new technologies, norms of governance and information flow evolve as well. The growing tradition of GKC analysis of a cooperative governance schema offers a way to uncover the contributing elements related to a shift in privacy expectations.

Our approach relies on the GKC framework to identify emerging communities in a given context and then use the CI framework to pose questions about what information flows they consider appropriate. Our methodology bridges the two frameworks by quantifying the effect of each of the elements on the collective norms by measuring how each factor affects the appropriateness of information flows in a given context. This allows researchers to gauge the effect of various factors on the formation of the norms and could be employed to structure future case studies in other contexts to understand norm formation. Our study shows that omitting a condition has an effect on appropriateness; different condition values vary the levels of appropriateness. We observed a similar effect for aims and consequences. In this sense, beyond the specific methodological contributions this gauging introduces, the design also offers a path toward overarching conceptual questions regarding norm formation. Through meta-analysis of cases structured through this approach, it would be possible to better understand privacy norm formation across contexts.

9.4.2 *Practical*

The GKC-CI method is useful in emerging contexts, such as IoT, which often lack established norms. We first identify the various exogenous variables that act as a proxy to understanding respondents' disposition towards privacy. For example, certain respondents tend to be concerned about privacy and are actively pursuing ways to improve it for themselves. They read privacy policies, disable third party sharing, and find ways to circumvent the system whenever possible. Our CI analysis of the flows they deem acceptable confirms it: on average they tend to disallow flows, with notable exceptions when specific conditions, aims, and consequences align with social expectations. Another community perceives the polar opposite. They rarely read privacy policies, embrace third party sharing and don't disable the tracking functionalities – all in the name of convenience and efficiency.

Furthermore, many respondents across interest groups perceive "anonymity" to be ineffective governance of information flows. "Anonymity" thus further fragments the overarching community of IoT users. In contrast to "consent," "anonymity" modifies information, rather than flow, impacting the association between information type and subject. Results indicate that adding "anonymity" as governance does not meaningfully impact perceptions of acceptability or behaviors.

Our results illustrate that governance of IoT should necessarily specify all parameters of the CI framework in structuring information flows, with clear identification of aims and conditions in the transmission principles. Practically, this means that when introducing new technology, it is possible to gauge the various factors using our methodology to reveal factors that have an effect on the acceptability of newly generated flows.

Furthermore, our results confirm previous findings that respondents (n=159) look for privacy policies to understand the privacy implications (e.g., Martin and Nissenbaum, 2016), however, some indicated in their comments that privacy policies are difficult to comprehend. Online forums and discussion with family were the other leading responses.

This result has practical implications with respect to how privacy related information could be structured and communicated so that users more intuitively understand. We propose that IoT manufacturers should clearly define all parameters according to CI and include institutional components within the transmission principle when prescribing information transfers. This could also offer a more informative and constructive discussion on the forums, with all the parameters stated explicitly.

9.5 CONCLUSION

We live in an age of great innovation! In the blink of an eye, information packets traverse the world; with a click of a button, information reaches millions of people. Things evolve at great speed and we, as a society, are looking for ways to keep apace with it. This forces us to adapt to the new reality and reconsider established concepts, such as the notion of privacy.

The GKC-CI method builds on the strength of two privacy theories. We use GKC to describe rules specific to a given context (rules-on-the-books and rules-in-use) and to understand users' strategies and norms. We use CI to gauge the appropriateness of information flows resulting from existing practices (rules-in-use) and/or prescribed by policy (rules-on-the-books).

Our results show diversity in respondents' privacy understanding and expectations around IoT devices. By gauging the information flows resulting from various practices employed by the Internet-connected systems, we can further see the importance of contextual elements to gain deeper insights into their appropriateness. Specifically, we use the expressive language of GKC to further describe CI transmission principles. Results from survey questions that addressed CI and institutional aspects illustrate how more detailed conceptualizations of transmission principles, deconstructed using the attributes within the institutional grammar, highlight what aspects yield differences in respondents' opinions of information flows. This in turn helps to illuminate how particular aspects of institutional governance improve perceptions of these information flows to engender trust in governance.

ACKNOWLEDGMENTS

This project was supported by National Security Agency (NSA) Award (#H98230-18-D-006). Sincere thanks to Helen Nissenbaum and Jessie Garrett Taft for their help in finalizing, funding, and deploying the survey.

REFERENCES

Apthorpe, Noah, Yan Shvartzshnaider, Arunesh Mathur, Dillon Reisman, and Nick Feamster. "Discovering Smart Home Internet of Things Privacy Norms Using Contextual Integrity." *Proceedings of the ACM on Interactive, Mobile, Wearable and Ubiquitous Technologies* 2, no. 2 (2018): 59.

Bhatia, Jaspreet, and Travis D. Breaux. "Semantic Incompleteness in Privacy Policy Goals." In *2018 IEEE 26th International Requirements Engineering Conference (RE)*, pp. 159–169. IEEE, 2018.

Borkowski, Stephen, Carolyn Sandrick, Katie Wagila, Carolin Goller, Chen Ye, and Lin Zhao. "Magicbands in the Magic Kingdom: Customer-Centric Information Technology Implementation at Disney." *Journal of the International Academy for Case Studies* 22, no. 3 (2016): 143.

Crawford, Sue ES and Elinor Ostrom. "A grammar of institutions." *American Political Science Review* 89, no. 3 (1995): 582–600.

Frischmann, Brett M., Michael J. Madison, and Katherine Jo Strandburg, eds. *Governing knowledge commons*. Oxford University Press, 2014.

Geeng, Christine and Franziska Roesner. "Who's In Control?: Interactions In Multi-User Smart Homes." In *Proceedings of the 2019 CHI Conference on Human Factors in Computing Systems*, p. 268. ACM, 2019.

Gorham, Ashley E., Helen Nissenbaum, Madelyn R. Sanfilippo, Katherine Strandburg, and Mark Verstraete. "Legitimacy in Context." At Privacy Law Scholars Conference (PLSC), University of California-Berkeley, 2019.

Joh, Elizabeth E. "The new surveillance discretion: Automated suspicion, big data, and policing." *Harv. L. & Pol'y Rev*. 10 (2016): 15.

Kumar, Deepak, Kelly Shen, Benton Case, Deepali Garg, Galina Alperovich, Dmitry Kuznetsov, Rajarshi Gupta, and Zakir Durumeric. "All Things Considered: An Analysis of IoT Devices on Home Networks." In *28th {USENIX} Security Symposium ({USENIX} Security 19)*, pp. 1169–1185. 2019.

Manikonda, Lydia, Aditya Deotale, and Subbarao Kambhampati. "What's up with Privacy?: User Preferences and Privacy Concerns in Intelligent Personal Assistants." In *Proceedings of the 2018 AAAI/ACM Conference on AI, Ethics, and Society*, pp. 229–235. ACM, 2018.

Martin, Kirsten. "Information technology and privacy: conceptual muddles or privacy vacuums?." *Ethics and Information Technology* 14, no. 4 (2012): 267–284.

Martin, Kirsten and Helen Nissenbaum. "Measuring privacy: an empirical test using context to expose confounding variables." *Colum. Sci. & Tech. L. Rev.* 18 (2016): 176.

Nissenbaum, Helen. *Privacy in context: Technology, policy, and the integrity of social life*. Stanford University Press, 2009.

Okoyomon, E., Samarin, N., Wijesekera, P., Elazari Bar On, A., Vallina-Rodriguez, N., Reyes, I., . . . & Egelman, S. (2019). On The Ridiculousness of Notice and Consent: Contradictions in App Privacy Policies. Privacy Law Scholars Conference (PLSC 2019), University of California, Berkeley, May 30–31, 2019. https://blues.cs.berkeley.edu/wp-content/uploads/2019/05/conpro19-policies.pdf

Sanfilippo, Madelyn, Brett Frischmann, and Katherine Strandburg. "Privacy as Commons: Case Evaluation Through the Governing Knowledge Commons Framework." *Journal of Information Policy* 8 (2018): 116–166.

Selbst, Andrew D. "Contextual expectations of privacy." *Cardozo L. Rev.* 35 (2013): 643.

Shvartzshnaider, Yan, Madelyn Sanfilippo, and Noah Apthorpe. "Privacy Expectations In the Wild: Integrating Contextual Integrity and Governing Knowledge Commons for Empirical Research." http://ssrn.com/abstract=3503096

Shvartzshnaider, Yan, Schrasing Tong, Thomas Wies, Paula Kift, Helen Nissenbaum, Lakshminarayanan Subramanian, and Prateek Mittal. "Learning privacy expectations by crowdsourcing contextual informational norms." In *Fourth AAAI Conference on Human Computation and Crowdsourcing*. 2016.

Tanczer, Leonie, Isabel Lopez Neira, Simon Parkin, Trupti Patel, and George Danezis. "Gender and IoT Research Report." University College London, white paper (2018): www.ucl.ac.uk/steapp/sites/steapp/files/giot-report.pdf

Valdez, André Calero and Martina Ziefle. "The users' perspective on the privacy-utility trade-offs in health recommender systems." *International Journal of Human-Computer Studies* 121 (2019): 108–121.

Zimmer, Michael. "Addressing Conceptual Gaps in Big Data Research Ethics: An Application of Contextual Integrity." *Social Media+ Society* 4, no. 2 (2018): https://doi .org/2056305118768300AU: DOI no?

Zou, Yixin, Abraham H. Mhaidli, Austin McCall, and Florian Schaub. " 'I've Got Nothing to Lose': Consumers' Risk Perceptions and Protective Actions after the Equifax Data Breach." In *Fourteenth Symposium on Usable Privacy and Security ({SOUPS} 2018)*, pp. 197–216. 2018.

10

Designing for the Privacy Commons

Darakhshan J. Mir

10.1 INTRODUCTION

This chapter frames privacy enforcement processes through the lens of governance and situated design of sociotechnical systems. It considers the challenges in formulating and designing privacy as commons (as per the Governing Knowledge Commons framework (Sanfilippo, Frischmann, and Strandburg 2018)) when privacy ultimately gets enacted (or not) in complex sociotechnical systems.

Privacy has traditionally (in computing, legal, economic, and other scholarly communities) been conceptualized in an individualistic framing, often as a private good that is traded off against other goods. In this framing, meaningful decision-making processes about one's data are available to oneself, and any resulting decisions are assumed to impact only one's own self. While social scientists have articulated and studied social conceptualizations of privacy (Petronio and Altman 2002; Altman 1975), the dominant public and scholarly discourse on privacy has been that of individualized control, with characterizations such as informed consent, and "notice and choice" being particularly prominent.

An important conceptualization of the social nature of privacy that has found expression in policy and technical practices is due to Helen Nissenbaum, whose articulation of privacy as *Contextual Integrity* (Nissenbaum 2009) rests on the notion of information flows between social actors within a specific social context. The Contextual Integrity (CI) framework states that privacy is preserved when any arising information flows comply with *contextual informational norms* and, conversely, privacy is violated when contextual norms are breached. In other words, flows are appropriate when they comply with (privacy) norms and (prima facie) inappropriate when these norms are disrupted. While CI is a powerful framework that foregrounds social conceptualizations of privacy, the contextual norms themselves are exogenous to it. Yet, the fundamentally political question of who has the power and authority to decide what is appropriate is inextricably linked to high-level moral and political values of a society, and the contextual functions, purposes, and values that practices, as per CI, must serve. In order to directly engage with these questions, the Governing

Knowledge Commons (GKC) framework considers privacy as the governance of these informational norms (Sanfilippo, Frischmann, and Strandburg 2018). It draws attention to the political and procedural aspects of governing these rules (or norms) of appropriateness.

Scholarly commitments to the characterization of privacy as governance and constitution of appropriate informational norms raise several theoretical, conceptual, empirical, and technical questions. This chapter explores questions that such orientations generate in the conceptualization, design, implementation, and production of technical artifacts and surrounding sociotechnical systems that enable these information flows. If attention to considerations of governance of informational norms is important, then it must find an expression in the design and conceptualization of sociotechnical systems, where information flows occur. These emergent questions reside at a rich interface between different disciplines such as communication theory, sociology, law, and computer science – including the sub-discipline of human–computer interaction (HCI).

As a computer scientist, my objective of mapping these research directions is two-fold: one, to frame richer, more politically and normatively grounded questions for computer scientists to engage with. Even as CI has found expression in privacy scholarship within the discipline of computer science, including HCI and software engineering, existing literature review shows (Benthall, Gürses, and Nissenbaum 2017; Badillo-Urquiola, Page, and Wisniewski 2018) that computer scientists have largely not engaged with the normative aspects of CI. Benthall et al. (Benthall, Gürses, and Nissenbaum 2017) and Badillo-Urquiloa et al. (Badillo-Urquiola, Page, and Wisniewski 2018), with the latter being focused on HCI researchers, call upon computer scientists to engage with the normative elements of CI. In this chapter, I reinforce this calling by highlighting the normative valence of the governance of informational norms, and outline a set of research directions that such orientations open up for privacy researchers who locate themselves in computer science. Second, by examining conceptualizations and practices in computer science, the GKC framework has an opportunity to make connections to existing literature in computer science, particularly one that conceptually aligns with the philosophy of the commons approach, yet might not have a similar theoretical and conceptual articulation. This is especially pertinent as the commons approach seeks to "systematize descriptive empirical case studies of real-world contexts." Finding points of injection into the design and architecture of sociotechnical systems both expands the purview of the GKC approach as well as provides opportunities to construct additional empirical case studies.

Consequently, I identify six distinct research directions pertinent to the governance and formulation of privacy norms, spanning an examination of how tools of design could be used to develop design strategies and approaches to formulate, design, and sustain a privacy commons, and how specific technical formulations and approaches to privacy can serve the governance of such a privacy commons.

First, I examine if the tools and methodologies of design can be used to explore questions of governance and procedural legitimacy both to assess the appropriateness of entrenched norms or rules-in-use, and to handle previously unresolved, hidden, un-surfaced ethical disagreements. Second, I examine what opportunities one of these design methodologies, *Participatory Design* (Muller 2009), with its political and ideological commitments to democratic decision-making, presents in the formulation and governance of privacy norms by communities in specific contexts. This direction lays out participatory decision-making about privacy as a normative goal to achieve. Third, I explore questions that arise from the relationship between privacy literacy, civic learning, and models of participatory governance. Relatedly, fourth I propose the empirical study of relationships between privacy norms and individuals' privacy expectations and preferences, and how participation and effective modes of community engagement can shape the latter. Fifth, I identify questions related to the capacities of computational techniques to automatically extract informational norms from human sentences that consist of privacy policies formulated through a participatory process. Sixth, I examine how a technical conceptualization of privacy, differential privacy (Dwork 2006), that provides a mathematical guarantee of plausible deniability to an individual can operate within the larger normative framing of governance.

The rest of the chapter is organized as follows. The next section discusses social conceptualizations of privacy. Following this, I outline existing literature on the operationalization of social notions of privacy in the design and implementation of technical systems, finally leading to a section that elaborates on the six research directions identified previously.

10.2 SOCIAL CONCEPTUALIZATIONS OF PRIVACY

The dominant public and scholarly discourse on privacy has been that of individualized control, with characterizations such as informed consent, and "notice and choice" being particularly prominent. Two conceptual underpinnings of this individualistic framing, namely, access to meaningful decision-making and the largely localized impact of sharing one's data, are insufficient when considering the larger social contexts in which privacy is or is not enacted. Meaningful decisions to share (or not share) one's data are contingent upon the availability of informative disclosures about how such data will be shared and processed. In reality, we have little to no control or understanding over what information about ourselves we exude, where it travels, who has access to it, the processes through which other parties or individuals share this information, the ways in which it is made actionable, and how we should respond to these situations on an individual level besides by opting out of services and becoming a "digital recluse". Furthermore, even if informative disclosures are made, and understood as such by the affected population, any resulting decisions people make are largely superfluous since access to services is typically only available in exchange for information that individuals must provide about themselves.

Additionally, individuals' lives, and, therefore, data are interlinked with each other in underlying social contexts animated by the social, communal, professional, civic, and commercial links they have with other individuals, entities, and institutions. Consequently, our privacy (or the lack thereof) is inherently linked. This becomes amply clear when privacy is considered within the context of predictive analytic power of data, including their correlational analyses – inferences about aspects of individuals' lives from data on other individuals are precisely possible because of the underlying networked nature of our personal information. Locating its origin in the networked nature of our social relationships, Marwick and boyd capture aspects of this inherently social nature of privacy using the concept of "Networked Privacy" (Marwick and boyd 2014).

One of the earlier and more comprehensive articulations of the social dimensions of privacy is due to Regan (1986, 2000). She comprehensively outlines three dimensions of the social nature of privacy: that *privacy is a common value*, with all individuals having an appreciation of privacy to some extent, and with cultures and communities having a shared perception of privacy; that *privacy is a public value* in that it is crucial in supporting democratic political processes, and in "the forming of a body politic or public" (P. M. Regan 2015); and that *privacy is a collective value* in that one person is unlikely to have privacy unless all people have a similar level of privacy echoing the conceptualization of "networked privacy" by Marwick and boyd (Marwick and boyd 2014). Other scholars have recognized the need to deemphasize the individualized narrative of privacy by arguing that privacy is a "public good" (Fairfield and Engel 2017; P. M. Regan 2015, 2016) – something that requires public coordination for its protection – and that legal and regulatory tools should be "redesigned to focus less on individual knowledge and empowerment and more on facilitating groups' collective protection of their privacy" (Fairfield and Engel 2017). In another powerful departure from individualistic framings, Cohen argues that "protecting privacy effectively requires willingness to depart more definitively from subject-centered frameworks in favor of condition-centered frameworks" (Cohen 2019).

In a seemingly orthogonal recognition (from the approaches summarized above) of the social nature of privacy, Nissenbaum's articulation of privacy as *Contextual Integrity* (Nissenbaum 2009) rests on the notion of information flows between social actors within a specific social context. As discussed in the previous section, CI rests on the notion of appropriate information flows that are regulated by contextual informational norms. A norm is conceptualized to be "well-formed" if it is composed of five parameters: sender, recipient, information subject, attribute (information type), and a transmission principle. For example, in the healthcare context, senders, recipients, and subjects are social actors within this sphere, such as physicians, nurses, patients, therapists, etc., and attributes could consist of elements such as diagnoses, prescriptions, and test results. Transmission principles are expressed as a condition under which the information flow can occur, such as *with permission of the subject, under confidentiality*, etc. According to CI, when information flows comply with entrenched informational norms, privacy is respected, and when flows violate norms, privacy is violated.

While it might seem on the surface that informational norms (whether in policy or in technical practice) merely act as tools that regulate the appropriateness of the flow of information concerning an individual, key to the CI framework is the recognition that "legitimate" contextual informational norms are not determined individually (even though the flows themselves might involve information about specific individuals); rather these are socially constructed by our shared understanding, as members of a society, of contextual goals, values, and ends. Information flows do not occur in a vacuum but purportedly to achieve specific contextual goals and outcomes in distinct social contexts. Privacy as CI rests on this notion of socially constructed informational norms that have achieved "settled accommodation" (Nissenbaum 2019) among a group, network, or community. It also provides a normative yardstick to evaluate the appropriateness of novel information flows that could reflect evolving societal norms, against high-level moral and political values, and the extent to which these novel or evolving information flows align with the values, end, and goals of the social context they occur in.

In all of these characterizations of privacy seen above, the social versus individual dimensions of privacy (or to what extent each characterization lies on the social vs. individual spectrum) is actuated by the underlying values inherent in these characterizations and the origins of these values. As we shall see later, and elsewhere in this chapter, the GKC framework aims to understand the sources and conflicts in values in addition to locating shared values.

Among social conceptualizations of privacy, Nissenbaum's CI framework is particularly prominent, because of its descriptive and evaluative power, and because by virtue of finding expression into the logics of software system design, it is actionable in the design of technical systems. See for example Barth et al.'s (2006) work on expressing information flows and their appropriateness using first order temporal logic.

The GKC framework draws attention to the political and procedural aspects of governing these rules (or norms) of appropriateness. By foregrounding the perspective of governance, the norms of information flow can no longer be deemed to be exogenous to a specific context, but demand an engagement with aspects of procedural legitimacy of these norms – how are the norms of appropriateness in specific contexts constituted, who has a say in the process, who is excluded, how are these norms governed, and if, how, and by whom is compliance with these norms enforced? The GKC approach positions actors as members of a community rather than individuals acting within a broad social sphere subject to norms and rules that are largely deemed to be exogenous to the context. Sanfilippo et al. state that the most important difference between the knowledge commons framework and the CI framework is that the latter "envisions actors as individual participants in a broadly defined social context, such as education, healthcare, or the commercial market, while the knowledge commons framework envisions actors as members of a 'community' involved in producing or managing a set of resources, and in producing (or at least co producing) the applicable rules-in-use within a broader context ordinarily accounted for as part of the background environment." Sanfilippo et al., argue that:

> this shifts the focus from questions of consistency with externally defined norms and rules to questions of community governance involving not only what background norms and rules are in forces in a specific action arena but also how and by whom those rules are determined. (Sanfilippo, Frischmann, and Strandburg 2018, 127)

The GKC framework fortifies CI by further directing attention away from individuals' perceptions or experiences about privacy to the consideration of these perceptions and experiences in the context of governance, placing privacy squarely in the political and normative realm. While individuals feel the impacts of information flows, the networked nature of these impacts, and their enactment in, often, contested social contexts, necessitates an approach that returns their consideration to the normative and political sphere.

10.3 ENGAGING WITH UNDERLYING TECHNICAL PROCESSES

In this section I review literature on the motivations and means to build privacy-preserving capacities in technical systems, particularly those that embrace social conceptualizations of privacy.

In his book "Code: And other Laws of Cyberspace," Lawrence Lessig (2000) argues that in addition to the law, social norms, and the market, the underlying architecture that enables digital environments, namely "code," regulates cyberspace, making an argument for citizens to demand that any resulting technology reflect values that they would like to see being upheld in a democratic society:

> But underlying everything in this book is a single normative plea: that all of us must learn at least enough to see that technology is plastic. It can be remade to do things differently. And that if there is a mistake that we who know too little about technology should make, it is the mistake of imagining technology to be too plastic, rather than not plastic enough. We should expect – and demand – that it can be made to reflect any set of values that we think important. The burden should be on the technologists to show us why that demand can't be met. (Lessig 2000, 32)

Gürses and van Hoboken (2018) argue that public attention on privacy concerns is mainly focused on the step when digital artifacts reach consumers, and that as a result any strategies that address these concerns are conceptualized for this interface of technology consumption. They propose exploring ways in which interventions can be injected prior to any potential consumption – at the stage of production of such technologies. Shining a spotlight on the stages of production of software – the backbone of any technical artifact – can help scholars "better engage with new configurations of power" that "have implications for fundamental rights and freedoms, including privacy." They articulate privacy governance as the "combination of technical, organizational and regulatory approaches" for the governance of privacy. They use the term "end-users" to underline the limited agency typically users of software services have in designing the privacy and other affordances of such systems, making the argument that in addition to paying more attention to the production stages of software, privacy scholarship should also focus on the functionality that the software offers and how it impacts end-users' activities.

The recognition of the importance of integrating and operationalizing conceptualizations of privacy in the design of technical products led to the development of the Privacy by Design (PBD) framework (Cavoukian and others 2009; Gürses, Troncoso, and Diaz 2011). PBD takes a proactive approach to privacy by ensuring that privacy-preserving capacities are upheld and privacy-harming ones are extenuated, during the design of a technical artifact. It relies on design of a product as a means of complying with privacy policies – which may be articulated through regulations or law – rather than a reactive system such as one that imposes penalties. The PBD paradigm foregrounds the technical design process to create an artifact that is protective of privacy from the "ground-up".

Gürses et al. (Gürses, Troncoso, and Diaz 2011) point out that while a commitment to principles of PBD is finding growing traction in regulatory settings, there is little common, concrete understanding of how these principles translate to technical and design practice. They argue that an interpretation of these principles "requires specific engineering expertise, contextual analysis, and a balancing of multilateral security and privacy interests." Systematically locating these principles and their translation in the practice of engineering sociotechnical systems has led to the expression of PBD in the emerging field of privacy engineering (Gürses and Alamo 2016).

However, the operationalization of social conceptualizations of privacy in the privacy engineering process remains an underexplored area. Gürses and Alamo (Gürses and Alamo 2016) assert that a future important direction for privacy engineering would be to conduct empirical studies that are cognizant of different *contextual* challenges when the tools, techniques, and methodologies of privacy engineering are used. In 2015, the Computing Community Consortium undertook a PBD initiative to identify appropriate conceptualizations of privacy and to operationalize these conceptualizations effectively in the engineering process, with contextual integrity merging as a prominent concept.

Even as CI has been used by computer scientists (in contexts within and outside privacy engineering), a recent literature review finds that they have largely not engaged with the normative elements of CI (Benthall, Gürses, and Nissenbaum 2017). This finding holds true even for HCI researchers (Badillo-Urquiola, Page, and Wisniewski 2018). Even as HCI engages more deeply with questions of technology embedded in social and cultural contexts, Badillo-Urquiloa et al. find that HCI researchers too have not engaged deeply with the critical and normative aspects of CI, and HCI researchers must engage more deeply with the normative aspects of CI to "inform their research design, design new sociotechnical systems, and evaluate whether CI can be used as an actionable framework for translating users' privacy norms into usable systems." Many of the research directions identified in this chapter, directly speak to these recommendations.

10.4 RESEARCH DIRECTIONS

In this section, I map six research directions pertinent to the design of sociotechnical systems when considering the GKC framework. First, I examine if the tools and methodologies of design can be used to explore questions of governance and procedural legitimacy both to assess the appropriateness of entrenched norms or rules-in-use and to handle previously unresolved, hidden, un-surfaced ethical disagreements. Second, I examine what opportunities one of these design methodologies, Participatory Design, with its political and ideological commitments to democratic decision-making, presents in the formulation and governance of privacy norms by a community in a specific context. This direction lays out participatory decision-making about privacy as a normative goal to achieve. Third, I explore questions that arise from the relationship between privacy literacy, civic learning, and models of participatory governance. Relatedly, fourth I propose the empirical study of relationships between privacy norms and individuals' privacy expectations and preferences, and how participation and effective modes of community engagement can shape the latter. Fifth, I identify questions related to the capacities of computational techniques to automatically extract informational norms from human sentences that consist of privacy policies formulated through a participatory process. Sixth, I examine how a technical conceptualization of privacy, differential privacy, that provides a mathematical guarantee of plausible deniability to an individual can operate within the larger normative framing of governance. In the following subsections, I expand on these six research directions.

10.4.1 *Design Paradigms to Examine the Legitimacy of Privacy Rules-in-Use*

As discussed in the previous section, the alignment of PBD with privacy engineering could make the former an important enactor of privacy-preserving capabilities of a sociotechnical system. Wong and Mulligan (Wong and Mulligan 2019) outline the important place PBD has come to occupy in the privacy policy sphere, owing to its inclusion in the EU's General Data Protection Regulation, the United States

Federal Trade Commission's privacy policy recommendations, and other privacy advisory and regulatory institutions. They argue that PBD is currently, largely, dominated by engineering approaches that assume that privacy is pre-defined and exogenous to the design process, whereas HCI has a rich collection of design methodologies and tools that are capable of identifying relevant conceptualizations of privacy and related values *within* the design process. Such approaches, they further argue, are largely absent from policy-making and practice of PBD. Furthermore, even within HCI, they find that most PBD approaches use design and associated principles "to solve a privacy problem" or "to support or inform privacy decision making", and that "design to explore people and situations and to critique, speculate, or present critical alternatives" – design approaches available from the field of HCI – are largely absent from both the policy-making and the practice dimensions of PBD. They argue that the latter are particularly pertinent when the "conception of privacy that ought to guide design is unknown or contested" (Wong and Mulligan 2019). This resonates with the GKC framework:

> The commons governance perspective encourages us to look behind the curtain to investigate the *origins* and dynamic characters of both nominal rules and rules-in-use and to interrogate the potentially contested legitimacy of the formal and informal processes that produce them. We believe that issues of procedural legitimacy and distinctions between nominal rules and rules-in-use are central both to descriptive understanding of privacy and to normative evaluation and policy making. Governance and legitimacy may be particularly important for the most perplexing privacy issues, which often involve overlapping ethical contexts or contested values. (Sanfilippo, Frischmann, and Strandburg 2018, 118–119)

Both approaches emphasize the contested nature of privacy and the procedural aspects of exploring and uncovering these contestations. An important question that a synthesis of this shared emphasis raises is: what kinds of design paradigms in computer science, generally, but HCI and adjoining disciplines, specifically, provide a way for questions of governance and procedural legitimacy to enter into the design and implementation of technology that mediates or enables information flows? How can the tools and methodologies of design be employed to explore questions of governance and procedural legitimacy both to assess the appropriateness of entrenched norms or rules-in-use, and to handle previously unresolved, hidden, un-surfaced ethical disagreements?

Gurses and van Hoboken argue that contextual integrity while not tied down to concepts of time and location requires "looking back in time" to identify entrenched social norms that govern the "appropriate" information flows, in order to enable an informed and reflective design of novel socio-technical systems. Utilizing such a lens on norms, and considering the GKC framework, what can the tools and methodologies of design reveal about the procedural legitimacy of entrenched privacy norms and values?

One way forward toward exploring this question further is contained in the approaches outlined by Wong and Mulligan (2019), who map out the purposes for which design is employed in relation to privacy in the existing HCI literature. On examining 64 scholarly publications in HCI venues that use design in relation to privacy, they find that 56 percent use design "to solve a privacy problem," where "privacy is a problem that has already been well-defined outside of the design process," and 52 percent use design "to inform and support decision-making," which foregrounds the individualized framing of privacy by focusing on providing information to users to enable them to make privacy-preserving decisions, or on the creation of tools and processes so that designers can incorporate privacy more easily in their practice. Only 22 percent used design "to explore people and situations" where design and other methodologies are used to explore what conceptualizations of privacy in varying social and cultural contexts are "at play" – an approach that has "implications for design". Finally, only 11 percent use design to "to critique, speculate or present critical alternatives," where questions such as "what should be considered as privacy?," "privacy for whom?," and "how does privacy emerge from technical, social, and legal entanglements" are considered. The latter two orientations are particularly well suited to the surfacing of privacy conceptualizations in relation to surrounding social, cultural, and political factors, yet are under-explored in the literature. These design approaches have the potential to provide tools to bring procedural legitimacy "into play in assessing whether the rules-in-use for personal information are normatively appropriate" (Sanfilippo, Frischmann, and Strandburg 2018). Furthermore, these approaches directly relate to the three distinct ways identified by Sanfilippo et al. in which procedural legitimacy is in play the GKC framework: first, whether the procedures that construct the rules-in-use are deemed to be legitimate by diverse community members, and aid them in achieving their objectives; second, whether the governance practices account for the interests and needs of "impacted outsiders"; and third, whether the "exogenous rules and norms" to which a community is subject are responsive to member needs and interests.

In particular, three design methodologies are well positioned to explore these orientations: (a) speculative design, where design is undertaken to present critical alternatives (Wong and Khovanskaya 2018; Auger 2013; DiSalvo, Jenkins, and Lodato 2016); (b) value centered design, where design is used to achieve certain human values (Friedman 1997; Shilton 2018); and (c) participatory design (Muller 2009), where design is undertaken not only for, but by impacted stakeholders.

In this section, I outline one possible direction that directly opens up points of engagement between privacy as governance of privacy rules and speculative design methodologies. DiSalvo et al. (2016) use speculative design in the context of "civic tech" as "a way to explore potential, alternative, and future conditions by articulating their existence in generative forms, with a particular focus on the complications of governance and politics disposed by computational technologies." The tools of speculative design can speak directly to aspects of governance that the commons approach focuses on.

To summarize, design paradigms in HCI provide potent tools to explore questions of procedural legitimacy of rules-in-use in the commons governance framework. In addition to achieving, what Wong and Mulligan (2019) consider important, namely, broadening the notion of design in PBD, these orientations could build important bridges between the PBD framework and the GKC framework.

10.4.2 *Formulation and Governance of Privacy Norms via Participatory Design*

In this subsection, I explore the framework of Participatory Design (PD) in detail to consider the opportunities it presents for democratic governance of privacy norms. PD as a design methodology has historically had clear political commitments to democratic ideals. Pilemalm (2018) notes that PD developed in the late 60s and early 70s (as cooperative design) with the intention of involving citizens in urban areas in Scandinavia in the planning and design of their living environments. Soon, PD entered workplaces in Scandinavia with the intention of making workplaces more democratic, and empowering workers to participate in and influence their working conditions and workplace technology through the use of collaborative design processes between the workers and the designers (Bjerknes et al. 1987; Ehn 1988; Simonsen and Robertson 2012). Often, this occurred by assisting workplace unions in devising technological "control activities and policies" (Asaro 2000). Subsequent "generations" of PD, particularly its variants in the United Kingdom and North America were more focused on involving users and other stakeholders in the process of design of technologies to create better systems, an adoption that largely found resonance in HCI (Muller 2009). Several studies since then have argued to actively re-introduce the political and ideological dimensions of PD, highlighting the importance of democracy as a core political ideal to PD (Beck 2002; Kanstrup 2003).

Regan's argument (Regan 1986; 2015) that privacy is both a collective and a democratic value lends credence to the idea of using democratic processes to determine which norms or rules regarding privacy should be in use, how they should be governed, how the appropriateness of specific privacy rules should be evaluated, and by whom. As Sanfilippo et al. articulate:

> Like substantive appropriateness, procedural legitimacy is contextual. Legitimacy, as consensus about social good or appropriateness as reached through participatory decision-making of all potentially impacted, is itself a normative goal that may be addressed through commons institutions. (Sanfilippo, Frischmann, and Strandburg 2018, 127)

Scholarly and political commitments to democratic decision-making in the governance of privacy takes us down the route of exploring connections to PD, and its democratic and political ideals, in particular. Some preliminary attempts in this direction are due to Mir et al. (2018) and Shilton et al. (2008). Yet, at the time of writing this chapter, there is almost no work on operationalizing PD to conceptualize privacy. There is much important work to be done in this direction, such as determining which privacy rules-in-use in specific contexts are normatively appropriate, what the characteristics of the community are that determine these rules-in-use, how communities and other stakeholders, particularly dynamic ones, can negotiate around conflicting values such as privacy. In this section, I examine the affordances of PD to speak to such concerns.

While PD processes have largely been absent both in the shaping of privacy policy and in exploring contested aspects of privacy, privacy scholarship can learn and adapt from the vast body of literature that *does* envision using participatory, democratic processes in shaping and determining aspects of public policy. Such adaptations are especially pertinent in cases where technology (including potentially privacy-invasive technology) is employed within contexts that are democratic by their very nature, such as several decision-making processes employed by states, cities, municipalities, and public services, a context that is often dubbed as "civic tech." In such contexts, participants' relationship to the technology in question is more appropriately framed as that of a citizen rather than a consumer. For example, Pilemalm (2018) studies the role of PD in public sector contexts, including civic engagement and "we-government" initiatives. He presents case studies showing that after addressing the challenges and practical difficulties of involving civil citizens, PD can be employed in the design of technologies in the public sector and lead to empowerment of citizens involved by both including them in designing the products that impact them and enhancing their understanding and skills.

In particular, the democratic framing of PD harkening back to its historical roots had led several PD researchers and practitioners to view PD as a process that interrogates issues of power and politics with the ultimate aim of enhancing democratic ideals, mutual learning and empowerment of the participants (Ehn 1988). While PD flourished as a practice and value-based design system (Shilton 2018) in the context of unionized workers in the Scandinavian workplace, the changing nature of work organizations and the adoption of PD outside Scandinavia led to the adoption of PD beyond the workplace. In particular Teli et al. (2018) remark that the adoption of PD in the early 2000s extended beyond the "renewed workplace" – workplaces they term as arising out of "transformations in the mode of production toward post-Fordism" – to domains considered to be constituting the "public realm" (Huybrechts, Benesch, and Geib 2017). This expression continues in what DiSalvo et al. (2012) call community-based PD, where the participants are not workers, but rather citizens interested in community-related issues, and the context involves negotiations among multiple parties with heterogeneous, and often conflicting values (Grönvall, Malmborg, and Messeter 2016). As Grönvall and coauthors remark, in such settings:

> Infrastructure is not viewed as a substrate that other actions are based upon, but rather as an on-going appropriation between different contexts with many different stakeholders and practices with negotiation of potentially conflicting agendas and motivations for participation. In community-based PD settings, contrasting and conflicting values are unavoidable and do not only need to be explicitly addressed in the PD process, but can act as drivers for PD negotiation processes. (Grönvall, Malmborg, and Messeter 2016)

Grönvall et al. present three case studies to demonstrate how design interventions enable the participants to become aware of other participant's attitudes toward the collaboration at hand as well as their values. The case studies illustrate how even as PD as a process can enable a consensus and an understanding, the dynamic nature of the participant population leads to a continuously changing landscape of values as each participant brings in their own roles, stances, and values into these collaborations. They remark that:

> the driving force in design is rarely a shared vision among stakeholders of a future made possible through design activities. Rather the driving force in our cases has been the plurality of dynamic values, and a continuous negotiation of values in agonistic spaces; not to reconcile value differences, but to reshape and achieve a productive co-existence between them, allowing new practices among project participants to form. (Grönvall, Malmborg, and Messeter 2016)

Lodato and DiSalvo (2018) consider PD in the context of institutions operating in the public realm, examining the constraints produced through employing PD in working with or through these institutions – what they call "institutional constraints," and are ultimately interested in understanding such institutions through the lens of PD.

PD, when employed in the so-called public realm, raises questions about who the participants are, who is considered to be part of the community, how those boundaries are drawn, and who is left out of the "participation." For example, Lodato and DiSalvo claim that:

> A central concern of PD is the distribution of power – authority, control, decision-making, etc. – to underrepresented bodies, populations, and people in the design, use, and deployment of products, services, and systems in work and public life. (Lodato and DiSalvo 2018)

Since PD aims to enhance democratic decision-making, mutual learning between designers and participants, and empowerment of participants, Bossen et al. (2016) consider the question of evaluating whether PD processes indeed achieve these goals. They present a framework to systematically evaluate PD projects for these goals paying attention to the purpose of the evaluation, who conducts and leads the evaluation, who participates, the methods used, and the audience for the evaluation. These criteria help understand questions of participation, legitimacy, and empowerment in PD.

There is some literature on the commonalities between Commons Design and Participatory Design; here I briefly review that literature to explore ideas pertinent to the design of a privacy commons. Marttila et al. (2014) examine the connections between the literature on commons (for example, using Ostrom's framework (Ostrom 1990)) and PD, with the aim of developing design strategies and approaches to designing the commons. They argue that both PD and the commons literatures "build upon stakeholders and communities' capabilities and right to act and decide upon their future." They point out how while Ostrom's "design principles"(Ostrom 1990) for long-enduring commons were not intended to provide a framework to design a commons, nevertheless, they can be integrated in the PD process "to develop a nuanced understanding of design agency and its interplay with multiple mechanisms of collective action" (Marttila, Botero, and Saad-Sulonen 2014).

Such orientations are also available (and arguably, direly needed) for the conceptualizations and implementations of privacy. However, such engagements open up questions about efficiency of processes, and scalability of solutions, two framings that technologists are particularly attuned to.

In his book titled the "Smart Enough City" (Green 2019), Ben Green presents an example that instead works with an alternative concept: "meaningful inefficiencies" that he borrows from civic media scholars (Gordon and Walter 2016). Green cites work by Gordon and coauthors (Gordon and Baldwin-Philippi 2014) to create Community PlanIt (CPI),[1] an online, multiplayer game to promote engagement, deliberation, and decision-making within communities. The game is focused not on making the process of deliberation and engagement efficient, but rather to recognize that these are necessarily inefficient processes, and to design such platforms for "meaningful inefficiencies" that highlight aspects of community member engagement, coordination, and reflection:

> Instead of being gamified with a rigid structure that funnels users to predetermined ends, CPI embraces play to enable exploration and deliberation. Every user is tasked with responding to open-ended prompts, and in order to see the responses of others, one must first submit one's own answer. Such game mechanics lead to positive and reflective deliberation that one participant called "the back and forth that you don't get in a town hall meeting." Players also noted that the game encouraged them to reflect on their own opinions and appreciate alternative viewpoints. "I think it forced you to really think about what you wanted to say in order to see other people's opinions," said one participant. "Whenever I found out that I was like the minority . . . it just made me think of why do people think the other idea is better," added another. "I put my comment and someone disagreed with it," remarked another player, before adding, "I don't really know who's right, but I feel like it made me really think about what I thought prior." Through these interactions, players developed their capacities to reflect on their positions and emerged with deeper trust in the community. (Green 2019, 54)

[1] https://elab.emerson.edu/projects/community-planit

Could community engagement platforms that are designed to enhance civic engagement and are embedded appropriately in the civic, social, and cultural contexts of communities, such as Community PlanIt, be deployed to develop models of participatory governance of information norms? This question is inextricably linked to the larger goals of PD – that of enhancing democratic ideals, mutual learning and empowerment of the participants. The next section will delve into some of the literature on "civic learning" and reflective decision-making that enables participants to negotiate around and make collective decisions about issues impacting them.

10.4.3 *Privacy Literacy, Civic Leaning, and Participatory Governance*

Questions of participation in mechanisms of governance lead to underlying questions about people's understanding of the information flow landscape, their perception of their roles in it, and what kinds of coordination and deliberation mechanisms enable people to engage meaningfully in such participatory frameworks. In relation to the GKC framework, "adequate" privacy literacy may be viewed as "attributes of the community members" (Strandburg, Frischmann, and Madison 2017). Community members can effectively govern the privacy commons only when they understand the underlying information flows and consequences of appropriate and inappropriate flows.

An important question that such considerations raise is: What kinds of (pedagogical) tools can be used to enhance people's understanding of the data ecosystem and its implications? As Regan outlines, "the goal here would be to make visible the privacy implications which to date have effectively remained invisible to those affected" (P. Regan 2016). Here, Kumar (2018) offers some preliminary research directions by outlining the possibility of using CI as an educational tool. This stems from an earlier study Kumar conducted with her co-authors (Kumar et al. 2017), where CI was used as an analytical tool to understand how children used digital devices and how they both understood and navigated privacy concerns online. The study provided evidence that children (especially over ten) largely understand how the parameters of CI affect norms of information flow, and in particular, they had an understanding of actors and attributes, even as they don't use the same terminology. Based on this, Kumar suggests exploring CI as a tool for privacy education (Kumar 2018). In related studies, Martin and Nissenbaum (2015) use survey-based methods to show that people typically understand the parameters of an informational norm, and frame their privacy expectations in view of the context in which the information flow occurs, as well as how the information is transmitted and used, and who the senders and receivers of this information are (Martin 2012).

While Kumar is largely interested in privacy literacy for children, with the objective of equipping children to make better decisions about their privacy, a larger additional question worth examining would be to understand whether and how CI can be used as an educational tool to equip adults (and, potentially, children) to better understand information flows within a larger governance context.

Much work in the privacy literacy space has focused on the understanding and empowerment of individual actors with respect to their privacy – another place where individualistic, subject-centered notions of privacy have gained traction. As Park notes:

> In the digital era, the idea encompasses critical understanding of data flow and its implicit rules for users to be able to act. Literacy may serve as a principle to support, encourage, and empower users to undertake informed control of their digital identities. In short, to exercise appropriate measures of resistance against the potential abuse of personal data, it may be that users should be able to understand data flow in cyberspace and its acceptable limits of exposure. (Park 2013, 217)

However, as Cohen (2019) argues, to consider effective responses to the erosion of privacy, scholarship and practice needs to shift from "subject-centered" to "condition-centered" frameworks. In this vein, literacy can also be broadly conceptualized as the building of capacity for an individual to act in a deliberative democratic system, a direction that remains under-explored in studies of privacy literacy. Gordon and Baldwin-Phillipi (2014) call this "civic learning". They present two case studies, in which the online game Community PlanIt (CPI) was deployed in a community to enhance civic-engagement with support from local community organizations. One was part of a district wide planning process in the Boston Public Schools and the second as part of a master planning process in Detroit, Michigan. On assessing the impact of CPI in both case studies, they concluded that the gaming platform allowed what they term as "civic learning" to occur. This has important implications for privacy governance and privacy literacy: what kinds of tools and systems can help build individuals' capacities as engaged, informed, and empowered citizens in the governance of privacy rules?

10.4.4 *Empirical Studies of Privacy Norms and Their Relation to Individuals' Expectations and Preferences*

A focus on procedural legitimacy of informational norms raises another related important question: how can community members' expectations and preferences of privacy be used to assess the legitimacy of contextual informational norms?

This calls for ways of empirically studying such expectations and preferences, not merely at an individual level, but at a group level. In prior work (Shvartzshnaider et al. 2016) survey-based methods were used to measure users' expectations and preferences of privacy to determine whether or not specific information flows are appropriate. However, as Benthall at al. outline:

> In CI, appropriateness is a function of social norms, and these norms do codify social expectations and values. Certainly, in some cases user expectations will track social expectations. But though they are related, we caution researchers against conflating social norms with user expectations and preferences. This is because individual users are more prone to becoming unreflectively habituated to a new technology than society as a whole. Also, individual user preferences may at times be opposed to the interests of society. We have identified elaborating on the relationship between individual preferences and social norms as a way to improve CI. (Benthall, Gürses, and Nissenbaum 2017, 44)

Since the GKC approach seeks to further direct attention from the individual, an important research direction is to explore how individuals' understanding, expectations, and preferences regarding privacy change in a group setting, and how such changes reflect on the larger governance procedures, particularly when these processes are democratic and participatory in nature?

In her articulation of privacy as a Common Good (P. M. Regan 2002; 2015), Regan raises an important and nuanced point to differentiate between "groups" and "individuals in a group" as a unit of analysis. She also poses the question of probing how individuals in groups differ from individuals acting individually in regards to privacy, highlighting that focusing on individuals who act and are aware of their actions and experiences as members of a group rather than merely as individuals acting in isolated capacities will aid our understanding of privacy behaviors and consequent "privacy actions and inactions." A consequent key problem Regan identifies is to create avenues to help individuals realize that they are not merely individuals but members of a group both being impacted by the actions of others in the privacy dimension and affecting other people's privacy. This has close connections to the idea of civic learning explored in the previous section. She recommends drawing on the work of sociologists, social psychologists, and communication scholars who study individual behavior in groups. This line of investigation is also open and available to computer science researchers, particularly those in HCI.

10.4.5 *Calibrating Norm Evaluation and Enforcement Engines for Dynamic Sources of Norms*

Technical systems that implement CI usually express informational norms in formal systems, and operationalize these norms on information flows that act on specific data exchange between actors in a particular context. Such systems typically rely on norm evaluation and enforcement engines that check whether the information flows are consistent with the supplied norms (Barth et al. 2006; Chowdhury et al. 2013). An important research consideration that the governance perspective raises is related to the design and architecture of CI norm evaluation and enforcement engines (along with accompanying human–computer interfaces) that are more suited for dynamic deliberative sources of these norms rather than static sources such as laws and policies, as has been the case in prior work (Barth et al. 2006).

Shvartzshanider et al. (2018) provide important directions here – they use natural language processing techniques such as dependency parsing to automatically extract the parameters of CI from individual sentences. Their approach extracts the CI norm parameters based on the syntactic structure of a single sentence, and uses an accompanying reading comprehension model to incorporate a semantic understanding of the larger scope in order to incorporate it into the CI parameters. They apply their techniques on a corpus that contains website privacy policies in natural text alongside annotations by law students. By supplementing this process with crowdsourcing, they demonstrate that information flows can be automatically extracted from natural text and can be made more precise by appropriate crowdsourcing techniques. While they use a corpus of website privacy policies for this purpose, an open direction is to use natural language processing to infer the parameters of privacy norms from privacy policies generated in a more participatory setting.

10.4.6 *Normative Considerations in Differential Privacy*

Contextual Integrity could provide a normative framework to embed technical notions such as differential privacy within it (Dwork 2006). To the best of the author's knowledge, there is no existing work that considers the appropriateness (or not) of releasing specific functions of a database from the perspective of CI. The GKC framework could further engage with these questions of appropriateness by considering aspects of governance of these rules of appropriateness.

Differential privacy (DP) is primarily suitable for settings where there is interest in releasing an aggregate function of a dataset consisting of data from individuals. This could include simple functions such as averages or more complex machine learning predictors. As Dwork and Roth state:

> "Differential privacy" describes a promise, made by a data holder, or curator, to a data subject: "You will not be affected, adversely or otherwise, by allowing your data to be used in any study or analysis, no matter what other studies, data sets, or information sources, are available." (Dwork and Roth 2013, 5)

This is a more intuitive explanation of an underlying mathematical guarantee of plausible deniability, modulated by a privacy parameter, that has been called epsilon in the literature (Dwork 2006; Dwork and Roth 2013). For a detailed non-technical discussion of differential privacy consult Wood et al.'s (2018) primer.

Even though the DP guarantee targets individuals, functions that could be potentially publicly released or shared are computed over a dataset consisting of several individuals. Such a guarantee might, therefore, be meaningful to examine within the context of community governance and deliberation about sharing of data or functions of data more widely. For example, access to information that furthers understanding of medical ailments has a different normative valence than that of aggregation and prediction for commercial purposes such as online advertising and applications that might intentionally or unintentionally enact discrimination. Communities are likely to evaluate the appropriateness of sharing aggregate functions for these two purposes in different ways. For example, many polls indicate that the public views sharing of personal health data with researchers to be different from sharing such data with other more commercializing applications, indicating the need for context-specific attention to such details. On surveying personally controlled health records (PCHRs) users, Weitzman et al. found that 91 percent were willing to share medical information for health research with such willingness "conditioned by anonymity, research use, engagement with a trusted intermediary, transparency around PCHR access and use, and payment" (Weitzman, Kaci, and Mandl 2010). In survey-based research conducted at the Pew Center, Madden and Rainie (2015) found that only 76 percent of respondents say they are "not too confident" or "not at all confident" that data on their online activity held by the online advertisers who place ads on the websites they visit will remain private and secure.

If sharing data at an aggregate level for, say, medical research purposes is deemed to be appropriate, DP can be employed within a governance framework to achieve the guarantee of plausible deniability for individual community members, and to consider questions about what are appropriate aggregate functions that should be shared with people outside the community. By paying attention to the larger normative elements of the use, purpose, and politics of aggregation, DP can be a powerful and effective tool to disrupt what Cohen terms "semantic continuity" (Cohen 2019).

Several other research directions open up when we consider embedding DP within the larger normative elements of the commons framework: what kinds of interfaces will enable citizens (without a deep mathematical background) to understand the larger guarantees of DP, and make good governance decisions? Bullek et al.'s (2017) preliminary work on making the core guarantees of DP understandable and accessible to the larger public provides one step in this direction. Further research that examines groups as units of analysis, rather than only individuals, along with considering contextual dimensions of the settings in which communities might want to share aggregate data, is needed here.

10.5 CONCLUSION

To conclude, attention toward aspects of governance, particularly its participatory orientations, opens a host of research directions that are ripe to be explored by computer scientists. Designing sociotechnical systems for the privacy commons is important scholarly work, which demands interdisciplinary engagements as well as orienting computer scientists toward such considerations. It is my hope that this chapter will be helpful in charting out some of these research directions.

REFERENCES

Altman, Irwin. 1975. "The Environment and Social Behavior: Privacy, Personal Space, Territory, and Crowding." Brooks/Cole Publishing Company, Monterey California.

Auger, James. 2013. "Speculative Design: Crafting the Speculation." *Digital Creativity* 24 (1): 11–35. https://doi.org/10.1080/14626268.2013.767276.

Badillo-Urquiola, Karla, Xinru Page, and Pamela Wisniewski. 2018. "Literature Review: Examining Contextual Integrity within Human-Computer Interaction." *Available at SSRN* 3309331.

Barth, A., A. Datta, J. C. Mitchell, and H. Nissenbaum. 2006. "Privacy and Contextual Integrity: Framework and Applications." In *2006 IEEE Symposium on Security and Privacy (S&P'06)*, 15 pp. 184–198. Berkeley/Oakland, CA: IEEE. https://doi.org/10.1109/SP.2006.32.

Beck, Eevi. 2002. "P for Political: Participation Is Not Enough." *Scandinavian Journal of Information Systems* 14 (1). https://aisel.aisnet.org/sjis/vol14/iss1/1.

Benthall, Sebastian, Seda Gürses, and Helen Nissenbaum. 2017. "Contextual Integrity through the Lens of Computer Science." *Foundations and Trends in Privacy and Security* 2 (1): 1–69.

Bjerknes, Gro, Pelle Ehn, Morten Kyng, and Kristen Nygaard. 1987. *Computers and Democracy: A Scandinavian Challenge*. Gower Pub Co.

Bossen, Claus, Christian Dindler, and Ole Sejer Iversen. 2016. "Evaluation in Participatory Design: A Literature Survey." In *Proceedings of the 14th Participatory Design Conference: Full Papers – Volume 1*, 151–160. PDC '16. New York, NY, USA: ACM. https://doi.org/10.1145/2940299.2940303.

Bullek, Brooke, Stephanie Garboski, Darakhshan J. Mir, and Evan M. Peck. 2017. "Towards Understanding Differential Privacy: When Do People Trust Randomized Response Technique?" In *Proceedings of the 2017 CHI Conference on Human Factors in Computing Systems*, 3833–3837. CHI '17. New York, NY, USA: ACM. https://doi.org/10.1145/3025453.3025698.

Cavoukian, Ann and others. 2009. "Privacy by Design: The 7 Foundational Principles." *Information and Privacy Commissioner of Ontario, Canada* 5.

Chowdhury, Omar, Andreas Gampe, Jianwei Niu, Jeffery von Ronne, Jared Bennatt, Anupam Datta, Limin Jia, and William H Winsborough. 2013. "Privacy Promises That Can Be Kept: A Policy Analysis Method with Application to the HIPAA Privacy Rule." In *Proceedings of the 18th ACM Symposium on Access Control Models and Technologies*, 3–14. ACM.

Cohen, Julie E. 2019. "Turning Privacy Inside Out." *Theoretical Inquiries in Law* 20 (1). www7.tau.ac.il/ojs/index.php/til/article/view/1607.

DiSalvo, Carl, Andrew Clement, and Volkmar Pipek. 2012. "Communities: Participatory Design for, with and by Communities." In *Routledge International Handbook of Participatory Design*, 202–230. Routledge.

DiSalvo, Carl, Tom Jenkins, and Thomas Lodato. 2016. "Designing Speculative Civics." In *Proceedings of the 2016 CHI Conference on Human Factors in Computing Systems*, 4979–4990. CHI '16. New York, NY, USA: ACM. https://doi.org/10.1145/2858036.2858505.

Dwork, Cynthia. 2006. "Differential Privacy." In *Proceedings of the 33rd International Conference on Automata, Languages and Programming – Volume Part II*, 1–12. ICALP'06. Berlin, Heidelberg: Springer-Verlag. https://doi.org/10.1007/11787006_1.

Dwork, Cynthia and Aaron Roth. 2013. "The Algorithmic Foundations of Differential Privacy." *Foundations and Trends® in Theoretical Computer Science* 9 (3–4): 211–407. https://doi.org/10.1561/0400000042.

Ehn, Pelle. 1988. "Work-Oriented Design of Computer Artifacts." PhD Thesis, Arbetslivscentrum.

Fairfield, Joshua and Christoph Engel. 2017. "Privacy as a Public Good." In *Privacy and Power*, edited by Russell A. Miller, 95–128. Cambridge: Cambridge University Press. https://doi.org/10.1017/CBO9781316658888.004.

Friedman, Batya, ed. 1997. *Human Values and the Design of Computer Technology*. Stanford, CA, USA: Center for the Study of Language and Information.

Gordon, Eric and Jessica Baldwin-Philippi. 2014. "Playful Civic Learning: Enabling Lateral Trust and Reflection in Game-Based Public Participation." *International Journal of Communication* 8: 759–786.

Gordon, Eric and Stephen Walter. 2016. "16. Meaningful Inefficiencies: Resisting the Logic of Technological Efficiency in the Design of Civic Systems." *The Playful Citizen*, 310.

Green, Ben. 2019. *The Smart Enough City: Putting Technology in Its Place to Reclaim Our Urban Future*. MIT Press.

Grönvall, Erik, Lone Malmborg, and Jörn Messeter. 2016. "Negotiation of Values As Driver in Community-Based PD." In *Proceedings of the 14th Participatory Design Conference: Full Papers – Volume 1*, 41–50. PDC '16. New York, NY, USA: ACM. https://doi.org/10.1145/2940299.2940308.

Gürses, S. and J. M. del Alamo. 2016. "Privacy Engineering: Shaping an Emerging Field of Research and Practice." *IEEE Security Privacy* 14 (2): 40–46. https://doi.org/10.1109/MSP.2016.37.

Gürses, Seda and Joris van Hoboken. 2018. "Privacy after the Agile Turn." The Cambridge Handbook of Consumer Privacy. April 2018. https://doi.org/10.1017/9781316831960.032.

Gürses, Seda, Carmela Troncoso, and Claudia Diaz. 2011. "Engineering Privacy by Design." *Computers, Privacy & Data Protection* 14 (3): 25.

Huybrechts, Liesbeth, Henric Benesch, and Jon Geib. 2017. "Institutioning: Participatory Design, Co-Design and the Public Realm." *CoDesign* 13 (3): 148–159.

Kanstrup, Anne Marie. 2003. "D for Democracy: On Political Ideals in Participatory Design." *Scand. J. Inf. Syst.* 15 (1): 81–85.

Kumar, Priya. 2018. "Contextual Integrity as a Conceptual, Analytical, and Educational Tool for Research," 5.

Kumar, Priya, Shalmali Milind Naik, Utkarsha Ramesh Devkar, Marshini Chetty, Tamara L. Clegg, and Jessica Vitak. 2017. "'No Telling Passcodes Out Because They'Re Private': Understanding Children's Mental Models of Privacy and Security Online." *Proc. ACM Hum.-Comput. Interact.* 1 (CSCW): 64: 1–64: 21. https://doi.org/10.1145/3134699.

Lessig, Lawrence. 2000. *Code and Other Laws of Cyberspace*. New York, NY, USA: Basic Books, Inc.

Lodato, Thomas and Carl DiSalvo. 2018. "Institutional Constraints: The Forms and Limits of Participatory Design in the Public Realm." In *Proceedings of the 15th Participatory Design Conference: Full Papers – Volume 1*, 5: 1–5:12. PDC '18. New York, NY, USA: ACM. https://doi.org/10.1145/3210586.3210595.

Madden, Mary and Lee Rainie. 2015. "NUMBERS, FACTS AND TRENDS SHAPING THE WORLD." Pew Research Center. www.pewinternet.org/2015/05/20/americans-attitudes-about-privacy-security-and-surveillance/.

Martin, Kirsten E. 2012. "Diminished or Just Different? A Factorial Vignette Study of Privacy as a Social Contract." *Journal of Business Ethics* 111 (4): 519–539. https://doi.org/10.1007/s10551-012–1215-8.

Martin, Kirsten E. and Helen Nissenbaum. 2015. "Measuring Privacy: An Empirical Test Using Context To Expose Confounding Variables." SSRN Scholarly Paper ID 2709584. Rochester, NY: Social Science Research Network. https://papers.ssrn.com/abstract=2709584.

Marttila, Sanna, Andrea Botero, and Joanna Saad-Sulonen. 2014. "Towards Commons Design in Participatory Design." In *Proceedings of the 13th Participatory Design Conference: Short Papers, Industry Cases, Workshop Descriptions, Doctoral Consortium Papers, and Keynote Abstracts – Volume 2*, 9–12. PDC '14. New York, NY, USA: Association for Computing Machinery. https://doi.org/10.1145/2662155.2662187.

Marwick, Alice E. and danah boyd. 2014. "Networked Privacy: How Teenagers Negotiate Context in Social Media." *New Media & Society* 16 (7): 1051–1067. https://doi.org/10.1177/1461444814543995.

Mir, Darakhshan J., Yan Shvartzshnaider, and Mark Latonero. 2018. "It Takes a Village: A Community Based Participatory Framework for Privacy Design." In *2018 IEEE European Symposium on Security and Privacy Workshops (EuroS&PW)*, 112–115. IEEE.

Muller, Michael J. 2009. "Participatory Design: The Third Space In HCI." Human-Computer Interaction. March 2, 2009. https://doi.org/10.1201/9781420088892–15.

Nissenbaum, Helen. 2009. *Privacy in Context: Technology, Policy, and the Integrity of Social Life*. Stanford, CA: Stanford University Press.

Nissenbaum, Helen. 2019. "Contextual Integrity Up and Down the Data Food Chain." *Theoretical Inquiries in Law* 20 (1): 221–56. https://doi.org/10.1515/til-2019–0008.

Ostrom, Elinor. 1990. *Governing the Commons: The Evolution of Institutions for Collective Action*. The Political Economy of Institutions and Decisions. Cambridge; New York: Cambridge University Press.

Park, Yong Jin. 2013. "Digital Literacy and Privacy Behavior Online." *Communication Research* 40 (2): 215–36. https://doi.org/10.1177/0093650211418338.

Petronio, Sandra and Irwin Altman. 2002. *Boundaries of Privacy: Dialectics of Disclosure*. Albany, UNITED STATES: State University of New York Press. http://ebookcentral.proquest.com/lib/bucknell/detail.action?docID=3408055.

Pilemalm, Sofie. 2018. "Participatory Design in Emerging Civic Engagement Initiatives in the New Public Sector: Applying PD Concepts in Resource-Scarce Organizations." *ACM Trans. Comput.-Hum. Interact.* 25 (1): 5:1–5: 26. https://doi.org/10.1145/3152420.

Regan, Priscilla. 2016. "Response to Privacy as a Public Good." *Duke Law Journal Online*, February, 51–65.

Regan, Priscilla M. 1986. "Privacy, Government Information, and Technology." *Public Administration Review* 46 (6): 629–34. https://doi.org/10.2307/976229.

Regan, Priscilla M. 2000. *Legislating Privacy: Technology, Social Values, and Public Policy*. University of North Carolina Press.

Regan, Priscilla M. 2002. "Privacy as a Common Good in the Digital World." *Information, Communication & Society* 5 (3): 382–405. https://doi.org/10.1080/13691180210159328.

Regan, Priscilla M. 2015. "Privacy and the Common Good: Revisited." In *Social Dimensions of Privacy: Interdisciplinary Perspectives*, edited by B. Roessler & D. Mokrosinska, 50–70,

Cambridge: Cambridge University Press. https://doi.org/10.1017/CBO9781107280557.004.

Sanfilippo, Frischmann and Strandburg. 2018. "Privacy as Commons: Case Evaluation Through the Governing Knowledge Commons Framework." *Journal of Information Policy* 8: 116. https://doi.org/10.5325/jinfopoli.8.2018.0116.

Shilton, Katie. 2018. "Values and Ethics in Human-Computer Interaction." *Foundations and Trends® Human–Computer Interaction* 12 (2): 107–71. https://doi.org/10.1561/1100000073.

Shilton, Katie, Jeff Burke, Deborah Estrin, Mark Hansen, and Mani B Srivastava. 2008. "Participatory Privacy in Urban Sensing." http://scholarworks.umass.edu/esence http://escholarship.org/uc/item/90j149pp.pdf.

Shvartzshanider, Yan, Ananth Balashankar, Thomas Wies, and Lakshminarayanan Subramanian. 2018. "RECIPE: Applying Open Domain Question Answering to Privacy Policies." In *Proceedings of the Workshop on Machine Reading for Question Answering*, 71–77.

Shvartzshnaider, Yan, Schrasing Tong, Thomas Wies, Paula Kift, Helen Nissenbaum, Lakshminarayanan Subramanian, and Prateek Mittal. 2016. "Learning Privacy Expectations by Crowdsourcing Contextual Informational Norms." In *Fourth AAAI Conference on Human Computation and Crowdsourcing*.

Simonsen, J., and T. Robertson. 2012. *Routledge International Handbook of Participatory Design*. Routledge International Handbooks. Taylor & Francis. https://books.google.com/books?id=l29JFCmqFikC.

Strandburg, Katherine J., Brett M. Frischmann, and Michael J. Madison. 2017. "The Knowledge Commons Framework." In *Governing Medical Knowledge Commons*, edited by Katherine J. Strandburg, Brett M. Frischmann, and Michael J. Madison, 9–18. Cambridge Studies on Governing Knowledge Commons. Cambridge University Press. https://doi.org/10.1017/9781316544587.002.

Teli, Maurizio, Peter Lyle, and Mariacristina Sciannamblo. 2018. "Institutioning the Common: The Case of Commonfare." In *Proceedings of the 15th Participatory Design Conference: Full Papers – Volume 1*, 6:1–6:11.PDC '18. New York, NY, USA: ACM. https://doi.org/10.1145/3210586.3210590.

Weitzman, Elissa R., Liljana Kaci, and Kenneth D. Mandl. 2010. "Sharing Medical Data for Health Research: The Early Personal Health Record Experience." *Journal of Medical Internet Research* 12 (2): e14. https://doi.org/10.2196/jmir.1356.

Wong, Richmond Y. and Vera Khovanskaya. 2018. "Speculative Design in HCI: From Corporate Imaginations to Critical Orientations." In *New Directions in Third Wave Human-Computer Interaction: Volume 2 – Methodologies*, edited by Michael Filimowicz and Veronika Tzankova, 175–202. Human–Computer Interaction Series. Cham: Springer International Publishing. https://doi.org/10.1007/978-3-319-73374-6_10.

Wong, Richmond Y. and Deirdre K. Mulligan. 2019. "Bringing Design to the Privacy Table: Broadening 'Design' in 'Privacy by Design' Through the Lens of HCI." In *Proceedings of the 2019 CHI Conference on Human Factors in Computing Systems*, 262:1–262: 17.CHI '19. New York, NY, USA: ACM. https://doi.org/10.1145/3290605.3300492.

Wood, Alexandra, Micah Altman, Aaron Bembenek, Mark Bun, Marco Gaboardi, James Honaker, Kobbi Nissim, David R O'Brien, Thomas Steinke, and Salil Vadhan. 2018. "Differential Privacy: A Primer for a Non-Technical Audience." *Vand. J. Ent. & Tech. L.* 21: 209.

Conclusion

Privacy as Knowledge Commons Governance

An Appraisal

Madelyn Sanfilippo, Katherine J. Strandburg and Brett M. Frischmann

The chapters in this book have explored how privacy commons, understood as the sharing and use of personal information, are governed, as well as how information subjects are sometimes excluded from governance. Our previous two books, *Governing Medical Knowledge Commons* (2017) and *Governing Knowledge Commons* (2014), collected case studies of commons governance aimed at promoting and sustaining innovation and creativity by sharing and pooling knowledge. While personal information is often shared and pooled for similar purposes, it is distinctive in several important respects. First, and foremost, personal information is inherently *about someone*, who arguably has a particularized stake in the way that information is shared, pooled and used. This relationship means that privacy commons governance may be ineffective, illegitimate or both if it does not appropriately account for the interests of information subjects. Second, personal information is often shared unintentionally or involuntarily as a side effect of activities aimed at other goals, possibly creating a schism between those seeking to pool and use personal information and the individuals most intimately tied to it. Third, in our current technological era, personal information often flows via commercial communication infrastructure. This infrastructure is owned and designed by actors whose interests may be misaligned or in conflict with the interests of information subjects or of communities seeking to pool, use and manage personal information for common ends. Finally, governing the flow of personal information can be instrumental and often essential to building trust among members of a community, and this can be especially important in contexts where it is a community interested in producing and sharing knowledge.

As the chapters in this volume illustrate, the distinctive characteristics of personal information have important implications for the observed features of commons governance and, ultimately, for legitimacy. Taken together, the studies in this volume thus deepen our understanding of privacy commons governance, identify newly salient issues related to the distinctive characteristics of personal information, and confirm many recurring themes identified in previous GKC studies.

VOICE-SHAPED, EXIT-SHAPED AND IMPOSED PATTERNS IN COMMONS GOVERNANCE OF PERSONAL INFORMATION

To organize some of the lessons that emerge from the GKC analysis of privacy, we harken back to patterns of governance that we identified in our privacy-focused meta-analysis of earlier knowledge commons studies (Sanfilippo, Frischmann and Strandburg, 2018). Though those earlier case studies were neither selected nor conducted using a privacy lens, the meta-analysis identified three patterns of commons governance: member-driven, public-driven and imposed. We observe similar patterns in the privacy-focused case studies gathered here. Reflecting on these new cases allows to refine our understanding of these governance patterns in three respects, which inform the analyses in sub-sections 1.1, 1.2 and 1.3, which illustrate and systematize some of the important patterns that we observe.

First, we hone our understanding of these patterns by drawing on A. O. Hirschmann's useful conceptions of 'voice' and 'exit' as distinctive governance mechanisms. What we previously termed 'member-driven' commons governance is characterized by the meaningful exercise of participant 'voice' in governing the rules-in-use (Gorham et al. 2020). Even when participants do not have a direct voice in governance, however, they may exert indirect influence by 'voting with their feet' as long as they have meaningful options to 'exit' if they are dissatisfied. The governance pattern that we previously characterized as 'public-driven' is associated with just such opt out capacity, driving those with direct authority to take participants' governance preference into account – it is in this sense 'exit-shaped'. Commons governance is 'imposed' when participants have neither a direct 'voice' in shaping rules-in-use nor a meaningful opportunity to 'exit' when those rules are not to their liking.

Second, as discussed in the Introduction to this volume, personal information can play two different sorts of roles in knowledge commons governance. Most obviously, as reflected in the cases studied in Chapters 2 through 5, personal information is one type of knowledge resource that can be pooled and shared. For example, personal health information from patients may be an important knowledge resource for a medical research consortium. In these cases, privacy is often an important objective to information subjects, as actors who may or may not be adequately represented in commons governance. But even when personal information is not pooled as a knowledge resource, the rules-in-use governing how personal information flows within and outside of the relevant community can have important implications for sustaining participation in a knowledge commons and for the legitimacy of its governance. Chapters 5 through 7 analyse this sort of situation. Either sort of privacy commons can be governed according to any of the three patterns we previously identified. Moreover, and independently, privacy commons governance can also be distinguished according to the role played by information subjects because personal information *about* one individual can be contributed, disclosed or collected by someone else. Thus, members who have a voice in commons governance might use personal information about unrepresented non-members to create a knowledge resource. Similarly, participants who opt to contribute to a knowledge commons might contribute information about non-participants who have neither a voice in the governance of their personal information nor any ability to opt out of contributing it. And, of course, imposed commons governance might be designed to force participants to contribute personal information 'without representation'.

Third, we note that even the more nuanced taxonomy presented here papers over many grey areas and complexities that are important in real-world cases. Governance patterns reside on a continuum in, for example, the extent to which governance institutions empower particular individuals and groups. Moreover, most shared knowledge resources are governed by overlapping and nested institutions that may follow different patterns. The often polycentric nature of resource governance, involving overlapping centres of decision-making associated with different actors, often with different objectives and values, is well-recognized in studies of natural resource commons (e.g. McGinnis, 1999; Ostrom, 1990). Polycentricity is equally important in knowledge commons governance. Thus, the rules-in-use that emerge in any given case may have complex origins involving interactions and contestation between different groups of commons participants and between commons governance and exogenous background institutions. Different aspects of a case may exhibit different governance patterns. Moreover, some participants may have a voice in shaping certain rules-in-use, while others encounter those same rules on a take-it-or-leave-it basis. This polycentricity means that some cases appear in multiple categories in the analysis mentioned later.

We also emphasize that our categorization of voice-shaped, exit-shaped and imposed commons governance is descriptive. The normative valence of any commons activity depends on its overall social impact. Thus, different governance patterns may be normatively preferable for different knowledge commons or even for different aspects of the same knowledge commons. In particular, as we explain below, any of the three governance patterns can be implemented in a way that accounts adequately or inadequately for the interests and concerns of personal information subjects. For example, while imposed commons governance associated with commercial infrastructure is notoriously unresponsive to information subject concerns, government-imposed commons governance often aims to bring the interests of information subjects into the picture.

Voice-shaped Commons Governance

In the voice-shaped governance pattern, those creating and using knowledge resources are also responsible for their governance. The success of voice-shaped commons arrangements depends on governance that encourages reciprocal contribution for a mutually beneficial outcome. Chapters 2, 4, 5, 6 and 7 in this book describe cases characterized at least in significant part by voice-shaped governance of personal information. In Chapters 2, 4 and 6 this voice-shaped governance is mostly informal, while Chapters 3 and 7 describe more formal governance structures. Cases exhibiting voice-shaped commons can be further characterized as illustrated in Table 11.1, which employs the distinctions based on source and use of personal information described above to categorize cases from this volume and from our earlier meta-analysis.

As illustrated in the top row of Table 11.1, voice-shaped commons governance is sometimes applied to create and manage a pool of personal information as a resource. In the cases listed in the upper left quadrant, members participate in governance of knowledge resources created by pooling *their own* personal information. That quadrant includes medical commons in which patients or their representatives have a direct voice in commons governance, including the MIDATA case explored in Chapter 2 and earlier-studied RDCRN cases, the previously studied LINK Indigenous Knowledge Commons, in which representatives of indigenous groups participate in governing information resources that they view as intimately related to their communities, as well as some aspects of the Facebook activist groups explored in Chapter 5.

In the cases listed in the upper right quadrant, members govern knowledge resources they create by contributing *other people's* personal information. In the

TABLE 11.1 *Voice-shaped commons breakdown (Case studies in this volume are in bold)*

	Information Subjects = Members	Information Subjects = Not Members
PI = Resource	Rare Disease Clinical Research Network LINK Indigenous Knowledge Commons Patient Innovation Project **MIDATA** (Ch. 2) **Facebook Activist Groups** (Ch. 5)	Biobanks Sentinel Initiative Open Neuroscience Movement Oncofertility Consortium **University Institutional Research** (Ch. 4) **Facebook Activist Groups** (Ch. 5)
PI = Collateral Flow	Online Creation Communities (some) Aviation Clubs Nineteenth-Century Newspaper Editors Congress Patient Innovation Project **Republic of Letters** (Ch. 6) **Chatham House** (Ch. 7) **Gordon Conferences** (Ch. 7) **Broadband ITAG** (Ch. 7) **Facebook Activist Groups** (Ch. 5)	

previously studied medical cases in that quadrant, for example, patient information is governed by consortia of physicians and medical researchers without direct patient involvement. Similarly, in Chapter 4 of this volume, Jones and McCoy describe institutional research by university administrators using a pool of student personal information. Governance of the sharing and use of student information is largely voice-shaped, in that many of the rules-in-use are determined by university personnel who contribute and use the information. Crucially, however, the student information subjects are not members of this governing community.

The distinction is normatively significant. While members may have altruistic concerns for non-member information subjects or be bound, as in the medical and education contexts, by background legal or professional obligations to them, voice-shaped governance is no guarantee that the concerns of non-members will be adequately addressed. Indeed, the NIH included patient representatives as governing members in the Rare Disease Clinical Research Network as a condition of government funding following complaints that patient interests had not been sufficiently represented in earlier consortia made up entirely of physicians and researchers.

That said, governance without the direct participation of information subjects does not necessarily give members free rein to share and use other people's personal information however they please. Personal health and education information, for example, is governed by applicable background privacy legislation, ethical rules and professional norms. Moreover, in some contexts commons members may be required to obtain the consent of information subjects before contributing their personal information to the pool. Consent, however, is not the same as participation in governance, a point we explore further below and in related work (Gorham et al.).

As illustrated in the bottom left quadrant of Table 11.1, voice-shaped commons governance may also be applied to collateral flows of members' personal information that occur in conjunction with or as a by-product of creating some other sort of shared knowledge resource. Appropriate governance of such collateral flows of personal information can be important for encouraging participation, improving the quality of other sorts of knowledge resources the group creates and otherwise furthering the goals and objectives of voice-shaped commons governance. The cases in Chapter 7 by Frischmann et al. illustrate how constraints on the flow of members' personal information to outsiders can incentivize diverse and open participation in creating other sorts of knowledge resources and improve their quality. Whether it is the Chatham House Rule's incredibly simple prohibition[1] on revealing the identity

[1] Despite the simplicity of the Chatham House Rule, there are variations in how it is applied. As law students learn in the first semester of law school, even simple rules require interpretation. Ambiguities arise, and thus lead to variances in applications across communities, with respect to questions, such as: *Who decides whether the Rule governs? To whom does the ban on revealing a speaker's identity or affiliation extend? Can identity be disclosed to someone bound by a duty of confidentiality? Can a speaker waive the Rule, and if so, under what circumstances?*

or affiliation of speakers or the more elaborate confidentiality rules adopted by Broadband Internet Technical Advisory Group (BITAG), privacy governance fosters knowledge production and sharing by members. Madison's Chapter 6 illustrates how informal norms against disclosing personal information in exchanges with other members created a venue for building a knowledge base through rational, scientific argument. The previously studied Patient Innovation Project similarly aims to create a pool of generalizable knowledge about medical innovations made by patients and caregivers, but personal information flows are an inevitable by-product of the sharing of innovations so intimately bound up with patients' medical conditions. Though the Patient Innovation Project governs these collateral flows of personal information in part by platform design, as discussed in the next sub-section, sub-communities have also developed more tailored, voice-shaped information sharing norms. The bottom right quadrant of Table 11.1 is empty, perhaps because collateral flow of non-member personal information that is not being pooled into a shared resource is rare.

The Facebook activist groups studied in Chapter 5 are included in three of the four quadrants in Table 11.1 because of the variety of personal information-based resources involved and the various ways in which intentional and collateral personal information flows affected participation in these groups. We can describe the governance of these pooled personal information resources and collateral flows as voice-shaped to the extent that contributors either participated actively in creating the mostly informal rules-in-use that emerged or viewed themselves as adequately represented by the groups' more actively involved leaders and organizers. Voice-shaped governance was only part of the story for these Facebook activist groups, however, as discussed in the sections on exit-shaped and imposed commons later.

In these cases, personal information was contributed directly to shared knowledge resources by those who posted personal narratives to the public Facebook pages, contributed photos, joined Facebook groups or signed up for events or email lists. These pooled knowledge resources were used to further the group's objectives by informing and persuading the public, facilitating communication of information to members and so forth. While much of this personal information pertained to the contributors, these cases are included in both left and right quadrants of the top row because it was also possible to contribute personal information pertaining to someone else. Indeed, this sort of behaviour occurred often enough that groups developed mechanisms for protecting potentially vulnerable non-participants from such disclosures through rules-in-use. These cases thus illustrate not only the potential for information subjects to be left out of voice-shaped governance, but also the fact that voice-shaped governance may nonetheless incorporate protections for non-members.

The Facebook activist groups of Chapter 5 are also represented in the bottom left quadrant of Table 11.1 because they adopted rules-in-use governing collateral personal information flow arising, for example, from the metadata identifying those who posted to the Facebook pages and the interactions between organizers behind the scenes. In some ways, the various interactions between personal information and participation parallel patterns observed within the Patient Innovation Project, a previous case study. With respect to Patient Innovation, however, personal information as a resource or as collateral flows always pertained to members, rather than non-member information subjects.

Exit-shaped Commons Governance

Exit-shaped commons governance, as we identified in Chapter 1, occurs when an individual or group creates an infrastructure for voluntary public participation in creating a shared knowledge resource. It thus differs from voice-shaped governance in that contributors to the knowledge resource do not participate directly in its governance. The key characteristic that distinguishes exit-shaped commons governance from imposed governance is that contributions are meaningfully voluntary. As a result, whoever governs the shared knowledge resource must do so in a way that will attract participants.

The characteristics of personal information surface distinctions among cases of exit-shaped commons governance similar to those we observed for voice-shaped governance, as illustrated in Table 11.2.

Before delving into the distinctions between cases in the different quadrants in Table 11.2, we focus on common features of exit-shaped commons governance. Most importantly, given that participation is meaningfully voluntary, designers of exit-shaped commons governance must ensure that potential participants will find it worth their while to contribute. As a result, even though contributors do not participate directly in governance, designers of exit-shaped commons cannot stray too far out of alignment with their interests. Trust is important. So, setting aside personal information for the moment, the need to attract participants means that the mental health chatbot must offer mental health assistance that, all things considered, is at least as attractive as alternatives. Galaxy Zoo and many online creation

TABLE 11.2 *Exit-shaped commons breakdown (Case studies in this volume are in bold)*

	Information Subjects = Public participants	Information Subjects = Others
PI = Resource	**Mental Health Chatbots** (Ch. 3) **Facebook Activist Groups** (Ch. 5) **IoT** (Ch. 9)	**Facebook Activist Groups** (Ch. 5) **IoT** (Ch. 9)
PI = Collateral Flow	Online creation communities Galaxy Zoo Patient Innovation Project **Facebook Activist Groups** (Ch. 5)	

communities have adopted rules favouring non-commercial use of their (non-personal) knowledge resources, presumably because potential contributors find those policies attractive. More limited forms of democratic participation adopted by some online communities may have served similar purposes.

Turning more specifically to the exit-shaped commons governance of personal information, Table 11.2, like Table 11.1, lists cases aiming to create a pool of personal information in the top row and cases involving only personal information flow collateral to other sorts of activities in the bottom row.

The Woebot mental health chatbot described by Mattioli in Chapter 3 appears in the top left quadrant because it creates of pool of personal information contributed by patients as they use the app. By using a therapy chatbot, patients receive mental health assistance, while simultaneously contributing their personal health information to a knowledge pool that can be used by the app's creators to improve its performance. Based on the analysis in Chapter 3, we categorize the governance of the personal information collected by the Woebot chatbot as exit-shaped. Governance of these personal information resources is not voice-shaped because it is physicians, not patients, who control the design of the app and the use of the associated personal information. Use of these chatbots, and the associated information pooling, does however currently appear to be meaningfully voluntary. Patients seem to have many viable alternative treatment options. Moreover, the chatbot's physician designers appear to have transparently committed to using the resulting knowledge pool only for research purposes and to improve the app's operation. It thus seems plausible that patients using the chatbot understand the ramifications of the chatbot's collection of their personal information, because interesting rules-in-use operationalize this intent in ways that align with patient expectations.

We categorize the Facebook activist groups discussed in Chapter 5 under exit-shaped governance, as well as voice-shaped governance. Informal governance by trusted leaders is a recurring theme in knowledge commons governance. Nonetheless, participation in these movements was so broad that it is virtually inevitable that some participants – especially those who joined at a later stage – experienced the rules-in-use and governance as essentially 'take it or leave it'. Like the more involved members discussed earlier, such participants could have posted personal information pertaining to themselves or to others. These groups were extremely successful in attracting large numbers of participants who contributed various sorts of personal information. While this success presumably reflects some satisfaction with the rules-in-use for personal information, later joining participants may not have viewed their choice to participate in these particular groups as entirely voluntary. As these groups became foci for expressing certain political views, their value undoubtedly rose relative to alternative protest avenues. This rich-get-richer phenomenon thus may have tipped the balance toward imposed governance, as discussed in the next sub-section.

The rules-in-use for collecting and employing personal information about users of Internet of Things (IoT) devices are largely determined by the commercial suppliers of 'smart' devices. The survey study by Shvartzshnaider et al., reported in Chapter 9, suggests that some device users have a sufficient understanding of the way that their personal information is collected and used by IoT companies that their decision to opt in by purchasing and using a given device or to opt out by not doing so are meaningfully voluntary. For this subset of users, the governance of IoT personal information resources may be categorized as exit-shaped and entered into the top left quadrant of Table 11.2. Notably, however, those users' choices to opt in may also result in the collection of personal information from bystanders, guests and others who have made no such choice. We thus also categorize the IoT in the top right quadrant of Table 11.2. Much as for mental health chatbots, diminishing opportunities for meaningful exit amid pervasive surveillance environments oriented around IoT may disempower users, tipping governance from exit-shaped to imposed, as we will discuss in the next sub-section. On the other hand, one very interesting observation of the Shvartzshnaider et al. study is that online IoT forums allow users to pool their experiences and expertise to create knowledge resources *about personal information collection* by smart devices and strategies to mitigate it (at least to some degree). Those forums may thus empower consumers and expand the extent to which the governance of personal information resources collected through the IoT is exit-shaped.

The cases in the bottom row of Table 11.2 involve exit-shaped governance of collateral flows of personal information associated with the creation of other sorts of knowledge resources. Galaxy Zoo and the online creation community cases identified in our earlier meta-analysis both fall into this category. We observed in our earlier meta-analysis that those systems governed the collateral flow of personal information, at least in part, by allowing anonymous or pseudonymous participation. Nonetheless, though anonymity was the norm, participants were not discouraged from strategically revealing personal information on occasion in order to establish credibility or expertise. This set of rules presumably encouraged public participation by protecting participants from potentially negative effects of exposing their personal information publicly online while still allowing them to deploy it strategically in ways that benefitted them and may have improved the quality of the knowledge resource. The Patient Innovation Project similarly involves collateral flows of personal information intertwined with information about medical innovations developed by patients and caregivers, though its rules-in-use are different. Though sub-community governance is partially voice-shaped, as discussed above, much of the governance of personal information flows depends on platform design and is thus categorized as exit-shaped.

As noted in the previous section, the Facebook activist groups discussed in Chapter 5 also developed rules-in-use to govern collateral flows of personal information associated with the creation of other sorts of knowledge resources. To the extent those rules-in-use applied to contributors who were not adequately represented in governance, they also constitute exit-shaped commons governance.

Notably, all of the previously studied cases in Table 11.2 appear in the bottom row and involved the creation of general knowledge resources not comprised of personal information. These previously studied knowledge commons were also designed to make the knowledge resources they created openly available. For these earlier cases, the designation 'public-driven' may have been ambiguous, conflating openness to all willing contributors with public accessibility of the pooled information or public-generated data sets. The studies categorized in the top row of Table 11.2 clarify that there is a distinction. When we speak of exit-shaped commons governance, we mean openness regarding contributors.

We thus emphasize again the importance of meaningful voluntariness as the key characteristic of exit-shaped commons governance. If participation is not meaningfully voluntary, commons governance becomes imposed, rather than exit-shaped – a very different situation, which we discuss in the next section. Meaningful voluntariness means that potential contributors have meaningful alternatives as well as a sufficient grasp of the ramifications of contributing to the knowledge pool. Exit-shaped commons governance must therefore be designed to attract contributors in order to succeed. The need to attract contributors forces governance to attend sufficiently to participants' interests. We do not, therefore, expect rules-in-use of open accessibility to emerge from exit-shaped commons governance of personal information pools because open availability would be likely to deter, rather than attract, potential contributors. In exit-shaped commons governance, rules-in-use regarding access to pooled resources are tools that designers can shape to attract participation. We would thus expect access rules to vary depending on the sorts of personal information involved and the goals and objectives of both potential participants and designers.

Of course, while meaningful voluntariness is the key to categorizing governance as exit-shaped, it is no guarantee of success. For example, one could imagine a version of the mental health chatbot that was completely transparent in its intentions to sell mental health information to advertisers or post it on the dark web. That sort of governance would be sufficiently voluntary to be classified as exit-shaped, but highly unlikely to attract enough participants to succeed.

Finally, it is important to note that while exit-shaped commons governance gives contributors some indirect influence over the rules-in-use, it does nothing to empower individuals whose personal information is contributed by others. Thus, cases in the upper right quadrant of Table 11.2 raise the same sorts of privacy concerns as cases in the upper right quadrant of Table 11.1. Just as members-driven governance may fail to attend to the interests of non-member information subjects, designers of exit-shaped governance may fail to attend to the interests of individuals whose personal information can be obtained without their participation.

Imposed Commons Governance

Imposed commons governance is similar to exit-shaped commons governance in that knowledge contributors do not have a voice in the rules-in-use that emerge, but differs significantly because contributors also do not opt for imposed governance in any meaningfully voluntary way. In other words, to the extent commons governance is imposed, contributors and information subjects alike lack both voice and the option to exit. While there is no bright line between voluntarily accepted and mandatory governance, one practical result is that imposed commons governance, unlike exit-shaped governance, need not be designed to attract participation. Thus, though designers might choose to take the interests and preferences of contributors into account, they need not do so.

Those with decision-making power over rules and governance are not always or necessarily the information subjects. Communities can include different membership groups and subgroups, and can rely on different existing infrastructures and technologies for collecting, processing and managing data. Governance associated with these infrastructure and external platforms are determined in design, by commercial interests, and through regulations, thus they will vary accordingly. Externally imposing commons governance requires power of some sort that effectively precludes contributors from opting out of participation. Such power may arise from various sources and can reside in either government or private hands.

One important source of power to impose commons governance over personal information is control and design of important infrastructure or other input resources needed to effectively create and manage the desired knowledge resources. This power is often associated with infrastructure because of network and similar effects that reduce the number of viable options. The Facebook activist groups study in Chapter 5 provides a good example of this source of privately imposed commons governance. Organizers repeatedly noted that they were displeased with certain aspects of Facebook's platform design and treatment of contributors' personal information. For these reasons, all three activist groups resorted to alternative means of communication for some purposes. Nonetheless, all concluded that they had no reasonable alternative to using Facebook as their central platform for communicating, aggregating and publicizing information. This example illustrates that complete market dominance is not required to empower a party to impose commons governance to some degree.

Another important source of imposed governance is the law, which is part of the background environment for every knowledge commons arrangement. (Of course, in a democracy, citizens ultimately create law, but on the time frame and scale of most knowledge commons goals and objectives, it is reasonable to treat legal requirements as mandatory and externally imposed.) Applicable law can be general or aimed more specifically at structuring and regulating the creation of particular knowledge resources. To create a useful categorization, we treat only the latter sorts of legal requirements as imposed commons governance. Thus, for example, while acknowledging the importance of HIPAA, and other health privacy laws, we do not classify every medical knowledge commons as involving imposed commons governance. We do, however, classify the specific government mandates of the previously studied Sentinel program as imposed governance. The power to impose governance through law is, of course, limited to governments. However, there are also parallels in corporate policies that, when imposed on employees and teams, are strictly enforced rules.

Commons governance may also be imposed through the power of the purse. For example, while medical researchers are not literally forced to accept government conditions on funding, such as those associated with the Rare Disease Clinical Research Network, their acceptance of those conditions is not meaningfully voluntary in the sense that matters for our categorization. While researchers could in principle rely entirely on other funding sources or choose a different occupation, the paucity of realistic alternatives empowers funding agencies to impose commons governance. Indeed, while there more often are viable funding alternatives in the private sector, large private funders may have similar power to impose governance in some arenas.

Collecting knowledge resources by surveillance is another way to elude voluntary exit and thus impose commons governance. Both governments and some sorts of private entities may be able to impose governance in this way. Many 'smart city' activities create knowledge resources through this sort of imposed governance. Private parties exercise this sort of power when they siphon off information that individuals contribute or generate while using their products or services for unrelated purposes. Internet giants such as Facebook and Google are notorious for pooling such information for purposes of targeting ads, but a universe of smaller ad-supported businesses also contribute to such pools. More recently, as discussed in Chapters 8 and 9, the IoT provides a similar source of private power to impose commons governance. Governments can accomplish essentially the same sort of thing by mandating disclosure. The earlier case study of Congress provides an interesting example of the way that open government laws create this sort of imposed commons governance.

Commons governance can also be imposed through control or constraint over contributor participation. This source of power can be illustrated by a thought experiment based on the mental health chatbots studied in Chapter 3. Mattioli's study suggests that patients' contributions of personal health information by using the current version of Woebot are meaningfully voluntary. If, however, a mental health chatbot's use were to be mandated or highly rewarded by insurance companies, its governance pattern would shift from exit-shaped to imposed.[2] A less obvious example of this type of power comes from the Facebook activist group study. While

[2] Meaningfully voluntary is thus doing significant work, and one might question whether this criterion is as useful and clear cut as it seems. Like the similar concept of informed consent, it may be fundamentally flawed because it is contingent, at least to a substantial degree, on the integrity and stability of individual's preferences and beliefs. Preferences and beliefs are, of course, malleable (i.e.

there might initially be several different groups vying to organize a national protest movement, as time goes on potential participants will naturally value being a part of the largest group. At some point, this rich-get-richer effect can implicitly empower the most popular group to impose its rules-in-use on later joiners.

Finally, and in a somewhat different vein, power to impose commons governance can stem from a party's ability to undermine contributor voluntariness by misleading individuals about the implications of contributing to a knowledge pool or using particular products or services. This concern has long been central to privacy discourse, especially in the private realm. Empirical studies have convinced many, if not most, privacy experts that privacy policies and similar forms of 'notice and consent' in the commercial context ordinarily do not suffice to ensure that participants understand the uses to which their personal information will be put. Facebook is only one prominent example of a company that has been repeatedly criticized in this regard. As another illustration, consider how the voluntariness of patients' use of the mental health chatbot would be eroded if its pool of personal information came under the control of private parties who wanted to use to target advertising or for other reasons unrelated to improving mental health treatment. If the implications of such uses were inadequately understood by patients, the chatbot's governance pattern might well shift from exit-shaped to imposed.

Table 11.3 lists cases that involve significant imposed governance. In most of these cases, imposed governance of some aspects of commons activity is layered with voice-shaped or exit-shaped governance of other aspects. The distinctions in Tables 11.1 and 11.2 based on information subjects' role in governance and on whether pooling personal information is a knowledge commons objective are less salient for categorizing imposed governance in which both contributors and information

TABLE 11.3 *Imposed commons governance*

Governance imposed upon:	Govt	Private
Actors	RDCRN Genome Commons Sentinel Initiative	
Resources	Open Neuroscience Movement Genome Commons **IoT Cybersecurity** (Ch. 8)	Galaxy Zoo **IoT Cybersecurity** (Ch. 8) **Facebook** (Ch. 5) **Personal IoT** (Ch. 9)

subject to manipulation, nudging through adjustments in the choice architecture, and other forms of techno-social engineering). See Frischmann and Selinger (2018). This is a significant challenge. Nonetheless, we believe Hirschmann's conception of exit and voice remain useful as a baseline for evaluation.

subjects have neither voice nor the capacity to exit. Instead, the columns in Table 11.3 distinguish between cases in which governance is imposed by government and cases in which it is imposed by private actors, while the rows differentiate between rules-in-use associated with actors and knowledge resources, including contribution, access to, and use of personal information resources. Overall, though governments must balance many competing interests and are not immune to capture, one would expect government-imposed governance to be more responsive than privately imposed governance to the concerns of information subjects.

With respect to imposed governance, it is also important to note that some of these cases highlighted efforts to contest these constraints, when they didn't align with information subjects' norms and values. Many of the efforts to create more representative rules-in-use or work arounds developed within existing knowledge commons, such as activists on Facebook (Chapter 5). Yet, occasionally, communities of information subjects emerged for the sole purpose of pooling knowledge about exit or obfuscation. For example, the formation of sub-communities of IoT users through online forums that wants to assert more control over the pools of user data generated through their use of smart devices. These users, rather than pooling personal information, create a knowledge resource aimed at supporting other users to more effectively decide whether or how to exit, as well as how to obfuscate the collection of personal information. In this sense, these forums allow information subjects, as actors, to cope with exogenously imposed governance by manufacturers, as well as publicly driven governance.

PRIVACY AS KNOWLEDGE COMMONS GOVERNANCE: NEWLY EMERGING THEMES

These new studies of privacy's role in commons governance highlight several emerging themes that have not been emphasized in earlier Governing Knowledge Commons (GKC) analyses. In the previous section we reflected on the role of personal information governance in boundary negotiation and socialization, the potential for conflicts between knowledge contributors and information subjects; the potential adversarial role of commercial infrastructure in imposing commons governance; and the role of privacy work-around strategies in responding to those conflicts. Additional newly emerging themes include: the importance of trust; the contestability of commons governance legitimacy; and the co-emergence of contributor communities and knowledge resources.

The Importance of Trust

Focusing on privacy and personal information flows reveals the extent to which the success of voice-shaped or exit-shaped commons governance depends on trust. Perhaps this is most obvious in thinking of cases involving voluntary contributions of personal information to create a knowledge resource. Whether commons governance is voice-shaped or exit-shaped, voluntary contribution must depend on establishing a degree of trust in the governing institutions. Without such trust, information subjects will either opt out or attempt to employ strategy to avoid full participation. Voice-shaped commons governance can create such trust by including information subjects as members. This is the approach taken by the Gordon Research Conferences, the BITAG, the MIDATA case and RDCRN consortia, for example. When a group decides to adopt the Chatham House Rule to govern a meeting, it creates an environment of trust. Exit-shaped commons governance must rely on other mechanisms to create trust. In the medical and education contexts, professional ethics are a potentially meaningful basis for trust. Trust might also be based in shared agendas and circumstances, as was likely the case for the informal governance of the Facebook activist groups. The studies in Chapters 6 and 7 illustrate the perhaps less obvious extent to which trust based on rules-in-use about personal information can be essential to the successful of knowledge commons resources that do not incorporate personal information. This effect suggests that mechanisms for creating and reinforcing trust may be of very broad relevance to knowledge commons governance far beyond the obvious purview of personal information-based resources.

The Contestability of Commons Governance Legitimacy

These privacy-focused studies draw attention to the role of privately imposed commons governance, especially through the design of commercial infrastructure. Previous GKC studies that have dealt with imposed commons governance have focused primarily on government mandates, while previous consideration of infrastructure has been mostly confined to the benign contributions of government actors or private commons entrepreneurs whose goals and objectives were mostly in line with those of contributors and affected parties. These cases also highlight the potentially contestable legitimacy of commons governance of all three sorts and call out for more study of where and when commons governance is socially problematic and how communities respond to illegitimate governance. The issue of legitimacy also demands further attention, of the sort reflected in Chapters 8 through 10 of this volume, to policy approaches for improving the situation.

While GKC theory has always acknowledged the possibility that commons governance will fail to serve the goals and values of the larger society, previous studies have focused primarily on the extent to which a given knowledge commons achieved the objectives of its members and participants. Concerns about social impact focused mainly on the extent to which the resources created by a knowledge commons community would be shared for the benefit of the larger society. These privacy commons studies help to clarify the ways in which knowledge commons governance can fail to be legitimate from a social perspective. They underscore the possibility that knowledge commons governance can be illegitimate and socially problematic even if a pooled knowledge resource is successfully created. This sort of governance failure demands solutions that go beyond overcoming barriers to cooperation. Various types of solutions can be explored, including the development of appropriate regime complexes discussed by Shackelford in Chapter 8, the participatory design approach discussed by Mir in Chapter 9, to the collaborative development of self-help strategies illustrated by the IoT forums discussed in Chapter 10, the imposition of funding requirements giving information subjects a direct voice in governance illustrated by the RDRCN, the development of privacy-protective technologies and infrastructures, and the imposition of more effective government regulation.

Co-emergence of Communities and Knowledge Resources

One of the important differences between the IAD and GKC frameworks is the recognition that knowledge creation communities and knowledge resources may co-emerge, with each affecting the character of the other. The privacy commons studies provide valuable illustrations of this general feature of knowledge commons, particularly in voice-shaped and some exit-shaped situations. In some cases, this co-emergence occurs because at least some participants are subjects of personal information that is pooled to create a knowledge resource. This sort of relationship was identified in earlier RDCRN case studies and is a notable feature of cases discussed in Chapters 2, 3 and 5. The Gordon Research Conferences and BITAG examples from Chapter 5 are perfect examples. Even when the knowledge resource ultimately created by the community does not contain personal information, however, participants' personal perspectives or experiences may be essential inputs that shape the knowledge resources that are ultimately created, as illustrated by the case studies discussed in Chapter 7 and in the earlier study of the Patient Innovation Project.

PRIVACY AS KNOWLEDGE COMMONS GOVERNANCE: DEEPENING RECURRING THEMES

The contributions in this volume also confirm and deepen insights into recurring themes identified in previous GKC studies (Frischmann, Madison and Strandburg, 2014; Strandburg, Frischmann and Madison, 2017). These privacy-focused studies lend support to many of those themes, while the distinctive characteristics of personal information add nuance, uncover limitations and highlight new observations which suggest directions for further research. Rather than re-visiting all of those earlier observations, this section first summarizes some recurring themes that are distinctively affected by the characteristics of personal information and then identifies some new themes that emerge from privacy commons studies.

Knowledge Commons May Confront Diverse Obstacles or Social Dilemmas, Many of Which are Not Well Described or Reducible to the Simple Free Rider Dilemma

When we developed the GKC framework more than ten years ago, our focus was on challenging the simplistic view that the primary obstacle to knowledge creation was the free rider dilemma, which had to be solved by intellectual property or government subsidy. We were directly inspired by Ostrom's demonstration that private property and government regulation are not the sole solutions to the so-called tragedy of the commons for natural resources. It became immediately clear from our early case studies, however, not only that there were collective solutions to the free rider problem for knowledge production, but that successful commons governance often confronted and overcame many other sorts of social dilemmas. Moreover, these other obstacles and dilemmas were often more important to successful knowledge creation and completely unaddressed by intellectual property regimes. Considering privacy and personal information confirms this observation and adds some new twists.

Among the dilemmas identified in the earlier GKC studies, the privacy-focused studies in this volume call particular attention to:

- *Dilemmas attributable to the nature of the knowledge or information production problem.*

As we have already emphasized, personal information flow and collection creates unique dilemmas because of the special connection between the information and its subjects, who may or may not have an adequate role in commons governance.

- *Dilemmas arising from the interdependence among different constituencies of the knowledge commons.*

When personal information is involved, these sorts of dilemmas reappear in familiar guises, but also with respect to particular concerns about the role of information subjects in governance.

- *Dilemmas arising from (or mitigated by) the broader systems within which a knowledge commons is nested or embedded.*

On the one hand, accounting for personal information highlights the important (though often incomplete) role that background law and professional ethics play in mitigating problems that arise from the lack of representation of information subjects' interests in commons governance. On the other hand, it draws attention to the ways in which infrastructure design, especially when driven by commercial interests, can create governance dilemmas related to that lack of representation.

- *Dilemmas associated with boundary management*

The studies in this volume identify the important role that privacy governance can play in governing participation and managing access boundaries for knowledge commons, often even when the relevant knowledge resources are not comprised of personal information.

Close Relationships Often Exist between Knowledge Commons and Shared Infrastructure

Earlier GKC case studies noted the important role that the existence or creation of shared infrastructure often played in encouraging knowledge sharing by reducing transaction costs. In those earlier studies, when infrastructure was not created collaboratively, it was often essentially donated by governments or 'commons entrepreneurs' whose goals and objectives were closely aligned with those of the broader commons community. While some studies of privacy commons also identify this sort of 'friendly' infrastructure, their most important contribution is to identify problems that arise when infrastructure owners have interests that conflict with the interests of information subjects. This sort of 'adversarial infrastructure' is often created by commercial entities and closely associated with the emergence of imposed commons governance. Undoubtedly, there are times when society's values are best served by embedding and imposing governance within infrastructure in order to constrain some knowledge commons from emerging, in competition with sub-communities' preferences; in these cases infrastructure operationalizes rules to prevent certain resources from being pooled or disseminated, such as by white supremacists or for terrorism, or the emergence of rules-in-use to prevent social harms, such as pornography. There is a special danger, however, that society's values will not be reflected in private infrastructure that takes on the role of imposing commons governance, as many of the privacy commons studies illustrate.

Knowledge Commons Governance Often Did Not Depend on One Strong Type or Source of Individual Motivations for Cooperation

Earlier GKC case studies largely presumed that contributing to a knowledge commons was largely, if not entirely, a voluntary activity and that commons governance had to concern itself with tapping into, or supplying, the varying motivations required to attract the cooperation of a sometimes diverse group of necessary participants. Privacy commons studies turn this theme on its head by emphasizing the role of involuntary – perhaps even coerced – contribution. Thus, a given individual's personal information can sometimes be contributed by others, obtained by surveillance or gleaned from other behaviour that would be difficult or costly to avoid. This possibility raises important questions about the legitimacy of commons governance that were not a central focus of earlier GKC case studies.

THE PATH AHEAD

The studies in this volume move us significantly forward in our understanding of knowledge commons, while opening up important new directions for future research and policy development. We mention just a few such directions in this closing section.

First, while the taxonomy of voice-shaped, exit-shaped and imposed commons governance emerged from studies of personal information governance, it is more broadly applicable. To date, GKC case studies have tended to focus on voice-shaped commons governance. More studies of exit-shaped commons governance would be useful, for knowledge commons aimed at pooling personal information and others. For example, it might be quite interesting to study some of the commercial DNA sequencing companies, such as 23andMe, which create pools of extremely personal genetic information, used at least partly for genetic research. There are currently a number of such companies, which seem to attract a fair amount of business. Without further study, it is unclear whether the behaviour of these entities is sufficiently clear to contributors to qualify them as exit-shaped commons governance. Moreover, these companies also collect a considerable amount of information that pertains to information subjects who are not contributors, making them a promising place to study those issues as well.

Second, we learned from these cases that the distinction between public- and voice-shaped governance is strongly associated with the differences between meaningful exit and voice, respectively. While these mechanisms are important in providing legitimacy (Gorham et al.), individual rules-in-use to establish exit and voice functions vary significantly across contexts. It is not yet clear what makes exit or voice meaningful in a given context. Future case studies should address the institutional structure, differentiating between specific strategies, norms and rules and seeking to associate particular governance arrangements with social attributes and background characteristics in order to understand when exit or voice solutions might work and the contextual nature of successful governance arrangements.

Third, many of these privacy commons case studies emphasized the complexity of governance arrangements, identifying many competing layers of rules-in-use and rules-on-the-books, which reflected the interests of different actors, including information subjects, private sector firms and government actors. These conflicting layers illustrate the polycentric nature of knowledge commons governance, providing an opportunity to reconnect to insights from natural resource commons in future case studies. Further, there is room for considerably more study of how adversarial (or at least conflicting) infrastructure design affects commons governance. Additional inquiries into communities' relationships with social media platforms would likely provide significant insight, as would case studies in smart city contexts.

While each of these directions should be explored in their own right, they are also reflected in supplementary questions added to the GKC framework, as represented in Table 11.4, and should be considered in future case studies.

TABLE 11.4 *Updated GKC framework (with supplementary questions in bold)*

Knowledge Commons Framework and Representative Research Questions	
	Background Environment
	What is the background context (legal, cultural, etc.) of this particular commons?
	What normative values are relevant for this community?
	What is the 'default' status of the resources involved in the commons (patented, copyrighted, open, or other)?
	How does this community fit into a larger context? What relevant domains overlap in this context?
	Attributes
Resources	What resources are pooled and how are they created or obtained?
	What are the characteristics of the resources? Are they rival or nonrival, tangible or intangible? Is there shared infrastructure?
	What is personal information relative to resources in this action arena?
	What technologies and skills are needed to create, obtain, maintain, and use the resources?
	What are considered to be appropriate resource flows? How is appropriateness of resource use structured or protected?
Community Members	Who are the community members and what are their roles, **including with respect to resource creation or use, and decision-making**?
	Are community members also information subjects?
	What are the degree and nature of openness with respect to each type of community member and the general public?
	Which non-community members are impacted?
Goals and Objectives	What are the goals and objectives of the commons and its members, including obstacles or dilemmas to be overcome?
	Who determines goals and objectives?
	What values are reflected in goals and objectives?
	What are the history and narrative of the commons?
	What is the value of knowledge production in this context?
	Governance
Context	What are the relevant action arenas and how do they relate to the goals and objective of the commons and the relationships among various types of participants and with the general public?
	Are action arenas perceived to be legitimate?
Institutions	What legal structures (e.g., intellectual property, subsidies, contract, licensing, tax, antitrust) apply?

TABLE 11.4 *(continued)*

	Knowledge Commons Framework and Representative Research Questions
	What other external institutional constraints are imposed? What government, agency, organization, or platform established those institutions and how? **How is institutional compliance evaluated?** What are the governance mechanisms (e.g., membership rules, resource contribution or extraction standards and requirements, conflict resolution mechanisms, sanctions for rule violation)? What are the institutions and technological infrastructures that structure and govern decision making? What informal norms govern the commons? What institutions are perceived to be legitimate? Illegitimate? How are institutional illegitimacies addressed?
Actors	**What actors and communities: are members of the commons, participants in the commons, users of the commons and/or subjects of the commons?** Who are the decision-makers and how are they selected? Are decision-makers perceived to be legitimate? **Do decision-makers have an active stake in the commons?** How do nonmembers interact with the commons? What institutions govern those interactions? Are there impacted groups that have no say in governance? **If so, which groups?**
	Patterns and Outcomes
	What benefits are delivered to members and to others (e.g., innovations and creative output, production, sharing and dissemination to a broader audience and social interactions that emerge from the commons)? What costs and risks are associated with the commons, including any negative externalities? Are outcomes perceived to be legitimate by members? By decision-makers? By impacted outsiders? **Do governance patterns regarding participation provide exit and/or voice mechanisms for participants and/or community members?** **Which rules-in-use are associated with exit-shaped, voice-shaped or imposed governance? Are there governance patterns that indicate the relative impact of each within the commons overall?**

REFERENCES

Frischmann, Brett M., Michael J. Madison and Katherine Jo Strandburg, eds. *Governing Knowledge Commons*. Oxford University Press, 2014.

Frischmann, Brett and Evan Selinger, *Re-Engineering Humanity*. Cambridge University Press, 2018.

Gorham, Ashley Elizabeth, Helen Nissenbaum, Madelyn R. Sanfilippo, Katherine J. Strandburg, and Mark Verstraete. "Social Media Is Not a Context: Protecting Privacy Amid 'Context Collapse'." Proceedings of American Political Science Association (APSA), 2020 Virtual Annual Meeting & Exhibition. September 10, 2020. http://tinyurl.com/ybfnz4bb.

McGinnis, Michael Dean. *Polycentricity and Local Public Economies: Readings from the Workshop in Political Theory and Policy Analysis*. University of Michigan Press, 1999.

Ostrom, Elinor. *Governing the Commons: The Evolution of Institutions for Collective Action*. Cambridge University Press, 1990.

Sanfilippo, Madelyn, Brett Frischmann, and Katherine Strandburg. Privacy as Commons: Case Evaluation through the Governing Knowledge Commons Framework, 8 *Journal of Information Policy* 116–66 (2018)

Strandburg, Katherine J., Brett M. Frischmann and Michael J. Madison, eds. *Governing Medical Knowledge Commons*. Cambridge University Press, 2017.

For EU product safety concerns, contact us at Calle de José Abascal, 56–1°, 28003 Madrid, Spain or eugpsr@cambridge.org.

www.ingramcontent.com/pod-product-compliance
Lightning Source LLC
LaVergne TN
LVHW011809200926
848484LV00005B/1113

* 9 7 8 1 1 0 8 4 8 5 1 4 2 *